WORLD CIVILIZATIONS

Sources, Images, and Interpretations

VOLUME I

Edited by
Dennis Sherman
JOHN JAY COLLEGE OF CRIMINAL JUSTICE, CITY UNIVERSITY OF NEW YORK

A. Tom Grunfeld
EMPIRE STATE COLLEGE, STATE UNIVERSITY OF NEW YORK

Gerald Markowitz
JOHN JAY COLLEGE OF CRIMINAL JUSTICE, CITY UNIVERSITY OF NEW YORK

David Rosner
BARUCH COLLEGE, CITY UNIVERSITY OF NEW YORK

Linda Heywood
HOWARD UNIVERSITY

McGRAW-HILL, INC.
New York   St. Louis   San Francisco   Auckland   Bogotá
Caracas   Lisbon   London   Madrid   Mexico City   Milan
Montreal   New Delhi   San Juan   Singapore   Sydney   Tokyo   Toronto

WORLD CIVILIZATIONS
Sources, Images, and Interpretations
Volume I

This book is printed on recycled, acid-free paper containing 10% postconsumer waste.

234567890 DOC DOC 90987654

ISBN 0-07-056831-6

This book was set in Caledonia by Ruttle, Shaw & Wetherill, Inc.
The editor was Pamela Gordon;
the production supervisor was Louise Karam.
The cover was designed by Carla Bauer.
The photo researcher was Barbara Salz.
Project supervision was done by Ruttle, Shaw & Wetherill, Inc.
R. R. Donnelley & Sons Company was printer and binder.

Cover painting: Court Ladies Preparing Newly Woven Silk. Chinese and Japanese Special Fund. Courtesy, Museum of Fine Arts, Boston.

Library of Congress Cataloging-in-Publication Data

World civilizations: sources, images, and interpretations / edited by
    Dennis Sherman; A. Tom Grunfeld . . . [et al.].
        p.   cm.
    Includes bibliographical references.
    ISBN 0-07-056831-6 (v. 1). —ISBN 0-07-056833-2 (v. 2).
    1. Civilization—History—Sources.   2. Civilization—History.
I. Sherman, Dennis.   II. Grunfeld, A. Tom.
CB69.W66   1994
909—dc20   93-34784

ABOUT THE AUTHORS

Dennis Sherman is professor of History at John Jay College of Criminal Justice, the City University of New York. He received his BA (1962) and JD (1965) degrees from the University of California at Berkeley and his PhD (1970) from the University of Michigan. He was visiting Professor at the University of Paris (1978–1979; 1985). He received the Ford Foundation Prize Fellowship (1968–1969, 1969–1970), a fellowship from the Council for Research on Economic History (1971–1972), and fellowships from the National Endowment for the Humanities (1973–1976). His publications include *A Short History of Western Civilization,* Seventh Edition (coauthor), *Western Civilization: Images and Interpretations,* Third Edition, *A Study Guide and Readings for the Western Experience* (1991), a series of introductions in the Garland Library of War and Peace, several articles and reviews on nineteenth-century French economic and social history in American and European journals, and short stories in literary reviews.

A. Tom Grunfeld is an Associate Professor of History at the State University of New York/Empire State College. He received his BA (1972) from the State University of New York/College at Old Westbury, his MA (1973) from the University of London/School of Oriental and African Studies and his PhD (1985) from New York University. He has received travel and research grants from the National Endowment for the Humanities (1984), the Research Foundation of the City University of New York (1985), and the State University of New York (1985, 1987, 1991). His publications include over 60 articles in journals published in a dozen countries, *The Making of Modern Tibet* (1987), and *On Her Own: Journalistic Adventures from the San Francisco Earthquake to the Chinese Revolution 1917–1927* (1993). He has lived in and traveled extensively throughout Asia since 1966.

Gerald Markowitz is Professor of History at the Graduate Center, John Jay College of the City University of New York. He received his PhD from the University of Wisconsin (1971). He received grants from the National Endowment for the Humanities (1975–77, 1987–89, 1992–94). His publications include *The Anti-Imperialists, 1898–1902* (1976), *Democratic Vistas: Post Offices and Public Art in the New Deal* (with Marlene Park) (1984), *Deadly Dust: Silicosis and the Politics of Industrial Disease* (with David Rosner) (1991), *Dying for Work: Safety and Health in the United States* (ed. with D. Rosner) (1987), *"Slaves of the Depression": Workers' Letters about Life on the Job* (ed. with D. Rosner) (1987), as well as numerous articles and reviews on American History.

David Rosner is Professor of History at Baruch College and the Graduate Center of the City University of New York. He received his PhD from Harvard University (1978). He received fellowships and grants from the National Endowment for the Humanities (1982–83, 1987–89, 1992–94), was a Josiah Macy Fellow in the History of Biology and Medicine (1973–1976) and was a John Simon Guggenheim Fellow (1987–88). His publications include *A Once Charitable Enterprise: Hospitals and Health Care in Brooklyn and New York, 1885–1915* (1982), *Deadly Dust: Silicosis and the Politics of Industrial Disease* (with Gerald Markowitz) (1991), *Dying for Work: Safety and Health in the United States* (ed. with G. Markowitz) (1987), *"Slaves of the Depression": Workers' Letters about Life on the Job* (ed. with G. Markowitz) (1987), as well as numerous articles and reviews on American History.

Linda Heywood is Associate Professor of African History at Howard University in Washington, D.C. She received her BA (1973) from Brooklyn College and her PhD (1984) from Columbia University. She was a Visiting Assistant Professor at Cleveland State University (1982–84). She received a Whiting Fellowship (1977) and a grant from Howard University Faculty Humanities Program (1990). Her publications include several articles on the economic and political history of central Angola. She is the coeditor of *Black Diaspora: Africans and Their Descendants in the Wider World,* Parts I and II (1988 revised editions). She is currently completing a manuscript entitled "Thwarted Power: The State and Transformation in Central Angola, 1840–1975."

We Look Backward,
All of Us,
To Know,
All of Us,
If We Can.

CONTENTS IN BRIEF

CONTENTS

TOPICAL CONTENTS

CROSS-CULTURAL CONTACTS

To A.D. 500

500–1500

1500–1700

ECONOMIC ACTIVITIES

To A.D. 500

500–1500

1500–1700

ENVIRONMENT AND GEOGRAPHY

To A.D. 500

GOVERNMENT AND POLITICS

1500–1700

IMPERIALISM AND COLONIZATION

To A.D. 500

500–1500

1500–1700

RELIGION

To A.D. 500

500–1500

1500–1700

SOCIAL LIFE AND SOCIAL STRUCTURE

To A.D. 500

500–1500

1500–1700

THOUGHT AND CULTURE

To A.D. 500

500–1500

PREFACE

This book provides a broad introduction to the sources historians use, the kind of interpretations historians make, and the evolution of civilizations throughout the world over the past six thousand years. A large selection of documents, photographs, and maps is presented along with introductions, commentaries, and questions designed to place each selection in a meaningful context and facilitate an understanding of its historical significance. The selections and accompanying notes also provide insights into how historians work and some of the problems they face.

A brief look at the task facing historians will supply a background to what will be covered in this book. To discover what people thought and did and to organize this into a chronological record of the human past, historians must search for evidence—for the sources of history. Most sources are written materials, ranging from government records to gravestone inscriptions, memoirs, and poetry. Other sources include paintings, photographs, sculpture, buildings, maps, pottery, and oral traditions. In searching for sources, historians usually have something in mind—some tentative goals or conclusions that guide their search. Thus, in the process of working with sources, historians must decide which ones to emphasize. What historians ultimately write is a synthesis of the questions posed, the sources used, and their own ideas.

The perspective in this book is not from western civilization or indeed from any particular civilization. The perspective is the course of human history as a whole, as it ebbs and flows over various parts of the globe. At the same time, the focus in each chapter will usually be on particular civilizations as they have risen, developed, and interacted with other civilizations of the world. The sources have been selected to provide an overall balance between political, economic, social, intellectual, religious, and cultural history. However, most chapters also stress certain topics of particular importance for understanding the history of a civilization. Therefore, for example, some chapters will have more sources on social and women's history, while others will emphasize political and religious history.

Structure of the Book

This book is divided into manageable chapters, the divisions based on how the different civilizations of the world have developed over time and within certain geographical contexts. There is also a **topical table of contents** that further facilitates cross-chapter comparisons between different civilizations and over time. All the chapters are organized the same way. Each chapter is broken into sections consisting of the following features:

Each chapter opens with a **chapter introduction,** in which the period of history and the general topics to be dealt with in the chapter are described. The introduction provides a brief sketch of some of the most important developments, but no effort is made to cover the period. Instead, the purpose is to introduce the topics, issues, and questions that the sources in the chapter focus on, and to place these sources in the historical context of the civilizations being examined.

The introduction is followed by a **time line,** showing the relevant dates, people, events, and developments of the period, to provide a historical context for the selections in the chapter.

The chapter time line is followed by the **primary sources.** These are documents written by individuals involved in the matter under investigation. Historians consider these documents their main building blocks for learning about and interpreting the past. They are pieces of evidence that show what people thought, how they acted, and what they accomplished. At the same time historians must criticize these sources both externally—to attempt to uncover forgeries and errors—and internally—to find the authors' motives, inconsistencies within the documents, and different meanings of words and phrases.

Each document is preceded by a **headnote.** The headnote provides some information on the nature of the source, places it in a specific historical context, and indicates its particular focus.

The headnotes end with suggestions of **points to consider.** These points are not simply facts to be searched for in the selection. Rather, they are designed to stimulate analytical thought about the selections and to indicate some of the uses of each source.

The primary sources are followed by visual sources, including maps, and then by **secondary sources.**

Secondary sources are documents written by scholars about the time in question. Usually, they are interpretations of what occurred based on examination of numerous primary documents and other sources. They reflect choices the authors have made and their own particular understandings of what has happened. Often there are important differences of opinion among scholars about how to understand significant historical developments. Secondary sources should therefore be read with these questions in mind: What sort of evidence does the author use? Does the author's argument make sense? What political or ideological preferences are revealed in the author's interpretation? How might one argue against the interpretation presented by the author? At times the distinction between primary and secondary documents becomes blurred, as when the author is a contemporary of the events he or she is interpreting. If a document by that author is read as an interpretation of what occurred, it would be a secondary source. As evidence for the assumption and attitudes of the author's times, however, the document would be a primary source.

Like the primary documents, all the secondary documents are preceded by headnotes and suggestions for points to consider.

Visual sources are paintings, drawings, sculpture, ceramics, photographs, buildings, monuments, coins, and so forth, that can provide valuable historical insights or information. Although they often include characteristics of secondary documents, they are usually most valuable when used in the same way as primary documents. In this book their purpose is not merely to supplement the documents or provide examples of the great pieces of art throughout history. It is to show how these visual materials can be used as sources of history and to provide insights difficult to gain solely through written documents. To this end, each visual source is accompanied by a relatively extensive interpretive description. Care should be taken in viewing these sources and using these descriptions. By their very nature, visual sources usually have a less clear meaning than written documents. Scholars differ greatly over how sources such as paintings, ceramics, and coins should be interpreted. Therefore, the descriptions accompanying the visual sources are open to debate. They are designed to show how it is possible for historians to use visual materials as sources of history—as unwritten evidence for what people thought and did in the past.

Maps often combine elements of primary documents, secondary documents, and visual sources. However, here they are usually used to help establish relationships, such as the connections between geographical factors and political developments, thereby enabling us to interpret what occurred differently than we could have if we had relied on written sources alone. As is the case with visual sources, each map is accompanied by an interpretive description. These descriptions indicate some of the ways maps might be used by historians.

Each chapter ends with **chapter questions.** These are designed to draw major themes of the chapter together in a challenging way. Answers to these questions require some analytical thought and the use of several of the selections in the chapter and even, occasionally, the use of sources from several chapters.

Since a book of this size can only sample what is available and outline what has occurred, this book is truly an introduction to the human past and its sources. Indeed, it is our hope that the materials presented here will reveal the range of sources that can be used to deepen our understanding of the human past and serve as a jumping-off point for further exploration into history and the historian's discipline.

McGraw-Hill and the authors would like to thank Edward Anson, University of Arkansas at Little Rock; Hines Hall, Auburn University; Udo Heyn, California State, Los Angeles; Thomas Kay, Wheaton College; Gretchen Knapp, State University of New York, Buffalo; Daniel Lewis, San Bernadino Valley College; Marilyn Morris, University of North Texas; Oliver Pollack, University of Nebraska, Omaha; Linda Walton, Portland State University; Lawrence Watkins, University of Kansas; John Weakland, Ball State University; Joseph Whitehorne, Lord Fairfax Community College; and Richard Williams, Washington State University for their many helpful comments and suggestions in reviewing this book.

Dennis Sherman
A. Tom Grunfeld
Gerald Markowitz
David Rosner
Linda Heywood

A NOTE ON CHINESE ROMANIZATION

From the first contacts of Europeans and Chinese there has been a problem in transliterating Chinese characters into the western alphabet. Many varied systems were developed. The romanization system most widely used in the English-speaking world was named after its nineteenth-century British creators, Wade and Giles.

In recent years there has been an attempt to develop a single transliteration which could be used universally. This system, adopted officially in the People's Republic of China in 1979, is known as *pinyin*. This system approximates the Chinese sounds more closely although it uses letters such as *q* and *x* in ways unfamiliar to most English speakers.

In this book we have used *pinyin,* but the first time a word appears, the Wade-Giles form will appear in brackets except for names particularly well known such as Sun Yat-sen, Chiang Kai-shek, Hong Kong, Tibet, etc.

ONE

Early Civilizations of Southwestern Asia and Northeastern Africa

What most historians call *civilization* began along major river valleys in the eastern hemisphere and along coastal areas in the western hemisphere. The earliest of these civilizations arose some five to six thousand years ago out of small agricultural villages in the river valleys of southwestern Asia and northeastern Africa, first in Mesopotamia near the Tigris and Euphrates rivers and shortly thereafter in Egypt around the Nile. In the delta of the Tigris-Euphrates river system, the Sumerians organized into city-states, the principal one being Ur. About 2340 B.C. the Sumerians were overwhelmed by the Akkadians from the north, and over the next two thousand years this area, a meeting point between Asia, Africa, and Europe, experienced great instability as in their turn the Babylonians, Hittites, Chaldeans, Medes, and Persians gained dominance. Egyptian civilization developed toward the end of the fourth millennium B.C. and is usually dated from about 3000 B.C., when the upper and lower Nile areas were unified under one king. Although there were some periods of change, as well as influence from peoples farther south, this was a remarkably stable civilization, lasting almost three thousand years.

In many respects the Mesopotamian and Egyptian civilizations were simi-

1

lar. Both were dependent on rivers and the rich soil deposited by periodic floods; both had to develop and maintain organized systems of irrigation and flood control. Both eventually had powerful kings and a priestly caste. Both believed in all-powerful gods who played an active role in the world. But there were also important differences between these two civilizations. Mesopotamia was not as well protected geographically as Egypt and was thus more open to attack. Her rivers were not as navigable, nor were the floods as regular as the Nile's. Her culture and religion reflected a sense of instability and pessimism in comparison to the stability and optimism that characterized Egyptian civilization.

Between these two areas there arose a number of smaller and politically less significant states, the most important of which were the Phoenician and the Hebrew states. The Phoenicians, a mercantile people, facilitated trade, established colonies, and spread Near Eastern culture. The Hebrews developed religious and ethical ideas that would provide a foundation for both Christian and Islamic civilizations.

A number of sources in this chapter deal with the origins, nature, and spread of the earliest civilizations. How should "civilization" be defined? Why did civilizations arise where and when they did? What were the main char-

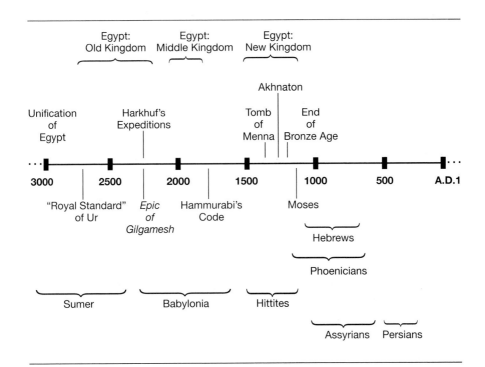

acteristics of these ancient civilizations? Through what processes did civilizations spread? Most of the remaining sources concern each of three civilizations: the Mesopotamians, the Egyptians, and the Hebrews. Sources concerning Mesopotamia center on the nature of that civilization and its legal system. The position of women in Mesopotamian societies, particularly compared to that of Egyptian women, is analyzed. The sources concerning Egypt provide insight into some of its main economic and social characteristics, the significance of the Pharaoh, and Egypt's connections to its southern neighbors. Sources concerning the Hebrews focus on their religion, which would become pivotal in the development of Western civilizations, and how it compared to other religions.

In sum, the sources in this chapter provide an introduction to the nature of civilization and its deep roots in southwestern Asa and northeastern Africa.

PRIMARY SOURCES

The Epic of Gilgamesh

Insight into a people's ideas about life and death can be gained by examining their myths and their literature. The Epic of Gilgamesh, *probably written in the latter part of the third millennium (2000s)* B.C., *was the great epic poem of Mesopotamia. Its hero, Gilgamesh, ruled the Sumerian city-state of Uruk around 2700* B.C. *The poem is about the mythical adventures this king, part god himself, has struggling with life, the gods, and death. In one adventure, Gilgamesh faces death by embarking on a search for immortality. As part of that search he descends into the Netherworld to find Utnapishtim, a human who has been granted immortality by the gods. In the following selection, Gilgamesh questions Utnapishtim, who tells him the story of the flood.*

> **Consider:** *The nature of the gods and their relations with humans; conclusions about life Mesopotamians might have come to reading or listening to this story; connections between this story and the biblical story of Noah and the flood.*

"Oh, father Utnapishtim, you who have entered the assembly of the gods, I wish to question you concerning the living and the dead, how shall I find the life for which I am searching?"

SOURCE: N. K. Sandars, trans., *The Epic of Gilgamesh*, 2nd rev. ed. (London: Penguin Books, 1972), copyright © N. K. Sandars, 1960, 1964, 1972.

Utnapishtim said, "There is no permanence. Do we build a house to stand for ever, do we seal a contract to hold for all time? Do brothers divide an inheritance to keep for ever, does the flood-time of rivers endure? It is only the nymph of the dragon-fly who sheds her larva and sees the sun in his glory. From the days of old there is no permanence. The sleeping and the dead, how alike they are, they are like a painted death. What is there between the master and the servant when both have fulfilled their doom? When the Annunaki,[1] the judges, come together, and Mammetun the mother of destinies, together they decree the fates of men. Life and death they allot but the day of death they do not disclose."

Then Gilgamesh said to Utnapishtim the Faraway, "I look at you now, Utnapishtim, and your appearance is no different from mine; there is nothing strange in your features. I thought I should find you like a hero prepared for battle, but you lie here taking your ease on your back. Tell me truly, how was it that you came to enter the company of the gods and to possess everlasting life?" Utnapishtim said to Gilgamesh, "I will reveal to you a mystery, I will tell you a secret of the gods."

"You know the city Shurrupak, it stands on the banks of Euphrates? That city grew old and the gods that were in it were old. There was Anu, lord of the firmament, their father, and warrior Enlil their counsellor, Ninurta the helper, and Ennugi watcher over canals; and with them also was Ea.[2] In those days the world teemed, the people multiplied, the world bellowed like a wild bull, and the great god was aroused by the clamour. Enlil heard the clamour and he said to the gods in council, 'The uproar of mankind is intolerable and sleep is no longer possible by reason of the babel.' So the gods in their hearts were moved to let loose the deluge; but my lord Ea warned me in a dream. He whispered their words to my house of reeds, 'Reed-house, reed-house! Wall, O wall, hearken reed-house, wall reflect; O man of Shurrupak, son of Ubara-Tutu; tear down your house and build a boat, abandon possessions and look for life, despise worldly goods and save your soul alive. Tear down your house, I say, and build a boat.'

"When I had understood I said to my lord, 'Behold, what you have commanded I will honour and perform, but how shall I answer the people, the city, the elders?' Then Ea opened his mouth and said to me, his servant, 'Tell them this: I have learnt that Enlil is wrathful against me, I dare no longer walk in his land nor live in his city; I will go down to the Gulf to dwell with Ea my lord. But on you he will rain down abundance, rare fish and shy wild-fowl, a rich harvest-tide. In the evening the rider of the storm will bring you wheat in torrents.' " . . .

"On the seventh day the boat was complete. . . .

"I loaded into her all that I had of gold and of living things, my family, my kin, the beasts of the field both wild and tame, and all the craftsmen. . . .

"For six days and six nights the winds blew, torrent and tempest and flood overwhelmed the world, tempest and flood raged together like warring hosts. When the seventh day dawned the storm from the south subsided, the sea grew

---

[1] Gods.

[2] God of wisdom and good fortune.

calm, the flood was stilled; I looked at the face of the world and there was silence, all mankind was turned to clay. The surface of the sea stretched as flat as a rooftop; I opened a hatch and the light fell on my face. Then I bowed low, I sat down and I wept, the tears streamed down my face, for on every side was the waste of water. I looked for land in vain, but fourteen leagues distant there appeared a mountain, and there the boat grounded; on the mountain of Nisir the boat held fast, she held fast and did not budge. . . . When the seventh day dawned I loosed a dove and let her go. She flew away, but finding no resting-place she returned. Then I loosed a swallow, and she flew away but finding no resting-place she returned. I loosed a raven, she saw that the waters had retreated, she ate, she flew around, she cawed, and she did not come back. Then I threw everything open to the four winds, I made a sacrifice and poured out a libation on the mountain top. Seven and again seven cauldrons I set up on their stands, I heaped up wood and cane and cedar and myrtle. When the gods smelled the sweet savour, they gathered like flies over the sacrifice. Then, at last, Ishtar also came, she lifted her necklace with the jewels of heaven that once Anu had made to please her. 'O you gods here present, by the lapis lazuli round my neck I shall remember these days as I remember the jewels of my throat; these last days I shall not forget. Let all the gods gather round the sacrifice, except Enlil. He shall not approach this offering, for without reflection he brought the flood; he consigned my people to destruction.'

"When Enlil had come, when he saw the boat, he was wrath and swelled with anger at the gods, the host of heaven, 'Has any of these mortals escaped? Not one was to have survived the destruction.' Then the god of the wells and canals Ninurta opened his mouth and said to the warrior Enlil, 'Who is there of the gods that can devise without Ea? It is Ea alone who knows all things.' Then Ea opened his mouth and spoke to warrior Enlil, 'Wisest of gods, hero Enlil, how could you so senselessly bring down the flood?" . . .

"Then Enlil went up into the boat, he took me by the hand and my wife and made us enter the boat and kneel down on either side, he standing between us. He touched our foreheads to bless us saying, 'In time past Utnapishtim was a mortal man; henceforth he and his wife shall live in the distance at the mouth of the rivers.' Thus it was that the gods took me and placed me here to live in the distance, at the mouth of the rivers."

The Laws of Hammurabi

Much information about the peoples of Mesopotamia comes from compilations of laws, prescriptions, and decisions that were written as early as the twenty-third century B.C. The best known of these are the Laws of Hammurabi (often referred to as the Code of Hammurabi), issued by an eighteenth-century Babylonian king who probably used older

SOURCE: James B. Pritchard, ed. *Ancient Near-Eastern Texts Relative to the Old Testament* (Princeton: Princeton University Press, 1950), pp. 166–168, 172, 175.

Sumerian and Akkadian laws. The laws refer to almost all aspects of life in Babylonia. The following selections are taken from this code, which originally had about 282 articles and included a lengthy prologue and epilogue.

> **Consider:** *The principles of justice reflected by these laws; the social divisions in Babylonian society disclosed in these laws; the political and economic characteristics of Babylonia revealed in this document.*

1: If a seignior[39] accused a(nother) seignior and brought a charge of murder against him, but has not proved it, his accuser shall be put to death.

✢

3: If a seignior came forward with false testimony in a case, and has not proved the word which he spoke, if that case was a case involving life, that seignior shall be put to death.

4: If he came forward with (false) testimony concerning grain or money, he shall bear the penalty of that case.

✢

6: If a seignior stole the property of church or state, that seignior shall be put to death; also the one who received the stolen goods from his hand shall be put to death.

✢

17: If a seignior caught a fugitive male or female slave in the open and has taken him to his owner, the owner of the slave shall pay him two shekels[48] of silver.

18: If that slave will not name his owner, he shall take him to the palace in order that his record may be investigated, and they shall return him to his owner.

19: If he has kept that slave in his house (and) later the slave has been found in his possession, that seignior shall be put to death.

✢

22: If a seignior committed robbery and has been caught, that seignior shall be put to death.

---

[39] The word *awēlum,* used here, is literally "man," but in the legal literature it seems to be used in at least three senses: (1) sometimes to indicate a man of the higher class, a noble; (2) sometimes a free man of any class, high or low; and (3) occasionally a man of any class, from king to slave. For the last I use the inclusive word "man," but for the first two, since it is seldom clear which of the two is intended in a given context, I follow the ambiguity of the original and use the rather general term "seignior," which I employ as the term is employed in Italian and Spanish, to indicate any free man of standing, and not in the strict feudal sense, although the ancient Near East did have something approximating the feudal system, and that is another reason for using "seignior."

[48] A weight of about 8 grams.

23: If the robber has not been caught, the robbed seignior shall set forth the particulars regarding his lost property in the presence of god, and the city and governor, in whose territory and district the robbery was committed, shall make good to him his lost property.

✿

48: If a debt is outstanding against a seignior and Adad has inundated his field or a flood has ravaged (it) or through lack of water grain has not been produced in the field, he shall not make any return of grain to his creditor in that year; he shall cancel his contract-tablet and he shall pay no interest for that year.

✿

53: If a seignior was too lazy to make [the dike of] his field strong and did not make his dike strong and a break has opened up in his dike and he has accordingly let the water ravage the farmland, the seignior in whose dike the break was opened shall make good the grain that he let get destroyed.

54: If he is not able to make good the grain, they shall sell him and his goods, and the farmers whose grain the water carried off shall divide (the proceeds).

141: If a seignior's wife, who was living in the house of the seignior, has made up her mind to leave in order that she may engage in business, thus neglecting her house (and) humiliating her husband, they shall prove it against her; and if her husband has then decided on her divorce, he may divorce her, with nothing to be given her as her divorce-settlement upon her departure. If her husband has not decided on her divorce, her husband may marry another woman, with the former woman living in the house of her husband like a maidservant.

142: If a woman so hated her husband that she has declared, "You may not have me," her record shall be investigated at her city council, and if she was careful and was not at fault, even though her husband has been going out and disparaging her greatly, that woman, without incurring any blame at all, may take her dowry and go off to her father's house.

✿

195: If a son has struck his father, they shall cut off his hand.

196: If a seignior has destroyed the eye of a member of the aristocracy, they shall destroy his eye.

197: If he has broken a(nother) seignior's bone, they shall break his bone.

198: If he has destroyed the eye of a commoner or broken the bone of a commoner, he shall pay one mina of silver.

199: If he has destroyed the eye of a seignior's slave or broken the bone of a seignior's slave, he shall pay one-half his value.

200: If a seignior has knocked out a tooth of a seignior of his own rank, they shall knock out his tooth.

201: If he has knocked out a commoner's tooth, he shall pay one-third mina of silver.

202: If a seignior has struck the cheek of a seignior who is superior to him, he shall be beaten sixty (times) with an oxtail whip in the assembly.

✿

209: If a seignior struck a(nother) seignior's daughter and has caused her to have a miscarriage, he shall pay ten shekels of silver for her fetus.

210: If that woman has died, they shall put his daughter to death.

211: If by a blow he has caused a commoner's daughter to have a miscarriage, he shall pay five shekels of silver.

212: If that woman has died, he shall pay one-half mina of silver.

Hymn to the Pharaoh

The history of Egypt and the institution of kingship have been traced back to the end of the fourth millennium B.C., when Upper and Lower Egypt were unified, apparently under one great conquering king. The Egyptian king, or pharaoh, was considered both a god and the absolute ruler of his country. These beliefs are reflected in laudatory hymns addressed to pharaohs. The following selection is from one of those hymns, dating from the reign of Sesostris III, who ruled from about 1880 to 1840 B.C.

> **Consider:** *The Egyptian perception of the pharaoh; what deeds or powers of the pharaoh seemed most important to the Egyptians.*

He hath come unto us that he may carry away Upper Egypt;
    the double diadem[1] hath rested on his head.
He hath come unto us and hath united the Two Lands; he
    hath mingled the reed (?)[2] with the bee.
He hath come unto us and hath brought the Black Land[3]
    under his sway; he hath apportioned to himself the Red
    Land.[3]
He hath come unto us and hath taken the Two Lands under
    his protection; he hath given peace to the Two Riverbanks.
He hath come unto us and hath made Egypt to live; he hath banished its
    suffering.
He hath come unto us and hath made the people to live; he hath caused the
    throat of the subjects to breathe.

SOURCE: Adolf Erman, *The Literature of the Ancient Egyptians,* trans. Aylward M. Blackman (London: Methuen & Co., Ltd, 1927), pp. 136–137. Reprinted by permission.

[1] That form of the diadem, in which the crown of Upper Egypt is inserted into that of Lower Egypt.

[2] The emblem of Upper Egypt, with which also its king is written, whereas the king of Lower Egypt is denoted in the writing by the bee.

[3] Egyptian and non-Egyptian territory.

He hath come unto us and hath trodden down the foreign
    countries; he hath smitten the Troglodytes[4] that knew
    not the dread of him.
He hath come unto us and hath (done battle for) his boundaries;
    he hath delivered them that were robbed. . . .
    (*A destroyed verse.*)
He hath come unto us, that we may (nurture up?) our children
    and bury our aged ones. . . .

---

[4] A people in the desert between Upper Egypt and the Red Sea, who plundered travelers. The king had just fought against them, as is evident from the following verse.

Egypt's Southern Neighbors
Harkhuf

The civilizations of the Nile valley usually encompassed two regions: Egypt in the north, from the Nile delta south to the Aswan, and the region to the south, from Aswan to modern Khartoum. The southern region was the land occupied by the Nubians or the Kushites of the Old Testament. Recent archaeological research has shown that this region shared the Pharaonic culture but had not developed as large a centralized state as Egypt. Throughout the period of Pharaonic Egypt, the two regions had extensive commercial relations and various episodes of collaboration and conflict. However, for much of the period of ancient Egyptian history the two regions were politically independent. The following excerpt, dating from around 2250 B.C., was written by Harkhuf, an Egyptian governor. Harkhuf is leading a trading expedition for the Pharaoh Mernere to Yam—a Nubian-controlled state to the south of Egypt. The text illustrates some of the more peaceful aspects of the relationship between Egypt and its southern neighbors.

> **Consider:** *The economic relationship between these two areas where cultural relations overlap; why Harkhuf had to bring troops and meet with local leaders; the religious status Egyptians gave the southern regions.*

The majesty of Mernere[1] my lord, sent me, together with my father, the sole companion, and ritual priest, Iri to Yam, in order to explore a road to this country. I did it in only seven months, and I brought all (kinds of) gifts from it. I was very greatly praised for it.

His majesty sent me a second time alone; I went forth upon the Elephantine road, and I descended [south from Egypt through lands to Yam in the Sudan,]

SOURCE: Excerpts from James Breasted, ed., *Ancient Records of Egypt*, vols. 1 and 4, (Chicago: University of Chicago Press).

[1] The Pharaoh Mernere (c2250 B.C.) who personally oversaw the subjection of the kings of lower Nubia.

being an affair of eight months. When I descended I brought gifts from this country in very great quantity. Never before was the like brought to this land. . . . I explored these countries. Never had any companion or caravan-conductor who went forth to Yam before this, done (it).

His majesty now sent me a third time to Yam; I went forth and I found the chief of Yam going to the land of Temeh to smite Temeh as far as the western corner of heaven. I went forth after him to the land of Temeh, and I pacified him, until he praised all the gods for the king's sake. . . .

I descended with 300 asses laden with incense, ebony, heknu, grain, panthers, ivory, throw-sticks, and every good product. Now when the chief of Irthet, Sethu, and Wawat[2] saw how strong and numerous was the troop of Yam, which descended with me to the court, and the soldiers who had been sent with me, (then) this [chief] brought and gave to me bulls and small cattle, and conducted me to the roads of the highlands of Irthet, because I was more excellent, vigilant . . . than any count, companion or caravan-conductor, who had been sent to Yam before. Now, when the servant there was descending to the court, one sent the . . . sole companion, the master of the bath, Khuni up-stream with a vessel laden with datewine, cakes, bread, and beer. The count, wearer of the royal seal, sole companion, ritual priest, treasurer of the god, privy councilor of decrees, the revered, Harkhuf.

[The king of Egypt, informed of Harkhuf's return from the south with various gifts, sent to Harkhuf the following instructions:]

Come northward to the court immediately; thou shalt bring this dwarf with thee, which thou bringest living, prosperous and healthy from the land of spirits, for the dances of the god, to rejoice and gladden the heart of the king of Upper and Lower Egypt, who lives forever. When he goes down with thee into the vessel, appoint excellent people, who shall be beside him on each side of the vessel; take care lest he fall into the water. When [he] sleeps at night appoint excellent people, who shall sleep beside him in his tent; inspect ten times a night. My majesty desires to see this dwarf more than the gifts of Sinai and of Punt.[3] If thou arrivest at court this dwarf being with thee alive, prosperous and healthy, my majesty will do for thee a greater thing than that which was done for the treasurer of the god, Burded in the time of Isesi, according to the heart's desire of my majesty to see this dwarf.

Commands have been sent to the chief of the New Towns, the companion, and superior prophet, to command that sustenance be taken from him in every store-city and every temple, without stinting therein.

---

[2] Lands south of Egypt.

[3] The areas along the Red Sea.

The Old Testament—
Genesis and Exodus

Squeezed between the larger kingdoms of Mesopotamia and Egypt were a number of small states. For the development of Western civilization, the most important of these states was in Palestine, where the Hebrews formed Israel and Judah. Although their roots extend further into the past, the Hebrews were originally led out of northeastern Egypt toward Palestine by Moses near the end of the second millennium B.C. The power of the Hebrew nation reached its height during the tenth and ninth centuries B.C., but the nation's importance rests primarily in the religion developed by the Hebrews. Judaism differed in many ways from other Near Eastern religions, particularly in its monotheism, its contractual nature, and its ethical mandates. These characteristics of Judaism are illustrated in the following selections from Genesis and Exodus.

> **Consider:** *The relationship between God and people illustrated in these selections; how these Hebrew beliefs compare with Egyptian beliefs; as a set of laws, how these selections compare with Hammurabi's Code.*

12. Now the Lord said to Abram, "Go from your country and your kindred and your father's house to the land that I will show you. And I will make of you a great nation, and I will bless you, and make your name great, so that you will be a blessing. I will bless those who bless you, and him who curses you I will curse; and by you all the families of the earth will bless themselves."

✽

19. On the third new moon after the people of Israel had gone forth out of the land of Egypt, on that day they came into the wilderness of Sinai. And when they set from Rephídim and came into the wilderness of Sinai, they encamped in the wilderness; and there Israel encamped before the mountain. And Moses went up to God, and the LORD called him out of the mountain, saying, "Thus you shall say to the house of Jacob, and tell the people of Israel: You have seen what I did to the Egyptians, and how I bore you on eagles' wings and brought you to myself. Now therefore, if you will obey my voice and keep my covenant, you shall be my own possession among all peoples; for all the earth is mine, and you shall be to me a kingdom of priests and a holy nation. These are the words which you shall speak to the children of Israel."

So Moses came and called the elders of the people, and set before them all these words which the LORD had commanded him. And all the people answered

SOURCE: *The Holy Bible: Revised Standard Version* (New York: Thomas Nelson, 1953). Genesis, p. 11; Exodus, pp. 75–77. Scripture quotations are from the Revised Standard Version Bible, copyright © 1946, 1952, 1971 by the Division of Christian Education of the National Council of the Churches of Christ in the U.S.A. Used by permission.

together and said, "All that the Lord has spoken we will do." And Moses reported the words of the people to the LORD.

°

20. And God spoke all these words saying,

"I am the Lord your God, who brought you out of the land of Egypt, out of the house of bondage.

"You shall have no other gods before me.

"You shall not make yourself a graven image, or any likeness of anything that is in heaven above, or that is in the earth beneath, or that is in the water under the earth; you shall not bow down to them or serve them; for I the LORD your God am a jealous God, visiting the iniquity of the fathers upon the children to the third and the fourth generation of those who hate me, but showing steadfast love to thousands of those who love me and keep my commandments.

"You shall not take the name of the LORD your God in vain; for the LORD will not hold him guiltless who takes his name in vain.

"Remember the sabbath day, to keep it holy. Six days you shall labor, and do all your work; but the seventh day is a sabbath to the LORD your God; in it you shall not do any work, you, or your son, or your daughter, your manservant, or your maidservant, or your cattle, or the sojourner who is within your gates; for in six days the Lord made heaven and earth, the sea, and all that is in them, and rested the seventh day; therefore the LORD blessed the sabbath day and hallowed it.

"Honor your father and your mother, that your days may be long in the land which the LORD your God gives you.

"You shall not kill.

"You shall not commit adultery.

"You shall not steal.

"You shall not bear false witness against your neighbor.

"You shall not covet your neighbor's house; you shall not covet your neighbor's wife, or his manservant, or his maidservant; or his ox, or his ass, or anything that is your neighbor's."

Now when all the people perceived the thunderings and the lightnings and the sound of the trumpet and the mountain smoking, the people were afraid and trembled; and they stood afar off, and said to Moses, "You speak to us, and we will hear; but let not God speak to us, lest we die." And Moses said to the people, "Do not fear; for God has come to prove you, and that the fear of him may be before your eyes, that you may not sin."

The Aton Hymn and Psalm 104: The Egyptians and the Hebrews

Despite characteristics that made them unique in the area, Hebrews were connected to and influenced by the Egyptians in many ways. Geographically, Palestine served as a buffer zone between Egypt and the large kingdoms of Mesopotamia. Historically, the formative ordeal of Moses and the Exodus stemmed from Egypt. Less apparent but of great importance were connections between Hebrew and Egyptian religious concepts and forms of expression. The following comparison of selections from the Egyptian Aton Hymn, composed in the fourteenth century B.C. during the rule of Akhenaton, who attempted to change some traditional religious views, and Psalm 104 from the Old Testament, written six or seven centuries later, illustrates striking parallels between the two documents.

Consider: *How the similarities between these two excerpts might be explained.*

THE ATON HYMN

When thou settest in the western
    horizon,
The land is in darkness like death . . .
Every lion comes forth from his den;

All creeping things, they sting.

At daybreak, when thou arisest in the
    horizon . . .
Thou drivest away the darkness . . .
Men awake and stand upon their
    feet . . .
All the world, they do their labor.
How manifold are thy works!
They are hidden from man's sight.
O sole god, like whom there is no
    other,
Thou hast made the earth
    according to thy desire.

PSALM 104

Thou makest darkness and it is night,
Wherein all the beasts of the forest
    creep forth.
The young lions roar after their prey.

The sun ariseth, they get them
    away . . .

Man goeth forth unto his work,
And to his labor until the evening.
O Jahweh, how manifold are thy
    works!
In wisdom has thou made them all;
The earth is full of thy riches.

SOURCE: Reprinted in *The Burden of Egypt* by John A. Wilson by permission of The University of Chicago Press. Copyright © 1951, p. 227.

VISUAL SOURCES

Sumer: The "Royal Standard" of Ur

This piece of art—made of shell, lapis lazuli, and red stone inlaid on the sides of a wooden box and found in a grave dating around 2700 B.C.—illustrates two aspects of Sumerian life: war and peace. In the bottom line of the first panel, reading from left to right, a wooden chariot charges the enemy and knocks him over. In the second line the infantry, with protective cloaks, helmets, and short spears, captures and leads off the enemy. In the third line soldiers on the right lead captives to the king in the center. The king, who has just alighted from his attended chariot on the left, towers over the rest. In the second panel the fruits of victory or of peace are enjoyed, at least by the court. In the bottom and middle lines produce, manufactured goods, and livestock are brought to a banquet by bearers and menials. In the top line the king on the left and his soldiers drink wine while attended by servants and serenaded by a harpist and female singer on the right.

Clearly, this offers evidence for what historians consider a civilized society. Agricultural products are shown. Various animals have been domesticated for specialized purposes. Important inventions such as the wheel are in use. Leisure activities have been cultivated as revealed by the harp, the rather formal banquet, and the existence of this piece of art itself (which may have been a box for a lyre). The society has been organized and displays some discipline as indicated by the use of chariots, the infantry, the porters, the musicians, the servants, and the banquet itself. Finally, the king represents centralized political authority that is directly tied to military prowess. Note that the sole female figure here is the singer.

*   **Consider:** *Why there is a lack of individual differences in the people portrayed in this picture; bases for social distinction in Sumerian society revealed in this scene; things or scenes missing from this that you might have expected to find; reasons why the artist chose to portray these particular scenes and to include only the things you see here.*

Egyptian Wall Paintings from the Tomb of Menna

This wall painting from the tomb of an Egyptian scribe, Menna, dating from the late fifteenth century B.C., illustrates the basis of Egyptian economic life. This pictorial record of a harvest should be read from bottom to top. In the bottom row, from left to right, commoners are harvesting wheat with sickles. The wheat is then carried in rope baskets past two girls fighting over remaining bits of wheat and past two laborers (one of whom is playing a flute), who are taking a break under a date tree, to where the wheat is being

Photo 1-1

The British Museum

threshed and raked out by laborers. In the second row, from right to left, oxen tread on the wheat, separating the kernels from the husks, and laborers remove the chaff by scooping up the wheat and allowing it to fall in the wind. The grain is then brought to the supervising scribe, Menna, standing in a kiosk. Menna is aided by subordinate recording scribes. In the top row, from left to right, the fields are being measured by ropes as a basis for assessing taxes. In the center Menna watches as subordinates line up and whip those who have apparently failed to pay their taxes or adequately perform their duties. Finally, the grain is stacked for shipment and carried off in a boat.

Photo 1-2

Elliot Erwitt/Magnum

The harvest seems plentiful, and Egyptian society is tightly organized around it—from the gathering, processing, and shipping of the wheat to the assessing of taxes and enforcement of laws. Menna's authority is denoted by his size, by his placement in a kiosk, and by the symbols of power placed in his hand and immediately around him. The importance of writing in early societies is also demonstrated: Menna and his immediate subordinates are in an authoritative position in part because they can write, a skill connected here to the ability of the central authority to organize the economy and exact taxes. Finally, this wall painting reveals part of the nature of Egyptian religious beliefs. The scene is painted on the inside of a tomb. Thus the paintings were not for the living public, as the tombs were not to be visited, but for the dead or the world of the dead. This implies a belief that there were strong connections between the world, what one did in it, and the afterlife.

> **Consider:** *The evidence for the existence of a civilized society here; the similarities and differences between this and the "Royal Standard" of Ur.*

The Environment and the Rise of Civilization in Southwestern Asia and Northeastern Africa

These three maps relate weather, vegetation, agricultural sites, and civiization in south-western Asia and northeastern Africa. The first map shows the average annual rainfall in modern times (although weather patterns may have changed over the last five thousand years, it is likely that they have not changed greatly). The second map shows some of the vegetation patterns and a number of the earliest agricultural sites that have been discovered in the same area. The third map shows patterns of civilization in this part of the world.

Together, these maps indicate a tendency for early agricultural sites to locate in areas of substantial rainfall and subtropical woodland, both appropriate for cereal farming.

Map 1-1   Rainfall

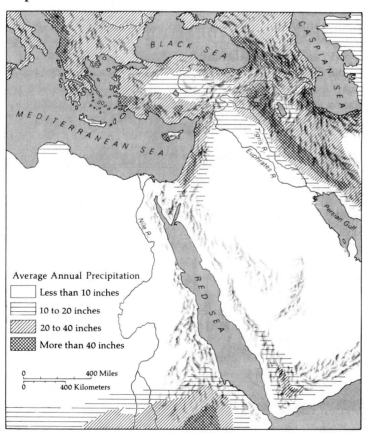

Average Annual Precipitation

Less than 10 inches
10 to 20 inches
20 to 40 inches
More than 40 inches

0   400 Miles
0   400 Kilometers

Map 1-2   Vegetation and Agricultural Sites

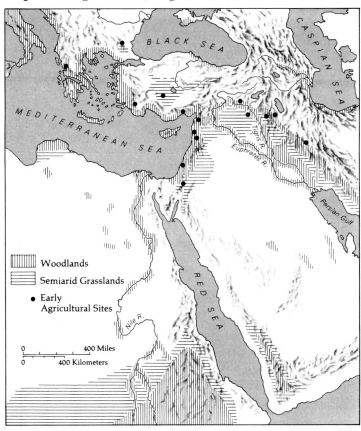

These areas often eventually supported the development of civilizations. Yet the earliest civilizations generally do not fall in these areas, but rather in areas of low rainfall that have a narrow strip of subtropical woodland along riverbanks. The rivers could compensate for the lack of rain, but this presented the challenge of developing irrigation systems along with corresponding social and political organization, which is what happened in the earliest civilizations of Mesopotamia and Egypt.

> **Consider:** *How geographic and climatic factors help explain the rise of civilization in Mesopotamia and Egypt; how geographic and climatic factors facilitated the growth of settlements in some areas but not the blossoming of those settlements into large, organized societies.*

Map 1-3   Civilization

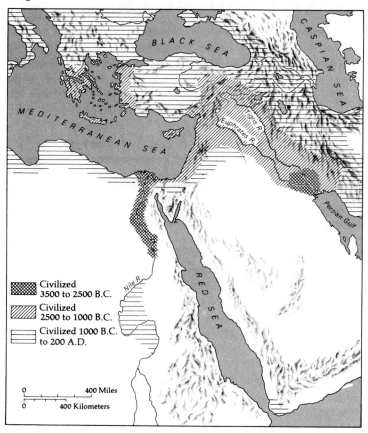

SECONDARY SOURCES

The Agricultural Revolution
Robert J. Braidwood

Human beings populated parts of the earth for thousands of years before the first civiliza-
tions arose five or six thousand years ago. The causes for this relatively rapid transforma-
tion in the condition of human beings have been interpreted in a variety of ways. How-
ever, most historians and anthropologists point to the agricultural revolution of the
Neolithic Age, in which—through the domestication of plants and animals—human be-
ings became food producers rather than hunters and food gatherers, as the central devel-
opment in this transformation to civilization. In the following selection, Robert J. Braid-
wood, an archaeologist and anthropologist, analyzes the agricultural revolution, its
spread, and its significance.

> **Consider:** *The origins or causes of the agricultural revolution; Braidwood's rejec-*
> *tion of environmental determinism and his acceptance of cultural differentiation*
> *and specialization; connections between agriculture and the beginnings of cities.*

Tool-making was initiated by pre-*sapiens* man. The first comparable achievement
of our species was the agricultural revolution. No doubt a small human population
could have persisted on the sustenance secured by the hunting and food-gathering
technology that had been handed down and slowly improved upon over the 500
to 1,000 millennia of pre-human and pre-*sapiens* experience. With the domestication of plants and animals, however, vast new dimensions for cultural evolution
suddenly became possible. The achievement of an effective food-producing technology may not have predetermined subsequent developments, but they followed
swiftly: the first urban societies in a few thousand years and contemporary industrial civiization in less than 10,000 years.

The first successful experiment in food production took place in southwestern
Asia, on the hilly flanks of the "fertile crescent." Later experiments in agriculture
occurred (possibly independently) in China and (certainly independently) in the
New World. The multiple occurrence of the agricultural revolution suggests that
it was a highly probable outcome of the prior cultural evolution of mankind and
a peculiar combination of environmental circumstances. It is in the record of
culture, therefore, that the origin of agriculture must be sought.

SOURCE: Robert J. Braidwood, "The Agricultural Revolution," *in* C. C. Lamberg-Karlovsky, ed.,
Hunters, Farmers, and Civilizations: Old World Archaeology. Copyright © 1979 by W. H.
Freeman and Company. Reprinted with permission.

Not long ago the proponents of environmental determinism argued that the agricultural revolution was a response to the great changes in climate which accompanied the retreat of the last glaciation about 10,000 years ago. However, the climate had altered in equally dramatic fashion on other occasions in the past 75,000 years, and the potentially domesticable plants and animals were surely available to the bands of food-gatherers who lived in southwestern Asia and similar habitats in various parts of the globe. Moreover, recent studies have revealed that the climate did not change radically where farming began in the hills that flank the fertile crescent. Environmental determinists have also argued from the "theory of propinquity" that the isolation of men along with appropriate plants and animals in desert oases started the process of domestication.

In my opinion there is no need to complicate the story with extraneous "causes." The food-producing revolution seems to have occurred as the culmination of the ever increasing cultural differentiation and specialization of human communities. Around 8000 B.C. the inhabitants of the hills around the fertile crescent had come to know their habitat so well that they were beginning to domesticate the plants and animals they had been collecting and hunting. At slightly later times human cultures reached the corresponding level in Central America and perhaps in the Andes, in southeastern Asia and in China. From these "nuclear" zones cultural diffusion spread the new way of life to the rest of the world.

As the agricultural revolution began to spread, the trend toward ever increasing specialization of the intensified food-collecting way of life began to reverse itself. The new techniques were capable of wide application, given suitable adaptation, in diverse environments. Archaeological remains at Hassuna, a site near the Tigris River somewhat later than Jarmo, show that the people were exchanging ideas on the manufacture of pottery and of flint and obsidian projectile points with people in the region of the Amouq in Syro-Cilicia. The basic elements of the foodpro-ducing complex—wheat, barley, sheep, goats and probably cattle—in this period moved west beyond the bounds of their native habitat to occupy the whole eastern end of the Mediterranean. They also traveled as far east as Anau, east of the Caspian Sea. Localized cultural differences still existed, but people were adopting and adapting more and more cultural traits from other areas. Eventually the new way of life traveled to the Aegean and beyond into Europe, moving slowly up such great river valley systems as the Dnieper, the Danube and the Rhone, as well as along the coasts. The intensified food-gatherers of Europe accepted the new way of life, but, as V. Gordon Childe has pointed out, they "were not slavish imitators: they adapted the gifts from the East . . . into a new and organic whole capable of developing on its own original lines." Among other things, the Europeans appear to have domesticated rye and oats that were first imported to the European continent as weed plants contaminating the seed of wheat and barley. In the comparable diffusion of agriculture from Central America, some of the peoples to the north appear to have rejected the new ways, at least temporarily.

By about 5000 B.C. the village-farming way of life seems to have been fingering down the valleys toward the alluvial bottom lands of the Tigris and Euphrates.

Robert M. Adams believes that there may have been people living in the lowlands who were expert in collecting food from the rivers. They would have taken up the idea of farming from people who came down from the higher areas. In the bottom lands a very different climate, seasonal flooding of the land and small-scale irrigation led agriculture through a significant new technological transformation. By about 4000 B.C. the people of southern Mesopotamia had achieved such increases in productivity that their farms were beginning to support an urban civilization. The ancient site at Ubaid is typical of this period.

Thus in 3,000 or 4,000 years the life of man had changed more radically than in all of the preceding 250,000 years. Before the agricultural revolution most men must have spent their waking moments seeking their next meal, except when they could gorge following a great kill. As man learned to produce food, instead of gathering, hunting or collecting it, and to store it in the grain bin and on the hoof, he was compelled as well as enabled to settle in larger communities. With human energy released for a whole spectrum of new activities, there came the development of specialized nonagricultural crafts. It is no accident that such innovations as the discovery of the basic mechanical principles, weaving, the plow, the wheel and metallurgy soon appeared.

Bronze Age Cities and Civilizations
C. C. Lamberg-Karlovsky

Most historians agree that civilization started in Mesopotamia and Egypt some five or six thousand years ago. However, historians—as well as archaeologists and anthropologists—have had difficulty agreeing upon a definition of "civilization." Part of the problem is to define civilization without being overly swayed by what we value most about our own cultures and societies. Another problem is to agree upon which traits are most crucial in a definition—be they writing, urbanization, or something else. In the following selection, C. C. Lamberg-Karlovsky surveys some of the problems in defining civilization.

Consider: *How "civilization" might be defined; the differences between the various definitions in this selection.*

What is civilization? The word *civilization* is by no means an old word or concept. Boswell reported that in 1772 he urged Johnson to insert the word in his dictionary, but the doctor declined; he preferred the older word *civility*, which, in being derived from the Latin *civitas*, reflects the world of the city dweller. V. G. Childe

SOURCE: C. C. Lamberg-Karlovsky, "Bronze Age Cities and Civilizations: Introduction," *in* C. C. Lamberg-Karlovsky, ed., *Hunters, Farmers, and Civilizations: Old World Archaeology.* Copyright © 1979 by W. H. Freeman and Company. Reprinted with permission.

. . . provided a list of material inventions that he believed were responsible for transforming people into urban dwellers: writing, use of animals for traction, wheeled carts, the plow, metallurgy, standard units of weight and volume, sailing boats, surplus production, specialization of craftsmen, irrigation technology, and mathematics. However, such a list is of very little help in defining a civilization, and it adds absolutely nothing to our understanding of how and why these inventions came about in the first place.

At neolithic Çayönü Tepesi about 7000 B.C. . . . there was metallurgy; sailing was already evident in Europe by 5000 B.C., as was irrigation at neolithic Beidha, Palestine; and specialized craftsmen may be posited as the artists of the Paleolithic. It is quite clear that neither a single criterion nor any list of criteria will succeed in defining civilization. Yet, if any single invention stands out as creating a dramatic change in social organization, I think it must be writing.

An attempt to define civilization made at a symposium held in 1958 at the Oriental Institute of the University of Chicago was perhaps more successful than others. . . . At that symposium the anthropologist Clyde Kluckhohn argued that there were three essential criteria for civilization: (1) towns containing 5,000 or more people, (2) writing, and (3) monumental ceremonial centers. The Assyriologist I. Gelb stated, "I have reached the conclusion that writing is of such importance that civilization cannot exist without it, and, conversely, that writing cannot exist except in a civilization." I would agree with this, were it not for the Inca and Maya of the New World, peoples who lacked full writing and yet cannot be denied the status of civilization, however one chooses to define the concept. Robert M. Adams, . . . an archaeologist and anthropologist, perhaps came closest to a working definition. He argued for a definition of civilization as a society with functionally interrelated set of social institutions, which he listed as:

1. Class stratification, each stratum marked by a highly different degree of ownership or control of the main productive resources.
2. Political and religious hierarchies complementing each other in the administration of territorially organized states.
3. Complex division of labor, with full-time craftsmen, servants, soldiers, and officials existing alongside the great mass of primary, peasant producers.

Professor Adams' criteria thus concentrated on sociological phenomena that, when found working together, constitute a civilization.

Freedom in the Ancient World: Civilization in Sumer

Herbert J. Muller

Historians generally see the development of cities as a sign of transformation into a civilized state and indeed an essential component of being civilized. Some of the earliest cities were formed by the Sumerians in the valley of the Tigris and Euphrates rivers, where settlers had already developed irrigation systems. In the following selection Herbert J. Muller analyzes the social and political significance of cities and irrigation systems for the Sumerians, and focuses on the problems that civilization brought.

> **Consider:** *Why cities and irrigation systems require new systems of legal and political control, why Muller believes that the increased wealth and opportunity created by civilization was not an unmitigated benefit to the Sumerians.*

We must now consider the problems that came with civilization—problems due not so much to the sinful nature of man as to the nature of the city. "Friendship lasts a day" ran a Sumerian proverb; "kinship endures forever." The heterogeneous city was no longer held together by the bonds of kinship. Even the family was unstable. "For his pleasure: marriage," ran another proverb; "on his thinking it over: divorce." Hence the Sumerians could no longer depend on the informal controls of custom or common understanding that had sufficed to maintain order in the village. They had to supplement custom by political controls, a system of laws, backed by both force and moral persuasion. In this sense the city created the problem of evil. Here, not in Eden, occurred the Fall.

More specifically, the rise of civilization forced the social question that is still with us. By their great drainage and irrigation system the Sumerians were able to produce an increasing surplus of material wealth. The question is: Who was to possess and enjoy this wealth? The answer in Sumer was to be the invariable one: Chiefly a privileged few. The god who in theory owned it all in fact required the services of priestly bailiffs, and before long these were doing more than their share in assisting him to enjoy it, at the expense of the many menials beneath them. Class divisions grew more pronounced in the divine household, as in the city at large. The skilled artisans of Sumer, whose work in metals and gems has hardly ever been surpassed, became a proletariat, unable to afford their own products. . . . And outside its walls the city created still another type of man—the peasant. The villager had been preliterate, on a cultural par with his fellows; the peasant was illiterate, aware of the writing he did not know, aware of his dependence on the powers of the city, and liable to exploitation by them. Altogether,

---

SOURCE: Excerpted from pp. 33–35 in *Freedom in the Ancient World* by Herbert J. Muller. Copyright © 1961 by Harper & Row, Publishers, Inc. Reprinted by permission of HarperCollins Publishers.

the urban revolution produced the anomaly that would become more glaring with the Industrial Revolution. As the collective wealth increased, many men were worse off, and many more felt worse off, than the neolithic villager had been.

Similarly the great irrigation system posed a political problem: Who would control the organization it required, exercise the power it gave? The answer was the same—a privileged few. As the temple estate grew into a city, the priesthood needed more secular help, especially in time of war. Sumerian legend retained memories of some sort of democratic assembly in the early cities, but it emphasized that after the Flood "kingship descended from heaven." The gods had sent kings to maintain order and to assure the proper service of them upon which the city's welfare depended. This was not a pure heavenly boon, judging by the Sumerian myth of a Golden Age before the Flood: an Eden of peace and plenty in which there was no snake, scorpion, hyena, lion, wild dog, wolf—"There was no fear, no terror. Man had no rival." At any rate, the divinely appointed king ruled as an absolute monarch, and might be a terror. With him descended a plague of locusts—the tax collectors. Again civilization meant an anomaly: as the collective achieved much more effective freedom, many individuals enjoyed less freedom than prehistoric villagers had.

Women of Egypt and the Ancient Near East
Barbara S. Lesko

In the early Egyptian and Mesopotamian civilizations, women had greater access to valued political, religious, and economic positions than in civilizations that followed. What explains the changes that would make societies in the Near East more dominated by men and more oppressive to women? Barbara S. Lesko, an Egyptologist, addresses this question in the following excerpt. Here her focus is on the centuries toward the end of the third millennium and the beginning of the second millennium.

> **Consider:** *What three factors explain the decline of women's status and freedoms; how Egypt and early Sumer differed from later societies such as Assyria; other possible explanations for the decline of women's status and freedoms.*

What was the real cause of the rise of patriarchy, which became increasingly oppressive to women in the Near East after Sumerian civilization waned? Several

---

reasons suggest themselves. The first is militarism. In an early agrarian society like Egypt where internal disputes were effectively handled by the strong, centralized government, where wars usually took place beyond the borders, where no standing army existed during the first 1500 years of recorded history, and where invasion seldom affected the country, women continually shared the burdens, full rights, and obligations of citizens. However, in the newer societies, founded by the sons of ever-vigilant and suspicious desert nomads, where warfare between cities was frequent and invasion by outside hostile forces familiar, militarism developed, excluding women and rendering them dependent. Second, where commercialism held sway at the same time—as in Assyria—the worst examples of patriarchy were found. Commerce based on private initiative first appears on a well developed scale in the Old Babylonian period where the first concerted effort by men to control women for financial gain is also documented. This is seen not only in the laws of Hammurabi but in institutions like that of the cloistered *Naditu* women. Coupled with virulent militarism, as in Assyria, the rise of commercialism had a devastating effect on women's rights. In Egypt large scale commerce long remained a virtual monopoly of the state, so its impact on society remained less significant.

We might further point out that, even during the somewhat militaristic Egyptian empire of the New Kingdom, women's status and freedoms did not diminish significantly. This introduces a third factor: confidence. A supremely confident nation can afford tolerance. Egypt had confidence in its gods, in the eternity of life, and in the bounty of its land. Sumer, in its early formative years, shared these advantages too. Not so the subsequent societies. It is the threatened male and the threatened society—like Assyria, surrounded on three sides by deadly enemies, and weak impoverished Israel—which created such a restricted role for their women.

Chapter Questions

1. What characteristics of the societies discussed in this chapter fit with what we usually consider as civilized?
2. How would you explain the rise of these civilizations and their similarities?
3. Evaluate the relative importance of geographic, economic, and other factors in the differing natures of these early civilizations.
4. Drawing from both primary and secondary documents, describe some of the most likely of ancient peoples' assumptions and attitudes about the world, about their societies, and about women. How might some of these assumptions and attitudes differ in the various societies of the area?

TWO

India,
to A.D. 500

The earliest civilization in the Indian subcontinent arose in the Indus river valley around 2500 B.C. We know that large cities, such as Harappa in Northern Punjab and Mohenjo-daro further south, were formed and we can discern an organized society ruled by strong central government. However, their writings, and much else about this early civilization, remain a mystery, as does its collapse sometime between 1750 B.C. and 1500 B.C.

Soon thereafter Aryans, warrior nomads from Central Asia, migrated southeast into the Indus Valley, subdued the indigenous Dravidians, and planted the seeds of the caste system. When Aryan military expansion ended, priests gained influence and established Brahmanism. Our knowledge of these Aryans comes from stories in the *Vedas* (Divine Knowledge), a collection of popular wisdom, folklore, and religious beliefs. Later the *Brahmanas* and the *Upanishads* were written as guides to Vedic rituals and then popularized by wandering priests.

Out of these beliefs and practices Hinduism would emerge after the sixth century B.C. as a religion, a philosophy, and a guide to life. This same period of time would also witness a flourishing of new religions—Jainism and Buddhism—with messages of personal salvation becoming more accessible to the populace.

Meanwhile, India was developing a sophisticated civilization with vigorous urban centers and large territorial states ruled by hereditary kings who were supported by a hereditary priesthood. India's greatest ruler of the period was the Maurya king Asoka (273–232 B.C.) who encouraged the arts, Buddhism, paternal government, and public works. When the Maurya period ended in 185 B.C. anarchy resulted in northern India until the Kushans arrived from Central Asia to rule the region. Southern India remained an area of small prosperous kingdoms. Kushan reign was ended in the fourth century by the Guptas, who created what many believed was a relatively humane and gentle society.

The sources in this chapter focus on three broad themes. The first is the nature of India's social order during this long period. Emphasis is on the caste system, marriage, sex, and the role of women. The second theme involves religious precepts and philosophical traditions. Here Buddhism and Jainism are examined. The final theme is the development of Indian culture which brings elements of the first two themes together and emphasizes the problems of finding commonalities among a history of such mixed peoples, traditions, and teachings.

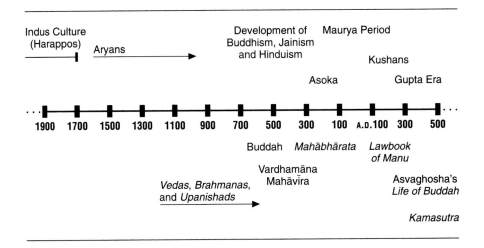

PRIMARY SOURCES

The Lawbook of Manu: The Caste System

With the advent of Brahmanism came the entrenchment of a new social order based on the teaching from the Rig-Veda, *which had decreed the division of the population into four distinct castes: Brahman (priests), Kshatriyas (warriors), Vaisyas (merchants, bureaucrats), and Shudras (menial workers). Subcastes, which eventually numbered in the hundreds, were based on skin color. Caste status was hereditary and intermarriage forbidden. There was no way to change one's caste status. The following two readings deal with this caste system.*

The first reading in this section is from the Manu Smriti *(Lawbook of Manu) which was said to be written around* A.D. *200 by the sage Manu as a guide to the domestic, religious, and social duties for all Hindus. It describes the creation of the different castes or classes and how they are part of the universe which the deity created.*

> **Consider:** *The ways the various castes are distinguished; the connections between religious beliefs and the established social order.*

But in the beginning he assigned their several names, actions, and conditions to all (created beings), even according to the words of the Veda.

He, the Lord, also created the class of the gods, who are endowed with life, and whose nature is action; and the subtile class of the Sādhyas, and the eternal sacrifice.

But from fire, wind, and the sun he drew forth the threefold eternal Veda, called *Rik,* Yajus, and Sāman, for the due performance of the sacrifice.

Time and the divisions of time, the lunar mansions and the planets, the rivers, the oceans, the mountains, plains, and uneven ground,

Austerity, speech, pleasure, desire, and anger, this whole creation he likewise produced, as he desired to call these beings into existence. . . .

Whatever he assigned to each at the (first) creation, noxiousness or harmlessness, gentleness or ferocity, virtue or sin, truth or falsehood, that clung (afterwards) spontaneously to it.

As at the change of the seasons each season of its own accord assumes its distinctive marks, even so corporeal beings (resume in new births) their (appointed) course of action.

But for the sake of the prosperity of the worlds, he created the Brāhman, the

SOURCE: F. Max Müller, ed., *The Sacred Books of the East,* vol. xxv (Oxford: At the Clarendon Press, 1886), pp. 12–14, 24.

Kshatriya, the Vaishya, and the Shūdra to proceed from his mouth, his arms, his thighs, and his feet. . . .

To Brāhmans he assigned teaching and studying (the Veda), sacrificing for their own benefit and for others, giving and accepting (of alms).

The Kshatriya he commanded to protect the people, to bestow gifts, to offer sacrifices, to study (the Veda), and to abstain from attaching himself to sensual pleasures. . . .

The Vaishya to tend cattle, to bestow gifts, to offer sacrifices, to study (the Veda), to trade, to lend money, and to cultivate land.

One occupation only the land prescribed to the Shūdra, to serve meekly even these (other) three castes.

The Mahābhārata

The second reading is from the Mahābhārata *(ca. 900 B.C.–A.D. 200), the world's longest poem with 100,000 couplets depicting a heroic conflict between two royal families. This excerpt describes the hierarchical social order which was believed to guarantee peace and prosperity. The episode is meant to demonstrate the harmony that results from the practice of this social order.*

> **Consider:** *Why societies attempt to create hierarchical social orders and whether they are solutions to the perceived problems they are meant to address.*

Bhīsma said: "I shall discourse on duties that are eternal. The suppression of wrath, truthfulness of speech, justice, forgiveness, begetting children upon one's own wedded wives, purity of conduct, avoidance of quarrel, simplicity, and maintenance of dependents—these nine duties belong to all the four orders (equally). Those duties, however, which belong exclusively to Brāhmanas, I shall now tell thee! Self-restraint,O king, has been declared to be the first duty of Brāhmanas. Study of the Vedas, and patience in undergoing austerities, . . . while engaged in the observance of his own duties, without doing any improper act, wealth comes to a peaceful Brāhmana possessed of knowledge, he should then marry and seek to beget children and should also practise charity and perform sacrifices. It has been declared by the wise that wealth thus obtained should be enjoyed by distributing it (among deserving persons and relatives). . . . I shall also tell thee, O Bhārata, what the duties are of a Kshatriya. A Kshatriya, O king, should give but not beg, should himself perform sacrfices but not officiate as a priest in the sacrifices of other's. He should never teach . . . but study. . . . He should protect the people. Always exerting himself for the destruction of robbers and wicked people, he should put forth his prowess in battle. . . . Persons conversant with the

SOURCE: Protap Chundra Roy, trans., *The Mahābhārata of Krishna-Dwaipayona Vyaa* (Calcutta: Bharata Press, 1883), pp. 81–83.

old scriptures do not applaud that Kshatriya who returns unwounded from battle. This has been declared to be the conduct of a wretched Kshatriya. There is no higher duty for him than the suppression of robbers. . . . I shall now tell thee, O Yudhishthira, what the eternal duties of the Vaishya are. A Vaishya should make gifts, study the Vedas, perform sacrifices, and acquire wealth by fair means. With proper attention he should also protect and rear all (domestic) animals as a sire protecting his sons. . . . The Creator, having created the (domestic) animals, bestowed their care upon the Vaishya. . . . I shall tell thee what the Vaishya's profession is and how he is to earn the means of his sustenance. If he keeps (for others) six kine, he may take the milk of one cow as his remuneration; and if he keeps (for others) a hundred kine, he may take a single pair as such fee. If he trades with other's wealth, he may take a seventh part of the profits (as his share). A seventh also is his share in the profits arising from the trade in horns, but he should take a sixteenth if the trade be in hoofs. If he engages in cultivation with seeds supplied by others, he may take a seventh part of the yield. This should be his annual remuneration. A Vaishya should never desire that he should not tend cattle. . . . I should tell thee, O Bhārata, what the duties of a Shudra are. The Creator intended the Shudra to become the servant of the other three orders. . . . By such service of the other three, a Shudra may obtain great happiness. He should wait upon the three other classes according to their order of seniority. A Shudra should never amass wealth, lest, by his wealth, he makes the numbers of the three superior classes obedient to him. By this he would incur sin. With the king's permission, however, a Shudra, for performing religious acts, may earn wealth. . . . It is said that Shudras should certainly be maintained by the (three) other orders. Worn out umbrellas, turbans, beds and seats, shoes, and fans, should be given to the Shudra servants. Torn clothes, which are no longer fit for wear, should be given away by the regenerate classes unto the Shudra. . . . The Shudra should never abandon his master whatever the nature or degree of the distress into which the latter may fall. If the master loses his wealth, he should with excessive zeal be supported by the Shudra servant. A Shudra cannot have any wealth that is his own. Whatever he possesses belongs lawfully to his master.

The Lawbook of Manu: Marriage and Sexual Activity

The Hindu caste system not only divided Indian society into various social orders, it proscribed the rules of marriage and sexual activity. This is revealed in the following two selections. The first is from the Manu Smriti *(Lawbook of Manu) and focuses on the rules of marriage. The second is from the* Kamasutra *(300–600 A.D.), the standard work on*

SOURCE: F. Max Müller, ed., *The Sacred Books of the East,* vol. xxv (Oxford: At the Clarendon Press, 1886).

sexual activity, and delineates rules of sexual activity. In each case, the rules apply only to men, as women are expected to be obedient and loyal.

> **Consider:** *How marriage and sexual activity reflect the broader social order; the relative status of men and women in this society.*

Let the twice-born man,[1] having bathed, with the permission of his teacher and performed the stated ceremonies on his return home, marry a wife of the same caste, endowed with auspicious marks. . . . In connecting himself with a wife, the ten following families are to be avoided however great or rich in kine, goats, sheep, gold, and grain. The family which neglects rites, which has no males, in which the Veda is not read, and the members of which have thick hair on the body, or have piles, or are afflicted with consumption, indigestion, epilepsy, white or black leprosy. Let him not marry a maiden with reddish hair or having a redundant member; one who is sickly, nor one without hair or with excessive hair, nor a chatterbox or one who has red eyes. Nor one named after a star, a tree, or a river, nor one called after barbarians or a mountain, nor one named after a bird, a snake, or a slave, nor one with a name causing terror. Let him choose for his wife a maiden free from bodily defects, who has a pleasant name, who walks gracefully like a *hamsa* or elephant; whose hair is moderate, teeth small, and body soft. . . .

For the first marriage of a twice-born man, a woman of the same caste is approved; but for those who through lust marry again the following females are to be preferred. A Sudra woman only must be the wife of a Sudra, she and a Vaishya, of a Vaishya; these two and a Kshatriya of a Kshatriya; those two and a Brahmani, or a Brahman. Twice-born men, marrying, through folly, low caste women, soon degrade their families and children to the state of Sudras. A Brahman who takes a Sudra woman to his bed, goes to the lower course; if he beget a child by her, he loses his Brahmanhood. . . .

—Women are to be honoured and adorned by their fathers, brothers, husbands, and brothers-in-law, who desire much prosperity. . . . When women are miserable, that family quickly perishes; but when they do not grieve, that family ever prospers. Houses, cursed by women not honoured, perish utterly as if destroyed by magic.

---

[1] Members of the Brahman, Kshatriya, and Vaishya castes who are "born again" upon ritual initiation of maturity.

The Kamasutra

The practice of Kama by the men in the four castes with women of similar castes who are virgins in accordance with the rules of ancient texts is conducive to progeny, besides bringing them a good name and being accepted as legal and binding. However, marital relationship with a woman of higher caste, who has

---

SOURCE: S. C. Upadhyaya, *Kama Sutra of Vatsyayana* (Tarqporevala, 1984), pp. 89–91.

already been married once, is absolutely forbidden. Union with women who are of lower caste, or who are excommunicated, or with those once married and later deserted or widowed, or with courtesans, is neither commended nor condemned, since this relationship is entered into for mere pleasure. . . .

Therefore Nayikas[1] are of three kinds: the maiden, the woman once married and later deserted or widowed, and the courtesan.

. . . however, there is yet a fourth type of Nayika, Pakshiki: one who is already married to another, but who is resorted to for some special reason (i.e., other than the reasons of procreation or pleasure). . . .

Physical union with the following is strictly forbidden:

One who suffers from leprosy, . . .
    who is mentally deranged, . . .
    who is morally depraved, . . .
    who divulges secrets, . . .
    whose charms of youth have faded altogether, . . .
    who is very white, . . .
    who is very dark, . . .
    who emits foul smell, . . .
    who is a near relative, . . .
    who is a friend of one's wife, . . .
    who is a recluse, . . .
    who is the wife of a friend, . . .
    who is the wife of a Brahmin, . . .
    who is the wife of a ruler. . . .

The followers of Babhravya opine that a woman who has had intimate relations with five men, becomes fit to resort to. . . .

But Gonikaputra dissents from this view and urges that even if this is the case, that woman should not be resorted to if she happens to be the wife of a relative, of a friend, of a learned Brahmin, or of a king.

Friendship develops in nine different ways:

With one who has been a playmate in childhood,
that engendered by mutual obligation,
from similarity of temperament and habit,
from being co-students,
with one who knows the other's lapses,
with one who knows the other's secrets,
from mutual acknowledgement of each other's lapses and secrets,
with the child of the nurse,
with one who is brought up together. . . .

---

[1] "Nayika" Any woman fit to be enjoyed without sin, for either of the two purposes—procreation or pleasure.

Thus a prudent man who has a large circle of friends, who performs his duties conscientiously and who is aware of the propriety of time and place, can win over a woman effortlessly, even though she be unapproachable.

The Book of Sermons: The Teachings of Jainism

The Jains, a religious sect founded toward the end of the sixth century B.C., had a great deal of influence on Indian culture. Their emphasis on nonviolence (ahimsa), many-sided- ness (the parable of six blind men touching an elephant which taught respect for all views), and their devotion to secular learning contributed enormously to the development of literature, science, and mathematics.

The Jain philosophy is one of rigorous asceticism. Jains, like Brahmins and Buddhists, believe that only a life of self-denial, discipline, penance, and nonviolence can allow an individual to escape from successive reincarnations. Jains rejected the caste system. Jains follow the teachings of Vardhamana Mahavira ("The Great Hero") who lived about the same time as Buddha and, like his more famous contemporary, left a prosperous home in search of salvation. When he achieved it he became a kevalin *(completed soul) and a* jina *(conqueror).The word Jain comes from this second appellation.*

The following two sources relate to the practice of Jainism. The first is from the opening verses of Sutrakrtanga *(The Book of Sermons) which is considered the epitome of Jainist teachings. The second is from the* Uttarāchyayana Sūtra *(Book of Later Instructions) and is meant to portray the ideal attitude that all good Jains should adopt.*

> **Consider:** *The kind of person a proper Jain should be; the importance of nonvio- lence, disparagement of human emotions, and impassiveness toward life in these beliefs.*

One should know what binds the soul, and, knowing, break free from bondage.

What bondage did the Hero declare, and what knowledge did he teach to remove it?

He who grasps at even a little, whether living or lifeless, or consents to another doing so, will never be freed from sorrow.

If a man kills living things, or slays by the hand of another, or consents to another slaying, his sin goes on increasing.

The man who cares for his kin and companions is a fool who suffers much, for their numbers are ever increasing.

All his wealth and relations cannot save him from sorrow.

Only if he knows the nature of life, will he get rid of karma.

SOURCE: *Sources of Indian Tradition,* Theodore de Bary, et al., eds., (Columbia University Press, New York, 1966) p. 56. Reprinted by permission of the publishers.

The Book of Later Instructions: Jainian Ideals

If another insult him, a monk should not lose his temper,
For that is mere childishness—a monk should never be angry.
If he hears words harsh and cruel, vulgar and painful,
He should silently disregard them, and not take them to heart.
Even if beaten he should not be angry, or even think sinfully,
But should know that patience is best, and follow the Law.
If someone should strike a monk, restrained and subdued,
He should think, "[It might be worse—] I haven't lost my life!" . . .
If on his daily begging round he receives no alms he should not be grieved,
But think, "I have nothing today, but I may get something tomorrow!" . . .
When a restrained ascetic, though inured to hardship,
Lies naked on the rough grass, his body will be irritated,
And in full sunlight the pain will be immeasurable,
But still, though hurt by the grass, he should not wear clothes.
When his limbs are running with sweat, and grimed with dust and dirt
In the heat of summer, the wise monk will not lament his lost comfort.
He must bear it all to wear out his karma, and follow the noble, the supreme Law.
Until his body breaks up, he should bear the filth upon it.

The Life of Buddha: The Origins of Buddhism

Not long after Buddhism spread, it suffered a religious schism. Theravada (believers in the teaching of the elders) closely adhered to Buddha's original teachings while Mahayana (greater vehicle) wanted to humanize their teachings to better appeal to the people among whom they proselytized. The Mahayanists contemptuously referred to the Theravada as Hinayana (lesser vehicle). In the fifth century, worship of female deities associated with a female cult emerged. Later called Tantric Buddhism, it is still practiced in Nepal, Tibet, and Mongolia and is centered in huge monasteries inhabited by large monk populations.

Theravada followers believed the Buddha was a teacher and not a divine being. They taught that enlightenment is only possible by individual action; priests, rituals, and ceremonies are of little help. Mahayana believers taught that enlightenment was more readily available to all with the help of clergy, through rituals, ceremonies, liturgies, fasts, and

---

SOURCE: *Sources of Indian Tradition*, Theodore de Bary, et al., eds. (Columbia University Press, New York, 1966) pp. 64–65. Reprinted by permission of the publishers.
SOURCE: Paul Carus, *The Gospel of Buddha* (Chicago and London: The Open Court Publishing Company, 1915), pp. 39–43.

the possession of sacred objects such as holy water. Theravada Buddhism would become popular in Ceylon (now Sri Lanka) and in Southeast Asia. Mahayana Buddhism would spread to Tibet, China, Korea, and Japan.

The following two selections reveal some of the major precepts of Buddhism. The first selection is from a Sanskrit text, The Life of Buddha, *by Asvaghosha (ca. 420 A.D.) and concerns teachings all Buddhists accept. It refers to a time when the Buddha, upon attaining enlightenment, described how others could do so as well.*

> **Consider:** *The nature of Buddhist teachings; the ways such teachings might appeal to the people of India who were seeped in the teachings of Brahmanism.*

The Bodhisatta . . . gave himself up to meditation. All the miseries of the world, the evils produced by evil deeds and the sufferings arising therefrom, passed before his mental eye, and he thought:

Surely if living creatures saw the results of all their evil deeds, they would turn away from them in disgust. . . .

They crave pleasure for themselves and they cause pain to others; when death destroys their individuality, they find no peace; their thirst for existence abides and their selfhood reappears in new births.

Thus they continue to move in the coil and can find no escape from the hell of their own making. And how empty are their pleasures, how vain are their endeavors! . . .

The world is full of evil and sorrow, because it is full of lust. Men go astray because they think that delusion is better than truth. Rather than truth they follow error, which is pleasant to look at in the beginning but in the end causes anxiety, tribulation, and misery."

And the Bodhisatta began to expound the Dharma. The Dharma is the truth. The Dharma is the sacred law. The Dharma is religion. The Dharma alone can deliver us from error, from wrong and from sorrow. . . .

The Enlightened One recognized that ignorance was the root of all evil. . . .

The cause of all sorrow lies at the very beginning; it is hidden in the ignorance from which life grows. Remove ignorance and you will destroy the wrong appetences that rise from ignorance; destroy these appetences and you will wipe out the wrong perception that rises from them. Destroy wrong perception and there is an end of errors in individualized beings. Destroy the errors in individualized beings and the illusions of the six fields will disappear. Destroy illusions and the contact with things will cease to beget misconception. Destroy misconception and you do away with thirst. Destroy thirst and you will be free of all morbid cleaving. Remove the cleaving and you destroy the selfishness of selfhood. If the selfishness of selfhood is destroyed you will be above birth, old age, disease, and death, and you will escape all suffering.

The Enlightened One saw the four noble truths which point out the path that leads to Nirvāna or the extinction of self:

The first noble truth is the existence of sorrow.

The second noble truth is the cause of suffering.

The third noble truth is the cessation of sorrow.

The fourth noble truth is the eightfold path that leads to the cessation of sorrow. This is the Dharma. This is the truth. This is religion. . . .

There is self and there is truth. Where self is, truth is not. Where truth is, self is not. Self is the fleeting error of samsāra; it is individual separateness and that egotism which begets envy and hatred. Self is the yearning for pleasure and the lust after vanity. Truth is the correct comprehension of things; it is the permanent and everlasting, the real in all existence, the bliss of righteousness.

The existence of self is an illusion, and there is no wrong in this world, no vice, no evil, except what flows from the assertion of self. . . .

The attainment of truth is possible only when self is recognized as an illusion. Righteousness can be practised only when we have freed our mind from passions of egotism. Perfect peace can dwell only where all vanity has disappeared.

The Mahayana Tradition: The Compassion of a Bodhisattva

Mahayanists believed that the perfect Buddhist would renounce as selfish the opportunity to advance into Nirvana and instead return to earth as a bodhisattva *(being of wisdom) to help others achieve Nirvana. This excerpt describes the compassion of a bodhisattva.*

Consider: *Why most, if not all, religions have theories of redemption.*

The bodhisattva is endowed with wisdom of a kind whereby he looks on all beings as though victims going to the slaughter. And immense compassion grips him. His divine eye sees . . . innumerable beings, and he is filled with great distress at what he sees, for many bear the burden of past deeds which will be punished in purgatory, others will have unfortunate rebirths which will divide them from the Buddha and his teachings, others must soon be slain, others are caught in the net of false doctrine, others cannot find the path (of salvation), while others have gained a favorable rebirth only to lose it again.

So he pours out his love and compassion upon all those beings, and attends to them, thinking, *I shall become the savior of all beings, and set them free from their sufferings.*

SOURCE: *Sources of Indian Tradition,* Theodore de Bary, et al., eds. (Columbia University Press, New York, 1966), pp. 161–162. Reprinted by permission of the publishers.

VISUAL SOURCES

Gateway at Sāñchī

Throughout much of Asia, Buddhists built statues, temples, caves, stupas, monasteries and pillars. Buddhist believers, like practitioners of many other religions, liked to build enormous structures to propagate and celebrate their religion. Often these structures were meant to tell a story drawing from the life of Buddha and/or his teachings. This attempt to make art more accessible to the daily lives of the people was a direct result of the religious leaders' desire to sustain current membership and to appeal to potential converts.

The example used here comes from a gateway at Sāñchī, an Indian city northeast of the city of Bhopal. Built in the early first century B.C., this is one of the most preserved and superb examples of this type of Buddhist architecture in India. The earthiness and sensuousness of this style would later be attacked by more puritanical religious forces, who would use their influence to change the art into something more "sacred."

> **Consider:** *How religion spreads its influence by the construction of large and magnificent structures; the impression such a structure might have on people.*

Geography and Linguistic Divisions: The Indian Subcontinent

The Indian subcontinent was, historically, a large number of states, tribal groups, principalities, and fiefdoms. These various peoples had different cultural attributes, the most obvious being the many languages they spoke.

The first group of identifiable languages were the Indo-Aryan languages brought by Aryan invaders in the second millennium B.C. The most important of these became known as Sanskrit. Although originally confined to limited areas in India, Sanskrit would spread and play a major role in the development of the national language of India, Hindi, which is a heavily Sanskritized version of ancient Hindustani. Other versions of Indo-Aryan languages also developed such as Bengali (the national language of Bangladesh), Assamese, and Oriya. Later, the Muslim invasion would bring Arabic and Persian, which together evolved into Urdu, today the national language of Pakistan.

While other languages and linguistic divisions have changed, this map reveals how culturally and socially complex the Indian subcontinent has become.

> **Consider:** *The problems facing rulers in India who try to unify and govern large areas in the subcontinent.*

Photo 2-1

Ananda K. Coomaraswamy, *History of Indian and Indonesian Art*, E. Weyke, 1927, New York.
Courtesy of The Research Libraries, New York Public Library.

Map 2-1   Principal Languages

SECONDARY SOURCES

Aspects of Ancient Indian Culture
A. L. Basham

As each new ethnic or religious group gained power in India, they attempted to alter the political structure according to their beliefs. Throughout this early period the India we recognize today was a collection of small states ruled in their own unique ways. When conquerors came along and united assorted parts of this region, conflicting notions of governing caused confusion and, sometimes, conflict. Eventually, as a definitive Indian culture emerged, so did ideas of political governance. This excerpt from Aspects of Ancient Indian Culture *by the well-known historian of India, A. L. Basham, examines the different interpretations of kingship in ancient Indian political life and how those interpretations fit into the evolving cultural traditions.*

Consider: *How these different political values, institutions, and philosophies conflict with each other and how they agree.*

It is well known that in certain parts of India, at certain times, there were forms of government that we can justifiably call republics, whether of democratic or oligarchical constitution, but these were never the standard form of government in classical India. . . . Kingship came into existence, in order to preserve as much as was possible of the age of gold, in a period of universal degeneration. There are a number of legends with this purport, which seem to have replaced earlier legends which, as we can gather from the Vedic literature, told of the appointment of the first king of the gods as a war leader, chosen by his peers to lead them in war against the demons. . . . [A]s settled regional kingdoms were established, . . . there appeared the doctrine of kingship as a means of preserving society, rather than as a means of preserving the tribe from external attack. The new legends were no doubt inspired by the great fear of anarchy. . . . Particularly significant are two legends, one of which tells us that in a time of anarchy in the distant past, men met together and made an agreement to keep the peace and to expel evildoers. The agreement was not kept and conditions became worse than before, and so mankind in a body waited on Brahmā, the High God, and asked his help. He ordained Manu as the first king. Manu first refused to become king on account of the difficulty and the cruelty involved in his task, but the people persuaded him with promises of shares of their crops and herds and a share of their religious merit also. Here we see the king as a divinely ordained being, decreed by God to meet human need at human request, in order to save man's life from being "mean, brutish and short." The king enjoys his authority partly by human consent, but partly also by divine decree.

The other story . . . gives us a rather different picture. Again we have the account of the decline of the world. The Vedas were forgotten, the religious rituals were no longer performed, but it was the gods who suffered rather than men, and it was the gods, not the men, who approached Brahmā to put things right. Brahmā composed the archetypal text on polity, and then the gods turned to Visnu, the ruler of heaven, and asked him to ordain a king. He created the first king out of his own mind, a miraculous and a supernatural being, to rule over men, and to ensure that they fulfilled their religious duties. . . . The king is here the servant of the gods rather than the servant of men.

At the other extreme, we have the Buddhist legend . . . of "The Great Elected One" . . . chosen at an enormous gathering of the people at a time when private property and the family were no longer being respected. He was appointed in order to maintain law and order, and he was expected to depend for his livelihood on a share of the crops and herds, which he received in return for his services. Thus he held office as a social servant, and the legend is a very early version of the widespread and well-known doctrine of social contract. . . .

Thus in ancient India there were at least three major concepts of the nature of kingship as well as others of less importance, and they existed side by side. . . . As far as orthodox Hindu texts are concerned, however, there is no question that the most influential of these concepts was that of the royal divinity. We must always remember that the *Mahābhārata,* the *Rāmāyana,* and the law book of Manu, which emphasize the doctrine of royal divinity, were influential in most parts of India. . . . We must also remember that the doctrine of the royal divinity does not necessarily imply that "the king can do no wrong." We do find statements to this effect in certain texts, . . . but in general the ancient Indian conception of divinity was very different from that of the modern West. Brahmans are gods on earth; husbands are gods to their wives; teachers are gods to their students. . . . Thus incarnate divinity is almost commonplace. The fact that the original king came down from heaven as the son of Vishnu perhaps did not make much difference in practice.

Etymologically the word *rājya,* "kingdom," implies merely "that which pertains to or comes from the king." It seems to me very doubtful whether any real concept of the State in the modern sense, as something distinct from the king and his officers, existed in ancient India. . . .

Thus the primary purpose of the king, and of the government as an extension of the king, is the protection of the social order. This is done with the aid of *danda,* "punishment" or "coercion," because, as Manu put it so tersely, "a sinless man is hard to find. . . .

So the king, the people, the land and the natural phenomena in ancient India were thought of as united in a way quite transcending all rational explanation, and we should not look for rational explanations of ancient beliefs. . . .

This ancient Indian idea was closely linked up with the doctrine of Karma, and it is something very different from the organic theory of the State. All things in the kingdom, not merely the people, but the phenomena of nature and all that the kingdom contains, are members one of another. Righteousness brings blessings and material welfare. The righteousness of the people has an effect on the weather. The king is a very exceptional being and is divine, therefore his righteousness has a very special effect on the weather and the other phenomena. The king shares this characteristic with learned and pious Brahmans and particularly holy and powerful ascetics. It was thought to be very good to have a specially saintly ascetic in the neighbourhood, because he would bring prosperity to the district. I think this is still believed by many simple and less well-educated Indians.

The king is responsible for the protection of the order of the society, but he also has the responsibility of "pleasing the people." . . .

The king's positive duty of pleasing the people was expressed in many ways. It was an element in his system of justice. It led to the encouragement of agriculture and irrigation, the fixing of fair prices, famine relief, medical help, the care of widows, the promotion of religion, which gave various practical benefits to the people as well as spiritual ones, and the holding of what in later India were called "tamashas."

Another very significant aspect of the king's activity . . . is Kāma, pleasure. The king fulfils the aim of Dharma by his protection and his justice; he fulfils the aim of Artha by promoting the material welfare of his subjects. And in the time left to him from his many duties he is perfectly entitled to enjoy life in whatever way is legitimately possible. In the *Aitareya Brāhmana*, composed well before the time of the Buddha, the king is referred to as *viśām attā*, "the eater of the people," that is the enjoyer of the people, or of whatever the people can provide for him in the way of goods and services. Elsewhere, he is their *bhoktā*, literally their "enjoyer." What is the implication of these terms? In many texts and inscriptions of medieval India, we find phrases which refer to a given king as having won the sea-girt earth as a bride in a *svayaṁvara*, the bride's choice of ancient heroic days. The king was in some sense not merely the father of his people, but also the husband of the land and all it contained.

Cultural Continuity in India
W. Norman Brown

Not surprisingly, one of the more complicated tasks in the development of Indian civiliza-
tion was maintaining continuity in the face of so much diversity. However, Indian cul-
ture, throughout its history, did have a common theme that facilitated this task: the
search for the spiritual aspects of life. In the following selection, W. Norman Brown, an
American professor of Sanskrit and Indian history, analyzes the question of how India
was able to maintain cultural continuity while exploring the issue of the traditional Indian
concern with spiritual matters.

> **Consider:** *What Brown identifies as the key to Indian cultural continuity; the na-*
> *ture of a society that emerges from different cultural and religious traditions; what*
> *such a society must do to maintain cultural continuity.*

Since the third millennium B.C. India has had a highly developed civilization, and we can see that this has had a continuity through successive periods with many variations from then to the present. The variation has often been great, so that today's phenomenon looks little like its antecedent, though caused by it, two or three or four thousand years ago, while there are also many differentiations in separate localities. Yet there must be something which in each successive periodic reincarnation of the civilization has caused the new existence of the civilization, something which in terms of the Buddhist doctrinal analogy corresponds to consciousness. To identify that something, assuming that it really is present, is the problem which I suggest deserves our attention. Its identification would contribute to our understanding of the process of Indian civilization, its past and its present, and give some hint, however slight or vague, of its future. . . .

It would be possible to compile a catalogue of many hundreds of cultural items appearing in ancient Indian civilization which are then reborn or at least reappear in always altering fashion in succeeding periods during centuries, even millennia. Such a catalogue doubtless would not answer the question of what has given Indian civilization its special character and vitality, the element corresponding to the "consciousness" of Buddhist thought, without which new existences would not come into being, existences which, though new, are yet dependent upon preceding existences. Nor is that element likely to be identified even if we could classify the details of Indian civilization into categories by ethnic source, that is determine which were developed by Indo-Aryans, or by Dravidians, or by some other ethnic group, hoping in this way to identify a given people as the author of characteristic Indian civilization. . . .

[T]he determining element is the Indian concern with religio-philosophical

SOURCE: W. Norman Brown, *Cultural Continuity in India.* JAS, 20:4 (August 1961), pp. 429–433.

investigation and its application to life. This is the search for metaphysical truth, the nature of the cosmos, of god, of the human soul, and of the Absolute and man's relation to it. The answer is in line with the common Indian view today that India throughout its history, down to and including the present, has been engrossed in the quest for the spiritual—in contrast with the West, which is considered to be preoccupied with "materialism." Aside from this bit of cultural chauvinism there is support for the general idea of India's especially intensive interest in religio-philosophic activity in the long history of speculative thought and religious teaching, so voluminously recorded in Indian literature from its beginnings in the Rig Veda, its blossoming in the Upanishads and in the Jain and Buddhist scriptures, and its wide ramification and varying development thereafter until our own day. . . .

Possibly we can take another step forward by looking at one of the values of Hinduism more closely. I am thinking of duty, and the unusual stress put upon correct action. Again, we can say nothing about this in the Harappa culture, but we can see it in the Rig Veda and still more markedly in the ritual worship described in the Yajur Veda and the Brāhmaṇas. In this ritual every detail must be perfect and the priests are a highly trained fraternity with specialized duties painstakingly learned and performed with the finest exactitude. The doctrine of rebirth and karma, the most characteristic of all Indian religious teachings, employs this notion to its fullest. Every person's slightest action is a determinant of his future state, and the literature in thousands of passages points out in minute detail the correspondence between deed and result. In caste practice, behavior is the primary consideration; it must always accord with prescription, not only with respect to important matters such as marriage selection and birth and death ceremonies, but also with respect to such small ones as eating, speaking to or approaching others, or even the style of tonsure. Behavior far outweighs dogma in Hinduism, which may vary widely even for members of the same caste without objection from one's fellows. But not so with action! Infringement there results in penalty, which may extend to expulsion from the caste, social death.

Correct or right behavior is viewed as a personal responsibility or duty with a most significant meaning to Hundus, Buddhists, and Jains. . . . There was no such thing as a single universal standard of duty. Not all people were or could rationally be expected to comprehend the same ideas or to live by the same codes. Each caste could quite legitimately frame its own rules for fulfilling its caste function—within limits, of course; that is, so long as the observance of them did not interfere with another caste in the fulfilling of its function and the observance of its rules. This was the adjustment that made it possible for contradictory doctrines and conflicting codes to dwell side by side in peaceful coexistence. Divergency of duty was expected, accepted, and legitimized on what might seem to others to be a scale of astounding amplitude.

Other large or basic values of Indian civilization might be cited for examination, such as truth and *ahiṅsā,* which have already been mentioned, or the attitude toward law as something not made by man, not even by the king—the Bṛhad

Āraṇyaka Upanishad says law is "king over the king"—not invented by kings or by the gods or even by God, but existing before and independently of them all. Should we think that any such value or a whole set of values has constituted the feature giving Indian civilization its vitality throughout history? I repeat that I should not want to make a positive asseveration that it has, but I think the possibility may at least be worthy of consideration, and, in that case, the identification, description, and application of these values deserve deep study.

The Discovery of India: What Is Hinduism?
Jawaharlal Nehru

Since Indian culture is derived from such a variety of sources, a common theme in Indian literature explores the question of what an Indian is. The following selection is from a book by one of India's most prominent twentieth century intellectuals and political leaders, the first Prime Minister of independent India, Jawaharlal Nehru. Having decided to oppose Indian support for Britain's war effort in the 1940s, Nehru and most other Congress Party leaders were imprisoned for the duration of the war. To Nehru and his eleven companions in Ahmadnagar Fort prison camp from 1942–1945, this was an opportunity to have wide-ranging discussions on the history and culture of India. One of the results of those discussions was a book Nehru wrote entitled The Discovery of India. *The following selection from this book attempts to explain what Hinduism is.*

> **Consider:** *The difficulties in forging a national identity from a culture that derives from so many varied traditions; what Nehru identifies as the central elements of twentieth century Hinduism and whether this applies to the Hinduism of the distant past.*

The word Hindu does not occur at all in our ancient literature. The first reference to it in an Indian book is, I am told, in a tantric work of the eighth century A.D., where "Hindu" means a people and not the followers of a particular religion. . . . The word is clearly derived from Sindhu, the old, as well as the present, Indian name for the Indus. From this Sindhu came the words Hindu and Hindustan, as well as Indos and India. . . . The use of the word Hindu in connection with a particular religion is of very late occurrence.

The old inclusive term for religion in India was *Arya dharma*. Dharma really means something more than religion. It is from a root word which means to hold together; it is the inmost constitution of a thing, the law of its inner being. It is an ethical concept which includes the moral code, righteousness, and the whole range of man's duties and responsibilities. *Arya dharma* would include all the

SOURCE: J. Nehru, *The Discovery of India* (New York: The John Day Company, 1946), p. 63–67. Copyright © 1946. Used by permission of Jawaharlal Nehru Memorial Fund.

faiths (Vedic and non-Vedic) that originated in India; it was used by Buddhists and Jains as well as by those who accepted the Vedas. Buddha always called his way to salvation "the Aryan Path." . . .

Hinduism, as a faith, is vague, amorphous, many-sided, all things to all men. It is hardly possible to define it, or indeed to say definitely whether it is a religion or not, in the usual sense of the word. . . . Its essential spirit seems to be to live and let live. Mahatma Gandhi has attempted to define it: "If I were asked to define the Hindu creed, I should simply say: Search after truth through non-violent means. A man may not believe in God and still call himself a Hindu. Hinduism is a relentless pursuit after truth. . . . Hinduism is the religion of truth. Truth is God. Denial of God we have known. Denial of truth we have not known."

For our cultural tradition, we see in the past that some inner urge toward synthesis, derived essentially from the Indian philosophic outlook, was the dominant feature of Indian cultural and even racial development. Each incursion of foreign elements was a challenge to this culture, and it met it successfully by a new synthesis and a process of absorption. This was also a process of rejuvenation and new blooms of culture arose out of it, the background and essential basis, however, remaining much the same. C. E. M. Joad has written about this: "Whatever the reason, it is a fact that India's special gift to mankind has been the ability and willingness of Indians to effect a synthesis of many different elements both of thoughts and peoples, to create, in fact, unity out of diversity."

Chapter Questions

1. As is common among ancient civilizations, much of the early history of India is based on legend and is difficult to verify. Nevertheless, what sorts of insights about Indian civilization do these sources provide? How might these sources be used?

2. According to the sources in this chapter, what are the main religious precepts or attitudes in Indian civilization prior to A.D. 500?

3. Religion serves many functions in every society and religious teachings usually have some social significance in addition to their theological concepts. Explain how Hindu teachings about *karma* and the caste system minimize political conflict.

4. Drawing on sources from this and the previous chapter, explain how Indian ideals and religious ideas compare with those of southwest Asian and northeast African societies.

THREE

China, to A.D. 500

According to legend, Chinese civilization began in the northern region around the Yellow River about 2700 B.C. According to historical data, Chinese civilization began with the founding of the Shang Dynasty sometime between 1800 and 1500 B.C. As an example of the extraordinary unbroken continuity of this civilization, much of the Chinese writing used during the Shang can be deciphered by present-day readers of Chinese.

The earliest dynasties (the Shang, ca. 1600?–1027? B.C., and the Zhou [Chou], Western and Eastern, 1027?–256 B.C.) ended with a period of interstate warfare (the Warring States period, 403–221 B.C.) that also saw a flourishing of philosophies and thought known as the "Hundred Schools." Much of Chinese history would be influenced by the philosophies and doctrines of these schools of thought, particularly the Confucian, Dao (Tao), and Legal. The most important was the Confucian school. It emphasized conformity under authority, reinforced by tradition and validated by moral excellence; proper social hierarchy, respect for social superiors, and moderation in behavior all flow from this principle. If political leaders were virtuous and people followed Confucian teachings, it argued, then a good government and a good society would be the rule. Daoism (Taoism) was another school, whose teachings stressed the need for harmony with nature. Life was to be enjoyed and made as simple as possible. Daoists rejected high office; wise men, they argued, minded their own business. The third school, the Legalists, taught that the rulers, for the most part, ignore the wishes of the people since the people know little about ruling. Legalists did, however, understand the power of an angry populace. Legalists were always striving for a strengthening of government control over the state and the people, while Confucianists looked to reconstitute forms from the past.

The Warring States period ended in 221 B.C. with the unification of China by Qin Shi Huangdi (Ch'in Shi Huang Ti), the first emperor of the Qin [Ch'in] Dynasty. The Qin lasted only about twenty years, to be followed by the Han which, institutionally and geographically, allowed China to reach its maturity and created the nation we are familiar with today. From the Han came the institution of an imperial dynasty ruling a united China through a single emperor, supported by a hierarchical social order and a governmental bureaucracy; a system which would last for some two thousand years. Indeed, the Han Dynasty became the model by which succeeding dynasties were judged. So important was the Han that the Chinese people use its name to identify their ethnicity.

The sources in this chapter center on three themes. The first is Chinese society. Here questions concerning the nature of social attitudes, the importance of kinship, and the role of women will be examined. The second theme is Chinese politics. Here the focus will be on questions concerning Chinese

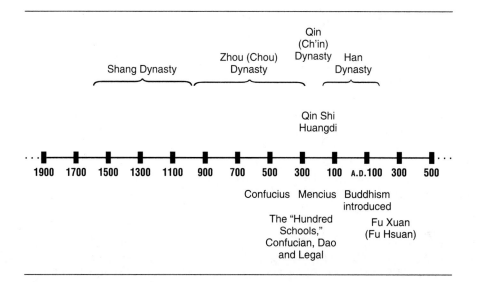

political theory, attitudes toward the political system, and ideas about the good ruler. Finally, many of the sources will explore aspects of the Chinese schools of thought, particularly Confucianism and Daoism, two of the most influential. Together, the sources should provide a picture of an early civilization that was sophisticated and already developing unusually long-lasting traditions.

PRIMARY SOURCES

The Analects: The Confucian School

Confucius (ca. 551–479 B.C.) played the most important role in the explicit interpretation of Chinese culture. His influence cannot be overstated. An itinerant teacher of the sixth and fifth centuries B.C., Confucius rarely wrote down his thoughts. Unfortunately we have lost most of his teachings and the Analects *is considered the only reliable source. Although the authorship of the* Analects *is usually attributed to Confucius, some believe they were written after his death by his students and added to centuries later.*

The main purpose of the teachings was to bring order and stability to what Confucius correctly saw as a chaotic society. In order to create this harmonious community, Confucius taught that all Chinese must act properly, obey their superiors, know their rightful place in society and, above all else, practice filial piety (unquestioning obedience to the family elders). The following excerpt from the Analects *exemplifies his teachings on proper behavior, humanity, and filial piety.*

Consider: *What Confucius' image of the proper gentleman was; the type of society these ideas described.*

Confucius said, "The gentleman concerns himself with the Way; he does not worry about his salary. Hunger may be found in plowing; wealth may be found in studying. . . .

"When he eats, the gentleman does not seek to stuff himself. In his home he does not seek luxury. . . . He may be considered a lover of learning.

. . . "First he behaves properly and then he speaks, so that his words follow his actions."

SOURCE: Reprinted with the permission of The Free Press, a division of Macmillan, Inc. from *Chinese Civilization and Society*, Patricia Buckley Ebrey. Copyright © 1981 by The Free Press.

"The gentleman does not worry and is not fearful. . . .

. . ."The gentleman reveres three things. He reveres the mandate of Heaven; he reveres great people; and he reveres the words of the sages. . . .

. . ."The gentleman must exert caution in three areas. When he is a youth and his blood and spirit have not yet settled down, he must be on his guard lest he fall into lusting. When he reaches the full vigor of his manhood in his thirties and his blood and spirit are strong, he must guard against getting into quarrels. When he reaches old age and his blood and spirit have begun to weaken, he must guard against envy.

. . ."The gentleman understands integrity; the petty person knows about profit.

. . ."In his personal conduct he was respectful; in serving his superiors he was reverent; in nourishing the people he was kind; in governing the people he was righteous. . . .

"The gentleman aspires to things lofty; the petty person aspires to things base. . . .

"The gentleman looks to himself; the petty person looks to other people." . . .

Zi Zhang (Tzu-chang) asked Confucius about humanity. Confucius said, "If an individual can practice five things anywhere in the world, he is a man of humanity . . . reverence, generosity, truthfulness, diligence, and kindness. If a person acts with reverence, he will not be insulted. If he is generous, he will win over the people. If he is truthful, he will be trusted by people. If he is diligent, he will have great achievements. If he is kind, he will be able to influence others."

. . .Confucius said, "When you go out, treat everyone as if you were welcoming a great guest. Employ people as if you were conducting a great sacrifice. Do not do unto others what you would not have them do unto you. . . ."

Zi Yu (Tzu Yu) inquired about filial piety. Confucius said, "Nowadays, filial piety is considered to be the ability to nourish one's parents. But this obligation to nourish even extends down to the dogs and horses. Unless we have reverence for our parents, what makes us any different?

. . . "When your father is alive, observe his intentions. When he is deceased, model yourself on the memory of his behavior. If in three years after his death you have not deviated from your father's ways, then you may be considered a filial child. . . .

"Do not offend your parents. . . . When your parents are alive, serve them according to the rules of ritual and decorum. When they are deceased, give them a funeral and offer sacrifices to them according to the rules of ritual and decorum.

. . . "When your father and mother are alive, do not go rambling around far away. If you must travel, make sure you have a set destination.

. . . "It is unacceptable not to be aware of your parents' ages. Their advancing years are a cause for joy and at the same time a cause for sorrow." . . .

The Duke of She said to Confucius, "In my land there is an upright man. His father stole a sheep, and the man turned him in to the authorities." Confucius replied, "The upright men of my land are different. The father will shelter the son and the son will shelter the father. Righteousness lies precisely in this."

A Confucian Poem: The Role of Women

Society, Confucius taught, must be hierarchical and based on five key relationships: father/son, ruler/subject, husband/wife, elder brother/younger brother, and friend/friend. These relationships were superior to other relationships, with subordinates reverent and obedient to superiors. Women, especially, were ascribed subordinate status. Confucius said little about women but considered them distinctly inferior to men in spite of their necessary reproductive function. The societal structure that he recommended gave them virtually no power or voice. This is illustrated in a poem by a noted Chinese poet and philosopher of the Western Jin (Chin) Dynasty, Fu Xuan (Fu Hsuan), 217–278 A.D.

Consider: *The characteristics of a Chinese woman's place in the Confucian order; what was expected of her.*

How sad it is to be a woman:
Nothing on earth is held so cheap.
Boys stand leaning at the door
Like Gods fallen out of Heaven.
Their hearts brave the Four Oceans,
The wind and dust of a thousand miles.
No one is glad when a girl is born:
By *her* the family sets no store.
When she grows up, she hides in her room
Afraid to look a man in the face.
No one cries when she leaves her home—
Sudden as clouds when the rain stops.
She bows her head and composes her face,
Her teeth are pressed on her red lips:
She bows and kneels countless times.
She must humble herself even to the servants.
His love is distant as the stars in Heaven,
Yet the sunflower bends toward the sun.
Their hearts more sundered than water and fire—
A hundred evils are heaped upon her.
Her face will follow the years' changes:
Her lord will find new pleasures.
They that were once like substance and shadow
Are now as far as Hu from Qin (Ch'in).
Yet Hu and Qin shall sooner meet
Than they whose parting is like Can (Ts'an) and Chen (Ch'en).

SOURCE: From *One Hundred and Seventy Chinese Poems* by Arthur Waley, trans. Copyright ©
1919 and 1947 by Arthur Waley. Reprinted by permission of Alfred A. Knopf, Inc.

Buddhist Song: The Stages of a Woman's Life

The introduction of Buddhism in China during the first and second centuries A.D. did not improve attitudes toward women or their position in society. The third selection is a Buddhist song describing the ideal stages of a woman's life. This text was found among ancient Buddhist writings unearthed from the caves at Dunhuang (Tun-huang). The theme of this song—the transience of life—is a common Buddhist teaching.

> **Consider:** *What, according to this song, women should be happy doing; how this compares with or reinforces the previous source.*

At ten, like a flowering branch in the rain,
She is slender, delicate, and full of grace.
Her parents are themselves as young as the rising moon
And do not allow her past the red curtain without a reason.

At twenty, receiving the hairpin, she is a spring bud.
Her parents arrange her betrothal; the matter's well done.
A fragrant carriage comes at evening to carry her to her lord.
Like Hsiao-shih [Xiaso Shi] and his wife, at dawn they depart with the clouds.

At thirty, perfect as a pearl, full of the beauty of youth,
At her window, by the gauze curtain, she makes up in front of the mirror.
With her singing companions, in the waterlily season,
She rows a boat and plucks the blue flowers.

At forty, she is mistress of a prosperous house and makes plans.
Three sons and five daughters give her some trouble.
With her ch'in not far away, she toils always at her loom,
Her only fear that the sun will set too soon.

At fifty, afraid of her husband's dislike,
She strains to please him with every charm,
Trying to remember the many tricks she had learned since the age of sixteen.
No longer is she afraid of mothers- and sisters-in-law.

At sixty, face wrinkled and hair like silk thread,
She walks unsteadily and speaks little.
Distressed that her sons can find no brides.
Grieved that her daughters have departed for their husbands' homes.

At seventy, frail and thin, but not knowing what to do about it,
She is no longer able to learn the Buddhist Law even if she tries.

SOURCE: Reprinted with the permission of The Free Press, a division of Macmillan, Inc. from *Chinese Civilization and Society*, Patricia Buckley Ebrey. Copyright © 1981 by The Free Press.

In the morning a light breeze
Makes her joints crack like clanging gongs.

At eighty, eyes blinded and ears half-deaf,
When she goes out she cannot tell north from east.
Dreaming always of departed loves,
Who persuade her to charm the dying breeze.

At ninety, the glow fades like spent lightning.
Human affairs are no longer her concern.
Lying on a pillow, solitary on her high bed,
She resembles the dying leaves that fall in autumn.

At a hundred, like a cliff crumbling in the wind,
For her body it is the moment to become dust.
Children and grandchildren will perform sacrifices to her spirit.
And clear moonlight will forever illumine her patch of earth.

How to Be a Good Ruler
Mencius

Confucian doctrine was altered and amplified by many of his disciples. The most important of these disciples, Mencius (371–289 B.C.), was born about one hundred years after Confucius' death. Mencius' teachings have survived to a greater extent than Confucius'. Mencius was sometimes known as the "tender-minded" Confucian as a result of his attempts to describe a rational and more humane form of autocratic rule.

Confucian thought was designed not only to create a better social order for the people, but also to create a more harmonious and benign structure of government. Power, in a Confucian state, was held by the educated—learning made them the most suited. A Confucian social structure had, from the top down, intellectuals/scholars who ruled over everyone; farmers, since they grew the food needed for survival; artisans who made things that were essential, though less important than food; and merchants, at the bottom because they produced nothing—only making money for themselves as middlemen. Rulers did not rule by divine right but by a temporary commission from a higher order that could be withdrawn at any time. As long as the ruler behaved humanely and provided for the livelihood of the people, the people would support him and he enjoyed the "Mandate of Heaven." When rulers acted otherwise they were seen as losing the mandate of heaven and the people were justified in overthrowing them, as they often did.

The following selection is from Mencius' writings and relates a conversation between Mencius and King Xuan (Hsuan) of Qi (Ch'i) on the former's concepts of a benign ruler.

SOURCE: D. C. Lau, trans., *Mencius* (London: Penguin Books, 1970), pp. 54–59. Copyright © D. C. Lau, 1970.

Consider: *Mencius' argument that the king has failed to be a kind ruler; why a change in the king's attitude would be better for all the people, including the king; Mencius' notion of the influences of the people.*

'How virtuous must a man be before he can become a true King?'

'He becomes a true King by bringing peace to the people. This is something no one can stop.'

'Can someone like myself bring peace to the people?'

'Yes.'

'How do you know that I can?'. . .

. . . '[A]ll you have to do is take this very heart here and apply it to what is over there. Hence one who extends his bounty can bring peace to the Four Seas; one who does not cannot bring peace even to his own family. There is just one thing in which the ancients greatly surpassed others, and that is the way they extended what they did . . .

'It is by weighing a thing that its weight can be known and by measuring it that its length can be ascertained. It is so with all things, but particularly so with the heart . . .

'Perhaps you find satisfaction only in starting a war, imperilling your subjects and incurring the enmity of other feudal lords?'

'No. Why should I find satisfaction in such acts? I only wish to realize my supreme ambition.'

'May I be told what this is?'

The King smiled, offering no reply.

'Is it because your food is not good enough to gratify your palate, and your clothes not good enough to gratify your body? Or perhaps the sights and sounds are not good enough to gratify your eyes and ears and your close servants not good enough to serve you? Any of your various officials surely could make good these deficiencies. It cannot be because of these things.'

'No. It is not because of these things.'

'In that case one can guess what your supreme ambition is. You wish to extend your territory, . . . to bring peace to the barbarian tribes on the four borders. Seeking the fulfilment of such an ambition by such means as you employ is like looking for fish by climbing a tree.'

'Is it as bad as that?' asked the King.

'It is likely to be worse. If you look for fish by climbing a tree, though you will not find it, there is no danger of this bringing disasters in its train. But if you seek the fulfilment of an ambition like yours by such means as you employ, after putting all your heart and might into the pursuit, you are certain to reap disaster in the end.'

'Can I hear about this?'

'If the men of Tsou [Zhou] and the men of Chu were to go to war, who do you think would win?'

'The men of Chu.'

'That means that the small is no match for the big, the few no match for the many, and the weak no match for the strong. . . .

'Now if you should practise benevolence in the government of your state, then all those in the Empire who seek office would wish to find a place at your court, all tillers of land to till the land in outlying parts of your realm, all merchants to enjoy the refuge of your market-place, all travellers to go by way of your roads, and all those who hate their rulers to lay their complaints before you. This being so, who can stop you from becoming a true King? . . .

'Only a Gentleman can have a constant heart in spite of a lack of constant means of support. The people, on the other hand, will not have constant hearts if they are without constant means. Lacking constant hearts, they will go astray and fall into excesses, stopping at nothing. To punish them after they have fallen foul of the law is to set a trap for the people. How can a benevolent man in authority allow himself to set a trap for the people? Hence when determining what means of support the people should have, a clear-sighted ruler ensures that these are sufficient, on the one hand, for the care of parents, and, on the other, for the support of wife and children, so that the people always have sufficient food in good years and escape starvation in bad; only then does he drive them towards goodness; in this way the people find it easy to follow him. . . .

. . . 'Exercise due care over the education provided by village schools, and discipline the people by teaching them duties proper to sons and younger brothers, and those whose heads have turned grey will not be carrying loads on the roads. When the aged wear silk and eat meat and the masses are neither cold nor hungry, it is impossible for their prince not to be a true King.'

Eminence in Learning: The Legalist School
Han Fei Zi (Han Fei Tzu)

The major philosophical roots of Chinese civilization are Confucian. However, a compet-ing school—the Legalists—had considerable influence as well.

There were major differences. The Confucianists believed that people were born good and, if educated adequately, would practice proper behavior, thus obviating the need for written laws. Legalists believed humans to be inherently selfish and antisocial, not to be trusted by their rulers. Benevolent government may have worked in the past, Legalists argued, but now was the time for the people to be governed by strict laws and punish-ments administered by a strengthened bureaucratic organization.

Han Fei Zi (Han Fei Tzu) (ca. 280–233 B.C.) was one of the more forceful exponents of the Legalist school, the only nobleman among early Chinese philosophers. His writings

SOURCE: Burton Watson, *Basic Writings of Mo Tzu and Han Fei Tzu.* Copyright © 1967 Columbia University Press, New York. Reprinted with the permission of the publishers.

were designed to preserve and strengthen the state and are often compared to Machiavelli's The Prince *in that both are guides for princely political behavior. Han's writings are, perhaps, the fullest illustration of Legalist thought. In the end, the Legalists overestimated the amount of repression the Chinese people would bear and their policies were never fully applied although they had a strong and lasting influence on Chinese politics for two millennia.*

Consider: *Han's views of the Chinese people; his views of how they should best be ruled.*

Because the ruler gives equal ear to the learning of fools and imposters and the wranglings of the motley and contradictory schools, the gentlemen of the world follow no fixed policy in their words and no constant code of action in their behavior. As ice and live coals cannot share the same container for long, or winter and summer both arrive at the same time, so, too, motley and contradictory doctrines cannot stand side by side and produce a state of order. If equal ear is given to motley doctrines, false codes of behavior, and contradictory assertions, how can there be anything but chaos? If the ruler listens and acts in such a way, he will surely govern his people in the same absurd fashion.

When the scholars of today discuss good government, many of them say, "Give land to the poor and destitute so that those who have no means of livelihood may be provided for." Now if men start out with equal opportunities and yet there are a few who, without the help of unusually good harvests or outside income, are able to keep themselves well supplied, it must be due either to hard work or to frugal living. If men start out with equal opportunities and yet there are a few who, without having suffered from some calamity like famine or sickness, still sink into poverty and destitution, it must be due either to laziness or to extravagant living. The lazy and extravagant grow poor; the diligent and frugal get rich. Now if the ruler levies money from the rich in order to give alms to the poor, he is robbing the diligent and frugal and indulging the lazy and extravagant. If he expects by such means to induce the people to work industriously and spend with caution, he will be disappointed.

Now suppose there is a man who on principle refuses to enter a city that is in danger, to take part in a military campaign, or in fact to change so much as a hair of his shin, though it might bring the greatest benefit to the world. The rulers of the time are sure to honor him, admiring his wisdom, praising his conduct, and regarding him as a man who despises material things and values his life. Now the ruler hands out good fields and large houses and offers titles and stipends in order to encourage the people to risk their lives in his service. But if he honors and praises a man who despises material things and values life above everything else, and at the same time expects the people to risk their lives and serve him to the death, he will be disappointed.

Then there are other men who collect books, study rhetoric, gather bands of disciples, and devote themselves to literature, learning, and debate. The rulers of the time are sure to treat them with respect, saying, "It is the way of the former kings to honor worthy men." The farmers are the ones who must pay taxes to the officials, and yet the ruler patronizes scholars—thus the farmer's taxes grow heavier and heavier, while the scholars enjoy increasing reward. If the ruler hopes, in spite of this, that the people will work industriously and spend little time talking, he will be disappointed. . . .

Although the ruler of a state whose power is equal to yours may admire your righteousness, you cannot force him to come with tribute and acknowledge your sovereignty; but although one of the marquises within your borders may disapprove of your actions, you can make him bring the customary gifts and attend your court. Thus he who has great power at his disposal may force others to pay him court, but he whose power is weak must pay court to others. For this reason the enlightened ruler works to build up power. In a strict household there are no unruly slaves, but the children of a kindly mother often turn out bad. From this I know that power and authority can prevent violence, but kindness and generosity are insufficient to put an end to disorder.

When a sage rules the state, he does not depend on people's doing good of themselves; he sees to it that they are not allowed to do what is bad. If he depends on people's doing good of themselves, then within his borders he can count less than ten instances of success. But if he sees to it that they are not allowed to do what is bad, then the whole state can be brought to a uniform level of order. Those who rule must employ measures that will be effective with the majority and discard those that will be effective with only a few. Therefore they devote themselves not to virtue but to law. . . .

When the shaman priests pray for someone, they say, "May you live a thousand autumns and ten thousand years!" But the "thousand autumns and ten thousand years" are only a noise dinning on the ear—no one has ever proved that such prayers add so much as a day to anyone's life. For this reason people despise the shaman priests. Similarly, when the Confucians of the present time counsel rulers, they do not praise those measures which will bring order today, but talk only of the achievements of the men who brought order in the past. They do not investigate matters of bureaucratic system or law, or examine the realities of villainy and evil, but spend all their time telling tales of the distant past and praising the achievements of the former kings. And then they try to make their words more attractive by saying, "If you listen to our advice, you may become a dictator or a king!" They are the shaman priests of the rhetoricians, and no ruler with proper standards will tolerate them. Therefore the enlightened ruler works with facts and discards useless theories. He does not talk about deeds of benevolence and righteousness, and he does not listen to the words of scholars.

Nowadays, those who do not understand how to govern invariably say, "You must win the hearts of the people!" If you could assure good government merely by winning the hearts of the people, then there would be no need for men like Yi Yin and Kuan Chung [Guan Zhong]—you could simply listen to what the people say. The reason you cannot rely upon the wisdom of the people is that they have the minds of little children. If the child's head is not shaved, its sores will spread;

and if its boil is not lanced, it will become sicker than ever. But when it is having its head shaved or its boil lanced, someone must hold it while the loving mother performs the operation, and it yells and screams incessantly, for it does not understand that the little pain it suffers now will bring great benefit later.

Now the ruler presses the people to till the land and open up new pastures so as to increase their means of livelihood, and yet they consider him harsh; he draws up a penal code and makes the punishments more severe in order to put a stop to evil, and yet the people consider him stern. He levies taxes in cash and grain in order to fill the coffers and granaries so that there will be food for the starving and funds for the army, and yet the people consider him avaricious. He makes certain that everyone within his borders understands warfare and sees to it that there are no private exemptions from military service; he unites the strength of the state and fights fiercely in order to take its enemies captive, and yet the people consider him violent. These four types of undertaking all insure order and safety to the state, and yet the people do not have sense enough to rejoice in them.

Daoist Writings: "The Wise Judge" and "Social Connections"

Often one can tell more about the nature of a society through the writings of its critics than from its official papers. In China, the elite culture was Confucian, as was the design of the government. Daoist (Taoist) philosophers became social critics, voicing the complaints of the people through popular culture.

The following Daoist tales, the first from the Yuan Dynasty (1279–1368 A.D.) and the second from the Qing (Ch'ing, 1662–1912 A.D.), are directed at the county magistrate, the lowest official in the traditional bureaucracy and the administrator an ordinary person would encounter most often. Consequently, this official became the target for much of the people's anger. "The Wise Judge" is meant to pay tribute to a good magistrate, while "Social Connections" shows the harm an incompetent official can do.

> **Consider:** *The differences between the official view of Confucian society as portrayed by the elite and the society portrayed in these Daoist folktales; the lessons the reader, or hearer, of these tales is supposed to learn.*

THE WISE JUDGE

Early one morning, a grocer on his way to market to buy vegetables was surprised to find a sheaf of paper money on the ground. It was still dark, and the dealer tucked himself out of the way and waited for daylight so he could examine the money he had picked up. He counted fifteen notes worth five ounces of silver

SOURCE: Moss Roberts, *Chinese Fairy Tales and Fantasies.* Copyright © 1979 by Moss Roberts. Reprinted by permission of Pantheon Books, a division of Random House, Inc.

and five notes worth a string of one thousand copper coins each. Out of this grand sum he took a note, bought two strings' worth of meat and three strings' worth of hulled rice, and placed his purchases in the baskets that hung from his shoulder pole. Then he went home without buying the vegetables he had set out to buy.

When his mother asked why he had no vegetables, he replied, "I found this money early in the morning on my way to market. So I bought some meat and hulled rice and came home."

"What are you trying to put over on me?" his mother asked angrily. "If it were lost money, it couldn't be more than a note or two. How could anyone lose a whole sheaf? It's not stolen, is it? If you really found it on the ground, you should take it back."

When the son refused to follow his mother's advice, she threatened to report the matter to the officials. At that he said, "And to whom shall I return something I found on the road?"

"Go back to the place where you found the money," said his mother, "and see if the owner comes looking for it. Then you can return it to him." She added, "All our lives we've been poor. Now you've bought all this meat and rice; such sudden gains are sure to lead to misfortune."

The vegetable dealer took the notes back to where he had found them. Sure enough, someone came looking for the money. The dealer, who was a simple country fellow, never thought to ask how much money had been lost. "Here's your money," he said and handed it over. Bystanders urged the owner to reward the finder, but the owner was such a miser that he refused, saying, "I lost thirty notes. Half the money is still missing."

With such a large difference between the amounts claimed, the argument went on and on until it was brought to court for a hearing. The county magistrate Nie Yidao (Nieh Yi-tao) grilled the vegetable dealer and saw that his answers were basically truthful. He sent secretly for the mother, questioned her closely, and found that her answers agreed with her son's. Next he had the two disputing parties submit written statements to the court. The man who had lost money swore that he was missing thirty five-ounce bills. The vegetable dealer swore that he had found fifteen five-ounce bills.

"All right, then," said Nie Yidao, "the money found is not this man's money. These fifteen bills are heaven's gift to a worthy mother to sustain her in old age." He handed the money to mother and son and told them to leave. Then he said to the man who had lost his money, "The thirty bills you lost must be in some other place. Look for them yourself." Nie Yidao dismissed him with a good scolding, to the outspoken approval of all who heard it.

SOCIAL CONNECTIONS

Old Fei, a farmer, had applied himself to his acres and become tolerably rich. His only regret in life was that he had no friends in high society.

One day during a terrible rainstorm Fei's daughter-in-law was washing vegetables by the riverbank when a small boat anchored beside a willow. Inside there was a scholar sheltering under the dripping mat awning of the boat. His clothes and shoes were drenched; his two attendants were even worse off. The boatman told the daughter-in-law that the passenger's name was Fei and that he held a degree of the second rank. . . .

The old farmer gathered up rain gear and hurried to the boat. "What a storm!" he said to the scholar. "Would you care to take refuge in our poor quarters, honorable sir?" Cold and hungry, the scholar gladly accepted. . . . Together they traced the family genealogy, behaving as if they were indeed one happy family.

Old farmer Fei gave orders for a banquet. . . .

When dinner was announced, old Fei invited the scholar to the table. . . . The old farmer raised his cup and said, "This brew has been aged five years. We offer it today especially for my honored younger brother." The scholar thanked him profusely, and soon both Feis were warm with spirits. The scholar for his part gave a full account of his pedigree and connections. . . . Anyone associated with me would be immune from misfortune of any kind."

Old farmer Fei took it in with enthusiasm and reverence. The meal ended, and so did the rains. . . . The scholar said goodbye. . . .

Next day, wearing his best clothes and taking a multitude of servingmen, the farmer set sail. He reached the city and called on the scholar, who received him cordially. From then on their friendship deepened. Produce from farmer Fei's fields was frequently presented to scholar Fei. . . . The grateful scholar was pained that he could not do something useful in return for the food he had taken. Finally, however, he came up with an idea and consulted a certain police constable with whom he was on close terms. The policeman arranged for a certain bandit to commit a crime and frame farmer Fei for it. Soon the farmer found himself in jail.

Seeking help, the farmer's son rushed to the home of the scholar. "Your father has treated me so generously," the scholar said tearfully, "that I would spare nothing to save him. But his offense is not light. This isn't something I can take care of by putting in a word. We're involved with a bunch of real crooks here— what's the best way to deal with this, I wonder?"

The son said, "If there's any way to free my father, we'll follow your instructions to the letter." The scholar told him how much to pay to bribe this official and that official—how much for the magistrate's clerk, the constable, and last of all, the bandit. Paying off the higher-ups and the lower-downs would cost five thousand ounces of silver.

Now, the wealth of a farmer is in his land; there is little cash. Unable to raise the entire amount, the son was forced to give all the deeds for the land and buildings to the scholar, who took possession of the property in the name of other officials. He even circulated petitions and instructions to his superiors and inferiors to milk the son from every possible angle. To meet these demands the farmer's son was reduced to "netting sparrows and unearthing rats," as they say—doing any odd jobs that would turn a penny. At last when the household was stripped clean, the father was set free. One year had gone by.

While in prison, the farmer felt ever grateful to the scholar for keeping him in mind. Old Fei often remarked that he was lucky to know the young man. . . .

When the farmer had calmed himself, he fell to wondering why a bandit he had never met could have wreaked such vengeance upon him. So he killed a chicken and took it with some wine back to the jail to feast the bandit and ask the cause of his hatred.

"I ruined you and your family," the bandit said, "yet you have come to feed me. You must be an honorable man. I can no longer conceal the truth, which is that your brother the scholar instructed the constables to do everything." Hearing this, the old farmer realized at last what had happened. He dashed to the graduate's house but time and again was told that scholar Fei was away on business.

Unable to vent his anger there, the old farmer went home and laid the blame on his daughter-in-law. "If it were not for you," he said, "this disaster would never have happened." "Your surnames happened to be the same," she replied, "so I mentioned it to you. I didn't ask you to get involved with the man."

In his anguish the old farmer cursed her, and she was so outraged that she hanged herself. The son, furious at seeing his wife dead for no reason, also hanged himself. And old Fei, having now neither home nor descendants, put the cord around his own neck too.

VISUAL SOURCES

A Chinese House

A people's architecture, like its art, is a direct manifestation of its culture. A close examination of any recurring architectural theme can reveal a great deal about the cultural pattern of its builders.

In traditional China, the most important unit that a person belonged to was the family. The first loyalties were to the family and no virtue was more important than filial piety. The Confucian ideal—lived by only a very small percentage of the population in reality— was to have three or four generations of a single family living under the same roof. The traditional Chinese house was designed to express these beliefs.

Examining this drawing of a typical Chinese dwelling, notice the difference between the plainness of the outside and the lavishness of the interior courtyards. Each building is created to represent a hierarchical pattern—again a manifestation of traditional Chinese culture. The building facing south onto the larger courtyard houses the senior members of the family. The buildings on the east and west house married sons and their families.

Photo 3-1

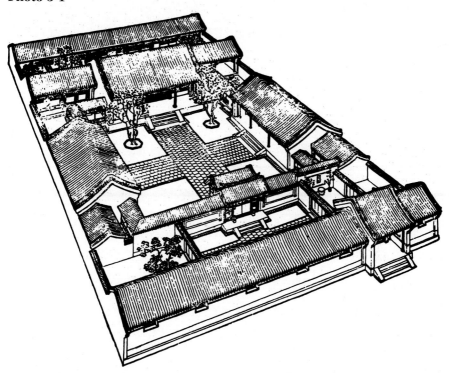

Ronald C. Knapp, *The Chinese House. Craft, Symbol, and the Folk Tradition.* (Oxford, U.K.: Oxford University Press, 1990.)

> **Consider:** *The contradiction between the sense of seclusion of such a dwelling, with its encompassing perimeter walls, and the openness of its interior.*

Chinese Bureaucracy

When China was first unified under the Qin (Ch'in) Dynasty in 221 B.C., a national government, and a nation, was created that lasted until A.D. 1911. One of the most remarkable features of this government was the creation of a complex bureaucracy—a political, administrative, and military organization run by people chosen by merit and paid for by compulsory taxes and labor services. Unlike the preceding quasi-feudal forms of government, this bureaucratic form of government ran on written rules and used written documents to carry on its business. As indicated by this chart, each position had its responsibilities clearly delineated, and only the proper performance of those duties allowed the entire structure to operate smoothly. The establishment of this system did not mean that all Chinese agreed with it. For the next century and more there was conflict between local rulers attempting to increase their power and the bureaucrats struggling to preserve

Chinese Bureaucracy

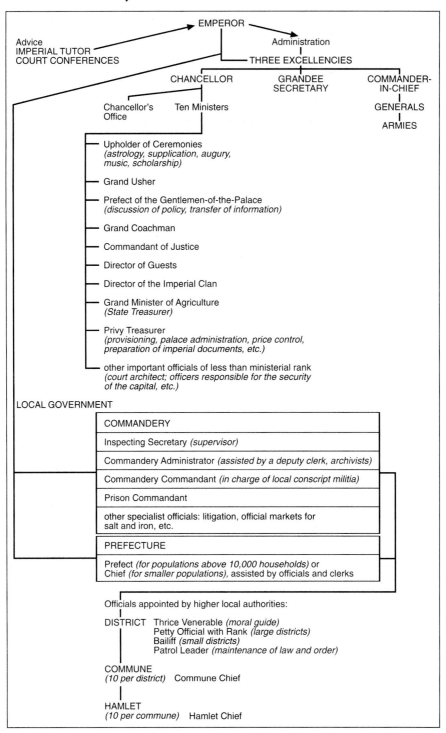

EMPEROR

Advice
IMPERIAL TUTOR
COURT CONFERENCES

Administration
THREE EXCELLENCIES

CHANCELLOR   GRANDEE   COMMANDER-
              SECRETARY   IN-CHIEF

Chancellor's   Ten Ministers   GENERALS
Office   ARMIES

- Upholder of Ceremonies
  *(astrology, supplication, augury,
  music, scholarship)*

- Grand Usher

- Prefect of the Gentlemen-of-the-Palace
  (discussion of policy, transfer of information)

- Grand Coachman

- Commandant of Justice

- Director of Guests

- Director of the Imperial Clan

- Grand Minister of Agriculture
  (State Treasurer)

- Privy Treasurer
  *(provisioning, palace administration, price control,
  preparation of imperial documents, etc.)*

- other important officials of less than ministerial rank
  *(court architect; officers responsible for the security
  of the capital, etc.)*

LOCAL GOVERNMENT

COMMANDERY
Inspecting Secretary *(supervisor)*
Commandery Administrator *(assisted by a deputy clerk, archivists)*
Commandery Commandant *(in charge of local conscript militia)*
Prison Commandant
other specialist officials: litigation, official markets for salt and iron, etc.
PREFECTURE
Prefect *(for populations above 10,000 households)* or Chief *(for smaller populations)*, assisted by officials and clerks

Officials appointed by higher local authorities:

DISTRICT   Thrice Venerable *(moral guide)*
            Petty Official with Rank *(large districts)*
            Bailiff *(small districts)*
            Patrol Leader *(maintenance of law and order)*

COMMUNE
(10 per district)   Commune Chief

HAMLET
(10 per commune)   Hamlet Chief

central rule. Over time, it was the national government, supported by this bureaucratic structure, that usually prevailed.

> **Consider:** *The advantages and disadvantages of this bureaucratic system compared to the rule of an individual or feudal power holder.*

China's Warring States

This period in Chinese history (481–221 B.C.) saw an increase in the state of anarchy in China. This situation had several consequences. It led to the rise of militarization, including the development of new weapons, new rules for war, and the conscription of large armies. It also increased the use of diplomacy as professional diplomats emerged to negotiate among neighboring states. Traditional aristocrats, who often died in the wars or had their states conquered by others, lost their place in society. They were often replaced by men of humbler origins who, during this chaotic time, were able to rise up the social ladder through their own deeds.

This map indicates the various states and their invasions (with dates) of each other. It also depicts the Great Wall, which had its origins in this period. The wall was built in different parts at different times largely to keep out non-Chinese invaders from the north. Out of this chaos emerged the Qin (Ch'in) Dynasty in 221 B.C., which united China for the first time under the Emperor Qin Shi Huangdi (Ch'in Shih Huang Ti).

> **Consider:** *The problems involved in unifying China and making it secure under the geopolitical circumstances.*

Map 3-1   The Warring States in China 481–221 B.C.

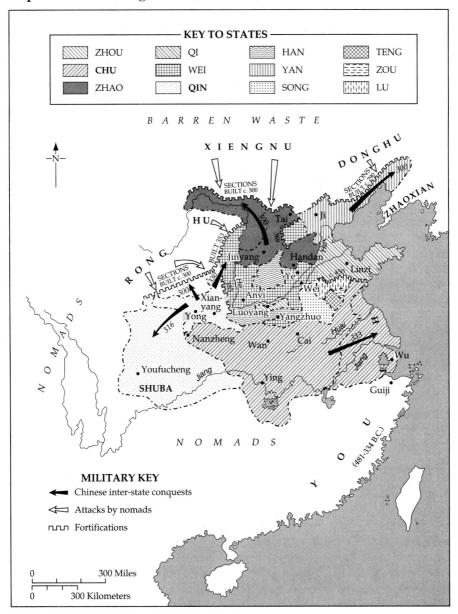

KEY TO STATES

ZHOU		QI		HAN		TENG	
CHU		WEI		YAN		ZOU	
ZHAO		**QIN**		SONG		LU	

BARREN WASTE

XIENGNU

DONGHU

ZHAOXIAN

SECTIONS
BUILT c. 300

SECTIONS
BUILT c. 300

—N—

HU

RONG

Tai
Ji

Jinyang
Handan
Linzi

BUILT 353

Ye
Wei

Xian-
yang
Anyi
Yong
Luoyang
Yangzhuo

Nanzheng
Wan
Cai
Huai
Jiang
Wu

Youfucheng
Jiang
Ying
Guiji

SHUBA

NOMADS

NOMADS

YOU
(481-334 B.C.)

MILITARY KEY

➤ Chinese inter-state conquests

⇦ Attacks by nomads

ⅎⅎⅎ Fortifications

0	300 Miles
0	300 Kilometers

SECONDARY SOURCES

Kinship in Chinese Culture
Evelyn S. Rawski

*The long, unbroken continuity of Chinese culture led to considerable interminging be-
tween elite culture (that is, the culture of the rulers, the landowners, the bureaucrats) and
the popular culture of the people. The central facet of the culture became the family unit
and, by extension, the ancestors. Add to this emphasis on family the concept of filial piety
as the most integral Confucian teaching and it is clear that understanding kinship is vital
to understanding Chinese culture. The reading below is by an American historian of Chinese culture, Evelyn S. Rawski, and concerns the power of kinship and its principal position in Chinese life.*

> **Consider:** *The nature of a society where the principal loyalties are to a family,
> even through its dead ancestors, rather than to a political entity; how domestic
> architecture reflects fundamental principles of Chinese social life; how Buddhism
> challenged the family-centered orientation of Chinese society.*

The Chinese from very early times placed special emphasis on funerary ritual and
looked after the well-being of their dead ancestors. The earliest written materials,
inscribed on the so-called oracle bones, which were used for divination during the
Bronze Age, petition the ancestral spirits and nature gods for information and
help reflect the "developing cult of the dead." Not only did Chinese believe in a
continuity of ties beyond death; they assumed that the ancestors had special entry
into the world of the gods and were able to intercede on behalf of their descendants. . . . The ritual primacy of death and its accompaniment, ancestor worship,
persists to the present day. . . .

The kinship group was a central focus for Chinese society. The family, conceived
not just as the group of living parents, siblings, spouse, and children but as the
male line of descent stretching back over many generations, appears as another
core element in Chinese culture for at least several millennia. A Chinese was thus
aware of himself as part of a collectivity, a group that persisted and endured over
generations. His first duty was to ensure the continuation of the line. The dominance of the male line—the marriage ideal was for brides to reside with the
groom's family—was also characteristically Chinese. . . .

Primacy of the male descent line, consciousness of the unbroken linkage of
ancestors to the current household, and concern for the well-being of the dead

Source: Ching-I Tu, ed. *Tradition and Creativity. Essays on East Asian Civilization* (New
Brunswick: Rutgers University Press, 1987), pp. 42–51.

are among the most fundamental assumptions, orientations, and social preferences expressed by Chinese of all social strata over a long historical span. One of the most impressive pieces of material evidence to support this statement lies in the domestic Chinese house plan. . . . Most Chinese lived in one-story structures built around courtyards. A peasant's house could consist of only one or two rooms; a landlord's house might have several hundred rooms with connecting courtyards. Whatever the size and locality, all houses shared one feature: the central room was used for offerings to ancestors, and as a reception room for guests.

. . . In its most typical form, the Chinese house was also walled. Within these walls, the layout of rooms and living space represented what Nelson Wu has called "graduated privacy." Outside the front gate was the world of strangers; the wall separated the "inner" family circle from the larger society. Treatment of outsiders was also finely differentiated. Peddlers were permitted into the gate to show their wares; friends and relatives were invited into the courtyard and the reception room. Behind the reception room were the private rooms, where women congregated. The use of living space thus reflected important social divisions. . . .

The Shang conceived of a paramount deity, Ti [Di], the predecessor of Heaven (*T'ien*) [Tian], which supplanted Ti with the Chou [Zhou] conquest of the eleventh century B.C. Ti ruled the cosmic order, as did the king the human society. The universal king derived his authority and legitimacy from this supreme deity, and an essential element of the king's role was to offer sacrifice to Ti and subsequently to T'ien. The special relationship between the supreme deity and the universal king was the linchpin of the cosmic order. Later elaborated as the "Mandate of Heaven," it served as the basis of legitimacy for the dynastic form of government that prevailed in China until 1911. The "Mandate of Heaven" concept shaped the behavior not only of rulers but of rebels, and it became an accepted part of popular culture in stories of the auspicious signs attending the birth of dynastic founders, or appearing at critical points in their lives. . . .

Buddhism was introduced into China during the Han dynasty in the first and second centuries A.D. and became influential in the fourth century among the ruling elite in North China and the Han Chinese elites in the Yangtze delta. . . .

Buddhism had a profound influence on the beliefs of ordinary Chinese. Buddhist notions of sin and judgment were incorporated into Chinese folk religion. Buddhist deities, imported into China, became important foci for worship. . . .

Buddhism also presented values that challenged the family-centered orientation of Chinese society. Its depiction of exemplars such as Miao-shan, or the devout Mu-lien [Mu-lian], who demonstrates his filiality by saving his wicked mother from hell, indicated its willingness to compromise with Chinese values in order to win acceptance; but the central value of renouncing worldly ties, including family ties, remained to serve as an alternative for those who could not or would not fit into the mainstream. The monastery and the nunnery existed as refuges for a small minority of individuals fleeing the normal life-course, but many more Chinese, who joined lay Buddhist associations, were influenced by the Buddhist teachings praising celibacy and advocating a vegetarian diet. These and other messages were conveyed to believers in sectarian *pao-chüan* [bao-juan] in the Ming and Ch'ing [Qing] periods: a text like the *Liu Hsiang pao-chüan*, [*Liu Xieng bao-juan*] with a Miao-shan type of heroine, portrays a woman who pursues spiritual salvation rather than a normal married life; it argues that children should be filial to their mothers because of the suffering and pollution that these women have borne in childbirth. For women, the goal of a pious life is to be reborn in the next life as a man; these texts not only express an antimarriage bias, but also the resentment of a woman's lot.

China's Cultural Heritage
Richard J. Smith

In trying to understand the development of Chinese culture, scholars have frequently commented on the interplay between a growing, diverse, multiethnic geographical area with the development of a centralized bureaucratic government run by scholar-officials. How did these highly structured governments function? One of the answers is in the cultural need for order (zhi) in societal and personal relations as evidenced in the philosophy of Confucius, the establishment of a centralized bureaucracy, and Chinese attitudes toward conformity and collective responsibility.

This innate fear of chaos and disorder (luan) allowed for a strong centrally controlled China by giving Chinese a clearly defined cultural identity and a sense of solidarity with their leaders. It also made the social and political order so rigid that it was slow in adapting to the rapid changes which would engulf China in later centuries.

In his study of China's cultural heritage, Rice University sinologist Richard J. Smith tried to understand the "holism of the Chinese cultural vision—the conviction that 'all strains of thought, all institutions [and] all forms of behavior should embody and express a common set of values.'" To that end, Smith examines three related themes in this excerpt: cognition, ethics, and ritual.

> **Consider:** *The creation of a cultural identity; its importance to both the leaders and the led and its importance in unifying a people.*

How did the Chinese order their vast cultural world, which embraced "all under Heaven"? . . .

Three related themes serve as the interpretive foundation [to this question]. . . . The first is cognition, the way the Chinese viewed the world around them. Despite the complexity of this outlook, with its intersecting Confucian, Buddhist, and Taoist elements and elaborate interplay between elite and popular conceptions of reality, we can identify at least one construct, or paradigm, that transcended ideology and class. Sometimes described as "complementary bipolarity," this view-

SOURCE: Richard J. Smith, *China's Cultural Heritage: The Ch'ing Dynasty, 1644–1912* (Boulder, Westview Press, 1983), pp. 3–7.

point was expressed by the well-known, but much abused, concepts of *yin* and *yang*. . . .

In traditional times, *yin* and *yang* were used in three main senses, each of which may be illustrated by the following excerpts from *Hung-lou meng* [Hong lou meng] (Dream of the Red Chamber), China's greatest and most influential novel. In a colorful conversation with her maidservant, Kingfisher, Shih Hsiang-yün [Shi Xiangyun] remarks: "Everything in the universe is produced by the forces of *yin* and *yang*. . . . All the transformations that occur result from the interaction of *yin* and *yang*. . . . When *yang* is exhausted, it becomes *yin,* and when *yin* is exhausted, it becomes *yang*. . . . *Yin-yang* is a kind of force in things that gives them their distinctive form. For example, Heaven is *yang* and Earth is *yin*; water is *yin*, fire is *yang*; the sun is *yang,* the moon is *yin*." "Ah yes," replies Kingfisher, "that's why astrologers call the sun the *"yang* star" and the moon the *"yin* star." After a lengthy discussion of several other such associations and correlations, Kingfisher ends the conversation by observing: "You're *yang* and I'm *yin*. . . . That's what people always say: the master is *yang* and the servant is *yin*. Even I can understand that principle."

Yin and *yang* were, then, (1) cosmic forces that produced and animated all natural phenomena; (2) terms used to identify recurrent, cyclical patterns of rise and decline, waxing and waning; and (3) comparative categories, describing dualistic relationships that were inherently unequal but invariably complementary. Virtually any aspect of Chinese experience could be explained in terms of these paired concepts, ranging from such mundane sensory perceptions as dark and light, wet and dry to abstractions such as real and unreal, being and nonbeing. *Yin-yang* relationships involved the notion of mutual dependence and "harmony based on hierarchical difference." *Yin* qualities were generally considered inferior to *yang* qualities, but unity of opposites was always the cultural ideal.

Perhaps no other major civilization in world history has had such a pervasive, tenacious, and essentially naturalistic world view—an accommodating outlook contrasting sharply with the familiar religious dualisms of good and evil, God and the Devil, which are so prominent in the ancient Near Eastern and Western cultural traditions. . . .

The second major theme of this study is ethics, an abiding cultural concern, as a glance at any Chinese political, social, or philosophical tract will clearly indicate. Like the concepts of *yin* and *yang*, ethical terms pervade virtually every area of traditional Chinese culture, including music and the arts. The modern Chinese philosopher Chang Tung-sun [Zhang Dongsun] tells us that the most numerous terms in the Chinese language come from the related realms of kinship and ethics, and the index to Fung Yu-lan's [Feng Youlan] well-known abridged history of Chinese philosophy states apologetically, "So much of Chinese philosophy is ethical that a complete list of 'ethical' references would be almost impossible."

Yet it is not only the pervasiveness of ethical concerns in China that is striking. It is also the essentially nonreligious source of basic moral values. In sharp contrast to many other cultural traditions, the Chinese moral order was essentially secular in nature. Although Chinese philosophers perceived a fundamental unity between the mind of Heaven and the mind of Man, the ethical system prevailing in China throughout the entire imperial era did not emanate from any supernatural authority. The major institutional religions of late imperial times—Buddhism and Religious Taoism—made no major contribution to the preexisting core of Confucian values, although they did play an important role in reinforcing secular norms. . . .

Supernatural authority might always be invoked in China, but in the ideal Confucian world it was considered unnecessary. . . .

Ritual [li] provides the third major theme . . . in a sense uniting the other two themes with itself. Like art, ritual may be viewed as a kind of "language" that celebrates man-made meaning. It indicates the way a culture group represents its situation to itself, how (in the words of Clifford Geertz) it links "the world as lived and the world as imagined." As a cultural performance, ritual articulates in symbolic action the concerns of the illiterate masses as well as those of the literate elite. Of course, there are many different kinds and definitions of ritual, but in its broadest sense the term may be said to include all forms of artificially structured social behavior, from the etiquette of daily greetings to solemn state ceremonies and religious sacrifices.

Such a broad definition accords well with traditional Chinese usage. Although the term *li* never completely lost either its original religious and mystical connotations or its close association with music as a source of moral cultivation, by late imperial times *li* had come to embrace all forms of sacred and secular ritual, as well as the entire body of social institutions, rules, regulations, conventions, and norms that governed human relations in China. *Li* has been variously translated as standards of social usage, mores, politeness, propriety, and etiquette, but no single term does justice to the wide range of its meanings and manifestations. . . .

No major aspect of Chinese life was devoid of ritual significance, and ritual specialists were ubiquitous at all levels of society. Everyone from emperor to peasant recognized the importance of ritual in preserving status distinctions, promoting social cohesion, sanctifying ethical norms, and transmitting tradition. Closely linked to both cosmology and law, ritual in China performed the function Geertz assigns to "sacred symbols" in synthesizing moral values, aesthetics, and world view.

Chapter Questions

1. Drawing from the sources in this chapter, compare and contrast the Confucian, Dao, and Legal schools of thought. Together, how do they provide insights into the nature of Chinese civilization?

2. Using sources from this chapter and the previous chapter on India, compare the Chinese schools of thought with Indian religious teachings. What does this comparison reveal about the similarities and differences between these two civilizations?

3. What do the sources in this chapter reveal about China's social and political order? In what ways were kinship and the role of women important? What do the various schools of thought tell us about the ideals and the realities of political rule?

4. Using materials from the first three chapters on the civilizations of southwestern Asia and northeastern Africa, India, and China, what sorts of assumptions and attitudes about the world, about people's place in the world, and about social order might people in these civilizations hold in common? How might some of these assumptions and attitudes differ?

FOUR

The Mediterranean Basin: Greek Civilization

Although the roots of Western civilization stretch to the civilizations of the ancient Near East, the birth of the West can more easily be recognized in Greek civilization. Before reaching its apex during the fifth and fourth centuries B.C., Greek civilization had a long developmental history. Two related civilizations preceded the Greeks: the Minoans (Achaeans), who developed a sophisticated maritime civilization based on the island of Crete during the third and second millennia, and the Mycenaeans, a militaristic Indo-European people who rose to prominence on the Greek mainland during the second millennium. Both of these Bronze Age peoples fell before the invading Dorians between 1200 and 1000 B.C. After three centuries of cultural decline, the Greeks emerged and entered into a period of vigorous growth. Commerce expanded and the Greeks colonized lands from the Black Sea to the western Mediterranean. At the same time, the city-states entered into a period of political evolution and cultural development.

During the fifth and fourth centuries B.C., Greek civilization reached its apex. Two city-states in particular became prominent: Sparta and Athens. The Spartans developed a tighty organized, militaristic, land-based state, dominating the Peloponnesian Peninsula. Athens developed a relatively open, democratic, maritime state, dominating Attica and supporting commercial and cultural expansion. In short, each represents an extreme of the many political and social forms embraced by the various Greek city-states.

This chapter surveys Greek civilization as it evolved from the Bronze Age civilizations of the Mycenaeans and Minoans (second millennium B.C.) through the Classical Age (550–323 B.C.) to the Hellenistic Age (323–31 B.C.). Four overlapping topics are discussed. The first concerns early Greek history, particularly the fall of Greece's Bronze Age civilizations, the importance of the Homeric epics, and the later expansion of the Greeks through migration, colonization, and trade.

The second topic concerns the nature of the *polis,* for the Greeks the appropriate context for the good life as well as the center of social, economic, religious, and cultural life. How should it be ruled? What was the proper balance between the individual and the state? Here the ideals and realities of Greek politics, particularly the contrasts between Athens and Sparta, will be examined.

The third topic concerns the nature of Greek thought. How abstract and rationalistic was it? What central ideas and ways of thinking are revealed in their literature, philosophy, and science?

The fourth topic concerns the nature of Greek civilization and society in general. How true is the traditional perception of the Greeks, and especially the Athenians, as being balanced, democratic, individualistic, and open? To

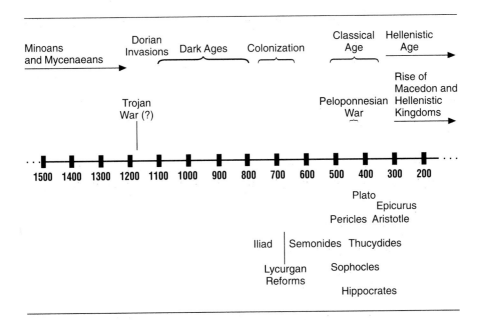

what extent did Greek realities approach Greek ideals? Here, in particular, Greek attitudes toward women and the importance of slavery will be examined.

In many ways Greek civilization provided a foundation for the civilizations that would later arise in the West. This is particularly so for Roman civilization, which came to prominence as Greece declined and which will be the subject of the next chapter.

PRIMARY SOURCES

The Iliad
Homer

Homer's Iliad, *a work of literature and an important cultural, religious, and social source on Greek civilization, is one of our few historical documents from the early period of Greek history. Most likely orally composed or assembled during the ninth or eighth century* B.C., *it refers to the great war between the Achaeans (Greeks of the Mycenaean Age) and the Trojans (occupants of a city in Asia Minor near the mouth of the Hellespont), probably fought in the thirteenth century* B.C. *The social and political conditions described in the* Iliad *are a mixture of traditions during Mycenaean times and typical practices during the ensuing "Dark Ages." The following selection refers to a shield being formed by Hephaistos, the Greek god of metalworking. The shield is decorated by scenes of two cities. In the first city, which is at peace, a trial is taking place. Around the second one, which is being besieged, are signs of a prosperous economy.*

> **Consider:** *The political characteristics of these cities, the basis on which this trial will be decided; the economic characteristics of the second city.*

On it he wrought in all their beauty two cities of mortal
    men. And there were marriages in one, and festivals.
They were leading the brides along the city from their maiden chambers
    under the flaring of torches, and the loud bride song was arising.
The young men followed the circles of the dance, and among them
    the flutes and lyres kept up their clamour as in the meantime
    the women standing each at the door of her court admired them.

SOURCE: Reprinted from Homer, *The Iliad*, trans. by Richmond Lattimore, by permission of The University of Chicago Press. Copyright © 1977, pp. 388–390.

The people were assembled in the market place, where a quarrel
    had arisen, and two men were disputing over the blood price
    for a man who had been killed. One man promised full restitution
    in a public statement, but the other refused and would accept nothing.
Both then made for an arbitrator, to have a decision;
    and people were speaking up on either side, to help both men.
But the heralds kept the people in hand, as meanwhile the elders
    were in session on benches of polished stone in the sacred circle
    and held in their hands the staves of the heralds who lift their voices.
The two men rushed before these, and took turns speaking their cases,
    and between them lay on the ground two talents of gold, to be given
    to that judge who in this case spoke the straightest opinion.
But around the other city were lying two forces of armed men
    shining in their war gear. For one side counsel was divided
    whether to storm and sack, or share between both sides the property
    and all the possessions the lovely citadel held hard within it.
But the city's people were not giving way, and armed for an ambush.
Their beloved wives and their little children stood on the rampart
    to hold it, and with them the men with age upon them, but meanwhile
    the others went out. And Ares led them, and Pallas Athene.
These were gold, both, and golden raiment upon them, and they were
    beautiful and huge in their armour, being divinities,
    and conpicuous from afar, but the people around them were smaller.
These, when they were come to the place that was set for their ambush,
    in a river, where there was a watering place for all animals,
    there they sat down in place shrouding themselves in the bright bronze.
But apart from these were sitting two men to watch for the rest of them
    and waiting until they could see the sheep and the shambling cattle,
    who appeared presently, and two herdsmen went along with them
    playing happily on pipes, and took no thought of the treachery.
Those others saw them, and made a rush, and quickly thereafter
    cut off on both sides the herds of cattle and the beautiful
    flocks of shining sheep, and killed the shepherds upon them. . . .
He made upon it a soft field, the pride of the tilled land,
    wide and triple-ploughed, with many ploughmen upon it
    who wheeled their teams at the turn and drove them in either
    direction. . . .
He made on it the precinct of a king, where the labourers
    were reaping, with the sharp reaping hooks in their hands. Of the
    cut swathes some fell along the lines of reaping, one after another,
    while the sheaf-binders caught up others and tied them with bind-ropes.
There were three sheaf-binders who stood by, and behind them
    were children picking up the cut swathes, and filled their arms with

them and carried and gave them always; and by them the king in
   silence and holding his staff near the line of the reapers, happily.
And apart and under a tree the heralds made a feast ready
   and trimmed a great ox they had slaughtered. Meanwhile the women
   scattered, for the workman to eat, abundant white barley.
He made on it a great vineyard and heavy with clusters,
   lovely in gold, but grapes upon it were darkened
   and the vines themselves stood out through poles of silver. About
   them he made a field-ditch of dark metal, and drove all around this
   a fence of tin; and there was only one path to the vineyard,
   and along it ran the grape-bearers for the vineyard's stripping.
Young girls and young men, in all their light-hearted innocence,
   carried the kind, sweet fruit away in their woven baskets,
   and in their midst a youth with a singing lyre played charmingly
   upon it for them, and sang the beautiful song for Linos
   in a light voice, and they followed him, and with singing and whistling
   and light dance-steps of their feet kept time to the music.

Poem on Women
Semonides of Amorgos

*There are few sources in this early period of Greek history that tell us about Greek atti-
tudes toward women. Most of the sources available were written by men, usually mentioning women only in passing. However, there is evidence that abuse of women was a
common theme in early Greek literature. The following selection is an example of this
theme. The selection is an excerpt from a poem about women by Semonides of Amorgos,
who lived on the island of Amorgos during the seventh century. The poem emphasizes
how different females are from men, describing nine negative types of women and one
positive type.*

> **Consider:** *What this indicates about Greek men's attitudes toward women; the
> ways in which the good woman differs from the bad woman according to Semoni-
> des.*

   In the beginning the god made the female mind separately. One he made from
a long-bristled sow. In her house everything lies in disorder, smeared with mud,
and rolls about the floor; and she herself unwashed, in clothes unlaundered, sits
by the dungheap and grows fat.

SOURCE: Hugh Lloyd-Jones, *Females of the Species: Semonides on Women.* (Park Ridge, New
Jersey: Noyes Press, 1975), pp. 30, 32, 34, 38. Copyright © 1975. Used by permission of Noyes
Publications.

❖

Another he made from a wicked vixen; a woman who knows everything. No bad thing and no better kind of thing is lost on her; for she often calls a good thing bad and a bad thing good. Her attitude is never the same.

❖

Another he made from a bitch, vicious, own daughter of her mother, who wants to hear everything and know everything. She peers everywhere and strays everywhere, always yapping, even if she sees no human being. A man cannot stop her by threatening, nor by losing his temper and knocking out her teeth with a stone, nor with honeyed words, not even if she is sitting with friends, but ceaselessly she keeps up a barking you can do nothing with.

❖

Another is from a bee; the man who gets her is fortunate, for on her alone blame does not settle. She causes his property to grow and increase, and she grows old with a husband whom she loves and who loves her, the mother of a handsome and reputable family. She stands out among all women, and a godike beauty plays about her. She takes no pleasure in sitting among women in places where they tell stories about love. Women like her are the best and most sensible whom Zeus bestows on men.

❖

Zeus has contrived that all these tribes of women are with men and remain with them. Yes, this is the worst plague Zeus has made—women; if they seem to be some use to him who has them, it is to him especially that they prove a plague. The man who lives with a woman never goes through all his day in cheerfulness; he will not be quick to push out of his house Starvation, a housemate who is an enemy, a god who is against us. Just when a man most wishes to enjoy himself at home, through the dispensation of a god or the kindness of a man, she finds a way of finding fault with him and lifts her crest for battle. Yes, where there is a woman, men cannot even give hearty entertainment to a guest who has come to the house; and the very woman who seems most respectable is the one who turns out guilty of the worst atrocity; because while her husband is not looking . . . and the neighbours get pleasure in seeing how he too is mistaken. Each man will take care to praise his own wife and find fault with the other's; we do not realize that the fate of all of us is alike. Yes, this is the greatest plague that Zeus has made, and he has bound us to them with a fetter that cannot be broken. Because of this some have gone to Hades fighting for a woman. . . .

Constitution of the Lacedaemonians

Xenophon

Sparta was one of the most powerful and well-known Greek city-states. Located on the Peloponnesian Peninsula, it developed a reputation during the seventh and sixth centuries B.C. for being conservative, disciplined, inward-loking, and devoted to military pursuits and strength. Much of this reputation derived from events during the middle of the seventh century when the helots, formerly the neighboring Messenians who had been conquered by the Spartans and subjected to serfdom, revolted against the far outnumbered Spartans. With great difficulty, the revolt was put down, but from that point on the Spartans committed themselves to preserving their dominance at all costs. Various constitutional reforms were instituted to ensure Spartan unity and military strength. Traditionally, these reforms were attributed to a perhaps legendary lawgiver, Lycurgus. Direct primary sources for these reforms are thin. The best evidence we have comes from Xenophon (434?–355? B.C.), an Athenian admirer of Sparta who wrote some two centuries after these occurrences. The following is a selection from his Constitution of the Lacedaemonians.

> **Consider:** *Xenophon's explanation for the extraordinary power and prestige of Sparta; the nature and purposes of Sparta's education system; how Sparta differed from other Greek city-states.*

I recall the astonishment with which I first noted the unique position of Sparta among the states of Hellas, the relatively sparse population, and at the same time the extraordinary power and prestige of the community. I was puzzled to account for the fact. It was only when I came to consider the peculiar institutions of the Spartans that my wonderment ceased. Or rather, it is transferred to the legislator who gave them those laws, obedience to which has been the secret of their prosperity. This legislator, Lycurgus, I admire, and hold him to have been one of the wisest of mankind. . . .

He insisted on the training of the body as incumbent no less on the female than the male; and in pursuit of the same idea instituted rival contests in running and feats of strength for women as for men. His belief was that where both parents were strong their progeny would be found to be more vigorous. . . .

Marriage, as he ordained it, must only take place in the prime of bodily vigour, this too being, as he believed, a condition conductive to the production of healthy offspring. . . .

But when we turn to Lycurgus, instead of leaving it to each member of the state privately to appoint a slave to be his son's tutor, he set over the young

---

SOURCE: Francis R. B. Godolphin, ed., *The Greek Historians*, Vol. II, trans. Henry G. Dakyns (New York: Random House, 1942), pp. 658–661, 666–669. Reprinted by permission.

Spartans a public guardian, the Paidonomos, to give him his proper title, with complete authority over them. . . .

Instead of softening their feet with shoe or sandal, his rule was to make them hardy through going barefoot. This habit, if practised, would, as he believed, enable them to scale heights more easily and clamber down precipices with less danger. . . .

Instead of making them effeminate with a variety of clothes, his rule was to habituate them to a single garment the whole year through, thinking that so they would be better prepared to withstand the variations of heat and cold.

Again, as regards food, according to his regulation the prefect, or head of the flock, must see that his messmates gathered to the club meal, with such moderate food as to avoid that heaviness which is engendered by repletion, and yet not to remain altogether unacquainted with the pains of penurious living. His belief was that by such training in boyhood they would be better able when occasion demanded to continue toiling on an empty stomach. . . .

On the other hand, in order to guard against a too great pinch of starvation, though he did not actually allow the boys to help themselves without further trouble to what they needed more, he did give them permission to steal this thing or that in the effort to alleviate their hunger. . . .

It is obvious, I say, that the whole of this education was intended to make the boys craftier and more inventive in getting in supplies, while at the same time it cultivated their warlike instincts. . . .

Furthermore, and in order that the boys should not want a ruler, even in case the guardian himself were absent, he gave to any citizen who chanced to be present authority to lay upon them injunctions for their good, and to chastise them for any trespass committed. . . .

We all know that in the generality of states everyone devotes his full energy to the business of making money: one man as a tiller of the soil, another as a mariner, a third as a merchant, whilst others depend on various arts to earn a living. But at Sparta Lycurgus forbade his freeborn citizens to have anything whatsoever to do with the concerns of moneymaking. As freemen, he enjoined upon them to regard as their concern exclusively those activities upon which the foundations of civic liberty are based. . . .

In Sparta, on the contrary, the stronger a man is the more readily does he bow before constituted authority. And indeed, they pride themselves on their humility, and on a prompt obedience, running, or at any rate not crawling with laggard step, at the word of command. Such an example of eager discipline, they are persuaded, set by themselves, will not fail to be followed by the rest.

Accordingly the ephors[1] are competent to punish whomsoever they choose: they have power to exact fines on the spur of the moment; they have power to depose magistrates in mid career, nay, actually to imprison and bring them to trial

---

[1] Elected magistrates.

on the capital charge. Entrusted with these vast powers, they do not, as do the rest of states, allow the magistrates elected to exercise authority as they like, right through the year of office; but, in the style rather of despotic monarchs, or presidents of the games, at the first symptom of an offence against the law they inflict chastisement without warning and without hesitation. . . .

And yet another point may well excite our admiration for Lycurgus largely. It had not escaped his observation that communities exist where those who are willing to make virtue their study and delight fail somehow in ability to add to the glory of their fatherland. That lesson the legislator laid to heart, and in Sparta he enforced, as a matter of public duty, the practice of every virtue by every citizen. And so it is that, just as man differs from man in some excellence, according as he cultivates or neglects to cultivate it, this city of Sparta, with good reason, outshines all other states in virtue; since she, and she alone, has made the attainment of a high standrd of noble living a public duty.

The History of the Peloponnesian War: Athens during the Golden Age
Thucydides

The first of the great Western historians lived in Greece during the Classical Age. They provide us with the most useful material available to trace events of the period. The greatest of these was Thucydides (471?–400? B.C.), a high-ranking and wealthy Athenian who was a general early in the war and who was later banished from Athens for twenty years for losing a campaign against the Spartans. In The History of the Peloponnesian War, *Thucydides traces the origins of the war, its course, and its consequences for the participants and for the Greek world in general. The following selection from this work is the famous eulogy delivered by the Athenian leader Pericles (490?–429 B.C.) during the winter of 431–430 B.C. for the Athenians killed during the first campaigns. In it Pericles compares the life and institutions of Athens with those of the enemy, Sparta, without mentioning the Spartans by name. He explains to his fellow Athenians what made Athens so great. This funeral oration provides a superb idealized description of the Athenian city-state at its height.*

> **Consider:** *The description of Athens, its institutions, and its people in this document; how Pericles compares Athens and Sparta and how a Spartan leader might reply; how Pericles defines the proper balance between Athenians' freedom as individuals and their commitments as citizens.*

SOURCE: From Francis R. B. Godolphin, ed., *The Greek Historians*, vol. I (New York: Random House, 1942), pp. 648–651. Reprinted by permission.

"I will speak first of our ancestors, for it is right and becoming that now, when we are lamenting the dead, a tribute should be paid to their memory. There has never been a time when they did not inhabit this land, which by their valour they have handed down from generation to generation, and we have received from them a free state. But if they were worthy of praise, still more were our fathers, who added to their inheritance, and after many a struggle transmitted to us their sons this great empire. And we ourselves assembed here today, who are still most of us in the vigour of life, have chiefly done the work of improvement, and have richly endowed our city with all things, so that she is sufficient for herself both in peace and war. Of the military exploits by which our various possessions were acquired, or of the energy with which we or our fathers drove back the tide of war, Hellenic or barbarian, I will not speak; for the tale would be long and is familiar to you. But before I praise the dead, I should like to point out by what principles of action we rose to power, and under what institutions and through what manner of life our empire became great. For I conceive that such thoughts are not unsuited to the occasion, and that this numerous assembly of citizens and strangers may profitably listen to them.

"Our form of government does not enter into rivalry with the institutions of others. We do not copy our neighbours, but are an example to them. It is true that we are called a democracy, for the administration is in the hands of the many and not of the few. But while the law secures equal justice to all alike in their private disputes, the claim of excellence is also recognised; and when a citizen is in any way distinguished, he is preferred to the public service, not as a matter of privilege, but as the reward of merit. Neither is poverty a bar, but a man may benefit his country whatever be the obscurity of his condition. There is no exclusiveness in our public life, and in our private intercourse we are not suspicious of one another, nor angry with our neighbour if he does what he likes; we do not put on sour looks at him which, though harmless, are not pleasant. While we are thus unconstrained in our private intercourse, a spirit of reverence pervades our public acts; we are prevented from doing wrong by respect for authority and for the laws, having an especial regard to those which are ordained for the protection of the injured as well as to those unwritten laws which bring upon the transgressor of them the reprobation of the general sentiment.

"And we have not forgotten to provide for our weary spirits many relaxations from toil; we have regular games and sacrifices throughout the year; at home the style of our life is refined; and the delight which we daily feel in all these things helps to banish melancholy. Because of the greatness of our city the fruits of the whole earth flow in upon us; so that we enjoy the goods of other countries as freely as of our own.

"Then, again, our military training is in many respects superior to that of our adversaries. Our city is thrown open to the world, and we never expel a foreigner or prevent him from seeing or learning anything of which the secret if revealed to an enemy might profit him. We rely not upon management or trickery, but upon our own hearts and hands. And in the matter of education, whereas they from early youth are always undergoing laborious exercises which are to make them brave, we live at ease, and yet are equally ready to face the perils which they face. And here is the proof. The Lacedaemonians come into Attica not by themselves, but with their whole confederacy following; we go alone into a neighbour's country; and although our opponents are fighting for their homes and we on a foreign soil, we have seldom any difficulty in overcoming them. Our enemies have never yet felt our united strength; the care of a navy divides our attention, and on land we are obliged to send our own citizens everywhere. But they, if they meet and defeat a part of our army, are as proud as if they had routed us all, and when defeated they pretend to have been vanquished by us all.

"If then we prefer to meet danger with a light heart but without laborious training, and with a courage which is gained by habit and not enforced by law, are we not greatly the gainers? Since we do not anticipate the pain, although, when the hour comes, we can be as brave as those who never allow themselves to rest; and thus too our city is equally admirable in peace and in war.

"For we are lovers of the beautiful, yet with economy, and we cultivate the mind without loss of manliness. Wealth we employ, not for talk and ostentation, but when there is a real use for it. To avow poverty with us is no disgrace; the true disgrace is in doing nothing to avoid it. An Athenian citizen does not neglect the state because he takes care of his own household; and even those of us who are engaged in business have a very fair idea of politics. We alone regard a man who takes no interest in public affairs, not as a harmless, but as a useless character; and if few of us are originators, we are all sound judges of a policy. The great impediment to action is, in our opinion, not discussion, but the want of that knowledge which is gained by discussion preparatory to action. For we have a peculiar power of thinking before we act and of acting too, whereas other men are courageous from ignorance but hesitate upon reflection. And they are surely to be esteemed the bravest spirits who, having the clearest sense both of the pains and pleasures of life, do not on that account shrink from danger. In doing good, again, we are unlike others; we make our friends by conferring, not by receiving favours. Now he who confers a favour is the firmer friend, because he would fain by kindness keep alive the memory of an obligation; but the recipient is colder in his feelings, because he knows that in requiting another's generosity he will not be winning gratitude but only paying a debt. We alone do good to our neighbours not upon a calculation of interest, but in the confidence of freedom and in a frank and fearless spirit.

"To sum up: I say that Athens is the school of Hellas, and that the individual Athenian in his own person seems to have the power of adapting himself to the most varied forms of action with the utmost versatility and grace."

Antigone
Sophocles

Much of our information about Greece comes from dramas, which played such an important educational, religious, and cultural role in Greek life. Sophocles (496?–406 B.C.), an Athenian of aristocratic birth and an important public official, was one of the greatest dramatists of the Classical Age. In Antigone, *which was first staged in 441 B.C., he focused on the conflicts between social obligation and individual convictions, between political and moral conscience. The first excerpt is a speech by Creon, King of Thebes, to his counselors. He refers to the recent strife in Thebes between the two sons of the tragically fallen King Oedipus. One of the sons, Polyneices, gathered Greek enemies of Thebes and attacked the city, which was defended by the other son, Eteocles. Both were killed in battle, and thus Creon, the brother of Oedipus, assumed the throne. A struggle arose between the strong-willed Antigone, Polyneices' sister, who felt compelled by dictates of blood and religion to give her brother a proper burial, and Creon, who felt that as ruler he had to uphold the authority of the state and punish rebellion. Here Creon justifies his decision to bury Eteocles honorably but to leave Polyneices unburied. In the second excerpt, Antigone justifies her burial of Polyneices and her disobeying the laws of the state.*

> **Consider:** *The attitudes and ideals revealed in this selection; Creon's view of the duties of the ruler and how these duties conflict with obligations of conscience and religion; how Antigone replies to Creon; how the relation between the individual and the state presented in this document compares with the same relation presented in Pericles' funeral oration.*

CREON. My lords: for what concerns the state, the gods
Who tossed it on the angry surge of strife
Have righted it again; and therefore you
By royal edict I have summoned here,
Chosen from all our number. I know well
How you revered the throne of Laius;
And then, when Oedipus maintained our state,
And when he perished, round his sons you rallied,
Still firm and steadfast in your loyalty.
Since they have fallen by a double doom
Upon a single day, two brothers each
Killing the other with polluted sword,
I now possess the throne and royal power
By right of nearest kinship with the dead.
　　There is no art that teaches us to know
The temper, mind or spirit of any man

SOURCE: *Sophocles: Three Tragedies*, trans. by H. D. F. Kitto (© Oxford University Press, 1962), pp. 8–9, 16–17, by permission of Oxford University Press.

Until he has been proved by government
And lawgiving. A man who rules a state
And will not ever steer the wisest course,
But is afraid, and says not what he thinks,
That man is worthless; and if any holds
A friend of more account than his own city,
I scorn him; for if I should see destruction
Threatening the safety of my citizens,
I would not hold my peace, nor would I count
That man my friend who was my country's foe,
Zeus be my witness. For be sure of this:
It is the city that protects us all;
She bears us through the storm; only when she
Rides safe and sound can we make loyal friends.
    This I believe, and thus will I maintain
Our city's greatness.—Now, conformably,
Of Oedipus' two sons I have proclaimed
This edict: he who in his country's cause
Fought gloriously and so laid down his life,
Shall be entombed and graced with every rite
That men can pay to those who die with honour;
But for his brother, him called Polyneices,
Who came from exile to lay waste his land,
To burn the temples of his native gods,
To drink his kindred blood, and to enslave
The rest, I have proclaimed to Thebes that none
Shall give him funeral honours or lament him,
But leave him there unburied, to be devoured
By dogs and birds, mangled most hideously.
Such is my will; never shall I allow
The villain to win more honour than the upright;
But any who show love to this our city
In life and death alike shall win my praise.

                              ❖

    CREON. You: tell me briefly—I want no long speech:
Did you not know that this had been forbidden?
ANTIGONE. Of course I knew. There was a proclamation.
CREON. And so you dared to disobey the law?
ANTIGONE. It was not Zeus who published this decree,
Nor have the Powers who rule among the dead
Imposed such laws as this upon mankind;
Nor could I think that a decree of yours—
A man—could override the laws of Heaven

Unwritten and unchanging. Not of today
Or yesterday is their authority;
They are eternal; no man saw their birth.
Was I to stand before the gods' tribunal
For disobeying *them*, because I feared
A man? I knew that I should have to die,
Even without your edict; if I die
Before my time, why then, I count it gain;
To one who lives as I do, ringed about
With countless miseries, why, death is welcome.
For me to meet this doom is little grief;
But when my mother's son lay dead, had I
Neglected him and left him there unburied,
That would have caused me grief; this causes none.
And if you think it folly, then perhaps
I am accused of folly by the fool.

The Republic
Plato

Various city-states in Classical Greece, and particularly Athens, have been admired for their democratic institutions and practices. Yet Plato (427?–347 B.C.), the greatest political theorist of the time, was a harsh critic of democracy. An aristocratic Athenian who grew up during the Peloponnesian War, Plato became embittered by the trial and death of his teacher, Socrates, in 399. After an extended absence from Athens, Plato returned in 386 and founded a school, the Academy, where he hoped to train philosopher-statesmen in accordance with his ideals expounded in The Republic. *In the following selection from that work, Plato employs the dialogue form to examine democracy and its perils. This represents more than abstract thoughts, for at the time it was written, there was a rivalry between democratic forms of government, best represented by Athens, and more struc-tured authoritarian forms, represented by Sparta.*

Consider: *The strengths and weaknesses of Plato's argument; how Plato's view of (Athenian) democracy compares with the view of Pericles (Thucydides).*

And then democracy comes into being after the poor have conquered their op-ponents, slaughtering some and banishing some, while to the remainder they give an equal share of freedom and power; and this is the form of government in which the magistrates are commonly elected by lot.

Source: M. J. Knight. ed., and B. Jowett, trans., A *Selection of Passages from Plato for English Readers* (Oxford, England: The Clarendon Press, 1895), pp. 80–82.

Yes, he said, that is the nature of democracy, whether the revolution has been effected by arms, or whether fear has caused the opposite party to withdraw.

And now what is their manner of life, and what sort of a government have they? For as the government is, such will be the man.

Clearly, he said.

In the first place, are they not free; and is not the city full of freedom and frankness—a man may say and do what he likes?

'Tis said so, he replied.

And where freedom is, the individual is clearly able to order for himself his own life as he pleases?

Clearly.

Then in this kind of State there will be the greatest variety of human natures?

There will.

This, then, seems likely to be the fairest of States, being like an embroidered robe which is spangled with every sort of flower. And just as women and children think a variety of colours to be of all things most charming, so there are many men to whom this State, which is spangled with the manners and characters of mankind, will appear to be the fairest of States.

Yes.

Yes, my good Sir, and there will be no better in which to look for a government. Why?

Because of the liberty which reigns there—they have a complete assortment of constitutions; and he who has a mind to establish a State, as we have been doing, must go to a democracy as he would to a bazaar at which they sell them, and pick out the one that suits him; then, when he has made his choice, he may found his State.

He will be sure to have patterns enough.

And there being no necessity, I said, for you to govern in this State, even if you have the capacity, or to be governed, unless you like, or to go to war when the rest go to war, or to be at peace when others are at peace, unless you are so disposed—there being no necessity also, because some law forbids you to hold office or be a dicast, that you should not hold office or be a dicast, if you have a fancy—is not this a way of life which for the moment is supremely delightful?

For the moment, yes.

And is not their humanity to the condemned in some cases quite charming? Have you not observed how, in a democracy, many persons, although they have been sentenced to death or exile, just stay where they are and walk about the world—the gentleman parades like a hero, and nobody sees or cares?

Yes, he replied, many and many a one.

See too, I said, the forgiving spirit of democracy, and the 'don't care' about trifles, and the disregard which she shows of all the fine principles which we solemnly laid down at the foundation of the city—as when we said that, except in the case of some rarely gifted nature, there never will be a good man who has not from his childhood been used to play amid things of beauty and make of them a joy and a study—how grandly does she trample all these fine notions of ours under her feet, never giving a thought to the pursuits which make a statesman, and promoting to honour any one who professes to be the people's friend.

Yes, she is of a noble spirit.

These and other kindred characteristics are proper to democracy, which is a charming form of government, full of variety and disorder, and dispensing a sort of equality to equals and unequals alike.

We know her well.

Medicine and Magic
Hippocrates

By the fifth century B.C. the Greeks had developed a scientific approach to knowledge. One of the many subjects reflecting this development was medicine. Hippocrates of Cos (460?–377 B.C.) founded a medical school that stressed careful observation and natural causes for disease. This method involved abandoning many religious or supernatural assumptions about diseases and rejecting various forms of divine healing. In the following selection attributed to Hippocrates, or at least his school, this approach is applied to the "sacred disease," the common term for epilepsy.

> **Consider:** *How scientific the assumptions in this document are; the points that might be rejected or applauded by modern doctors.*

I do not believe that the 'Sacred Disease' is any more divine or sacred than any other disease but, on the contrary, has specific characteristics and a definite cause. Nevertheless, because it is completely different from other diseases, it has been regarded as a divine visitation by those who, being only human, view it with ignorance and astonishment. This theory of divine origin, though supported by the difficulty of understanding the malady, is weakened by the simplicity of the cure consisting merely of ritual purification and incantation. If remarkable features in a malady were evidence of divine visitation, then there would be many 'sacred diseases.' Quotidian, tertian and quartan fevers are among other diseases no less remarkable and portentous and yet no one regards them as having a divine origin. I do not believe that these diseases have any less claim to be caused by a god than the so-called 'sacred' disease but they are not the objects of popular wonder. Again, no less remarkably, I have seen men go mad and become delirious for no obvious reason and do many strange things. I have seen many cases of people groaning and shouting in their sleep, some who choke; others jump from their

SOURCE: From Hippocrates, *The Medical Works of Hippocrates*, trans. John Chadwick and W. N. Mann, 1950. Courtesy of Charles C Thomas, Publisher, Springfield, Illinois, and Basil Blackwell, Publisher, Oxford, England.

bed and run outside and remain out of their mind till they wake, when they are as healthy and sane as they were before, although perhaps rather pale and weak. These things are not isolated events but frequent occurrences. There are many other remarkable afflictions of various sorts, but it would take too long to describe them in detail.

It is my opinion that those who first called this disease 'sacred' were the sort of people we now call witch-doctors, faith-healers, quacks and charlatans. These are exactly the people who pretend to be very pious and to be particularly wise. By invoking a divine element they were able to screen their own failure to give suitable treatment and so called this a 'sacred' malady to conceal their ignorance of its nature. . . .

They also employ other pretexts so that, if the patient be cured, their reputation for cleverness is enhanced while, if he dies, they can excuse themselves by explaining that the gods are to blame while they themselves did nothing wrong; that they did not prescribe the taking of any medicine whether liquid or solid, nor any baths which might have been responsible. . . .

It seems, then, that those who attempt to cure disease by this sort of treatment do not really consider the maladies thus treated of sacred or of divine origin. If the disease can be cured by purification and similar treatment then what is to prevent its being brought on by like devices? The man who can get rid of a disease by his magic could equally well bring it on; again there is nothing divine about this but a human element is involved. By such claims and trickery, these practitioners pretend a deeper knowledge than is given to others; with their prescriptions of 'sanctifications' and 'purifications', their patter about divine visitation and possession by devils, they seek to deceive. And yet I believe that all these professions of piety are really more like impiety and a denial of the existence of the gods, and all their religion and talk of divine visitation is an impious fraud which I shall proceed to expose. . . .

I believe that this disease is not in the least more divine than any other but has the same nature as other diseases and a similar cause. Moreover, it can be cured no less than other diseases so long as it has not become inveterate and too powerful for the drugs which are given.

Like other diseases it is hereditary. If a phlegmatic child is born of a phlegmatic parent, a bilious child of a bilious parent, a consumptive child of a consumptive parent and a splenetic child of a splenetic parent, why should the children of a father or mother who is afflicted with this disease not suffer similarly? The seed comes from all parts of the body; it is healthy when it comes from healthy parts, diseased when it comes from diseased parts. Another important proof that this disease is no more divine than any other lies in the fact that the phlegmatic are constitutionally liable to it while the bilious escape. If its origin were divine, all types would be affected alike without this particular distinction.

VISUAL SOURCES

Trade, Culture, and Colonization

This scene is from the inside of a Laconian cup dating from about 560 B.C. It shows King Arcesilas II of the Greek North African colony of Cyrene (a Dorian Greek colony originally founded by Thera around 630 B.C.) supervising the weighing and loading of a shipment of what is probably silphium, a medicinal plant exported from the area. On the left Arcesilas is sitting on the deck of a ship underneath a canopy, apparently arguing with his steward. On the right workers carry on the silphium and call out the weight while below workers fill the hold with it. Around are animals of the area: a lizard, a monkey, and birds.

This cup reflects the importance of trade for the Greeks and the role Greek colonies played in this. It also indicates a growing interconnectedness based on the Mediterranean—a familiarity with the shoreland areas in which Greeks had settled and contact with the cultures and environment they found there, as might be surmised by the use of a North African plant for medicinal purposes in the Greek homeland and by the large

Photo 4-1

Bibliothèque Nationale, Paris

number of cups similar to these that were being exported from Laconia. The words on the cup provide evidence for the spread of literacy among Greeks.

> **Consider:** *How this cup can be used as evidence for the importance of commerce and colonization in the Greek world; how commerce served as a medium for cultural diffusion throughout the Mediterranean basin.*

Migration and Colonization

These two maps reveal a number of relationships between history and geography in the Greek world. The first shows some of the dialects of the Greeks; the arrows indicate some of the probable directions of Greek migrations as traced by these dialects in the aftermath of the Dorian invasions between the thirteenth and tenth centuries B.C. The second shows

Map 4-1 Dialects

the extent of Greek settlement around the Mediterranean and Black Seas between 750 and 550 B.C. in comparison with the previously colonized or colonizing areas originating from Phoenicia and the relatively stable Etruscans in northern Italy. This map also distinguishes the Ionian, Dorian, and Aeolian origins of some of those Greek colonies.

Comparison of these two maps shows that there is a trend for colonies to be located near, or be logical geographic extensions of, the earlier migrations of Greeks. For example, as Dorians spread south and southeast to Thera, Crete, and Rhodes, so would future colonies extend further south, such as those in North Africa (Cyrenaica), and southeast, to, for example, Aspendus. Generally, the Ionians were the most mobile in face of the Dorian invasions and fled across the islands of the Aegean to the east and to the coast of Asia Minor. They were the most prolific colonizers in number and extent, stretching from Spain in the west to the extremes of the Black Sea in the north and east. Although colonies became independent city-states, some of the history of migrations and colonization affected future military alliances. For example, Greeks of the Ionic dialect tended to support each other in the Persian and Peloponnesian Wars.

The extent of Greek colonization suggests the importance of colonies for diffusing culture throughout the Mediterranean. Greeks often came into contact (at times through war) with the competing Phoenicians as well as with the established Etruscans and later the Romans in the western Mediterranean. All this helps explain how Greek and Greco-Roman civilization came to dominate most of the Mediterranean basin even when the Greeks were no longer a great military-political force and their colonies were no longer independent.

Map 4-2   Colonies

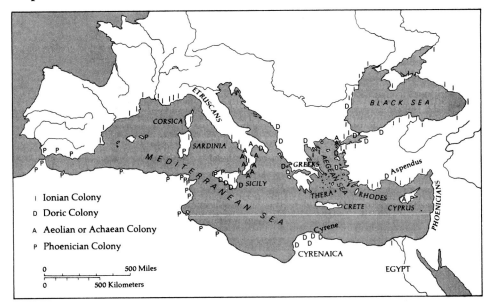

- ı Ionian Colony
- ᴅ Doric Colony
- ᴀ Aeolian or Achaean Colony
- ᴘ Phoenician Colony

Consider: *How the history and geography of Greek migrations and colonization helped diffuse culture in the ancient world; how a geographic analysis of dialects can shed light on the history of a civilization.*

SECONDARY SOURCES

Atlantis and Minoan Crete: An Archaeological Nexus
Jerome Pollitt

The highly developed Bronze Age civilizations of the Minoans and Mycenaeans seem to have collapsed suddenly between the thirteenth and twelfth centuries B.C. Indeed, the collapse was so complete that few records remain. This has forced historians and archaeologists to offer rather speculative interpretations for the fall. One interpretation links the fall of these civilizations to a great volcanic eruption on the Greek island of Thera (which, in turn, has been linked to the story of Atlantis sinking below the sea). In the following selection, Jerome Pollitt, an archaeologist and art historian from Yale University, challenges this interpretation and suggests another that links the fall of Minoan and Mycenaean civilizations to wider turmoil throughout the Mediterranean basin.

Consider: *How the volcanic eruption interpretation might be attacked; Pollitt's reasons for supporting the invasion interpretation.*

If we associate the presumed Thera disaster with the end of *both* Minoan and Mycenaean civilization, we must take into account the increasingly abundant evidence which demonstrates that the Mycenaean world did not collapse all at once. It is true that around 1200 B.C. there are signs of trouble in the Mycenaean world. Emergency fortifications and water supplies are built at Mycenae, Tiryns, and Athens (fortifications are built for protection from people, not volcanoes). Pylos, it is true, was destroyed by fire around 1200 B.C., but whatever the storm was, most Mycenaean centers seem to have weathered it. In Athens, civilization never came to an abrupt break. Mycenae and Tiryns seem to die of attrition

---

SOURCE: Jerome J. Pollitt, "Atlantis and Minoan Crete: An Archaeological Nexus," *Yale Alumni Magazine* (February 1970), pp. 28–29. Reprinted by permission.

around 1100 B.C., but in the century between 1200 B.C. and 1100 B.C. there is no single, great calamity. In fact, at times there are some signs of reviving prosperity. . . .

So, at this point in history our knowledge of what really happened at the end of the Greek Bronze Age is very much up in the air. I would like to compound the confusion by adding an observation of my own. To the archaeologist who looks beyond the confines of the Aegean toward other parts of the Mediterranean and Europe, it is clear that the period between 1250 B.C. and 1100 B.C. was an era of great turmoil and instability everywhere. In Asia Minor the once mighty Hittite Empire began to crumble. There are major destruction levels in Syria, Palestine, and on Cyprus. Egypt, during the reign of Ramses III in the early 12th century, suffered attacks from foreign hordes known collectively as the "Peoples of the Sea.". . .

Historians of the Greek Bronze Age more often look east rather than west, because it is from the east that the elements of so-called "higher" civilization emanated at this time. Yet Italy, at the end of the Bronze Age, has perhaps much to tell us about what happened in Greece. Around 1200 B.C. connections with the Aegean are shattered and here many sites are abandoned. In Sicily, the survivors of the Bronze Age Castelluccio and Thapsos cultures seem to flee up into the hills. On the Aeolian Islands, where a series of trading stations that seems to have passed on obsidian and metals to the Aegean has flourished for 2,000 years or more, civilization is all but annihilated.

In all these areas—Aegean, East, and West—there seems to be one consistent element that accompanies the turmoil and sets its stamp on it. This is the rite of cremation burial with certain types of swords, pins, and ornaments accompanying the cremation. . . . The aggregate of this rite and these implements, suddenly and in so many places at roughly the same time, must reflect more than just a coincidental change of custom. And the place where this combination of cremation, flange-hilted swords, and safety pins makes its earliest appearance is in the Urnfield cultures of the Balkans and central Europe.

The idea that the Bronze Age civilization of Greece might have been destroyed by an invasion from the north has been out of fashion for some time because, in the form in which it was originally proposed, it was simplistic and did not fit the archaeological evidence. But perhaps it is due for a comeback in an altered form. The picture of piratical groups of footloose Urn-fielders from central Europe, in concert perhaps with other disaffected elements of the Mediterranean population, attacking Egypt, driving the inhabitants of Crete and south Italy into the hills, sacking Pylos (causing the building of emergency fortifications in other Mycenaean cities), and starting a general chain reaction of piracy, civil strife, and economic dislocation throughout the Mediterranean, is not beyond the evidence.

The process may have resembled the invasion of the Roman Empire by semi-barbarian northerners from the third to the fifth centuries A.D. This was also a gradual process. There is no single archaeological stratum to mark where "the invaders" replaced the "established culture." But in several centuries a great and long-standing civilization passed from the scene.

The Greeks: Slavery
Anthony Andrews

It has long been known that the Greeks, like other ancient peoples, practiced slavery. But focusing only on the glories of Greece sometimes leads one to forget how much slavery existed at that time and the role slavery played in supporting the Greek style of life. A historian who takes this into account is Anthony Andrews, a professor at Oxford University who has written a major text on the Greeks. In the following selection he examines Greek assumptions about slavery and the relations between slaves and masters in the Greek world.

> **Consider:** *How this analysis undermines an image of Athens as an open, democratic, and just society; what distinctions might be made between slavery in different times and societies—such as between slavery in Athens and in eighteenth-century America.*

In the broadest terms, slavery was basic to Greek civilisation in the sense that, to abolish it and substitute free labour, if it had occurred to anyone to try this on, would have dislocated the whole society and done away with the leisure of the upper classes of Athens and Sparta. The ordinary Athenian had a very deeply ingrained feeling that it was impossible for a free man to work directly for another as his master. While it is true that free men, a well as slaves, engaged in most forms of trade and industry, the withdrawal of slaves from these tasks would have entailed a most uncomfortable reorganisation of labour and property. . . .

No easy generalisation is possible about the relations between slave and master in the Greek world, since the slave's view, as usual, is not known. In the close quarters of Greek domestic life, no distance could be preserved like that which English middle-class families used to keep between themselves and their servants—and the Greek was unlikely to refrain from talking under any circumstances. The closer relation of nurse and child, tutor and pupil, easily ripened into affection, nor need we doubt stories of the loyal slave saving his master's life on the battlefield, and the like. But at its best the relationship was bound to have unhappy elements, as that when a slave was punished it was with physical blows of the kind that a free man had the right to resent. . . .

The domestic slave who was on good terms with his master stood some chance of liberation, and the slave 'living apart' and practising his trade might hope to earn enough to buy his release. Manumission was by no means uncommon, though the practice and the formalities differed a good deal from place to place. The master often retained the right to certain services for a fixed period, or for his own lifetime. Some of those 'living apart' prospered conspicuously, giving rise to disgruntled oligarchic comment that slaves in the streets of Athens might be better dressed than free men. . . .

SOURCE: Anthony Andrews, *The Greeks* (New York: Random House, 1967), pp. 133, 138–139, 142.

But the domestic slave with a bad master was in poor case, with little hope of redress, and the prospects were altogether bleaker for those who were hired out to the mines and other work—and we are not given even a distorted reflection of their feelings. But, after the Spartans had fortified their post outside Athens in 413, Thucydides tells us that over 20,000 slaves deserted to the enemy, the bulk of them 'craftsmen' (the word would cover any sort of skilled labour and need not be confined to the miners of Laurium, though no doubt many of the deserters were from there). We do not know what promises the invaders had held out to them, still less what eventually became of them, but the suggestion is clear that the life of even a skilled slave was one which he was ready to fly from on a very uncertain prospect. . . .

In the generation of Socrates, when everything was questioned, the justice of slavery was questioned also. Isolated voices were heard to say that all men were equally men, and that slavery was against nature. The defence of Aristotle, that some were naturally slaves, incapable of full human reason and needing the will of a master to complete their own, rings hollow to us, quite apart from the accident that 'naturally free' Greeks might be enslaved by the chances of war. But this was a world in which slavery, in some form or other, was universal, and no nation could remember a time when it had not been so. It is not surprising that there was no clamour for emancipation. It has been convincingly argued that the margin over bare subsistence in Greece was so small that the surplus which was needed to give leisure to the minority could only be achieved with artificially cheap labour. If that is right, there was not much alternative for Greece. For Athens, it had come, by the opening of the sixth century, to a choice between reducing citizens to slavery or extensive import of chattel slaves from abroad. Only a greatly improved technology, something like an industrial revolution, coud effectively have altered these conditions.

Greek Realities
Finley Hooper

Most historians stress the intellectual and scientific accomplishments of the Greeks, above all their extraordinary use of reason. In recent years historians have been pointing to the less rational and individualistic aspects of the Greeks. Finley Hooper, author of Greek Realities *(1967), exemplifies this trend in the following selection by focusing on the context of the supernatural and the demand to conform that typified everyday life for most Greeks.*

SOURCE: Reprinted from *Greek Realities* by Finley Hooper, by permission of the Wayne State University Press. Copyright © 1967, pp. 1–3.

Consider: *Ways the primary documents support or refute Hooper's argument; whether, based on this interpretation and Andrews', it is a mistake to view the Greeks as democratic; the context Hooper is using for making his evaluation.*

For the most part, this history of the Greek people from the earliest times to the late fourth century B.C. is about a few men whose talents made all the others remembered. That would be true, in part, of any people. In ancient times, the sources of information about the average man and his life were very limited, yet one of the realities of Greek history is the wide disparity in outlook between the creative minority which held the spotlight and the far more numerous goatherders, beekeepers, olive growers, fishermen, seers, and sometimes charlatans, who along with other nameless folk made up the greater part of the population.

Romantic glorifications of Greece create the impression that the Greeks sought rational solutions and were imaginative and intellectually curious as a people. Actually, far from being devoted to the risks of rationality, the vast majority of the Greeks sought always the safe haven of superstition and the comfort of magic charms. Only a relatively few thinkers offered a wondrous variety of ideas in their tireless quest for truth. To study various opinions, each of which appears to have some element of truth, is not a risk everyone should take and by no means did all the ancient Greeks take it. Yet enough did, so as to enable a whole people to be associated with the beginnings of philosophy, including the objectivity of scientific inquiry.

The Greeks who belonged to the creative minority were no more like everybody else than such folks ever have been. . . .

They were restless, talkative, critical and sometimes tiresome. Yet their lives as much as their works reveal Greece, for better or for worse, in the way it really was. After Homer, lyric poets went wandering from place to place, in exile from their native cities; before the time of Aristotle, Socrates was executed. If the Greeks invented intellectualism, they were also the first to suppress it. They were, in brief, a people who showed others both how to succeed and how to fail at the things which men might try.

As has often been said, the first democratic society known to man originated in Greece. For this expression of human freedom the Greeks have deservedly received everlasting credit. Yet it is also true that democratic governments were never adopted by a majority of Greek states, and those established were bitterly contested from within and without. In Athens where democracy had its best chance, the government was always threatened by the schemes of oligarchical clubs which sought by any means possible to subvert it. Ironically, Athenian democracy actually failed because of the mistakes of those whom it benefited most, rather than through the machinations of men waiting in the wings to take over. Then, as now, beneath the surface of events there persisted the tension between the material benefits to be obtained through state intervention and the more dynamic vitality which prevails where individuals are left more free to serve and, as it happens, to exploit one another.

A historian must be careful in drawing parallels. The number of individuals in a Greek democracy whose freedom was at stake would be considerably fewer than nowadays. The history of ancient Greece came before the time when all men were created equal. Even the brilliant Aristotle accepted at face value the evidence that certain individuals were endowed with superior qualities. He saw no reason why all men should be treated alike before the law. In fact, he allowed that certain extraordinary persons might be above the law altogether. Some men seemed born to rule and others to serve. There was no common ground between them.

The egalitarian concept that every human being has been endowed by his creator with certain inalienable rights was not a part of the Greek democratic tradition. Pericles, the great Athenian statesman, said that the Athenians considered debate a necessary prelude to any wise action. At the same time, he had a narrow view as to who should do the debating. At Athens, women, foreigners and slaves were all excluded from political life. The actual citizenry was therefore a distinct minority of those living in the city.

In other Greek cities, political power continued to be vested in a small clique (an oligarchy) or in the hands of one man, and often with beneficial results. Various answers to the same political and social problems were proposed and because there were differences there were conflicts. Those who sought to reduce the conflicts also sought to curb the differences, the very same which gave Greek society its exciting vitality. Here we have one of the ironies of human history. Amid bitter often arrogant quarrelsomeness, the Greeks created a civilization which has been much admired. Yet, the price of it has been largely ignored. Hard choices are rarely popular. The Greeks provide the agonizing lesson that men do struggle with one another and in doing so are actually better off than when they live in collective submission to a single idea.

Chapter Questions

1. How should the historical usefulness of the various primary documents, particularly those that are usually considered pieces of literature, be evaluated? What problems might arise for historians who rely on literary documents for their interpretations of early Greek civilization?

2. Some of the documents have dealt with the nature of the city-state, emphasizing some of the tensions and changes the Greeks experienced. Basing your answers on the information and arguments presented in these sources, what do you think were the advantages and disadvantages for the Greeks of being organized into such relatively small, independent units?

3. On the one hand, the sources have focused on various admired characteristics of Greek civilization, such as their art, drama, democracy, political thought, science, and philosophy. On the other hand, the documents reveal certain

criticized qualities of Greek civilization, such as the relatively common occurrence of war, the nonegalitarian attitudes of the Greeks, the negative attitude toward women, and the support of slavery. Considering this, do you think that the Greeks have been overly romanticized or appropriately admired? Why?

4. Considering historical, geographic, and cultural factors, in what ways did the Greeks differ from earlier civilizations of the eastern hemisphere? How would you explain some of these differences?

FIVE

The Mediterranean Basin: Roman Civilization and the Origins of Christianity

Farther west from Greece in the Mediterranean basin, Roman civilization arose during the middle of the first millennium B.C. After gaining independence from the ruling Etruscans in 509 B.C., the Romans slowly established control over the Italian peninsula, the western Mediterranean, the whole Mediterranean basin, and large parts of Europe. In this process of expansion, the Romans borrowed freely from the Greeks, creating a Greco-Roman civilization that would endure for centuries.

Although Rome retained her republican form of government until the first century B.C., there was considerable political turmoil and struggle. After a century of "slow revolution," Augustus took command in 27 B.C. A variety of reforms transformed the Republic into the Empire. Rome entered a period of expansion, prosperity, cultural vigor, and relative political stability for most of the following two centuries.

During these first two centuries of the Empire, Christianity arose and spread. By the fourth century it was recognized as the state religion within the Roman Empire.

By then the Empire had experienced enormous difficulties. Despite various efforts to revive the Empire, it was split into a Western and an Eastern half toward the end of the fourth century. The West became increasingly rural, subject to invasion, and generally in decline; the East evolved into the long-lasting Byzantine Empire. By the end of the fifth century, a unified, effective Western Empire was little more than a memory.

This chapter deals with four main questions. First, what was the structure of the Roman state? This involves an examination of the Roman constitution and political institutions. Second, what was the nature of Roman society? A number of documents focus on the life of the aristocracy and the position of women in an attempt to address this question. Third, what was the nature and appeal of Christianity? Here early Christian writings and Roman reactions to the rise of Christianity will be examined. Fourth, how do we explain the "decline and fall" of Rome? This question will take us up to the rise of new civilizations in lands once controlled by Rome, which will be covered in following chapters.

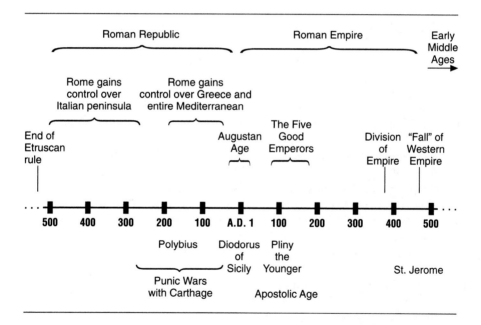

PRIMARY SOURCES

Histories: The Roman Constitution
Polybius

One of the Romans' greatest achievements was the development of political institutions that, despite problems, accommodated Rome's needs. Probably the best general description of these institutions during the Republic is provided by Polybius (205? B.C.–123 A.D.), a Greek politician and one of the greatest historians of the ancient world. He spent sixteen years in Rome, where he was in a position to observe the functioning of the Roman state and examine relevant documents. Part of his stated purpose in examining Rome's institutions was to explain why Rome had been so successful, particularly in comparison with his own Greek world. Some of his conclusions are presented in the following selection in which he describes the balanced nature of the Roman constitution.

> **Consider:** *The relative powers of the consuls, the Senate, and the people; the most important function of the Roman government according to Polybius; the potential dangers or sources of instability in such a constitution.*

As for the Roman constitution, it had three elements, each of them possessing sovereign powers: and their respective share of power in the whole state had been regulated with such a scrupulous regard to equality and equilibrium, that no one could say for certain, not even a native, whether the constitution as a whole were an aristocracy or democracy or despotism. And no wonder: for if we confine our observation to the power of the Consuls we should be inclined to regard it as despotic; if on that of the Senate, as aristocratic; and if finally one looks at the power possessed by the people it would seem a clear case of democracy. What the exact powers of these several parts were, and still, with slight modifications, are, I will now state.

The Consuls, before leading out the legions, remain in Rome and are supreme masters of the administration. All other magistrates, except the Tribunes, are under them and take their orders. They introduce foreign ambassadors to the Senate; bring matters requiring deliberation before it; and see to the execution of its decrees. If, again, there are any matters of state which require the authorisation of the people, it is their business to see to them, to summon the popular meetings, to bring the proposals before them, and to carry out the decrees of the majority.

SOURCE: Polybius, *Histories*, Vol. I, trans. Evelyn S. Shuckburgh (New York: Macmillan and Co., 1889), pp. 468–471.

In the preparations for war also, and in a word in the entire administration of a campaign, they have all but absolute power. It is competent to them to impose on the allies such levies as they think good, to appoint the Military Tribunes, to make up the roll for soldiers and select those that are suitable. Besides they have absolute power of inflicting punishment on all who are under their command while on active service: and they have authority to expend as much of the public money as they choose, being accompanied by a quaestor[1] who is entirely at their orders. A survey of these powers would in fact justify our describing the constitution as despotic,—a clear case of royal government. Nor will it affect the truth of my description, if any of the institutions I have described are changed in our time, or in that of our posterity: and the same remarks apply to what follows.

The Senate has first of all the control of the treasury, and regulates the receipts and disbursements alike. For the Quaestors cannot issue any public money for the various departments of the state without a decree of the Senate, except for the service of the Consuls. The Senate controls also what is by far the largest and most important expenditure, that, namely, which is made by the censors[2] every *lustrum*[3] for the repair or construction of public buildings; this money cannot be obtained by the censors except by the grant of the Senate. Similarly all crimes committed in Italy requiring a public investigation, such as treason, conspiracy, poisoning, or wilful murder, are in the hands of the Senate. Besides, if any individual or state among the Italian allies requires a controversy to be settled, a penalty to be assessed, help or protection to be afforded,—all this is the province of the Senate. Or again, outside Italy, if it is necessary to send an embassy to reconcile warring communities, or to remind them of their duty, or sometimes to impose requisitions upon them, or to receive their submission, or finally to proclaim war against them,—this too is the business of the Senate. In like manner the reception to be given to foreign ambassadors in Rome, and the answers to be returned to them, are decided by the Senate. With such business the people have nothing to do. Consequently, if one were staying at Rome when the Consuls were not in town, one would imagine the constitution to be a complete aristocracy: and this has been the idea entertained by many Greeks, and by many kings as well, from the fact that nearly all the business they had with Rome was settled by the Senate.

After this one would naturally be inclined to ask what part is left for the people in the constitution, when the Senate has these various functions, especially the control of the receipts and expenditure of the exchequer; and when the Consuls, again, have absolute power over the details of military preparation, and an absolute

---

[1] Official responsible for finance and administration.

[2] Officials responsible for supervising the public census and public behavior and morals.

[3] A ceremonial purification of the Roman population after the census every five years.

authority in the field? There is, however, a part left the people, and it is a most important one. For the people is the sole fountain of honour and of punishment; and it is by these two things and these alone that dynasties and constitutions and, in a word, human society are held together: for where the distinction between them is not sharply drawn both in theory and practice, there no undertaking can be properly administered,—as indeed we might expect when good and bad are held in exactly the same honour. The people then are the only court to decide matters of life and death; and even in cases where the penalty is money, if the sum to be assessed is sufficiently serious, and especially when the accused have held the higher magistracies. And in regard to this arrangement there is one point deserving special commendation and record. Men who are on trial for their lives at Rome, while sentence is in process of being voted,—if even only one of the tribes whose votes are needed to ratify the sentence has not voted,—have the privilege at Rome of openly departing and condemning themselves to a voluntary exile. Such men are safe at Naples or Praeneste or at Tibur, and at other towns with which this arrangement has been duly ratified on oath.

Again, it is the people who bestow offices on the deserving, which are the most honourable rewards of virtue. It has also the absolute power of passing or repealing laws; and, most important of all, it is the people who deliberate on the question of peace or war. And when provisional terms are made for alliance, suspension of hostilities, or treaties, it is the people who ratify them or the reverse.

These considerations again would lead one to say that the chief power in the state was the people's, and that the constitution was a democracy.

Such, then, is the distribution of power between the several parts of the state.

The Ethiopians
Diodorus of Sicily

Citizens of Greece and Rome looked to Egypt and the Nile Valley as the source of some of their religious and philosophical beliefs. Histories which linked Rome to Hellenism and to Egypt and the Nile Valley would have been read well into the early centuries of the Christian epoch.

The writings of Diodorus of Sicily, who wrote between 60 and 20 B.C., tell us much about areas on the frontiers of the Greek world and later Christian Roman world. His vision of the history of the Nile Valley civilization was probably shared by many people of his day. Both he and the authors he drew on included ancient Egyptian as well as Greek sources written since the fifth century B.C. and he himself spent some years in Egypt. The long tradition that the people Diodorus called "Ethiopians" (from the southern area of the Nile Valley occupying a kingdom called Meroe located on the borders of Roman Egypt)

SOURCE: *Diodorus of Sicily*, 3rd Book, Loeb Classical Library (Cambridge, Harvard University Press, 1939), III, 2-3, pp. 89–95.

*were the source of religion gave special importance to the cult of the Goddess Isis, whose
temples were found throughout the Roman world, and had a universal appeal that prefig-
ured Christianity's later spread.*

> **Consider:** *How this text compares with the texts on the Nile Valley in Chapter 1;
> the absence of religious exclusivism in the Mediterranean and Nile Valley at this
> time; the emphasis placed on the issues of origins and colonization.*

Now the Ethiopians, as historians relate, were the first of all men and the proofs
of this statement, they say, are manifest. For that they did not come into their
land as immigrants from abroad but were natives of it; . . . furthermore, that those
who dwell beneath the noon-day sun were, in all likelihood, the first to be generated by the earth, is clear to all . . . it is reasonable to suppose that the region
which was nearest the sun was the first to bring forth living creatures. And they
say that they were the first to be taught to honour the gods and to hold sacrifices
and processions and festivals and the other rites by which men honour the deity;
and that in consequence their piety has been published abroad among all men,
and it is generally held that the sacrifices practised among the Ethiopians are
those which are the most pleasing to heaven. As witness to this they call upon the
poet who is perhaps the oldest and certainly the most venerated among the Greeks;
for in the *Iliad* he represents both Zeus and the rest of the gods with him as
absent on a visit to Ethiopia to share in the sacrifices and the banquet which were
given annually by the Ethiopians for all the gods together . . . And they state that,
by reason of their piety towards the deity, they manifestly enjoy the favour of the
gods, inasmuch as they have never experienced the rule of an invader from abroad;
for from all time they have enjoyed a state of freedom and of peace one with
another, and although many and powerful rulers have made war upon them, not
one of these has succeeded in his undertaking. . . .

They say also that the Egyptians are colonists sent out by the Ethiopians, Osiris
having been the leader of the colony. . . . And the larger part of the customs of
the Egyptians are, they hold, Ethiopian, the colonists still preserving their ancient
manners. For instance, the belief that their kings are gods, the very special attention which they pay to their burials, and many other matters of a similar nature
are Ethiopian practices, while the shapes of their statues and the forms of their
letters are Ethiopian; for of the two kinds of writing which the Egyptians have,
that which is known as "popular" (demotic) is learned by everyone, while that
which is called "sacred" is understood only by the priests of the Egyptians, who
learn it from their fathers as one of the things which are not divulged, but among
the Ethiopians everyone uses these forms of letters. Furthermore, the orders of
the priests, they maintain, have much the same position among both peoples; for
all are clean who are engaged in the service of the gods, keeping themselves
shaven, like the Ethiopian priests, and having the same dress and form of staff,
which is shaped like a plough and is carried by their kings, who wear high felt
hats which end in a knob at the top and are circled by the serpents which they

call asps; and this symbol appears to carry the thought that it will be the lot of those who shall dare to attack the king to encounter death-carrying stings. Many other things are also told by them concerning their own antiquity and the colony which they sent out that became the Egyptians, but about this there is no special need of our writing anything.

Letters: The Daily Life of a Roman Governor
Pliny the Younger

For a cultured, well-to-do Roman gentleman, the period between A.D. 96 and 180, when the Empire was at its height, was a good time to live. This is reflected in the letters of Pliny the Younger (62?–113?), a lawyer who rose to the position of governor of Bithynia in Asia Minor. In the following letter he describes a typical day while vacationing at one of his Italian villas.

> **Consider:** *The kinds of activities most important to Pliny, at least during his stay at the villa; Pliny's view of his life and of people around him.*

To Fuscus Salinator

You want to know how I plan the summer days I spend in Tuscany. I wake when I like, usually about sunrise, often earlier but rarely later. My shutters stay closed, for in the stillness and darkness I feel myself surprisingly detached from any distractions and left to myself in freedom; my eyes do not determine the direction of my thinking, but, being unable to see anything, they are guided to visualize my thoughts. If I have anything on hand I work it out in my head, choosing and correcting the wording, and the amount I achieve depends on the ease or difficulty with which my thoughts can be marshalled and kept in my head. Then I call my secretary, the shutters are opened, and I dictate what I have put into shape; he goes out, is recalled, and again dismissed. Three or four hours after I first wake (but I don't keep to fixed times) I betake myself according to the weather either to the terrace or the covered arcade, work out the rest of my subject, and dictate it. I go for a drive, and spend the time in the same way as when walking or lying down; my powers of concentration do not flag and are in fact refreshed by the change. After a short sleep and another walk I read a Greek or Latin speech aloud and with emphasis, not so much for the sake of my voice as my digestion, though of course both are strengthened by this. Then I have

---

SOURCE: Reprinted by permission of the publishers and The Loeb Classical Library from Pliny the Younger, *Letters and Panegyricus*, vol. II, pp. 153–157, trans. by Betty Radice. Copyright © 1969 Harvard University Press.

another walk, am oiled, take exercise, and have a bath. If I am dining alone with my wife or with a few friends, a book is read aloud during the meal and afterwards we listen to a comedy or some music; then I walk again with the members of my household, some of whom are well educated. Thus the evening is prolonged with varied conversation, and, even when the days are at their longest, comes to a satisfying end.

Sometimes I vary this routine, for, if I have spent a long time on my couch or taking a walk, after my siesta and reading I go out on horseback instead of in a carriage so as to be quicker and take less time. Part of the day is given up to friends who visit me from neighbouring towns, and sometimes come to my aid with a welcome interruption when I am tired. Occasionally I go hunting, but not without my notebooks so that I shall have something to bring home even if I catch nothing. I also give some time to my tenants (they think it should be more), and the boorishness of their complaints gives fresh zest to our literary interests and the more civilized pursuits of town.

The Gospel According to St. Matthew

During the first and second centuries Christianity was one of many competing sects in the Empire. But by the fourth century it had become the most significant one and was finally adopted as the official faith of the Roman Empire. From a historical point of view, explaining the success of Christianity is a crucial problem. Part of the explanation comes from an analysis of the basic teachings of Christianity. One of the most useful texts for this purpose is found in the Gospel according to St. Matthew, written toward the end of the first century, about sixty years after the recorded occurrences. The rules for conduct and the general ethical message of Christianity are revealed in the following sermon of Jesus.

> **Consider:** *To whom this message was directed; the appeal of this message to people of those times; the differences in tone and content between these selections and the selections from the Old Testament in Chapter 1.*

5 Seeing the crowds, he went up on the mountain, and when he sat down his disciples came to him. And he opened his mouth and taught them, saying:

"Blesed are the poor in spirit, for theirs is the kingdom of heaven.

"Blessed are those who mourn, for they shall be comforted.

"Blessed are the meek, for they shall inherit the earth.

"Blessed are those who hunger and thirst for righteousness, for they shall be satisfied.

SOURCE: *The Holy Bible: Revised Standard Version* (New York: Thomas Nelson, 1953), pp. 5–8.

7 "Blessed are the merciful, for they shall obtain mercy.

8 "Blessed are the pure in heart, for they shall see God.

9 "Blessed are the peacemakers, for they shall be called sons of God.

10 "Blessed are those who are persecuted for righteousness' sake, for theirs is the kingdom of heaven.

11 "Blessed are you when men revile you and persecute you and utter all kinds of evil against you falsely on my account. 12 Rejoice and be glad, for your reward is great in heaven, for so men persecuted the prophets who were before you.

✺

27 "You have heard that it was said, 'You shall not commit adultery.' 28 But I say to you that every one who looks at a woman lustfully has already committed adultery with her in his heart. 29 If your right eye causes you to sin, pluck it out and throw it away; it is better that you lose one of your members than that your whole body be thrown into hell. 30 And if your right hand causes you to sin, cut it off and throw it away; it is better that you lose one of your members than that your whole body go into hell.

31 "It was also said, 'Whoever divorces his wife, let him give her a certificate of divorce.' 32 But I say to you that every one who divorces his wife, except on the ground of unchastity, makes her an adulteress; and whoever marries a divorced woman commits adultery.

✺

38 "You have heard that it was said, 'An eye for an eye and a tooth for a tooth.' 39 But I say to you, Do not resist one who is evil. But if any one strikes you on the right cheek, turn to him the other also; 40 and if any one would sue you and take your coat, let him have your cloak as well; 41 and if any one forces you to go one mile, go with him two miles. 42 Give to him who begs from you, and do not refuse him who would borrow from you.

43 "You have heard that it was said, 'You shall love your neighbor and hate your enemy.' 44 But I say to you, Love your enemies and pray for those who persecute you, 45 so that you may be sons of your Father who is in heaven; for he makes his sun rise on the evil and on the good, and sends rain on the just and on the unjust. 46 For if you love those who love you, what reward have you? Do not even the tax collectors do the same? 47 And if you salute only your brethren, what more are you doing than others? Do not even the Gentiles do the same? 48 You, therefore, must be perfect, as your heavenly Father is perfect."

✺

15 "Beware of false prophets, who come to you in sheep's clothing but inwardly are ravenous wolves. 16 You will know them by their fruits. Are grapes gathered from thorns, or figs from thistles? 17 So, every sound tree bears good fruit, but the bad tree bears evil fruit. 18 A sound tree cannot bear evil fruit, not can a bad tree bear good fruit. 19 Every tree that does not bear good fruit is cut down and thrown into the fire. 20 Thus you will know them by their fruits.

21 "Not every one who says to me, 'Lord, Lord,' shall enter the kingdom of heaven, but he who does the will of my Father who is in heaven. 22 On that day many will say to me, 'Lord, Lord, did we not prophesy in your name, and cast out demons in your name, and do many mighty works in your name?' 23 And then will I declare to them, 'I never knew you; depart from me, you evildoers.'

24 "Every one then who hears these words of mine and does them will be like a wise man who built his house upon the rock; 25 and the rain fell, and the floods came, and the winds blew and beat upon that house, but it did not fall, because it had been founded on the rock. 26 And every one who hears these words of mine and does not do them will be like a foolish man who built his house upon the sand; 27 and the rain fell, and the floods came, and the winds blew and beat against that house, and it fell; and great was the fall of it."

28 And when Jesus finished these sayings, the crowds were astonished at his teaching, 29 for he taught them as one who had authority, and not as their scribes.

The Fall of Rome
St. Jerome

The fall of the Roman Empire, though occurring over a long period of time, was experienced as a profound shock. Even those who were not part of the Roman power structure saw the invasions and decomposition of Rome as a catastrophe. This reaction can be found in the letters of St. Jerome (340?–420), who lived through much of the decline. St. Jerome, an ascetic for part of his life and a great doctor of the Church, spent most of his life in Jerusalem and is known for his translation of the Bible into Latin.

> **Consider:** *Why Jerome was so shocked and overwhelmed by what was happening; any evidence in these letters of an incompatibility between Christianity and the Roman Empire; the methods apparently used in an effort to avoid destruction by invaders.*

Nations innumerable and most savage have invaded all Gaul. The whole region between the Alps and the Pyrenees, the ocean and the Rhine, has been devastated by the Quadi, the Vandals, the Sarmati, the Alani, the Gepidae, the hostile Heruli, the Saxons, the Burgundians, the Alemanni and the Pannonians. O wretched Empire! Mayence, formerly so noble a city, has been taken and ruined, and in the church many thousands of men have been massacred. Worms has been destroyed after a long siege. Rheims, that powerful city, Amiens, Arras, Speyer, Strasburg,—all have seen their citizens led away captive into Germany. Aquitaine and the provinces of Lyons and Narbonne, all save a few towns, have been depopulated; and these the sword threatens without, while hunger ravages within.

SOURCE: From James Harvey Robinson, ed., *Readings in European History*, vol. I (New York: Ginn and Co., 1904), pp. 44–45.

I cannot speak without tears of Toulouse, which the merits of the holy Bishop Exuperius have prevailed so far to save from destruction. Spain, even, is in daily terror lest it perish, remembering the invasion of the Cimbri; and whatsoever the other provinces have suffered once, they continue to suffer in their fear.

I will keep silence concerning the rest, lest I seem to despair of the mercy of God. For a long time, from the Black Sea to the Julian Alps, those things which are ours have not been ours; and for thirty years, since the Danube boundary was broken, war has been waged in the very midst of the Roman Empire. Our tears are dried by old age. Except a few old men, all were born in captivity and siege, and do not desire the liberty they never knew. Who could believe this? How could the whole tale be worthily told? How Rome has fought within her own bosom not for glory, but for preservation—nay, how she has not even fought, but with gold and all her precious things has ransomed her life. . . .

Who could believe [Jerome exclaims in another passage] that Rome, built upon the conquest of the whole world, would fall to the ground? that the mother herself would become the tomb of her peoples? that all the regions of the East, of Africa and Egypt, once ruled by the queenly city, would be filled with troops of slaves and handmaidens? that today holy Bethlehem should shelter men and women of noble birth, who once abounded in wealth and are now beggars?

VISUAL SOURCES

The Geographic and Cultural Environment

This map shows some of the peoples and civilizations that occupied Italy and its immediately surrounding territory during the fifth century B.C. In the process of Rome's formation and expansion, the Romans came into direct and extended contact with these peoples. Before Rome became a dominant power, the Etruscans, Carthaginians (descendants of the Phoenicians), and Greeks had already established strong, literate, sophisticated civilizations. Understandably, then, as Rome expanded the Romans drew from and even copied many of the institutions and practices of these civilizations, particularly the closer Etruscans and Greeks. Other peoples, such as the Samnites, constituted a barrier to Roman expansion that the Romans overcame during the fifth, fourth, and third centuries B.C., usually by force of arms. Rome's geographic and cultural environment, therefore, played an important role in the development of the Roman Republic.

> **Consider:** *How the experience gained during the early years of the Roman Republic laid the foundations for later Roman imperialism.*

Map 5-1   Italy, Fifth Century B.C.

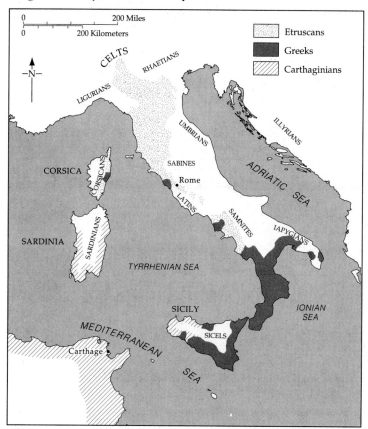

Carved Gemstone: Augustus and the Empire Transformed

This onyx gemstone with a carved relief scene, known as the Gemma Augustrea, portrays both a specific event and a general set of views during the early Roman Empire. Made between A.D. 10 and 20, it appears to commemorate a victory by the Romans over the Pannonians and Germans in A.D. 12. In the lower half, moving from right to left, a man and a woman are being dragged by auxiliary soldiers (probably Macedonian allies of the Romans). On the left four Roman soldiers raise a trophy; another barbarian couple will be tied to it. In the upper half, moving from left to right, Tiberius, who led the victorious Roman troops, descends from a chariot held by Victory. The youth in armor is probably his nephew Germanicus. In the center sit the goddess Roma and Augustus, between them the sign of Capricorn (the month of his conception) and below them an eagle (the bird of

Photo 5-1

Kunsthistorisches Museum, Vienna

the god Jupiter) and armor of the defeated. Augustus is being crowned as ruler of the civilized world by Oikoumene, while on the far right the bearded Ocean and the Earth with one of her children look on.

This scene is particularly revealing of political and religious information. It shows the transformation from the Republic to the Empire under a deified emperor in the making, for Augustus is being transformed into an equivalent of Jupiter and is clearly accepted by the rest of the gods. Moreover, his successor, Tiberius, appears to be in line for a similar fate. It also indicates the growing reach of the Roman Empire and the Romans' use of subordinate allies—the Macedonians—to exert their control. The religious figures and symbols, while Roman, also reveal affinities with Greek religious figures and symbols; artistically, the scene has a Hellenistic flavor. This is evidence for a merging of Roman and Greek cultures. Note also the balance between idealized form and realistic representation: The bodies are somewhat stylized, particularly Augustus' heroic body, but at the same time the individuals are clearly distinguished; these individuals were meant to be recognizable to the viewer.

> **Consider:** *The political implications of this scene; how contemporaries might have understood the message of this scene.*

Tomb Decoration: Death and Roman Culture

This tomb decoration, known as the Sarcophagus from Acilia, dates from the mid-third century. Here, a boy, perhaps the young Emperor Gordian III, is standing next to a number of other figures. To his right are perhaps his parents, and to his left important government officials (perhaps senators) as suggested by their costumes. The bundle of scrolls at the feet of the boy and the stance of the figures indicate a dedication to Classical philosophy or scholarship. Indeed, in this period, there were many tombs with scenes representing a commitment to or glorification of pagan culture—a wish by individuals to be remembered as devotees of philosophy or literature.

Photo 5-2

Museo Nationale delle Terme

This commitment to pagan culture is revealed both in what this tomb decoration shows and in what it does not show. Rather than showing mythical scenes, pagan gods, or Christian beliefs, it shows secular figures glorifying literature and philosophy. It is thus evidence for the continued strength of Classical pagan culture, at least among the elite, even during a period of decline for Rome. The style also indicates a continuing Classical balance between idealized forms and realistic representation. While the robes, the bearing, and the figures are stylized, there are clear individual differences, particularly in the head of the boy and in the balding individual to his left.

> **Consider:** *How this tomb decoration compares with the Tomb of Menna (Chapter 1) and with Christian beliefs.*

SECONDARY SOURCES

Roman Women
Gillian Clark

Until recently, most historians presented an image of Roman life that mentioned women only in passing. This void about the experience of Roman women is being filled by new scholarship, much of it written by feminist historians. In the following selection, Gillian Clark analyzes the position and experience of women during the late Republic and age of Augustus, emphasizing the political, legal, and social restraints on women.

> **Consider:** *Ways in which women might influence public life despite restraints placed on them; the characteristics of the good woman; how one might evaluate whether Roman women were happy.*

Women did not vote, did not serve as *iudices*,[1] were not senators or magistrates or holders of major priesthoods. They did not, as a rule, speak in the courts. . . . As a rule, women took no part in public life, except on the rare occasions when they were angry enough to demonstrate, which was startling and shocking. . . .

Women might, then, have considerable influence and interests outside their homes and families, but they were acting from within their families to affect a

SOURCE: Gillian Clark, "Roman Women," in *Greece and Rome*, vol. 28, pp. 206–207, 209–210. Copyright © 1981. Used by permission of Oxford University Press.

[1] Judges.

social system managed by men: their influence was not to be publicly acknowledged. Why were women excluded from public life? The division between arms-
bearers and child-bearers was doubtless one historical cause, but the reasons
publicly given were different. Women were alleged to be fragile and fickle, and
therefore in need of protection; if they were not kept in their proper place they
would (fragility and fickleness notwithstanding) take over. As the elder Cato . . .
said: . . .

'Our ancestors decided that women should not handle anything, even a private
matter, without the advice of a guardian; that they should always be in the power
of fathers, brothers, husbands. . . . Call to mind all those laws on women by which
your ancestors restrained their license and made them subject to men: you can
only just keep them under by using the whole range of laws. If you let them niggle
away at one law after another until they have worked it out of your grasp, until at
last you let them make themselves equal to men, do you suppose that you'll be
able to stand them? If once they get equality, they'll be on top.' . . .

A social system which restricted women to domestic life, and prevailing attitudes
which assumed their inferiority, must seem to us oppressive. I know of no evidence
that it seemed so at the time. The legal and social constraints detailed above may
have frustrated the abilities of many women and caused much ordinary human
unhappiness. But there evidently were, also, many ordinarily happy families where
knowledge of real live women took precedence over the theories, and women
themselves enjoyed home, children, and friends. There were some women who
enjoyed the political game, and who found an emotional life outside their necessary
marriages. And there were certainly women who found satisfaction in living up to
the standards of the time. They were, as they should be, chaste, dutiful, submissive,
and domestic; they took pride in the family of their birth and the family they had
produced; and probably their resolution to maintain these standards gave them
the support which women in all ages have found in religious faith. But the religious
feelings of Roman women, as opposed to the acts of worship in which they might
take part, are something of which we know very little. . . .

The son of Murdia, in the age of Augustus, made her a public eulogy . . . [which]
may make the best epitaph for the women who did not make the history books.

'What is said in praise of all good women is the same, and straightforward.
There is no need of elaborate phrases to tell of natural good qualities and of trust
maintained. It is enough that all alike have the same reward: a good reputation.
It is hard to find new things to praise in a woman, for their lives lack incident. We
must look for what they have in common, lest something be left out to spoil the
example they offer us. My beloved mother, then, deserves all the more praise, for
in modesty, integrity, chastity, submission, woolwork, industry, and trustworthiness
she was just like other women.'

The World of Ancient Times:
The Appeal of Christianity
Carl Roebuck

The beginnings of Christianity coincided with the establishment of the Empire under Augustus and the early emperors who succeeded him. Numerous attempts have been made to analyze Jesus and the rise of Christianity. In the following selection, Carl Roebuck of Northwestern University, author of a major text on the ancient world, views early Christianity from a historical perspective. He focuses on the appeal of Christianity and how it compares with other mystery religions of that period.

Consider: *Typical traits of mystery religions and how Christianity differed from other mystery religions; what other factors might help to explain the rise of Christianity in this early period.*

The appeal of early Christianity is to be understood in the same historical context as that of the mystery religions. In fact, Christianity had much in common with them: a God who had suffered, died, and had been resurrected; the rites of baptism and of the eucharist were mystical and shared by initiates; and not the least in that age were its miracles and visions. Men could find in Christianity the secure intimacy of a small group and a strong supernatural protector, Jesus, who would help them in their present distress and assure them of immortality. They could gain courage and assurance from the revelation and the common performance of the rites of worship.

There were also differences in Christianity from the mystery religions which added to its appeal and helped in its establishment. At the outset Jesus' teaching had enlarged the concept of God as a loving father; he had stressed the brotherhood of man and insisted on faith and personal goodness. As the Dead Sea scrolls have recently revealed, not all of this was peculiar to Jesus, but the Essene communities which shared much with early Christianity had taken to the desert, while Christianity developed an apostolic mission. The Christians retained a forceful code of conduct based on the Old Testament but, largely through the work of St. Paul, discarded the letter of the Mosaic Law. Some of its taboos and ritual practices, such as circumcision, were offensive to Gentiles. Thus, from the mid-first century Christianity had grown rapidly beyond its matrix of Judaism and had attracted Gentiles by its own qualities and by the zeal of its missionaries. In contrast to the mystery religions, Christianity developed the discipline and unity of a hierarchical organization, knit by political as well as religious ties.

SOURCE: Carl Roebuck, *The World of Ancient Times* (New York: Scribner's, 1966), pp. 679–680. Reprinted with permission of Macmillan Publishing Company.

The Later Roman Empire
A. H. M. Jones

Most historians who interpret the decline and fall of the Roman Empire focus on the Western half of the Empire. In fact, the Eastern half did not fall and would not, despite some ups and downs, for another thousand years. A. H. M. Jones, a distinguished British scholar of Greece and Rome, has emphasized the significance of the Eastern Empire's different fate for analyzing the decline and fall of the Western Empire. In the following selection, Jones compares conditions in the two halves of the Empire, criticizing those who have theorized that the fall in the West stemmed from long-term internal weaknesses.

Consider: *The primary cause for the collapse in the West according to Jones; other possible causes for the collapse in the West.*

All the historians who have discussed the decline and fall of the Roman empire have been Westerners. Their eyes have been fixed on the collapse of Roman authority in the Western parts and the evolution of the medieval Western European world. They have tended to forget, or to brush aside, one very important fact, that the Roman empire, though it may have declined, did not fall in the fifth century nor indeed for another thousand years. During the fifth century, while the Western parts were being parcelled out into a group of barbarian kingdoms, the empire of the East stood its ground. In the sixth it counter-attacked and reconquered Africa from the Vandals and Italy from the Ostrogoths, and part of Spain from the Visigoths. Before the end of the century, it is true, much of Italy and Spain had succumbed to renewed barbarian attacks, and in the seventh the onslaught of the Arabs robbed the empire of Syria, Egypt, and Africa, and the Slavs overran the Balkans. But in Asia Minor the empire lived on, and later, recovering its strength, reconquered much territory that it had lost in the dark days of the seventh century.

These facts are important, for they demonstrate that the empire did not, as some modern historians have suggested, totter into its grave from senile decay, impelled by a gentle push from the barbarians. Most of the internal weaknesses which these historians stress were common to both halves of the empire. The East was even more Christian than the West, its theological disputes far more embittered. The East, like the West, was administered by a corrupt and extortionate bureaucracy. The Eastern government strove as hard to enforce a rigid caste system, tying the *curiales* to their cities and the *coloni* to the soil. Land fell out of cultivation and was deserted in the East as well as in the West. It may be that some of these weaknesses were more accentuated in the West than in the East, but this is a question which needs investigation. It may be also that the initial

---

SOURCE: A. H. M. Jones, *The Later Roman Empire*, vol. II (Oxford, England: Basil Blackwell, 1964), pp. 1026–1027, 1062–1064, 1066–1067. By permission of Basil Blackwell, Oxford.

strength of the Eastern empire in wealth and population was greater, and that it could afford more wastage, but this again must be demonstrated. . . .

The East then probably possessed greater economic resources, and could thus support with less strain a larger number of idle mouths. A smaller part of its resources went, it would seem, to maintain its aristocracy, and more was thus available for the army and other essential services. It also was probably more populous, and since the economic pressure on the peasantry was perhaps less severe, may have suffered less from population decline. If there is any substance in these arguments, the Eastern government should have been able to raise a larger revenue without overstraining its resources, and to levy more troops without depleting its labour force. . . .

The Western empire was poorer and less populous, and its social and economic structure more unhealthy. It was thus less able to withstand the tremendous strains imposed by its defensive effort, and the internal weaknesses which it developed undoubtedly contributed to its final collapse in the fifth century. But the major cause of its fall was that it was more exposed to barbarian onslaughts which in persistence and sheer weight of numbers far exceeded anything which the empire had previously had to face. The Eastern empire, owing to its greater wealth and population and sounder economy, was better able to carry the burden of defence, but its resources were overstrained and it developed the same weaknesses as the West, if perhaps in a lesss acute form. Despite these weaknesses it managed in the sixth century not only to hold its own against the Persians in the East but to reconquer parts of the West, and even when, in the seventh century, it was overrun by the onslaughts of the Persians and the Arabs and the Slavs, it succeeded despite heavy territorial losses in rallying and holding its own. The internal weaknesses of the empire cannot have been a major factor in its decline.

Chapter Questions

1. In what ways do Roman political institutions help explain Rome's successful expansion and ability to control so much territory?

2. Drawing from the sources in this chapter and previous sources on Greece and the Hebrews, in what ways were conditions of Roman civilization conducive to the growth of Christianity? In what ways was Christianity nevertheless contradictory to Roman civilization?

3. How might the sources in this and the previous chapter be used to argue that Roman civilization drew heavily from Greek civilization? How might these same sources and others from Chapters 2 and 3 be used to compare Greco-Roman civilization with Indian and Chinese civilizations?

SIX

The Rise
of Islam

By the sixth century, unified Roman control over the Mediterranean basin had been shattered. Much of the northeastern part of the Empire would remain in the hands of the Eastern Roman Empire, which was evolving into the Byzantine Empire. To the south and east, major changes would soon take place that would have a great impact on world history.

In the seventh century, Islam arose among the nomads and city dwellers of the Arabian Desert. Led by their prophet, Muhammad, followers of Islam united most of the Arab world by the time of his death in 632. Over the course of the following century, these Islamic Arabs defeated the Persian Empire, took control of lands bordering the southern Mediterranean Sea from the Byzantine Empire, and were pushing farther east toward India and moving north into the Iberian peninsula. By the eighth century, much of the Mediterranean basin, formerly controlled by the Roman or Byzantine Empires, was under the authority of the Islamic Empire.

By the tenth and eleventh centuries, this Arabic empire would lose much of its political unity and initial zeal, but Islam would continue to expand in different ways in the following centuries—particularly farther south in Africa and farther east in Asia. Combining Arabic, Greco-Roman, Persian, and other sources, Islamic culture would become permanently established over large areas of the world.

The sources in this chapter will examine the rise and spread of Islam, particularly in the earlier period when it was so closely tied to Arabic civilization. In the process of doing this, the sources will address several fundamental questions. What was the nature of Islamic faith? What were some of the intellectual and cultural traditions that were valued in the Islamic world? What was the significance of the Arabic background to this rapid growth of Islam? What was the nature and position of law in Islamic societies? Was Islam oriented primarily toward the West or toward the East?

Together, the sources provide an introduction to this civilization, particularly in the areas around the Mediterranean, Africa, and the Middle East. In the following and subsequent chapters, Islam's expansion and influence farther east in Asia and farther south in Africa will be examined.

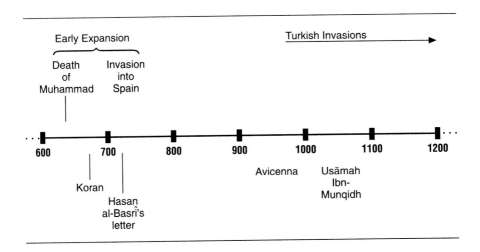

PRIMARY SOURCES

The Koran

The Koran is to the Islamic faith what the Bible is to Christianity. For believers it contains the word of Allah, God, as revealed to his prophet Muhammad and recorded by Muhammad's followers twenty years after Muhammad's death in 632. Over the next hundred years, Arab Muslims spread Islam and their own control from the Arabian peninsula north and east through the Persian Empire and parts of Asia Minor and west through North Africa as far as Spain. Islam did not reject all of Christianity or Judaism. According to the faithful, Muhammad was the last and most important of the prophets among whom were also included Moses and Jesus. The following selections from the Koran reveal some of the main beliefs and attitudes of the Islamic faith.

> **Consider:** *Attitudes toward struggle and dissent; how these selections compare with those from the Old and New Testaments in Chapters 1 and 5; Islamic views of women.*

SAY: HE IS ONE GOD;
God the Eternal.
He begetteth not, nor is begotten;
Nor is there one like unto Him.

✿

MAGNIFY the name of thy LORD, THE MOST HIGH,
Who created, and fashioned,
And decreed, and guided,
Who bringeth forth the pasturage,
Then turneth it dry and brown.

✿

It is not righteousness that ye turn your face towards the east or the west, but righteousness is [in] him who believeth in God and the Last Day, and the Angels, and the Scripture, and the Prophets, and who giveth wealth for the love of God to his kinsfolk and to orphans and the needy and the son of the road and them that ask and for the freeing of slaves, and who is instant in prayer, and giveth the alms; and those who fulfil their covenant when they covenant, and the patient in adversity and affliction and in time of violence, these are they who are true, and these are they who fear God.

SOURCE: Stanley Lane-Poole, *The Speech and Table-Talk of the Prophet Mohammed* (London: Macmillan, 1882), pp. 15, 32, 83, 133–137. J. M. Rodwell, trans., *The Koran* (London: J. M. Dent, 1871), pp. 411, 415.

SAY: We believe in God, and what hath been sent down to thee, and what was sent down to Abraham, and Ishmael, and Isaac, and Jacob, and the tribes, and what was given to Moses, and to Jesus, and the prophets from their Lord,—we make no distinction between any of them,—and to Him are we resigned: and whoso desireth other than Resignation [Islām] for a religion, it shall certainly not be accepted from him, and in the life to come he shall be among the losers.

✻

Fight in the path of God with those who fight with you;—but exceed not; verily God loveth not those who exceed.—And kill them wheresoever ye find them, and thrust them out from whence they thrust you out; for dissent is worse than slaughter; but fight them not at the Sacred Mosque, unless they fight you there: but if they fight you, then kill them: such is the reward of the infidels! But if they desist, then verily God is forgiving and merciful.—But fight them till there be no dissent, and the worship be only to God;—but, if they desist, then let there be no hostility save against the transgressors.

✻

Men are superior to women on account of the qualities with which God hath gifted the one above the other, and on account of the outlay they make from their substance for them. Virtuous women are obedient, careful, during *the husband's* absence, because God hath of them been careful. . . . *other* women who seem good in your eyes, marry *but* two, or three, or four; and if ye *still* fear that ye shall not act equitably, then one only; or the slaves whom ye have acquired: this will make justice on your part easier.

Letter to 'Umar II: Islamic Asceticism
Hasan al-Basrî

Islam, like other religions, had many followers who felt that their beliefs required a turning away from worldly concerns, the practice of austere self-discipline, and a more literal holding to the words of the Prophet. This is reflected in the following letter written by Hasan al-Basrî to the Caliph 'Umar II (717–720).

> **Consider:** *What the vision of proper behavior and concern for a believer of Islam is; connections made to Judaism and Christianity and what this reveals about the nature and appeal of Islam.*

SOURCE: Arthur J. Arberry, *Sufism* (London: George Allen & Unwin, Ltd., 1950), pp. 33–35.

Beware of this world with all wariness; for it is like a snake, smooth to the touch, but its venom is deadly. Turn away from whatsoever delights thee in it, for the little companioning thou wilt have of it; put off from thee its cares, for that thou hast seen its sudden chances, and knowest for sure that thou shalt be parted from it; endure firmly its hardships, for the ease that shall presently be thine. The more it pleases thee, the more do thou be wary of it; for the man of this world, whenever he feels secure in any pleasure thereof, the world drives him over into some unpleasantness, and whenever he attains any part of it and squats him down upon it, the world suddenly turns him upside down. And again, beware of this world, for its hopes are lies, its expectations false; its easefulness is all harshness, muddied its limpidity. And therein thou art in peril: or bliss transient, or sudden calamity, or painful affliction, or doom decisive. Hard is the life of a man if he be prudent, dangerous if comfortable, being wary ever of catastrophe, certain of his ultimate fate. Even had the Almighty not pronounced upon the world at all, nor coined for it any similitude, nor charged men to abstain from it, yet would the world itself have awakened the slumberer, and roused the heedless; how much the more then, seeing that God has Himself sent us a warning against it, an exhortation regarding it! For this world has neither worth nor weight with God; so slight it is, it weighs not with God so much as a pebble or a single clod of earth; as I am told, God has created nothing more hateful to Him than this world, and from the day He created it He has not looked upon it, so much He hates it. . . .

As for Muhammad, he bound a stone upon his belly when he was hungry; and as for Moses, the skin of his belly shewed as green as grass because of it all: he asked naught of God, the day he took refuge in the shade, save food to eat when he was hungered, and it is said of him in the stories that God revealed to him, "Moses, when thou seest poverty approaching, say, Welcome to the badge of the righteous! and when thou seest wealth approaching, say, Lo! a sin whose punishment has been put on aforetime." If thou shouldst wish, thou mightest name as a third the Lord of the Spirit and the Word (Jesus), for in his affair there is a marvel; he used to say, "My daily bread is hunger, my badge is fear, my raiment is wool, my mount is my foot, my lantern at night is the moon, my fire by day is the sun, and my fruit and fragrant herbs are such things as the earth brings forth for the wild beasts and cattle. All the night I have nothing, yet there is none richer than I!" And if thou shouldst wish, thou mightest name as a fourth David, who was no less wonderful than these; he ate barley bread in his chamber, and fed his family upon bran meal, but his people on fine corn; and when it was night he clad himself in sackcloth, and chained his hand to his neck, and wept until the dawn; eating coarse food, and wearing robes of hair. All these hated what God hates, and despised what God despises; then the righteous thereafter followed in their path and kept close upon their tracks.

Autobiography of an Islamic Scholar

Avicenna

Avicenna (980–1037) was an outstanding example of the many Islamic individuals who produced great creative and intellectual achievements. Known primarily as a philosopher, Avicenna was also a mathematician, physician, theologian, astronomer, and philologist. He wrote extensively, and some of his works were later translated and circulated in Europe. The following is a selection from his autobiography, indicating the breadth of his learning as well as aspects of social and cultural life in the Islamic world.

> **Consider:** *The attitude of Avicenna's family toward learning and knowledge; the most respected kinds of learning and intellectual authorities; ways an intellectual could survive or move up in the Islamic world.*

My father was a man of Balkh, and he moved from there to Bukhara during the days of Nuh ibn Mansūr; in his reign he was employed in the administration, being governor of a village-centre in the outlying district of Bukhara called Kharmaithan. Near by is a village named Afshana, and there my father married my mother and took up his residence; I was also born there, and after me my brother. Later we moved to Bukhara, where I was put under teachers of the Koran and of letters. By the time I was ten I had mastered the Koran and a great deal of literature, so that I was marvelled at for my aptitude.

Now my father was one of those who has responded to the Egyptian propagandist (who was an Ismaili); he, and my brother too, had listened to what they had to say about the Spirit and the Intellect, after the fashion in which they preach and understand the matter. They would therefore discuss these things together, whilst I listened and comprehended all that they said; but my spirit would not assent to their argument. Presently they began to invite me to join the movement, rolling on their tongues talk about philosophy, geometry, Indian arithmetic; and my father sent me to a certain vegetable-seller who used the Indian arithmetic, so that I might learn it from him. Then there came to Bukhara a man called Abū 'Abd Allāh al-Nātilī who claimed to be a philosopher; my father invited him to stay in our house, hoping that I would learn from him also. Before his advent I had already occupied myself with Muslim jurisprudence, attending Ismā'īl the Ascetic, so I was an excellent enquirer, having become familiar with the methods of postulation and the techniques of rebuttal according to the usages of the canon lawyers. I now commenced reading the *Isagoge* with al-Nātilī. When he mentioned

SOURCE: From A. J. Arberry, *Aspects of Islamic Civilization* (London: George Allen & Unwin Ltd., 1967), pp. 136–139. Reprinted by permission of George Allen & Unwin Ltd. and The University of Michigan Press.

to me the definition of *genus* as a term applied to a number of things of different species in answer to the question 'What is it?' I set about verifying this definition in a manner such as he had never heard. He marvelled at me exceedingly, and warned my father that I should not engage in any other occupation but learning. Whatever problem he stated to me, I showed a better mental conception of it than he. So I continued until I had read all the straightforward parts of Logic with him; as for the subtler points, he had no acquaintance with them.

From then onwards I took to reading texts by myself; I studied the commentaries, until I had completely mastered the science of Logic. Similarly with Euclid I read the first five or six figures with him, and thereafter undertook on my own account to solve the entire remainder of the book. Next I moved on to the *Almagest;* when I had finished the prolegomena and reached the geometrical figures, al-Nātilī told me to go on reading and to solve the problems by myself; I should merely revise what I read with him, so that he might indicate to me what was right and what was wrong. The truth is that he did not really teach this book; I began to solve the work, and many were the complicated figures of which he had no knowledge until I presented them to him, and made him understand them. Then al-Nātilī took leave of me, setting out for Gurganj.

I now occupied myself with mastering the various texts and commentaries on natural science and metaphysics, until all the gates of knowledge were open to me. Next I desired to study medicine, and proceeded to read all the books that have been written on this subject. Medicine is not a difficult science, and naturally I excelled in it in a very short time, so that qualified physicians began to read medicine with me. I also undertook to treat the sick, and methods of treatment derived from practical experience revealed themselves to me such as baffle description. At the same time I continued between whiles to study and dispute on law, being now sixteen years of age.

The next eighteen months I devoted entirely to reading; I studied Logic once again, and all the parts of philosophy. During all this time I did not sleep one night through, nor devoted my attention to any other matter by day. I prepared a set of files; with each proof I examined, I set down the syllogistic premises and put them in order in the files, then I examined what deductions might be drawn from them. I observed methodically the conditions of the premises, and proceeded until the truth of each particular problem was confirmed for me. Whenever I found myself perplexed by a problem, or could not find the middle term in any syllogism, I would repair to the mosque and pray, adoring the All-Creator, until my puzzle was resolved and my difficulty made easy. At night I would return home, set the lamp before me, and busy myself with reading and writing; whenever sleep overcame me or I was conscious of some weakness, I turned aside to drink a glass of wine until my strength returned to me; then I went back to my reading. If ever the least slumber overtook me, I would dream of the precise problem which I was considering as I fell asleep; in that way many problems revealed themselves to me whilst sleeping. So I continued until I had made myself master of all the sciences; I now comprehended them to the limits of human possibility. All that I learned during that time is exactly as I know it now; I have added nothing more to my knowledge to this day.

I was now a master of Logic, natural sciences and mathematics. I therefore returned to metaphysics; I read Aristotle's *Metaphysica,* but did not understand its contents and was baffled by the author's intention; I read it over forty times until I had the text by heart. Even then I did not understand it or what the author meant, and I despaired within myself, saying, 'This is a book which there is no way of understanding.' But one day at noon I chanced to be in the booksellers' quarter, and a broker was there with a volume in his hand which he was calling for sale. He offered it to me, but I returned it to him impatiently, believing that there was no use in this particular science. However, he said to me: 'Buy this book from me; it is cheap, and I will sell it to you for four dirhams. The owner is in need of the money.' So I bought it, and found that it was a book by Abū Nasr al-Fārābī *On the Objects of the Metaphysica.* I returned home and hastened to read it; and at once the objects of that book became clear to me, for I had it all by heart. I rejoiced at this, and upon the next day distributed much in alms to the poor in gratitude to Almighty God.

Now the Sultan of Bukhara at that time was Nūh ibn Mansūr, and it happened that he fell sick of a malady which baffled all the physicians. My name was famous among them because of the breadth of my reading; they therefore mentioned me in his presence, and begged him to summon me. I attended the sick-room, and collaborated with them in treating the royal patient. So I came to be enrolled in his service. One day I asked his leave to enter their library, to examine the contents and read the books on medicine; he granted my request, and I entered a mansion with many chambers, each chamber having chests of books piled one upon another. In one apartment were books on language and poetry, in another law, and so on; each apartment was set aside for books on a single science. I glanced through the catalogue of the works of the ancient Greeks, and asked for those which I required; and I saw books whose very names are as yet unknown to many—works which I had never seen before and have not seen since. I read these books, taking notes of their contents; I came to realize the place each man occupied in his particular science.

So by the time I reached my eighteenth year I had exhausted all these sciences. My memory for learning was at that period of my life better than it is now, but today I am more mature; apart from this my knowledge is exactly the same, nothing further having been added to my store since then.

Memoirs: Cultural Interactions
Usāmah Ibn-Munqidh

There was considerable interaction between Muslims and Europeans throughout the Mediterranean basin, but particularly where Islam had extended its control into Europe and above all, in the Christian Holy Lands where Europeans temporarily established feudal kingdoms during the times of the Crusades. Such interactions provide useful insights into the nature of both civilizations, as indicated in the following excerpt from an eleventh-century memoir written by Usāmah Ibn-Munqidh, an Islamic Syrian. Here he comments on the characteristics of the Franks, revealing much about his own culture in the process.

> **Consider:** *The Islamic customs and values revealed in this document; how this observer compares Muslims to Franks.*

Their lack of sense.—Mysterious are the works of the Creator, the author of all things! When one comes to recount cases regarding the Franks, he cannot but glorify Allah (exalted is he!) and sanctify him, for he sees them as animals possessing the virtues of courage and fighting, but nothing else; just as animals have only the virtues of strength and carrying loads. I shall now give some instances of their doings and their curious mentality.

In the army of King Fulk, son of Fulk, was a Frankish reverend knight who had just arrived from their land in order to make the holy pilgrimage and then return home. He was of my intimate fellowship and kept such constant company with me that he began to call me "my brother." Between us were mutual bonds of amity and friendship. When he resolved to return by sea to his homeland, he said to me:

> My brother, I am leaving for my country and I want thee to send with me thy son (my son, who was then fourteen years old, was at that time in my company) to our country, where he can see the knights and learn wisdom and chivalry. When he returns, he will be like a wise man.

Thus there fell upon my ears words which would never come out of the head of a sensible man; for even if my son were to be taken captive, his captivity could not bring him a worse misfortune than carrying him into the lands of the Franks. However, I said to the man:

> By thy life, this has exactly been my idea. But the only thing that prevented me from carrying it out was the fact that his grandmother, my mother, is so fond of him and

---

SOURCE: Philip K. Hitti, ed. and trans., *An Arab-Syrian Gentleman and Warrior in the Period of the Crusades: Memoires of Usāmah Ibn-Munqidh (Kitāb al-I'Tibār)* (New York: Columbia University Press, 1929), pp. 161, 164. Copyright © 1977 by Philip K. Hitti.

did not this time let him come out with me until she exacted an oath from me to the effect that I would return him to her.

Thereupon he asked, "Is thy mother still alive?" "Yes," I replied. "Well," said he, "disobey her not."

Another wants to show to a Moslem God as a child.—I saw one of the Franks come to al-Amīr Muʿīn-al-Din (may Allah's mercy rest upon his soul!) when he was in the Dome of the Rock and say to him, "Dost thou want to see God as a child?" Muʿīn-al-Din said, "Yes." The Frank walked ahead of us until he showed us the picture of Mary with Christ (may peace be upon him!) as an infant in her lap. He then said, "This is God as a child." But Allah is exalted far above what the infidels say about him!

Franks lack jealousy in sex affairs.—The Franks are void of all zeal and jealousy. One of them may be walking along with his wife. He meets another man who takes the wife by the hand and steps aside to converse with her while the husband is standing on one side waiting for his wife to conclude the conversation. If she lingers too long for him, he leaves her alone with the conversant and goes away.

VISUAL SOURCES

Manuscript Illuminations: Scenes from the Life of Muhammad

These three manuscript illuminations show scenes from the life of Muhammad. In the first, the boy Muhammad is being recognized as a prophet by the Christian monk, Bahira, on the right with two accompanying sages. Muhammad has already been recognized by followers on the left and is apparently even recognized by the bowing camels on the right. The recognition is confirmed by the anointing angel Gabriel above. In the second, Muhammad rides into a city backed up by armed followers and is apparently accepted by the city's inhabitants. Again, Muhammad's authority is shown by the presence of the angel Gabriel, who anoints him. In the third, Muhammad is preaching to his disciples during his final visit to Mecca. Both Muhammad and the disciples are displayed with halos.

These pictures disclose similarities and differences between the Islamic and Christian religions. These pictures come not from an illustrated Koran but from an early-fourteenth-century Islamic history book and are quite rare, for plastic or pictorial art was not sanctioned by Islamic theology; thus there developed no tradition of religious painting

Photo 6-1

مَعَهَ احَوالله وَكان نتجمع ملك الاحوال مَوَاضعة وَمناسبة لماقراه لخيرا نه الكتب وَراى خاتم النبوة بين كمفيه ثم سأل اباطالب عنه وقال لمن هذا الصبى

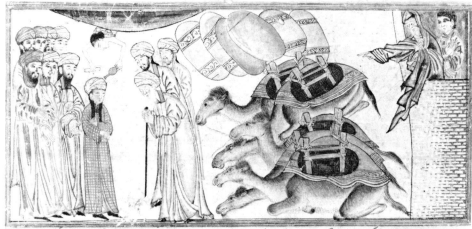

قال هوابى فقال ينبغى ان يكون لهاب لا يكون بل يكون والده قدقدح وَيكون نبها فقال هوابى اخى وكا نت امه حامله به ثم درج والدّ فقال لدحمدا صلى

Edinburgh University Library

Photo 6-2

وقطع جمع كلهم فقالوا الماخرج من بلادك فقال النبى عليه السلم ان لا ابدك لكم الآن مطلوكم وطلبكم لكن ارجعوا اولادكم وَمتركوا اموالكم وَسلاحكم وَسلبكم وَصواب لك وَكانوالجربون يسومهم باولدهم واهل المومسى كان بانه سوفا فانقعدوهمعر جوالى المدينة وَكان مولى الخراج محمدرس سلمة فمضوا ماولاد هم وَنسا همرسمية جعل جل الاخبار لده ابه

The Bettmann Archive

Photo 6-3

Edinburgh University Library

corresponding to the ecclesiastical art supported by the Christian Church. The content of the pictures reveals connections to Christianity: the recognition by Christian monks of Muhammad's authority, the importance of the biblical angel Gabriel, and even the use of halos to identify Muhammad and the disciples. The rapid spread of Islam by the legitimate use of arms is suggested in the second picture. The style of the pictures indicates the vast geographic extent of Islam by the fourteenth century, for it derives from Far Eastern, perhaps Mongolian, influence.

Consider: *The characteristics of Islam revealed by these scenes.*

The Spread of Islam in Africa

As this map reveals, the initial expansion of Islam in northern Africa during the seventh and eighth centuries was just the beginning of a long process of expansion. Certainly it was an uneven process and much depended on the barriers of terrain (such as the rain forest), distance (south and southeastern Africa), and resistance (Christian kingdoms in Nubia).

Consider: *Factors that facilitated the spread of Islam; factors that hindered its spread; the possible significance of the spread of Islam to sub-Saharan Africa.*

Map 6-1   The Spread of Islam in Africa

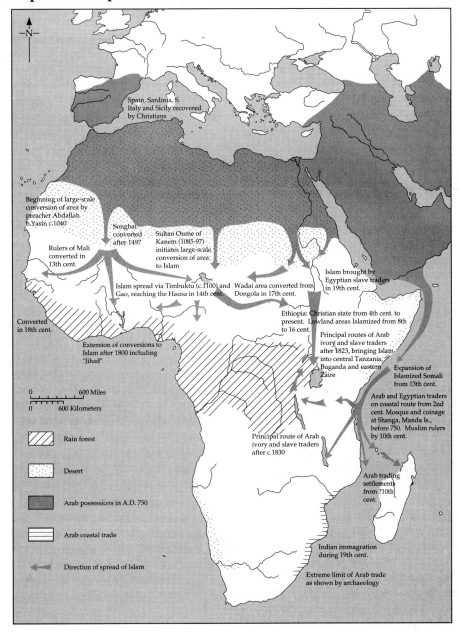

Spain, Sardinia, S. Italy and Sicily recovered by Christians

Beginning of large-scale conversion of area by preacher Abdallah b. Yasin c.1040

Songhai converted after 1497

Sultan Oume of Kanem (1085-97) initiates large-scale conversion of area to Islam

Rulers of Mali converted in 13th cent.

Islam brought by Egyptian slave traders in 19th cent.

Islam spread via Timbuktu (c.1100) and Gao, reaching the Hausa in 14th cent.

Wadai area converted from Dongola in 17th cent.

Converted in 18th cent.

Ethiopia: Christian state from 4th cent. to present. Lowland areas Islamized from 8th to 16 cent.

Extension of conversions to Islam after 1800 including "Jihad"

Principal routes of Arab ivory and slave traders after 1823, bringing Islam into central Tanzania, Buganda and eastern Zaire

Expansion of Islamized Somali from 13th cent.

Arab and Egyptian traders on coastal route from 2nd cent. Mosque and coinage at Shanga, Manda Is., before 750. Muslim rulers by 10th cent.

Principal route of Arab ivory and slave traders after c.1830

Arab trading settlements from ?10th cent.

0   600 Miles
0   600 Kilometers

Rain forest

Desert

Arab possessions in A.D. 750

Arab coastal trade

Direction of spread of Islam

Indian immigration during 19th cent.

Extreme limit of Arab trade as shown by archaeology

SECONDARY SOURCES

The Arabs in History
Bernard Lewis

Islam started as an Arabic religion, and its early conquests were made by Arabs. One of the questions that has concerned historians is the relative importance of Islam as a religion and the Arabs as a people in explaining the conquests and spread of Islam during the seventh and eighth centuries. In the following selection, Bernard Lewis, a historian of the Middle East, deals with this question and focuses particularly on the Arabic language as the key legacy of the early conquests.

> **Consider:** *Lewis' argument that the expansion was not of Islam, but of the Arab nation; what, according to Lewis, was the role of religion in the conquests; the significance of the Arabic language within the Islamic (or Arab) Empire.*

Initially the great conquests were an expansion not of Islam but of the Arab nation, driven by the pressure of over-population in its native peninsula to seek an outlet in the neighbouring countries. It is one of the series of migrations which carried the Semites time and again into the Fertile Crescent and beyond. The expansion of the Arabs is not as sudden as might at first appear. In periods when the dam holding the Arabs in their peninsula was too strong to allow a direct break-through, the pressure of over-population found partial relief in a steady infiltration of Arab elements into the border lands. There is much evidence of important Arab infiltration during the sixth and seventh centuries, in particular into the Euphrates basin, Palestine and south-east Syria. The Byzantine towns of Bosra and Gaza, to name but two, had important Arab populations even before the conquests, and there can be little doubt that the conquerors found many of their kinsmen already settled in the nearest of the countries they conquered.

The role of religion in the conquests is over-estimated by earlier writers and has perhaps been under-estimated by some modern scholars. Its importance lies in the temporary psychological change which it wrought in a people who were naturally excitable and temperamental, unaccustomed to any sort of discipline, willing to be persuaded, but never to be commanded. It made them for a time more self-confident and more amenable to control. In the Wars of Conquest it was the symbol of Arab unity and victory. That the driving force of the conquests was worldly rather than religious is shown by their outstanding figures—men of

SOURCE: Bernard Lewis, *The Arabs in History*, 3rd ed. (London: Hutchinson University Library, 1964), pp. 55–56, 132.

the type of Khālid and 'Amr, men whose interest in religion was perfunctory and utilitarian. With few exceptions the truly converted and the pietists played little part in the creation of the Arab Empire.

❋

The conquests made Arabic an imperial language, soon also the language of a great and diverse culture. Arabic expanded to meet these two needs, partly by borrowing new words and expressions, but mainly by development from within, forming new words from old roots, giving new meanings to old words. As an example of the process we may choose the Arabic word for "absolute", a notion quite unnecessary to the pre-Islamic Arabs. It is *mujurrad,* the passive participle of *jarrada,* to strip bare or denude, a term normally used of locusts and connected with the words *jarāda,* locust, and *jarīda,* leaf. The language created in this way possessed a vivid, concrete and pictorial vocabulary, with each term having deep roots in a purely Arab past and tradition. It allowed of the direct and uncushioned impact of ideas on the mind through concrete and familiar words and of unrestricted penetration to and from the deeper layers of consciousness.

The Arabic language, thus enriched, remained the sole instrument of culture for long after the fall of the purely Arab kingdom. With the language of the Arabs came their poetry as its classical model and the world of ideas embedded therein— concrete, not abstract, though often subtle and allusive; rhetorical and declamatory, not intimate and personal; recitative and spasmodic, not epic and sustained; a literature where the impact of words and form counted for more than the transmission of ideas.

It was the Arabisation of the conquered provinces rather than their military conquest that is the true wonder of the Arab expansion. By the eleventh century Arabic had become not only the chief idiom of everyday use from Persia to the Pyrenees, but also the chief instrument of culture, superseding old culture languages like Coptic, Aramaic, Greek and Latin. As the Arabic language spread, the distinction between Arab conqueror and Arabised conquered faded into relative insignificance, and while all who spoke Arabic and professed Islam were felt to belong to a single community, the term Arab was restricted once again to the nomads who had originally borne it or was used as a title of aristocratic descent with no great economic or social significance.

The Muslim Pattern of Conquest
W. Montgomery Watt

The speed with which the Muslims were able to conquer vast areas of land, particularly in Spain, has fascinated historians. In the following selection, W. Montgomery Watt, professor of Arabic and Islamic studies at the University of Edinburgh, provides an explana-

tion for the speed of the Muslim conquest. He points out that the Muslims had developed a pattern of conquest that had proved successful in the first campaigns of Muhammad. This same process was applied to Spain; thus the conquest may have come as a surprise to the Spanish inhabitants, but not to Muslims.

Consider: *The nature of the razzia and the Jihad and how Watt relates them to help explain the conquest of Spain; the motives for the Conquest of Spain according to Watt; the process that occurred in transforming a military victory into established political control.*

Although to the inhabitants of Spain the invasion of 711 may have come as a bolt from the blue, to the Muslims it was the normal continuation of a process that had been going on since the lifetime of Muhammad. This process came about through a transformation of the nomadic razzia. For centuries nomadic Arab tribes had been in the habit of making raids or razzias on other tribes. The usual aim was to drive off the camels or other livestock of the opponents. The favorite plan was to make a surprise attack with overwhelming force on a small section of the other tribe. In such circumstances it was no disgrace to the persons attacked if they made their escape; and so in many razzias there was little loss of life. Occasionally, however, things might take a more serious turn. After Muhammad went to Medina in 622 some of his followers, especially those who had emigrated with him from Mecca, began to engage in what were really razzias. Perhaps it was to encourage others to join in the razzias that the Qur'ān spoke of this as 'fighting in the way of God' or 'striving in the way of God'. The Arabic word for 'striving' or 'making efforts to secure a particular aim' is *jāhada* with the verbal noun *jihād*. While the latter can be used of moral and spiritual effort, it has come to be specially associated with fighting against the infidel and is then translated 'holy war'. Although this translation is appropriate, I propose to retain the term Jihād here, since there are differences between the Islamic conception of the Jihād and the Christian conception of the Crusade. . . .

From the standpoint of the Muslims, the crossing of the straits of Gibraltar in 711 was part of the process of expansion that had been going on for three-quarters of a century. It was one more in a series of raiding expeditions which had been pushing ever farther afield. These might be thought of as Jihād or 'striving in the way of God', but the acquiring of booty was a large part of the motive. After experiencing one or more such raiding expeditions the inhabitants of the countries traversed usually surrendered and became protected allies. Since it was too far for the Arabs to return to Arabia or even Damascus after each campaign, they established camp-cities such as Cairouan. These often became centres of administration and populous urban communities. From them further raiding expeditions went out, and in due course more advanced bases were established. This was what happened in Spain, except that existing towns were used as bases. Despite their limited manpower the Arabs were able within two or three years to occupy the chief towns and achieve a measure of pacification. The local population mostly submitted and received the status of protected allies.

SOURCE: W. Montgomery Watt, The Influence of Islam on Medieval Europe (Edinburgh University Press, 1972), pp. 5–6, 8.

Islamic Law
Hamilton A. R. Gibb

Intellectually, culturally, and politically, law was a pervasive force in the Islamic world. It helped to create needed cohesion among communities that had only recently been unified by force of arms or religious convictions. In the following selection, Hamilton A. R. Gibb, who has taught at Oxford and Harvard and is a recognized authority on the Islamic world, analyzes the significance of Islamic law in a comparative context.

> **Consider:** *The ways in which law was very important in the Islamic world; how the role of law in Islam compared with the role of law in the Roman world.*

The master science of the Muslim world was Law. Law, indeed, might be said to embrace all things, human and divine, and both for its comprehensiveness and for the ardour with which its study was pursued it would be hard to find a parallel elsewhere, except in Judaism.

But apart altogether from its intellectual preeminence and scholastic function, Islamic Law was the most far-reaching and effective agent in moulding the social order and the community life of the Muslim peoples. By its very comprehensiveness it exerted a steady pressure upon all private and social activities, setting a standard to which they conformed more and more closely as time went on, in spite of the resistance of ancient habits and time-honoured customs, especially amongst the more independent nomadic and mountain tribes. Moreover, Islamic Law gave practical expression to the characteristic Muslim quest for unity. In all essentials it was uniform, although the various schools differed in points of detail. To its operation was due the striking convergence of social ideals and ways of life throughout the medieval Muslim world. It went far deeper than Roman law; by reason of its religious basis and its theocratic sanctions it was the spiritual regulator, the conscience, of the Muslim community in all its parts and activities.

This function of law acquired still greater significance as political life in the Muslim world swung ever further away from the theocratic ideal of Mohammed and his successors. The decline of the Abbasid Caliphate in the tenth and eleventh centuries opened the door to political disintegration, the usurpation of royal authority by local princes and military governors, the rise and fall of ephemeral dynasties, and repeated outbreaks of civil war. But however seriously the political and military strength of the vast Empire might be weakened, the moral authority of the Law was but the more enhanced and held the social fabric of Islam compact and secure through all the fluctuations of political fortune.

At the end of the tenth century, the geographical area of Islam was but little wider than it had been in 750. But a great civilization had been built up, brilliant

---

SOURCE: *Mohammedanism: An Historical Survey* by Hamilton A. R. Gibb, pp. 9–11. Copyright © 1953. Reprinted by permission of Oxford University Press.

in intellectual life, wealthy and enterprising in economic life, powerfully cemented by an authoritative Law—the whole a visible embodiment of the temporal and spiritual might of Islam. As its military strength declined, it, like the Roman Empire six centuries before, fell gradually under the domination of the barbarians from beyond its frontiers, but also, like the Roman Empire, imposed upon the barbarians its religion, its law, and respect for its civilization.

The Eastern Orientation of Islam

Peter Brown

Westerners often assume that Islamic civilization centered around the Mediterranean and that if not for the resistance put up by Europeans and the Byzantine Empire, Islam would have extended its control to the lands north of the Mediterranean. In the following selection, Peter Brown of Oxford and the University of California disputes this view, arguing that Persia acquired great economic importance as the Mediterranean cities declined. In turn, the Islamic Empire became centered in Persia and was oriented toward the East rather than the West.

Consider: *How Persia pulled the Islamic Empire eastward; why, according to Brown, the foundation of Baghdad was more important than military defeats in halting the Arab advance on Europe.*

Mesopotamia regained a central position that it had lost since the days of Alexander the Great. Baghdad, with its circular city wall, owed nothing to the great cities of the Roman empire: It was an avatar of the round cities of Assyria and central Asia. The Mediterranean cities declined as the great caravans by-passed them, bringing trade by camel along the oceans of sand that stretched from the Sahara to the Gobi Desert. In North Africa and Syria, the villages that had sent their oil and grain across the sea to Rome and Constantinople disappeared into the sand. The Mediterranean coast, from being the heart of the civilized world, imperceptibly diminished in significance, as the numbed extremity of a great Eurasian empire.

For the new commercial opportunities were in Persian hands. And, in Persian hands, the eternal lure of Further Asia reasserted itself, as in the early Sassanian period. The mosque and the fire temple could be seen beside the market-places of Lohang and Canton. Chinese prisoners of war from central Asia brought the art of papermaking to Baghdad in 751. Sinbad the Sailor would not have considered the Mediterranean worth his trouble: for the wealth and interests of the Abbasid empire poured eastwards, down the Tigris and Euphrates, to the sea route that linked Basra directly with Canton.

SOURCE: Peter Brown, *The World of Late Antiquity* (New York: Harcourt Brace Jovanovich, Inc.; London: Thames and Hudson, Ltd., 1971), pp. 202–203.

The eastward pull of the vast mass of Persia in the Islamic empire was the salvation of Europe. It was not the Greek fire of the Byzantine navy outside Constantinople in 717, nor the Frankish cavalry of Charles Martel at Tours in 732, that brought the Arab war-machine to a halt. It was the foundation of Baghdad. With the establishment of the Abbasid califate, the slow-moving ideals of an organized and expensive imperial administration replaced the fearful mobility of the Beduin armies. In the new civilian world, the soldier was as much out of place as he had been among the otiose aristocrats of the fourth-century West. The bloodsucking relationships of the Holy War, by which the early Arabs had first impinged on the outside world, gave way to a meticulous diplomacy modelled on the protocol of the Persian *ancien régime.* At the court of the califs, the world appeared to revolve like clockwork round Baghdad, as in the dreamlike ceremonial of the king of kings. Just before he was crowned Roman emperor of the West in 800, Charlemagne received from Harun al-Rashid a great cloak and a pet elephant called Abul Abaz. Little did the Frankish monarch know it, but in this gift the calif had merely repeated the time-honoured gesture of Khusro I Anoshirwan when, at the great Spring festival, the king of kings had lavished gifts of animals and cast-off clothing on his humble servants.

In the western imagination, the Islamic empire stands as the quintessence of an oriental power. Islam owed this crucial orientation neither to Muhammad nor to the adaptable conquerors of the seventh century, but to the massive resurgence of eastern, Persian traditions in the eighth and ninth centuries.

Chapter Questions

1. Explain the appeal and the rapid spread of Islam during these early centuries.
2. In what ways might it be argued that politically, militarily, and culturally, Islam owed its success to its qualities as an Arab civilization?
3. Drawing on sources from this and previous chapters, how might Islamic civilization be compared with the Christian and Indian civilizations it was challenging?

SEVEN

India and Southeast Asia, 500–1500

While Islamic Arabs were forming their powerful empire around the Mediterranean basin and southwestern Asia during the centuries following the collapse of Roman civilization, Indian civilization was experiencing an extended period of political decline. From the late fifth century, northern India degenerated into a number of feuding dynasties and petty rival states. Hinduism, with its family system and caste structure, became stronger and further identified with Indian culture throughout this period until it became threatened by the spread of Islam in the eleventh century. Buddhism, which had been steadily weakening since the ninth century, was finally eliminated in India, replaced as the nation's second religion by Islam.

It was the eastward advance of Arab invaders that spread Islam as it moved across Asia. These invasions culminated in the expeditions of Amir Mahmud of Ghazni, a savage Turk whose swift horsemen easily overcame the plodding Indian war elephants. Eventually the Muslims gained control of northern India and established the Delhi Sultanate (1211–1504). The Muslim conquest profoundly affected Indian life in the fields of art, architecture, law, literature, and government and had important consequences for northern Indian society as a whole. Efforts to subdue the south were fruitless, as the Hindu kingdom of Vijaynagar was able to defend itself.

The early history of mainland Southeast Asia is the tale of various ethnic groups (Malays, Vietnamese, Mons, Khmers, Pyu-Burmans, Lao, Shan, Thai, Chams) migrating throughout the region and engaging in rivalries amongst themselves. Many of these peoples established their own societies in the centuries between 500 and 1500, such as the Thais in the eighth century, the Burmans in the ninth century, and the Vietnamese who regained their independence from China in the tenth century. The largest and most powerful of these were the Khmers, who established an empire based in Angkor that flourished from the ninth to the fourteenth centuries. The region was strongly influenced by both India and China, from which many of these peoples imported Buddhism, Hinduism, and Confucianism.

During this time period, although beginning later than its two major neighbors, the southeast Asian region began to develop into the nations which would emerge in the twentieth century. Using the teachings from the Indian and Chinese traditions, these peoples created states and cultures which gave them each an identifiable personality to be forged into nation states.

Religions and philosophies of life profoundly shaped the civilizations of India and Southeast Asia. Therefore, many of the sources in this chapter focus on the nature of Islam, Hinduism, and Sikhism. Some of these sources emphasize conflicts between religions, traditions, and schools of thought. Others focus on the social significance—especially for women—of Islam and

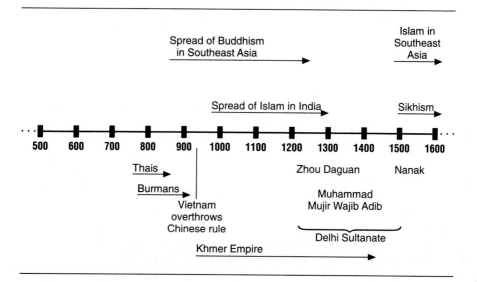

Hinduism in India as well as Buddhism and Confucianism in Southeast Asia. In addition, sources in this chapter will examine some of the political, social, and cultural characteristics of three of the civilizations that flourished in this area: northern India, Vietnam, and Cambodia.

PRIMARY SOURCES

The Key to Paradise: Islam in India
Muhammad Mujir Wajib Adib

During the eleventh century and thereafter, Islam spread across India and other parts of Asia. In India, Islam brought a new dimension to religious belief. Islam was monotheistic, while Hinduism was pantheistic. Islam believed humans lived only once and, therefore, life was vital, while Hinduism taught life was an evil illusion and the soul had to pass through successive reincarnations. Most importantly, Islam taught that all men were equal. Conversion to Islam, therefore, required teaching of its doctrines, particularly those that might be most appealing. This is exemplified by the following excerpt from the writings of Muhammad Mujir Wajib Adib, who lived in the fourteenth century. Here, he describes "The Key to Paradise" for an audience of Indians who were newly converted to Islam and unfamiliar with its teachings.

> **Consider:** *What might be attractive in Islamic teachings to Indians converting from Hinduism; how these teachings compare to other religious teachings.*

It is related that the Prophet said that whoever says every day at daybreak in the name of God the Merciful and Compassionate, "There is no god but God and Muhammad is His Prophet," him God Most High will honor with seven favors. First, He will open his spirit to Islam; second, He will soften the bitterness of death; third, He will illuminate his grave; fourth, He will show Munkar and Nakir, his best aspects; fifth, He will give the list of his deeds with His right hand; sixth, He will tilt the balance of his account in his favor; and seventh, He will pass him over the eternal bridge which spans the fire of hell into Paradise like a flash of lightning. . . .

Source: *Sources of Indian Tradition.* Theodore deBary, et al., eds., (Columbia University Press, New York, 1961) pp. 393–395. Reprinted by permission of the publishers.

In the illuminating commentary . . . it is set down that the servant of God should make the Qur'ān his guide and his protection. On the Day of Judgment the Qur'ān will precede him and lead him toward Paradise. Whoever does not diligently stay close to the Qur'ān but lags behind, the angel will come forth and striking him on his side will carry him off to hell. . . .

It is reported in tradition that one's rank in Paradise depends upon the extent of one's recitation of the Qur'ān. They say that everyone who knows how to read a small amount of the Qur'ān will enjoy a high position in Paradise and they say that the more one knows how to read it, the higher one's status in Paradise. . . . The Prophet said that on the night of his ascent to heaven he was shown the sins of his people. He did not see any greater sin than that of him who did not know and did not read the Qur'ān. . . .

It is reported in the *Salāt-i-Mas'ūdī* that Khwāja Imām Muhammad Taiyyar reported that on the morning of the Day of Resurrection, the people awaiting judgment will be deserving punishment. The angels will be hauling them up for punishment. They will say to young and old: "Come forth, you who were our followers in the world." Again they will say to the old weak ones: "You are the weak. It may be that God will have mercy on your weakness." Then they will go to the very edge of hell. When they say: "In the name of the merciful and compassionate God," the five-hundred-year-long fire of hell will avoid them. The Lord of Hell will address the fire: "Why do you not take them?" The fire will reply: "How can I take those who repeat the name of the Creator and remember Him as the Merciful and Compassionate?" God's voice will reach them, saying: "They are My servants and the fire is also My servant. He who honors My name, his name too I have held in higher esteem." On the blessings of saying: "In the name of the merciful and compassionate God," God said: "I have freed everyone in the name of God, the Merciful and the Compassionate.". . . Every believer who repeats that rubric, to him God will give refuge from the nineteen flames of hell. . . .

The Prophet was sitting down with his Companions around him with Abū Bakr Siddīq [Caliph after Muhammad's death] sitting at his right hand. A young man came in; the Prophet gave instructions that he should sit nearer to him than Abū Bakr. The Companions began to think this young man was a man of the highest distinction. After the young man had left they questioned the Prophet about it; Muhammad looked toward Abū Bakr and said: "O, chief of the Companions, do not be uneasy that I bade that young man to sit higher up than you." Abū Bakr said: "O Prophet of God, what was there to say? I obeyed your command quite willingly." The Prophet said, "O, Abū Bakr, be it known unto you that this young man has sent me a harvest of such quantity as no one else has done." Abū Bakr said, "But, O Prophet of God, this young man's only occupation is that of being your disciple." The Prophet said, "He is busy with his own affairs, but every day he says his prayers once during the day and once at night. I gave him a high place in our assembly because he says his prayers."

The Four Legs of the Realm
Muhammad Baquir Khan

By the beginning of the thirteenth century, Muslim invaders had gained control over northern India, replacing Hinduism with Islam and establishing the strong Delhi Sultanate (1211–1504). Islamic societies, like any other societies, tried to develop a form of government which not only suited them in a material sense, but which also adhered to their religious beliefs. Islamic invaders carried these ideas with them in their conquest of northern India.

The following two excerpts from early Indian Muslim texts describe Islamic ideas about good government, in theory if not always in practice.

> **Consider:** *The nature of good government according to these sources; potential political problems revealed by these documents; connections between religious and secular government.*

You should know that "pillars of the state," ministers, and other servants, are essential for sultans and kings. It is an unquestioned need of rulers to have capable counsellors and trusty officers who have the privilege of intimacy with the king's secrets, and have ability and authority for important undertakings. It is said that a realm has four legs. If one is missing the foundations of important transactions will not be firm. The first leg of the kingdom is the existence of great amīrs, who are the people of the sword and guard the frontiers of the kingdom and prevent the wickedness of enemies from affecting the king and the people. . . . Second are the capable finance officers and religious revenue officers who are the ornament of the kingdoms, the cause of the stable foundations of the sultanate, and the regulators of the affairs of the realm. . . . in some ways, the people of the pen aspire to superiority over the people of the sword, arguing first that the sword is only used for enemies and not for friends, whereas the pen is used both to benefit friends and to ward off enemies, something which the sword cannot do. . . . [T]he people of the sword in secret betray ambitions to be kings themselves. This is something which never happens with the people of the pen. . . .[T]he people of the sword empty the treasury, and the people of the pen fill it, and occasions of income are better than occasions of expenditure. . . . The third leg of the realm is the judge who, on behalf of the sultan, inquires into the state of the people, obtains justice for the weak from the strong, and abases and subdues the seditious and the forward. The fourth leg is the trusty intelligence officers who report continually the actions of the royal officials and the condition of the subjects. They bring to the royal notice any signs of harshness and negligence. For when infor-

---

SOURCE: *Sources of Indian Tradition*, Theodore deBary, et al., eds., (Columbia University Press, New York, 1961) pp. 499–502. Reprinted by permission of the publishers.

mation about the country and realm is hidden from the ruler, he is careless of friend or foe, good or evil, and everyone does as he likes. When the ruler is without information, the foundations of his sultanate become shaky from all the rebellions which spring up in all parts of the country.

Governmental Appointments
Barni

This second Islamic text on good government emphasizes the importance of making good governmental appointments.

In the appointment of intelligence officers, auditors, and spies, religious rulers have had good intentions and objects. First, when it becomes clear to the officers, judges, governors, and revenue collectors both far and near, that their good and bad actions will be brought to light, they do not demand bribes or accept presents or show favor or partiality. They do not depart from the path of righteousness or take to sinfulness and wrong-doing, and they are always fearful and trembling concerning their own private affairs. Owing to this caution on their part they may be safe from their real superior [God] and from their figurative superior [the sultan].

Secondly, when the people are convinced that the good and bad deeds of all classes are being reported to the king and that officeholders have been appointed for this particular purpose, they will behave like good subjects; they will neither conspire nor rebel nor attempt to overpower each other nor oppress the weak. Thirdly, if revenue collectors and accountants know that their actions will be brought to the notice of the king, they will refrain from stealing and misappropriating and thus remain secure from the ruler and escape dishonor and disgrace. Lastly, it will be an advantage even to the king's sons, brothers, and high officers if they are aware that the king will be informed of all their actions, for they will not then, presuming on their close relationship with the king, step beyond the bounds of justice in their dealings with their own people and strangers, or their slaves and servants. . . .

The intelligence officer should be truthful in speech, truthful in writing, reliable, well-born, worthy of confidence, sober and careful where he lives, and not much given to social and convivial intercourse so that his object, which is obtaining correct information for the king's business, may be attained. But if the intelligence officer is a thief, a man without rectitude, low-born, mean, a frequenter of every place and a caller at every door, corrupt, greedy, covetous, and reckless, then what

SOURCE: *Sources of Indian Tradition,* Theodore deBary, et al., eds., (Columbia University Press, New York, 1961). Reprinted by permission of the publishers.

should be the predicate of the ruler's intentions, his designs and his search for the welfare of his subjects, will become the opposite. For the dishonest and low-born intelligence officer, who is a master of intrigue and "wire-pulling," spins many lies that look like truth, and through his testifying to false information, affairs are thrown into disorder. Where benefits should be rendered, injuries are inflicted; men worthy of punishment are favored while men deserving of favor are punished.

Sikhism
Guru Nanak

The introduction of Islam would not be the last important religious change to affect India. The origins of Sikhism, which would gain many adherents in India, can be traced to Nanak, who lived in the late fifteenth and early sixteenth century. Nanak (1469–1539) was born near the city of Lahore and was strongly influenced by both Islamic and Hindu tradition. Inspired by earlier reformers of Islam, he visited the holy cities of Mecca and Medina. Dissatisfied with both religions, Nanak began to teach his own monotheistic ideas which eventually would come to be known as Sikhism and greatly influence Indian life. His teachings were written down in the Adi Granth *and were spread throughout northern India, especially in the province of Punjab. This selection from the* Adi Granth *contains excerpts from the morning prayer (*Japji*) which Sikhs believe carries the gist of their faith's teaching.*

> **Consider:** *Nanak's conception of god; his views on man preordained to be born sinful and finally brought to judgment.*

There is One God
His Name is Truth.
He is the Creator,
He is without fear and without hate.
He is beyond time Immortal,
His Spirit pervades the universe.
He is not born,
Nor does He die to be born again,
He is self-existent.
By the guru's grace shalt thou worship Him. . . .

Before time itself
There was Truth,
When time began to run its course
He became the Truth.

Source: *Hymns of Guru Nanak*, Khushwant Singh, trans. (Orient Longman Limited, India, 1969), Unesco Collection of Representative Works—Indian Series English translation © Unesco 1969, pp. 43–45, 60–62.

Even now, He is the Truth
And sayeth Nanak
Evermore shall Truth prevail.

1

Not by thought alone
Can He be known,
Though one think
A hundred thousand times;
Not in solemn silence
Nor in deep meditation.
Accumulation of the wealth of the world
Cannot appease the hunger for truth,
No, by none of these,
Nor by a hundred thousand other devices,
Can God be reached. . . .

2

By Him are all forms created,
But His ordinances we do not know,
By Him infused with life and blessed,
By Him are some to excellence elated,
Others born lowly and depressed.
By His writ some have pleasure, others pain;
By His grace some are saved,
Others doomed to die, re-live and die again.
His will encompasseth all, there be none beside. . . .

God is the Master, God is Truth,
His name spelleth love divine,
His creatures ever cry: 'O give, O give',
He the bounteous doth never decline.
What then in offering shall we bring
That we may see His court above?
What then shall we say in speech
That hearing may evoke His love?
In the ambrosial hours of a fragrant dawn
On truth and greatness ponder in meditation,
Through action determine how thou be born.
There the elect His court adorn,
And God Himself their actions honours;
There are sorted deeds that were done and bore fruit
From those that to action could never ripen.
This, O Nanak, shall hereafter happen. . . .

Air, water and earth,
Of these are we made.
Air like the Guru's word gives the breath of life
To the babe born to the great mother earth
Sired by the waters.
The day and night our nurses be
That watch over us in our infancy.
In their laps we play.
The world is our playground.
Our acts right and wrong at Thy court shall come to
        judgment,
Some be seated near Thy seat, some ever kept distant.
The toils have ended of those that have worshipped
        Thee,
O Nanak, their faces are lit with joyful radiance—
        many others they set free.

Traditional Vietnam
Nguyen Khac Vien

While Buddhism lost its followers in India, it did spread throughout east and southeast Asia where it came up against other belief systems. This was particularly the case with Vietnam, which had a long history of struggle with and domination by the Chinese. Vietnam came to be strongly influenced by Chinese culture and Confucian institutions. Confucianism, which Buddhism encountered in both China and Vietnam, was not a religion and therefore not a direct competitor of Buddhism. Nevertheless, adherents of the Confucian social order did not always welcome Buddhism, as revealed in the following selection. Nguyen Khac Vien is one of Vietnam's most respected historians. This excerpt from his book Traditional Vietnam *utilizes translations from original texts of the thirteenth century to explore the struggle between Buddhism, which is here the interloper, and Confucianism, which had become the dominant cultural model in Vietnam by that time.*

> **Consider:** *The class and occupation lines along which these struggles took place; the bases of the Confucian scholars' attacks on Buddhism.*

In 1070, Ly Thanh Ton had the "Temple of Literature" built, a school dedicated to Confucianism and his disciples, where the sons of high dignitaries received moral education and training in administration. In 1075, the first mandarin competitions took place, through which Confucian scholars could acceed to public

SOURCE: Nguyen Khac Vien, "Traditional Viet-Nam. Some Historical Stages," in *Vietnamese Studies* No. 21, Hanoi, 1969, pp. 54–57.

office; but they were open only to the sons of aristocratic families. In 1086, competitions were held to recruit members of the "Academy," whose task was to keep archives and write royal edicts. In 1089 the mandarin hierarchy was strictly organized. The appearance of Confucianism on the scene was the consequence of a double phenomenon: on the one hand the necessity to create a mandarin bureaucracy, on the other hand the increasing access of educated commoners to public office. At first, these men were given only subaltern positions, the higher offices being reserved for members of the royal family and of the aristocracy. . . .

. . . In the cultural field, Buddhist bonzes[1] were increasingly eclipsed by Confucian scholars. . . . The Confucian scholars more and more vigorously claimed positions in public life, in face of nobles of military origin, often uneducated, and Buddhist bonzes. In the 13th century, the ideological struggle between Buddhism and Confucianism became increasingly acute, a struggle which reflected the antagonism opposing the nobles, owners of great domains, to the fast-growing class of peasant-owners of popular origin. Besides, the great domains were shaken by revolts of serfs and domestic slaves at the close of the 13th century. Thus a dividing line was drawn between the aristocracy and the Buddhist clergy on one side, and on the other the class of peasant-owners allied with the serfs and slaves, having the Confucian scholars as their spokesmen in the ideological field.

> In face of Buddhism which affirmed the vanity, even the unreality of this world, preached renunciation, and directed men's minds towards supraterrestrial hopes, Confucianism taught that man is essentially a social being bound by social obligations. To serve one's king, honour one's parents, remain loyal to one's spouse until death, manage one's family affairs, participate in the administration of one's country, contribute to safeguarding the peace of the world, such were the duties prescribed by Confucianism to all. To educate oneself, to improve oneself so as to be able to assume all those tasks,—this should be the fundamental preoccupation of all men, from the Emperor, Son of Heaven, down to the humblest commoner.

The scholars directed their attacks not only against Buddhist beliefs, but also against the place granted them by the State and society. The historian Le Van Huu wrote:

> The first Ly king, hardly two years after his accession to the throne, at a time when the ancestral temples of the dynasty had not yet been consolidated, had already had eight pagodas built in the Thien Duc district, and many others restored in different provinces; he kept more than one thousand bonzes in the capital; much wealth and labour had thus been wasted! Those riches had not fallen from the sky, that labour had not been supplied by the gods; to do such things was to suck the blood and sweat of the people!

---

[1] Monks

The scholar Le Quat lamented:

> To implore Buddha's benediction, to dread his malediction—how had such beliefs become so deeply rooted in the hearts of men? Princes of the blood and common people alike squandered their possessions for the cult of Buddha, quite happy to give them away to pagodas, as if they had been given a guarantee for life in the other world. Wherever there was a house, one was sure to find a pagoda next to it; a crumbling pagoda was soon replaced by a new one; bells, pagodas, drums, towers, half of the population were engaged in making these things.

Truong Han Sieu also made a direct attack on the bonzes:

> Scoundrels who had lost all notion of Buddhist asceticism only thought of taking possession of beautiful monasteries and gardens, building for themselves luxurious residences, and surrounding themselves with a host of servants. . . . People became monks by the thousands, so as to get food without having to plough and clothes without having to weave. They deceived the people, undermined morality, squandered riches, were found everywhere, followed by numerous believers; very few of them were not real bandits.

But several centuries were to pass before Buddhism was eliminated from the scene, at least from public office, and Confucianism could stand alone. . . . No war of religion ever broke out in Viet-nam. By the 14th century, however, Confucianism had risen to pre-eminence.

An Account of Cambodia
Zhou Daguan (Chou Ta-kuan)

Traditionally, Chinese emperors were inward looking, far more interested in their own country than in the lands beyond their borders. However, on occasion, they did get information from travelers who happened into China. Marco Polo played that role during the Yuan (Mongol) Dynasty, for example. The Yuan Dynasty also had in its employ a Chinese official named Zhou Daguan (Chou Ta-kuan) who spent a year traveling in Cambodia during the height of the Khmer Empire's glory. These excerpts, probably the only extant account by an observer of that period, are from a report written in 1297 when Zhou had returned to China.

> **Consider:** *The characteristics of Khmer society; the Chinese officials' concern with trade in Cambodia; how the Khmer royal house ruled over its people.*

SOURCE: Zhou Daguan, *Memoires sur les Coutumes du Cambodge de Tcheou Ta-kouan* (Paris: A. Maisonneuve, 1951), pp. 19, 20, 26–28, 34–35.

There are two kinds of savages: those who know the language and are sold as slaves; the other are those who do not understand the language and could not adapt themselves to civilization. The latter have no permanent dwelling places, but, followed by their families, wander in the mountains carrying their few provisions in clay jars on their heads. If they find a wild animal, they will kill it with spears or bows and arrows, make a fire by striking stones together, cook the animal, eat it in common, and continue their wandering. . . . Savages are brought to do the work of servants. . . . Wealthy families may have more than a hundred; . . . The savages inhabit the wild mountains and belong to a different race; they are called *chuangs,* thieves. . . . Brought to the city, they never dare appear on the street. They are forced to live in the space under the houses which are built on stilts and when they come up into the house to do their work, they must first kneel and make the proper obeisance, prostrating themselves before they can advance. . . .

This country has its own language. Even though the sounds are fairly similar, the people of Champa and of Siam do not understand it. . . . The officials have an official style for their deliberations; the scholars speak in a literary manner; the Buddhist monks and Daoist priests have their own language; and different villages speak differently. It is absolutely the same as in China. . . .

In Cambodia, women attend to trade. Even a Chinese who arrives there and takes a woman will profit greatly from her trading abilities. They do not have permanent stores, but simply spread a piece of mat on the ground. . . . In small transactions, one pays in rice, grain, Chinese goods, and, lastly, fabrics; in large transactions they use gold and silver.

In a general way, the country people are very naïve. When they see a Chinese, they address him timidly, respectfully, calling him Fo—Buddha. . . . I do not think that Cambodia produces either gold or silver; and what the Cambodians value most is Chinese silver and gold, then silks, lightly patterned in two-toned threads.
. . .

The troops go naked and barefoot. They hold a lance in their right hand and a shield in their left. The Cambodians have neither bows nor arrows, war machines nor bullets, helmets nor armor. It is said that in the war against the Siamese everyone was obliged to fight, but they had no knowledge of tactics or strategy.

When the king leaves the palace, first comes the cavalry, leading his escort, followed by an array of standards, banners, and music. Next comes a troupe of palace girls, anywhere from three to five hundred, . . . holding large candles. . . . After them come more palace girls bearing the royal utensils of gold and silver. . . . Then come the palace girls who, armed with lance and shield, form the king's private bodyguard; . . . followed by carriages ornamented in gold and drawn by goats and horses. Ministers and nobles mounted on elephants look straight ahead. . . . After them in palanquins, carriages, and on elephants come the king's wives and concubines; . . . Behind them comes the king. . . . on the royal elephant, whose tusks are encased in gold. . . .

Twice each day the king holds an audience to conduct the affairs of government.

... Whoever desires to see the king—either officials or any private person—sits on the ground and awaits him. ... When all matters are disposed of, the king retires, the two palace girls let the curtain fall; everyone rises. Thus one sees that, though this country is barbarous and strange, they do not fail to know what it is to be a king.

VISUAL SOURCES

Trade along the Shores of the Indian Ocean

Although there were numerous contacts made between parts of India and other civiliza-tions well before the sixth century, long distances, geographic barriers, and the difficulties

Map 7–1   Trade along the Shores of the Indian Ocean

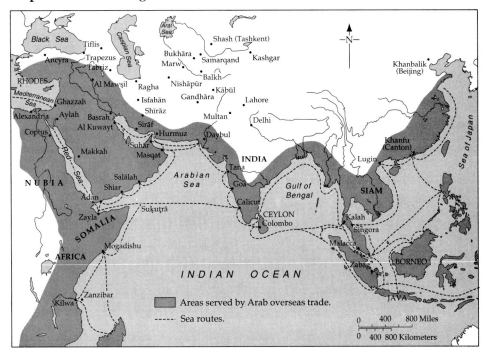

*of overland and long-distance sea travel often protected much of India from outside influ-
ences. But by the seventh century this subcontinent, and much of Southeast Asia, was
being pulled more and more into contact with lands far to the west and east by Arab
traders. As indicated by this map, these great traders headed south along the African
coast and east to India, Southeast Asia, and China. Their major commodities were spices
and gold. During the seventh and following centuries these extensive trade networks were
firmly established.*

> **Consider:** *How ideas, inventions, arts, crafts, and other cultural attributes might
> be interchanged along routes designed specifically for trade; how the northern In-
> dian Ocean might have played a role in this area of the world like the Mediterra-
> nean Sea played for Western civilization during Greek and Roman times.*

The Borobudur Stupa: An Oceangoing Ship

*The Arabs were not the only ones involved in the growing commerce along the shores of
the Indian Ocean. As revealed in this frieze from the Borobudur stupa (eighth century),
Indian traders sent their own ships out. This frieze shows an Indian ship arriving in Java.*

Photo 7–1

National Museum of Ethnology, The Netherlands

Such ships not only created commercial ties, but facilitated the spread of Buddhism and Indian culture to Southeast Asia during this period.

> **Consider:** *Why it might be important that this ship was Indian rather than Arabic; why the artist might have decided to depict this ship on the Borobodur stupa.*

SECONDARY SOURCES

Islam in India
Percival Spear

By the early eighth century, Islamic Arabs were on the borders of Islam, but it was not until the end of the twelfth and beginning of the thirteenth centuries that Islamic Turks swept into Hindu India. They established the Delhi Sultanate (1211–1504), gaining control of northern and northwestern India—particularly of the areas that would, centuries later, become present-day Pakistan. Scholars have debated the significance of Islam in India, often emphasizing the relative separateness of Hinduism and Islam. This debate, and the importance of Persian culture in the introduction of Islam into India, is reflected in the following selection by Percival Spear.

> **Consider:** *The importance of Persian culture for "Indian Islam"; the ways in which Hinduism and Islam influenced each other; why, nevertheless, there was much separateness between Hinduism and Islam.*

Indian Islam expressed itself in a distinctive culture which may be called Indo-Persian. The Muslim religion, modified by its Turkish and Afghan race-bearers, was further modified by the Persian culture by which all the invaders were more or less influenced. Persian was the language of official business and of polite society (as French was in England in the early Middle Ages). Persian literature was studied and cultivated by Hindus as well as Muslims; Persian manners became the standard of all Indian society. . . . The political side of the culture was an imperial tradition. The Muslims of India, as the result of much gifted leadership, felt themselves to be an imperial as well as a chosen race.

SOURCE: Percival Spear, *India: A Modern History*. (Ann Arbor: The University of Michigan Press, 1972), p. 101.

The separateness of Hinduism and Islam has been emphasized. The two bodies remained distinct for nine centuries, yet with so much intimate contact there was bound to be some mutual influence. As in the case of the Greeks, desire as to what is thought ought to be is apt to outrun recognition of what was. There was certainly mutual influence. Some of it was important but on neither side was it fundamental. On the Hindu side we find during the Muslim centuries a greater emphasis on the unity of God. We also find in the *bhakti* movements emphasis on such things as sin and forgiveness, which have a distinctly Judaic ring. A number of reforming movements have attacked caste. There have been a number of movements, of which Sikhism is the best known, which started by trying to bridge the gulf between the two communities; their basis was usually monotheism, no caste, and personal devotion. On the Muslim side we may say that the Indian atmosphere softened the original Turkish intolerance. Many Muslims were influenced by Hindu philosophy. In daily life saint worship and other Hindu practices established themselves, and the caste system made itself felt in marriage arrangements.

There was much give and take, but no fusion or synthesis. In daily life there was much day-to-day tolerance and consideration, but behind it all was a permanent tension between the two ways of life. Indo-Persian culture spread a mantle of elegance over the whole of Indian aristocratic society, but Hinduism and Islam remained apart.

Southeast Asia: A Geohistorical Perspective
Horace Stone

Southeast Asia may be a coherent geohistorical area, but its multiple ethnicities, cultures, religions, and societies makes trying to understand it as a whole a difficult task. The common traits of all these peoples are as numerous as their differences. Historians have learned that the geographic position of any nation has direct and critical consequences for its historical development. In the case of southeast Asia, critical factors were the monsoons and its central position between the sealane trade routes of India and China. When the traditional land routes between Europe, the Middle East, and east Asia were no longer feasible and merchants (and missionaries) began to travel by sea, southeast Asia began to flourish. In the following excerpt, historian Horace Stone analyzes the importance of geography for the history of Southeast Asia.

> **Consider:** *How changes in technology and knowledge can affect trade routes; how changing trade routes affected broad historical developments in southeast Asia.*

SOURCE: Horace Stone, *From Malacca to Malaysia, 1400–1965* (London: George Harrop & Co., 1966), pp. 11–17.

Until about two thousand years ago trade between India and China was carried on along the Great Silk Road, but then two things happened which caused more and more traders to turn to the sea route. The first was that in South India the people had learnt how to build large junks, and had learnt the 'secret' of the monsoons. The second was that fierce tribes in the centre of Asia were making the Old Silk Road dangerous for travellers. . . .

When these traders began to come in great numbers they found that the Malay Peninsula was a barrier to them when they wanted to travel to China from India. At first they stopped at ports on the west coast and carried their goods across to the east coast by using the rivers as much as they could. At a port on the east coast they could take ship again for China. Traders then began to leave home as soon as the monsoon blew steadily in the direction they wanted to go. At first they would not think of sailing out of the sight of land, but as time went on the shape of the Bay of Bengal became known, and the sailors steered a course straight across. The important thing to remember is that as soon as the monsoon began to show signs of changing they had to find somewhere to stop. If the traders wanted to sail all the way to China from India they would have to wait until the north-east monsoon had stopped and the south-west monsoon had started again—at least six months. These ships sailed slowly, and soon the traders began to plan their voyages so that they had time to reach ports on the way where they could stop. The next step came when they did not try to make the whole journey, but only went as far as the Malay Peninsula, to one of the markets that grew up there, such as Tun-sun, Langkasuka, or even Pahang. . . .

As the number of traders using the sea route from India to China grew, so did the number of river-system kingdoms. . . . The first of these 'empires' was Fu-nan, at the mouth of the Mekong river, in modern Cambodia. It lasted until just after A.D. 600, in the period when traders mostly used the routes crossing the Malay Peninsula, and fell, at the time when they began to travel all the way by sea, to attacks from the north. . . .

Missionaries followed the traders, in this case both Brahmanist and Buddhist. . . . Although Buddhism died out in India, it took root in many parts of South-east Asia, particularly in Thailand and in Java, where the great buildings of the Boro-budur are a "textbook in stone of the Buddhist religion."

The Legends of the Trung Sisters: Women and Revolution in Vietnam

Keith Weller Taylor

The history of Vietnam is one of repeated struggle against foreign invasion. Most often the invaders were Chinese and then Mongols from the north, but there were others as well. Not surprisingly, the historical heroes are those who were the bravest in the battles for independence. No one is more revered for their efforts than the Trung Sisters who, in A.D. 40, led an army of 90,000 and defeated the Chinese invaders. When the Chinese returned successfully three years later, the sisters committed suicide. Their story, and the pride and inspiration derived from it, is one of Vietnam's most important historical tales. The fact that they were women in a society that degraded women makes the story that much more interesting. In the passage that follows, American historian Keith Weller Taylor describes how the Trung sisters' story is told in Vietnam. He quotes from original Vietnamese sources and focuses on the importance of these legends for Vietnam's historical perspective.

Consider: *How Vietnamese scholars dealt with the contradiction of wanting to glorify the deeds and lives of Vietnamese patriots and the uncomfortable fact that they were women; the problems with writing history when patriotism is an important sentiment.*

Trung Trac and Trung Nhi were women; they gave one shout and all the prefectures of Cuu-chan, Nhat-nam, and Ho-p'u, along with sixty-five strongholds beyond the passes, responded to them, and, establishing the nation, they proclaimed themselves queens as easily as turning over their hands, which shows that our land of Viet was able to establish a royal tradition. What a pity that, for a thousand years after this, the men of our land bowed their heads, folded their arms, and served the northerners; how shameful this is in comparison with the two Trung sisters, who were women! Ah, it is enough to make one want to die!

In this comment, Le Van Huu . . . expresses deep anguish over what he interprets as male passivity and female initiative.

A fifteenth-century poet echoed this feeling of shame that it was the women rather than the men who had led the nation in such a time of crisis:

All the male heroes bowed their heads in submission;
Only the two sisters proudly stood up to avenge the country.

SOURCE: Keith Taylor, *Birth of Vietnam* (Berkeley: Regents of the University of California and the University of California Press, 1983), pp. 335–339.

In the same vein, a popular historical poem of the seventeenth century declared:

> The Han emperor was extremely furious:
> This insignificant speck of a Giao-chi!
> And it was not even a man,
> But a mere girl who wielded the skill of a hero!

By the nineteenth century, the sentiment had become even sharper:

> A woman proudly led a young nation;
> Even the Han emperor heard of it and was terrified.

. . . This combined ideal of romantic love and patriotism became important in Vietnamese thought in recent centuries.

The woman who fights for her country while mourning the battlefield death of her husband or lover is a compelling image in Vietnam. . . .

For the Vietnamese themselves, the importance of the Trung sisters in later centuries became closely associated with the sisters' spirit cult and with their prominent position in the pantheon of national spirits able to give supernatural aid in time of need. Ngo Si Lien, the fifteenth-century historian, expressed an appreciation of their posthumous role:

> Trung Trac, angry with the tyrannical Han governor, raising her hand and giving a shout, all but united and restored our country. Her heroic courage was not limited to her lifetime achievements of establishing the nation and proclaiming herself queen, but after her death she also resisted misfortune, for, in times of flood or drought, prayers to her spirit have never gone unanswered. And it is the same with her younger sister. Because they had both the virtue of scholars and the temperament of warriors, there are no greater spirits in all of heaven and earth. Should not all great heroes nurture an attitude of upright hauteur such as they had?

The Trung sisters' posthumous cult was popular in the independence period. It is recorded that, during a drought, King Ly Anh-tong (1138–75) went to the Trung sisters' ancestral temple and ordered Buddhist priests to pray for rain. The prayers were soon answered. As it rained, the king fell asleep and dreamed of "two pretty-faced women with willowy eyebrows wearing green robes over red garments with red crowns and sashes, astride iron horses, passing by with the rain." Astonished, the king asked the women who they were, and they replied, "We are the two Trung sisters; we have been sent from Heaven to bring rain." When the king awoke, he immediately ordered repairs to their ancestral temple and established rituals for offering sacrifices. . . . Kings of the Tran dynasty also honored the Trung sisters with posthumous imperial appointments in the thirteenth and early fourteenth centuries.

A commentary on the Trung sisters survives from Cao Huy Dieu, a scholar writing in 1715:

The imperial court was far away; local officials were greedy and oppressive. At that time the country of one hundred sons was the country of the women of Lord To. The ladies used the female arts against their irreconcilable foe; skirts and hairpins sang of patriotic righteousness, uttered a solemn oath at the inner door of the ladies quarters, expelled the governor, and seized the capital—the territories from Cuu-chan to Ho-p'u again saw the light of day. Were they not grand heroines?

From antiquity, women have played a conspiratorial role. For example, Empress Lü of Han and Empress Wu of T'ang were able to command China with loud threatening noises, like wind and thunder, but the rightful heirs of the one great heritage of the everlasting First Emperor [Ch'in Shih Huang Ti] were cheated, taken advantage of, treated contemptibly, and ridden roughshod over by women using deception and intimidation, who, in the end, were simply criminals, "gone forever."

On the other hand, our two ladies brought forward an army of all the people, and, establishing a royal court that settled affairs in the territories of sixty-five strongholds, shook their skirts over the Hundred Yüeh. In the south, they were proclaimed sovereign lords, in the same class as Martial Emperor Trieu [Chao T'o] and Southern Emperor Ly [Ly Bi], inspiring later generations to call them queens. Still, they did not follow the advice of others. They died at the defeat of Cam-khe in the spirit of uprightness and in purity of mind, towering in the midst of the vast universe, bringing men to their feet sighing affectionately over their memory. Were those hens that crowed at dawn during Han and T'ang even worthy of being the hibiscus-capped, green-gowned attendants of our two Trung ladies?

As a good moral historian, the commentator could not resist offering the usual explanation for failure: "They did not follow the advice of others." Scholar-officials, and their ideals, thrived only when rulers followed their advice; consequently, this is a typical comment, which was also an admonition to rulers in the writer's day.
. . .

The Trung sisters were leaders of a ruling class and of the society dominated by this class. They thereby became the symbolic guardians of the cultural heritage of the society. The significance of their guardianship has grown with the passing centuries. . . .

[Later literature] shows . . . that if the Trung sisters had not resisted, there would be no Vietnamese nation today, that the uprising of A.D. 40 effectively "froze" the Dong-son heritage in a moment of heroic courage, insuring that it would not degenerate and invite the scorn of later generations. The Trung sisters were the last of the pre-Chinese popular leaders; their deeds echoed across the centuries of Chinese rule, calling the Vietnamese back to an ancient inheritance.

Chapter Questions

1. Drawing from sources in this chapter, what might the impact of Islam have been on Indian civilization? In what ways might Islam have conflicted with Hinduism and with the Indian social and political order?

2. Several sources in this and previous chapters deal with religious beliefs that, at various times, spread in the Indian subcontinent. Among these beliefs, Buddhism, Hinduism, Sikhism, and Islam were the most important. Are there any fundamental similarities between these religious beliefs? How might these religious beliefs provide insights into the general nature of Indian civilization during this period?

3. How might geographical factors, travel, trade, and cross-cultural contacts have been of importance in the history of India and southeast Asia? What were some of the outside forces that shaped developments in these areas? How was southeast Asia particularly vulnerable to such forces?

EIGHT

China and Japan, 500–1500

Between 500 and 1500, China solidified its institutional structures along the Confucian lines and reaffirmed its sense of being at the center of civilization. The Sui (581–618) and Tang (T'ang) (618–907) Dynasties reunified China after centuries of division and invasion following the fall of the Han Dynasty in 220. Art and culture thrived. Buddhism gained great influence, becoming the dominant state ideology during the Tang. Later, Confucianism was reestablished but was unable to totally purge Buddhist and Daoist ideas, so they were absorbed and co-opted, creating a form of belief called neo-Confucianism. During the Song (Sung) Dynasty (960–1279), Confucian notions of government became entrenched. The civil service bureaucracy was firmly fixed, as was Confucian education and the examination system. While a considerable portion of the budget was spent on military matters, much went into the bribing of enemies. The Song was further weakened by a split in 1127 into two separate geographic areas ruled by different factions. These weaknesses allowed the invading Mongols to defeat the Jin Dynasty in the north and eventually establish their rule (Yuan Dynasty, 1279–1368) over all of China. The Mongols adapted to China's social and administrative order and, in the process, their rule became Sinicized. When military needs were neglected, the Mongols were overthrown by the ethnic Chinese Ming Dynasty in 1368. While they supported Confucian teachings, the Ming rulers became isolationist, cutting China off from most of its neighbors. They did allow trade across their borders but were little interested in the business.

The period of 500–1500 was one of consolidation for the Japanese as they developed their own culture and institutions. The earliest accounts of Japan appear in Chinese histories and our first indigenous written records of this civilization stem from the Yamato Period (ca. 300–710), a time when Chinese and Korean immigrants brought Chinese culture and political systems, along with Buddhism, to Japan. Japan's indigenous religion was Shinto, a personal religion with patron gods and reverence for ancestors. The Heian Period (794–1185) saw the court nobility dominate the political and cultural life of Japan. They promoted the arts, spread Buddhism, and led extravagant life-styles. Land became concentrated in the hands of the aristocracy and Buddhist monasteries, which eventually led to the creation of huge estates. The Kamakura Period (1185–1333) witnessed the beginning of warrior (*samurai*) rule which, by the seventeenth century, was based on a warrior code of conduct (*bushido*). Japan was now governed by a Shogun (supreme military commander), a system that was to last until 1867. The Emperor, residing in Kyoto, became the nominal ruler and high priest of the Shinto religion. It was also during this time that an economic and political system emerged that was very similar to European feudalism. The Ashikaga Period (1336–1573) was to be known as a time of warring states. Feudalism became entrenched with large estates governed by powerful lords (*daimyo*). The economy grew as

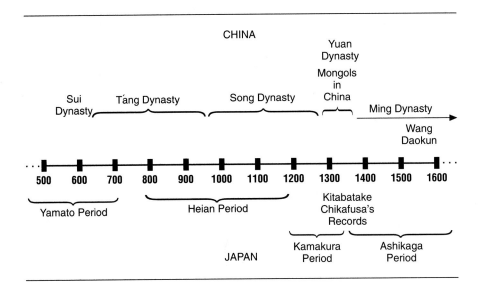

money began to be used and trade with China increased, leading to the establishment of commercial cities and market towns.

The sources in this chapter deal with some of the fundamental elements of Chinese and Japanese civilization during this period. For Japan, the focus is on the sense of uniqueness the Japanese fostered about themselves, particularly in comparison with China, and aspects of social history. For China, the focus is on the position of those who were not members of the elite, such as merchants, farmers, and members of rural society as a whole. In addition, some of the sources concern the family and the position of women in Japan and China.

PRIMARY SOURCES

The Biography of Zhu Jiefu (Chu Chieh-fu), Merchants in China
Wang Daokun (Wang Tao-k'un)

Historically, Chinese regarded merchants as being on the lowest rung of the social ladder because they produced nothing and made their money from other's labor. Yet at the same time the reality of Chinese society was that merchants, at least those with wealth, had, at times, enormous power. Nevertheless, they were always acutely aware of their social status and encouraged their sons to become scholars in order to escape their lowly social status.

This reading is a brief biography of a merchant drawn from a collection of such biographies compiled by Wang Daokun (Wang Tao-k'un, 1525–1593) who, although a scholar, was the grandson of salt merchants. The theme of this collection was to emphasize that even merchants could possess the moral and righteous values expected only of scholars.

> **Consider:** *How the merchant is positively portrayed, not only because he has business acumen which is not especially admired, but also because he possesses the Confucian virtues of morality and generosity which are admirable traits; how commercial disputes were handled.*

SOURCE: Patricia Buckley Ebrey, *Chinese Civilization and Society*, (New York: The Free Press, a Division of Macmillan, 1981).

Xing (Hsing) was a salt merchant who lived away from home at Wulin (Wu-lin). . . . [W]hen he returned home for his father-in-law's birthday, his primary wife became pregnant and gave birth to Jie Fu (Chieh-fu). In his early childhood, Chieh-fu lived in Wulin with his father and went to school there. . . . At the age of fourteen, he officially registered Wulin as his native place and was designated an official student of that place. Shortly thereafter, his father died at Wulin. His concubine took the money and hid it with some of her mother's relatives and would not return to her husband's hometown. Jie Fu wept day and night, saying, "However unworthy I may be, my late father was blameless." Finally the concubine arranged for the funeral and burial of her husband in his hometown. Thus, everything was done properly.

After the funeral, Jie Fu was short of funds. Since for generations his family had been in commerce, he decided not to suffer just to preserve his scholar's cap. Therefore he handed in his resignation to the academic officials and devoted himself to the salt business. He thoroughly studied the laws on salt merchandising and was always able to talk about the strengths and weaknesses of the law. . . . [A]ll the other salt merchants respected him as their leader.

. . . [S]alt affairs were handled by the Central Law Officer, who increased the taxes suddenly, causing great inconvenience for the merchants. They gathered in Jie Fu's house and asked him to serve as their negotiator. Jie Fu entered the office and stated the advantages and disadvantages of the new law eloquently in thousands of words. Leaning against his couch, the Central Law Officer listened to Jie Fu's argument and finally adopted his suggestion.

At that time, the merchants suffered greatly from two scoundrels who often took them to court in the hopes of getting bribes from them. During tense moments at trials the merchants usually turned to Jie Fu as their spokesman. Being lofty and righteous, he always disclosed the scoundrels' crimes and condemned them. The merchants thus esteemed Jie Fu for his virtue and wanted to give him a hundred taels of gold as a birthday present. But he protested: "Even if my acts have not been at the lofty level of a knight-errant, I did not do them for the sake of money." Thus, the merchants respected him even more and no longer talked about giving him money.

When there was a dispute among the merchants which the officials could not resolve, Jie Fu could always mediate it immediately. Even when one group would go to his house and demand his compliance with their views, he would still be able to settle the dispute by indirect and gentle persuasion. Hence, people both far and near followed each other, coming to ask him to be their arbitrator. Yet, after settling a dispute, Jie Fu would always step aside and never take credit himself.

The populace in Tunxi (T'un-hsi) city where Jie Fu lived was militant and litigious. When he returned home for his father's funeral, slanderous rumors were spread about him, but Jie Fu humbled himself and never tried to get back at the instigators. Later, when he grew rich rapidly, people became even more critical. Jie Fu merely behaved with even greater deference. . . .

Once Jie Fu bought a concubine in Wulin who bore a child after only a few months. His family was about to discard the child but Jie Fu upbraided them, saying, "I love my children dearly. How could I cause someone else's child to die in the gutter?" He brought the child up and educated him until he was able to support himself.

In the past many wealthy merchants in the eastern provinces had striven to associate themselves with the gentry. But for several years the merchants had been barely scraping by, limiting their access to such friendship. Yet when Jie Fu was in East Yue (Yüeh) for business he became acquainted with some members of the gentry there. He gained a reputation for his hospitality, and even when common people visited him they always received the best treatment. Some people came to rely upon Jie Fu as much as if he were a relative. If he did not offer them enough, they would complain, "You stupid little rich merchant, why are you so stingy with me?"

Jie Fu finally discontinued his salt business and ordered his son to pursue a different career. By that time he was already planning to retire to his hometown. Then a Central Law Officer who was appointed to inspect the salt business started to encourage secret informants. Soon Jie Fu was arrested, an enemy having laid a trap for him. However, the official could not find any evidence against him. But then He (Ho) whose son Jie Fu had once scolded, came forward to testify. Consequently, Jie Fu was found guilty. When the litigation against him was completed, he was sentenced to be a frontier guard at Dinghai (Ting-hai). The merchants said, in describing Jie Fu's case, "Beating the drum, the official seized a lamb and claimed it to be a tiger; pretending to net a big fish, he actually aimed at the big bird."

When Jie Fu received his sentence to enter the army, he controlled his feelings and immediately complied. His son, fearing his father would acquire a bad name, suggested that he send a petition to the Emperor. Jie Fu merely sighed and said, "Your father must have offended Heaven. The truth is that the Central Law Officer is a representative of his Heavenly Majesty, not that your father is falsely charged."

Frontier General Liu had heard of Jie Fu and therefore summoned him to work in his own encampment. At that time, a friend of the General's moved to Xindu (Hsin-tu) upon his retirement. The General sent Jie Fu to Xindu as his personal messenger but within a short time Jie Fu became seriously ill. He advised his son, Zhengmin (Cheng-min) "Your father's name has been recorded in the official labor records. Now he is about to die as a prisoner. Never let your father's example stop you from behaving righteously. Remember this." Then, at the age of sixty-five, he died.

The Lady Who Was a Beggar: Women in Chinese Society

Historically, Chinese viewed women as being decidedly inferior to men. They had no legal or civil rights. They could be, and frequently were, sold to men as wives or concubines. In Confucian thinking, sons were desirable since they stayed with their parents to look after them in their old age; girls left permanently to reside in and become part of their husband's household. In the countryside, to have a girl was colloquially referred to as having a "small happiness."

Additionally, families in northern China began to practice foot-binding which had begun during the Song (Sung) Dynasty (960–1279) among upperclass women. The practice, which quickly spread and was said to be sexually appealing to men, called for young girls to have their feet tightly bound to prevent growth. Women walked around on "lotus feet," which were stubs and were, for their entire lives, extraordinarily painful. It prevented mobility and encouraged dependency on men (Confucius taught that women should always obey men: fathers, husbands, sons) thereby reinforcing their inferior status.

What follows are excerpts from an anonymously written tale originally entitled "The Lady Who Was a Beggar" from the Song period. It is meant to convey how women are a marriage commodity always subject to the whims of their husbands and to be a frontal attack on the vice of snobbishness.

> **Consider:** *The roles of women and men portrayed in this story; the lessons the Chinese reader is to learn from this story; what this reveals about China's social structure.*

This is the "Song of the Rejected Wife," by a poet of former times. It likens the position of a wife to that of the blossom on the branch: the branch may be stripped of its blossom, but it will bloom again in the spring; the flowers, once they have left the branch, can never hope to return. Ladies, if you will listen to me, then serve your husband to the extent of your powers, share with him joy and sorrow, and follow one to the end. Unless you wish to lay up repentance in store, do not scorn poverty and covet riches, do not let your affections wander.

Let me tell you now of a famous statesman of the Han dynasty whose wife, in the days before he had made his name, left him. . . . In vain did she repent in later years. . . . His name was Zhu Maichen (Chu Mai-ch'en). . . . Of poor family, he had as yet found no opening, but lived, just himself and his wife, in a tumble-down cottage in a mean alley. Every day he would go into the hills and cut firewood to sell in the market-place for the few cash he needed to carry on existence. But he was addicted to study, and a book never left his hand. Though his back was bowed down under a weight of faggots, grasped in his hand would be a book. This

---

he would read aloud, rolling the phrases round his mouth, chanting as he walked along.

The townspeople were used to him, they knew Maichen was here with his firewood as soon as they heard the sound of intoning. . . . [T]here were always gangs of killers and street-urchins ready to make fun of him as he came along, intoning the classics with a load of faggots on his shoulders.

Maichen never noticed them. But one day when his wife went out of doors to draw water, she felt humiliated by the sight of these children making fun of Maichen with his burden. When he came home with his earnings she began to upbraid him: "If you want to study, then leave off selling firewood, and if you want to sell firewood then leave studying to others. When a man gets to your age, and in his right senses, that he should act like that and let children make fun of him! It's a wonder you don't die of shame."

"I sell firewood to save us from penury," replied Maichen, "and I study to win wealth and esteem. There is no contradiction there. Let them laugh!"

But his wife laughed at this. "If it's wealth and esteem you're after, then don't sell any more firewood. Who ever heard of a woodcutter becoming a mandarin? And yet you talk all this nonsense."

"Wealth and poverty, fame and obscurity, each has its time," said Maichen. "A fortune-teller told me my rise would begin when I had passed fifty." . . .

"Fortune-teller indeed!" said his wife. "He could see you were simple and deliberately made fun of you. You should pay no heed to him. By the time you're fifty you'll be past carrying firewood. Death from starvation, that's what's in store for you. . . . If you don't do as I say and throw those books away, I'm determined I won't stay with you. . . ."

"I am forty-three this year," said Maichen. "In seven years' time I shall be fifty. The long wait is behind us, you have only to be patient for a little longer. If you desert me now in such a callous fashion you will surely regret it in years to come."

"The world's not short of woodcutters," his wife rejoined. "What shall I have to regret? . . . It will count as a good deed if you release me now, for you will have saved my life."

Maichen realized that his wife had set her heart on leaving him and wouldn't be gainsaid. So he said, with a sigh, "Very well, then I only hope that your next husband will be a better man than Zhu Maichen." . . .

By the time Zhu Maichen reached his fiftieth birthday the Han Emperor Wudi (Wu-ti) had issued his edict summoning men of worth to serve their country. Maichen went to the Western Capital, submitted his name and took his place among those awaiting appointment. Meanwhile his abilities were brought to the notice of the Emperor by a fellow-townsman, Yanzhu (Yen Chu). Reflecting that Zhu Maichen must have intimate knowledge of the people of his native place and of their condition, the Emperor appointed him Prefect of Huiji (Hui-chi) and he rode off to take up his appointment.

Learning of the impending arrival of the New Prefect, the officials of Huiji mobilized great numbers of men to put the roads in order. Among these coolies was Zhu Maichen's marital successor; and at this man's side, attending to his food, was Maichen's ex-wife, barefoot and with matted hair. When the woman heard the din of the approach of the new Prefect and his suite, she tried to get a glimpse of him—and saw her former husband, Zhu Maichen.

Maichen also, from his carriage, caught sight of her and recognized his ex-wife. He summoned her and seated her in one of the carriages of his suite. . . .

His ex-wife went on kotowing and confessing. She had eyes but no pupils and had not recognized his worth; she would wish to return as humble slave or concubine; as such she would serve him to the end of her days. Zhu Maichen ordered a bucket of water to be brought and splashed on the floor. Then he told his wife: "If this spilt water can go back into the bucket, then you can come back to me." . . .

. . . Humiliated beyond measure, when she reached her piece of land she jumped in the nearby river and drowned herself.

Secret Societies in China

Throughout Chinese history, the farmers have established secret societies for a variety of purposes: for protection from the government and criminals, for religious purposes, for mutual help, and for political ends. Most importantly, for the ordinary people, these were groups in which they felt safe and supported against external forces to which they ordinarily felt vulnerable. One of the largest of these societies was the Hong (Hung) Society, organized in the middle of the seventeenth century, probably to try to overthrow the Manchu Qing (Ch'ing) Dynasty in order to foster the return of ethnic Chinese rulers. The Hong Society believed in patriotism, fraternity, chivalry, and traditional morality. Like other secret societies, it had secret initiation rites and ceremonies. The reading which follows is from these secret rituals, taken when a secret society member is initiated, and conveys the ideals and attitudes of the members.

> **Consider:** *How these societies could be useful to those joining them; potential problems facing such societies.*

We, sharing fortune and misfortune, are dedicated to the restoration of the Ming dynasty which belonged to Heaven and earth and all existence to the destruction of the barbarian bandits [the Manchus], and to waiting for the true mandate of Heaven. . . .

. . . After entering the Hong (Hung) Society, you must be of one body and one mind, each helping the other, and never allowing any distinction between one another to be made.

Tonight we worship Heaven as our father, earth as our mother, the sun as our

---

SOURCE: *Sources of Chinese Tradition,* Theodore deBary, et al., eds., (Columbia University Press, New York, 1960) pp. 652–656. Reprinted by permission of the publishers.

brother, and the moon as our sister. We also worship before our First Founding Father, the Five Founding Fathers, Ten-thousand Cloud Dragon, and others, and all spiritual beings of the Hung family. As we kneel in worship before the altar tonight, our minds and spirit are suddenly pure and clear. Each shall cut his finger, suck his blood, and take the oath of living and dying together. . . .

. . . Each shall show his sincerity and take the Thirty-six Oaths:

1. From the time I enter the Hong Society, your parents are my parents, your brothers and sisters are my brothers and sisters, your wife is my sister-in-law, and your sons and nephews are my sons and nephews. If I violate this oath, may I be destroyed by the five thunders. . . .

3. Whenever any of the Hong family Brothers in the provinces or abroad arrives, . . . he must be received, accommodated for the night, and given meals. . . .

5. Affairs of the Hong family may not be divulged or confided to one's father, son, brother, or relative. . . .

6. Brothers of the Hong family may not secretly act as leads for the arrest of a fellow Brother. Even if there is accumulated enmity, the matter should be presented to the Brethren for a just settlement, and by no means should hatred be retained in one's heart. . . .

7. Whenever a fellow Brother is in financial difficulty, a Brother must come to his assistance. He must do his best to provide the fellow Brother with money for his expenses or fare, whether the amount is large or small. . . .

9. If a Brother violates a fellow Brother's wife, daughter, or sister, may he be destroyed by the five thunders.

10. If a Brother appropriates a fellow Brother's money or property [entrusted to him for safe keeping], or deliberately fails to deliver the same as requested, may he perish under 10,000 swords.

11. If a Brother does not devote all his mind and energy when a fellow Brother entrusts his wife or children to his care, or important matters to his handling, may he be destroyed by the five thunders.

12. If anyone joining the Hong Society this evening lies about the date and hour of his birth, may he be destroyed by the five thunders. . . .

15. A Brother must not force a fellow Brother to sell him goods or force him out in order to make a sale. . . .

18. If a Brother is captured by a government official, he must bear the consequences for what he has done himself and must not involve a fellow Brother because of any enmity. . . .

19. When a fellow Brother is murdered or arrested, or when he has gone away for a long time, and the family he has left behind becomes destitute, a Brother must take steps to render assistance. . . .

20. When a fellow Brother is abused by others, a Brother must go forward to help him if he is in the right or arbitrate if he is in the wrong. . . .

23. A Brother must not fabricate stories or twist the words of fellow Brothers so as to set them apart. . . .
26. When a Brother's own brother is involved in a dispute or lawsuit with a fellow Brother of the Hong family, the Brother must try to reconcile them and must not render aid to either side. . . .
28. A Brother must not be jealous of the money or things acquired by a fellow Brother or plot to share his spoil. . . .
31. A Brother must not oppress people because of the power or the huge membership of the Hong family, and, what is more, he must not do violence and behave like a despot. . . .
34. A Brother must not accept or buy a fellow Brother's wife or concubine as his own spouse. Neither may he commit adultery with them. . . .
35. A Brother must be very careful in his speech and may not carelessly use the words, phrases, and other secrets of the Hong family, so as to prevent outsiders from penetrating our mysteries and to avoid inviting trouble with them. . . .
36. Whether a Brother is a scholar, a farmer, an artisan, or a merchant, he should attend to his own occupation. Having joined the Hong Society, the first emphasis must be loyalty to the Society and devotion to the Brethren, and the cultivation of fellowship with all Brothers within the four seas. When the time of uprising comes, all Brothers must be of one mind and united effort to destroy the Manchu role, restore the Ming empire as soon as possible, and avenge the burning of the Five Early Founding Fathers.
. . .

The Records of the Legitimate Succession of the Divine Sovereigns: Japanese Uniqueness
Kitabatake Chikafusa

One of the most central themes of Japanese culture is the teaching of Japanese uniqueness. The Japanese creation myth has the Sun Goddess, Amaterasu Omikami, creating the Japanese islands and people before anything else. Part of the reason for this quest for originality can be attributed to the desire of the Japanese to have something indigenous to counter having been so strongly influenced by Confucianism and Buddhism.

A good example of this theme can be found in The Records of the Legitimate Succes-

SOURCE: *Sources of Japanese Tradition,* Ryusaku Tsunda, et al., eds., (Columbia University Press, New York, 1961) pp. 274–280. Reprinted by permission of the publishers.

sion of the Divine Sovereigns, *the most important document to come out of medieval Japan. Written by Kitabatake Chikafusa (1293–1354) it was meant to reinforce the idea that Japan is a unique culture and that even Confucianism and Buddhism came from Shinto teachings, the indigenous religion of Japan. Part of its argument is based on the universally accepted notion that all Japanese Emperors have come from the same lineage. That, says the author, is proof of Japan's greatness.*

> **Consider:** *The arguments used to support Japanese uniqueness and primacy; the need for a people to have their own unique cultural roots, especially when those roots are borrowed from other teachings as in the case of Japan.*

Japan is the divine country. The heavenly ancestor it was who first laid its foundations, and the Sun Goddess left her descendants to reign over it forever and ever. This is true only of our country, and nothing similar may be found in foreign lands. That is why it is called the divine country. . . .

In the Age of the Gods, Japan was known as the "ever-fruitful land of reed-covered plains and luxuriant ricefields." . . . It is also called the country of the great eight islands. This name was given because eight islands were produced when the Male Deity and the Female Deity begot Japan. It is also called Yamato, which is the name of the central part of the eight islands. . . .

. . . Japan is the Land of the Sun Goddess, or it may have thus been called because it is near the place where the sun rises. . . .

. . . [S]ince Japan is a separate continent, distinct from both India and China and lying in a great ocean, it is the country where the divine illustrious imperial line has been transmitted. . . .

The creation of heaven and earth must everywhere have been the same, for it occurred within the same universe, but the Indian, Chinese, and Japanese traditions are each different. . . .

In China, nothing positive is stated concerning the creation of the world even though China is a country which accords special importance to the keeping of records. . . . In other works they speak of heaven, earth, and man as having begun in an unformed, undivided state, much as in the accounts of our Age of the Gods. . . .

The beginnings of Japan in some ways resemble the Indian descriptions, telling as it does of the world's creation from the seed of the heavenly gods. However, whereas in our country the succession to the throne has followed a single undeviating line since the first divine ancestor, nothing of the kind has existed in India. . . . China is also a country of notorious disorders. Even in ancient times, when life was simple and conduct was proper, the throne was offered to wise men, and no single lineage was established. . . . [S]ome of the rulers rose from the ranks of the plebeians, and there were even some of barbarian origin who usurped power. . . .

Only in our country has the succession remained inviolate, from the beginning of heaven and earth to the present. It has been maintained within a single lineage, and even when, as inevitably has happened, the succession has been transmitted collaterally, it has returned to the true line. This is due to the ever-renewed Divine Oath, and makes Japan unlike all other countries.

Tales of Uji: Dishonest Priests

Almost every culture has a tradition of oral literature that expresses the feelings and attitudes of the common people. Since elite cultural forms are withheld from the mass of the population, people resort to oral tales or music to express themselves. Often this litera-ture expresses disdain toward the elite of that society.

In Japan, A Collection of Tales from Uji *and* A Collection of Tales Old and New *represent the best of this tradition. It is believed that these collections date from the Kamakura period of the early thirteenth century, but some are clearly from the period prior to 1070 and are considered to be reflections of life among the people during the Heian period. This example is from the* Tales of Uji *and is meant to portray the people's dislike for dishonest priests.*

> **Consider:** *What this reveals about the attitudes of the common people in Japan; the importance of stories or tales for the popular culture of a society.*

HOW A PRIEST PUT THE MAGIC INCANTATION
OF THE BODHISATTVA ZUIGU[1] INTO HIS FOREHEAD

Again, long ago a very dignified-looking mountain priest came into a certain man's house and stood outside the retainers' duty-room, in a small courtyard enclosed by a screen. He had an air of great consequence, with an axe slung on his back and a conch-shell trumpet at his belt and in his hand a staff tipped with rings. When the retainers asked who he was, he replied, 'I spent some time on Hakusan, then I went to the Sacred Peak and I intended to perform devotions there for another two thousand days, but my food gave out and so I have come to beg alms. Please inform your master.' As he stood there, they observed that in the middle of his forehead he had a scar about two inches long extending up towards his hair, still newly healed and reddish. When one of the retainers wanted to know how he came to have this scar on his forehead, he assumed a tone of great dignity and said, 'That is where I put in the magic incantation of the Bodhisattva Zuigu.' 'What a wonderful thing', said the retainers to each other. 'You see many people who have cut off a finger or a toe, say, but who would have expected to come across someone who has broken open his forehead and put in the incantation of Zuigu?'

SOURCE: D. E. Mills, *A Collection of Tales from Uji. A Study and Translation of Uji Shui Monogatari* (Cambridge: Cambridge University Press, 1970), pp. 141–143.

[1] 'Zuigu' means "according to prayer." Bodhisattva Zuigu is one who sees that all prayers are answered.

Just then a young retainer of about sixteen or seventeen came running out, and taking one look at the priest, he burst out, 'Don't make me laugh! A fine one you'd be to put the Zuigu incantation into your forehead! You used to go and sneak into that house belonging to the metal-founder, directly to the east of young Gō's place in the Seventh Ward, and go to bed with the wife—till last summer the metal-founder came home and discovered you in bed with her. You didn't stop for anything, just bolted off up the street heading west. In front of my place you were cornered and had your head split open with a hoe. I saw it myself!' His words quite shocked the retainers, but the priest's face showed no sign of concern whatever. With an air of great solemnity and innocence, he said, 'That's when I seized the opportunity to put it in.' The whole crowd was convulsed with laughter, and the priest took advantage of this to slip away.

Lessons for Women
Ban Zhao (Pan Chao)

Every society determines customs of behavior or rules based on the historical develop-ment of that society, its religious and social beliefs, its socioeconomic condition, and so on. China had its share of these rules and none were more oppressive than those for women, since women were viewed as inferiors in traditional Chinese belief, in Confucian teach-ings, and in Buddhist belief.

In the first century A.D., *China's foremost female scholar, imperial historian, poet, and tutor of an empress, Ban Zhao, wrote out a series of "Lessons" that women were expected to follow. These "lessons" became the traditional standard of behavior for centuries.*

> **Consider:** *What these rules say about woman's perceived position in traditional Chinese society; what a set of rules for men might look like.*

HUMILITY

. . . Let a woman modestly yield to others; let her respect others; let her put others first, herself last. Should she do something good, let her not mention it; should she do something bad, let her not deny it. Let her bear disgrace; let her even endure when others speak or do evil to her. Always let her seem to tremble and to fear. (When a woman follows such maxims as these,) then she may be said to humble herself before others.

Let a woman retire late to bed, but rise early to duties; let her not dread tasks by day or by night. Let her not refuse to perform domestic duties whether easy or difficult. That which must be done, let her finish completely, tidily, and syste-

---

SOURCE: Nancy Lee Swann, *Pan Chao: Foremost Woman Scholar of China* (The Century Co., 1932), pp. 83–88.

matically. (When a woman follows such rules as these,) then she may be said to be industrious.

Let a woman be correct in manner and upright in character in order to serve her husband. Let her live in purity and quietness (of spirit), and attend to her own affairs. Let her love not gossip and silly laughter. Let her cleanse and purify and arrange in order the wine and the food for the offerings to the ancestors. (When a woman observes such principles as these,) then she may be said to continue ancestral worship.

No woman who observes these three (fundamentals of life) has ever had a bad reputation or has fallen into disgrace. If a woman fail to observe them, how can her name be honored; how can she but bring disgrace upon herself?

HUSBAND AND WIFE

If a husband be unworthy then he possesses nothing by which to control his wife. If a wife be unworthy, then she possesses nothing with which to serve her husband. If a husband does not control his wife, then the rules of conduct manifesting his authority are abandoned and broken. If a wife does not serve her husband, then the proper relationship (between men and women) and the natural order of things are neglected and destroyed. As a matter of fact the purpose of these two (the controlling of women by men, and the serving of men by women) is the same. . . .

WOMANLY QUALIFICATIONS

A woman (ought to) have four qualifications: (1) womanly virtue; (2) womanly words; (3) womanly bearing; and (4) womanly work. Now what is called womanly virtue need not be brilliant ability, exceptionally different from others. Womanly words need be neither clever in debate nor keen in conversation. Womanly appearance requires neither a pretty nor a perfect face and form. Womanly work need not be work done more skillfully than that of others.

To guard carefully her chastity; to control circumspectly her behavior; in every motion to exhibit modesty; and to model each act on the best usage, this is womanly virtue.

To choose her words with care; to avoid vulgar language; to speak at appropriate times; and not to weary others (with much conversation), may be called the characteristics of womanly words.

To wash and scrub filth away; to keep clothes and ornaments fresh and clean; to wash the head and bathe the body regularly, and to keep the person free from disgraceful filth, may be called the characteristics of womanly bearing.

With whole-hearted devotion to sew and to weave; to love not gossip and silly laughter; in cleanliness and order (to prepare) the wine and food for serving guests, may be called the characteristics of womanly work.

These four qualifications characterize the greatest virtue of a woman. No woman can afford to be without them. In fact they are very easy to possess if a woman only treasure them in her heart. The ancients had a saying: "Is Love afar off? If I desire love, then love is at hand!" So can it be said of these qualifications.

VISUAL SOURCES

Riverside Scene in Qing Ming (Ch'ing Ming) Festival
Zhang Zeduan (Chang Tse-tuan)

From a historical perspective, one of the more important art works from early China is "Riverside Scene on Qing Ming (Ch'ing Ming) Festival" by Zhang Zeduan (Chang Tse-tuan) which was drawn during the Northern Song (Sung) Dynasty (960–1127 A.D.). This enormous drawing is over seventeen feet long and depicts, in almost photographic fashion, one to one-and-a-half miles of the main streets of Bianjing (Pien Ching; modern day Kaifeng, the imperial capital at the time). Stretching from the rural countryside through the market streets to the outer walls of the city, the original scroll portrays 770 people, 90

Photo 8–1

"Social Sciences in China," No. 4, December 1981, Beijing, China.

animals, over 100 houses and 20 boats, leaving us with a vivid picture of life in a bustling market town of one million people during the tenth century. Using this scroll, along with written accounts of the period, historians can determine a great deal about population density, the nature of the economy (the drawing includes a wide array of merchants, artisans, peddlers, beggars, storytellers, prostitutes, street musicians, wealthy buyers, etc.), the clothing styles, the types of transportation used, and far more.

> **Consider:** *What this reveals about China's society and economy during this period.*

The Glory of the Samurai

No single group in Japanese life has attracted more attention than the samurai. To this day the samurai are major subjects for Japanese films, television, comic books, and fiction and are cited as an analogy for Japanese business prowess. "Samurai" in Japanese means "one who serves," and total loyalty to a leader was one of the most important required attributes. Samurai armies grew until the middle of the twelfth century when they took over the government of Japan by usurping the rule of the Emperor. Samurai then ruled, in one form or another, for the next seven hundred years.

Samurai deeds were glorified throughout Japan, and one of the favorite forms of this

Photo 8–2

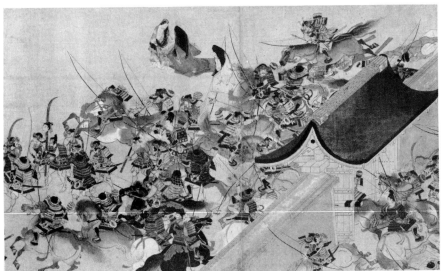

Fenollosa-Weld Collection, Museum of Fine Arts, Boston.

storytelling was lengthy scrolls on which were painted the depictions of samurai glory.
This particular example was done in the middle of the thirteenth century (Kamakura
period) and depicts the Heiji Insurrection that brought the samurai to power a century
earlier. It is a handscroll, ink and colors on paper, 41.3 cm. by 699.7 cm.

Consider: *How samurai values are represented in this painting.*

SECONDARY SOURCES

Daily Life in China in the Thirteenth Century
Jacques Gernet

In many ways life for the vast majority of Chinese—those 80 to 85 percent of the popula-
tion who lived in the rural areas—did not change for millennia. Art, literature, scientific
discovery, and early foreign contacts affected only the scholar-literati class and the small
number of urban residents. Nevertheless, there was a small measure of change as the
centuries progressed. In this reading, French sinologist Jacques Gernet describes daily life
during the middle of the thirteenth century.

Consider: *The nature of Chinese rural life; the ways in which collectivism played*
a role in rural life; how the political and legal systems worked in rural areas.

Winter was the only slack season. The men busied themselves with winnowing,
the women with weaving. They stayed up late and sometimes joined company to
save oil for the lamps. The rearing of silkworms and weaving were delicate and
absorbing tasks. As for the children, they were employed throughout the year in
looking after the buffaloes, feeding the animals in the yard (pigs, chickens, and
sometimes edible dogs), collecting firewood, which was always scarce, and fetching
water from the well. But in some villages there were schools for them in the
winter where they learnt the rudiments of writing and doing sums.

Peasant life, usually laborious and monotonous, did also have its moments of
relaxation and jollity. Such were the annual festivals, chief of which were the New

Source: Jacques Gernet, Trans., *Daily Life in China on the Eve of the Mongol Invasion*,
Copyright © 1962 by George & Allen Unwin, Ltd, Copyright © 1959 by Librairie Hachette.

Year festival, about the end of January or beginning of February, and that for the sacrifices to the god of the soil. The great festival of the god of the soil fell at the end of August or early in September. Its official date was the fifth day marked by the cyclical sign *wu* following the 'establishment of autumn', a date in the solar calendar corresponding approximately to August 7th. The villagers gathered together near a local sanctuary to watch games, theatrical entertainments, clowning and juggling, sometimes performed by wandering players specially hired for such great occasions. Pigs and chickens were killed, rice of superior quality was eaten, and everyone got drunk. The poorest among them borrowed in order to be able to celebrate in a fitting manner these special days of the year which influenced the fortune and happiness of everyone.

There was very little contact between the government and the rural population. The sub-prefect lived in town, within a fortified citadel containing his residence, the administrative offices, the audience-hall and the prison. He was a distant being who was hardly ever seen and who was surrounded by an aura of dazzling prestige. The State for its part did not interfere in the life of the peasant communities, or rather only did so for essential purposes; collecting taxes, collecting men for the forced labour that was demanded for public works, when sometimes as many as several hundred thousand men were required, and for taking defensive measures against subversive movements. For these, villages and families were held collectively responsible—and sometimes organized into groups of families with collective responsibility—so that whenever a rebellion broke out anywhere, the repression was terrible.

The principle underlying the whole administrative system in China was that above all, peace must reign. There was to be no stirring up of trouble: a sub-prefect who allowed disturbances to arise in his area of jurisdiction was a bad administrator, and it was he who was blamed, whatever the origin of the disturbances might have been. His immediate superiors ran a considerable risk of having their promotion retarded. From another point of view, the people administered were hesitant about referring to the public authorities for settling their differences, and it was only when all other solutions (compromise or arbitration) had failed that they presented themselves before the court of justice held by the sub-prefect. An accused person was immediately thrown into prison: even an innocent person wrongfully accused was guilty of having disturbed the peace of the locality and the tranquillity of the judge. Besides, since the idea of accusing him had arisen, his innocence was not complete. As for the accuser, he too was regarded with the greatest suspicion. Furthermore, it was expensive to have recourse to public justice, since an accusation could not be laid without making the usual offerings to the judge: it was a matter of decorum.

Chinese justice insisted on certain kinds of objective proof (a thief could not be condemned if the object stolen had not been found, nor a supposed murderer if there was no trace of violence on the corpse), but at the same time it was one of the most cruel systems of justice that have ever existed. All the penalties consisted of extremely severe corporal punishments. The accused were kept in prison for lengthy periods in wretched conditions. They received no nourishment except from their relations, who, however, were needed for work in the fields. Torture (whipping, beating, the iron collar and manacles) was normally employed to induce recalcitrant prisoners to confess. Also miscarriage of justice was comparatively frequent. In short, it was a system of justice apparently designed to discourage people from acquiring a taste for legal proceedings, and it is easy to understand why the peasants preferred to settle their quarrels among themselves, either by coming to an agreement, or by arbitration. Only the most serious cases came before the official courts of justice.

Collective responsibility, the cruelty of repressive measures, the authority of the elders of the village and the local district, the authority of heads of families, village solidarity and the horror of legal proceedings—these are the factors which explain why peace reigned in the countryside. Only a great famine or the most crying and widespread injustice stirred up troops of rebels. It was troops of this kind, inflamed with messianic hopes and grown to the size of veritable armies, that usually put an end to dynasties and sometimes swept one of their leaders to the throne of the Son of Heaven.

The Imperial Examination System
Ichisada Miyazaki

One of the central purposes of Confucian thought was to bring order out of chaos. Confucius taught that order could be accomplished through proper behavior, a widely accepted social stratification, and an education that taught people their proper place in society and how they should behave. Given these beliefs, it is not surprising that a system would be devised whereby government officials would be selected through merit based on educational accomplishments. This organized civil service, run by officials who had succeeded in passing a rigorous examination system based exclusively on the teachings of Confucius and various commentaries, developed during the Sui Dynasty (581–618) and was further developed during the Tang (T'ang) and Song (Sung) Dynasties that followed. It was not to be dismantled until 1905. In this selection, Ichisada Miyazaki analyzes China's civil service examinations and their connections to political and social aspects of China over the centuries.

> **Consider:** *What groups this system favored; who was excluded from the exams, in practice if not formally; why the system was introduced.*

Competition for a chance to take the civil service examinations began, if we may be allowed to exaggerate only a little, even before birth. On the back of many a

---

SOURCE: Ichisada Miyazaki, *China's Examination Hell. The Civil Service Examinations of Imperial China* Conrad Schirokaver, trans. (Weatherhill, New York and Tokyo, 1976) pp. 208–214.

woman's copper mirror the five-character formula "Five Sons Pass the Examinations" expressed her heart's desire to bear five successful sons. Girls, since they could not take the examinations and become officials but merely ran up dowry expenses, were no asset to a family; a man who had no sons was considered to be childless. . . .

Prenatal care began as soon as a woman was known to be pregnant. She had to be very careful then, because her conduct was thought to have an influence on the unborn child, and everything she did had to be right. She had to sit erect, with her seat and pillows arranged in exactly the proper way, to sleep without carelessly pillowing her head, . . . to abstain from strange foods, . . . to avoid unpleasant colors, and she spent her leisure listening to poetry. . . . These preparations were thought to lead to the birth of an unusually gifted boy. . . .

. . . From the very beginning he was instructed almost entirely in the classics, since mathematics could be left to merchants, while science and technology were relegated to the working class. A potential grand official must study the Four Books, the Five Classics, and other Confucian works, . . . to compose poems and write essays. . . . [Q]uestions in civil service examinations did not go beyond these areas of competence.

When he was just a little more than three years old, a boy's education began at home. . . . Formal education began at about seven years of age. . . . Boys from families that could afford the expense were sent to a temple, village, communal, or private school staffed by former officials who had lost their positions, or by old scholars who had repeatedly failed the examinations as the years slipped by. Sons of rich men and powerful officials often were taught at home by a family tutor in an elegant small room. . . . Instruction centered on the Four Books, beginning with the *Analects,* and the process of learning was almost entirely a matter of sheer memorization. . . .

Along with the literary curriculum, the boys were taught proper conduct, such as when to use honorific terms, how to bow to superiors and to equals, and so forth. . . . It was usual for a boy to enter school at the age of eight and to complete the general classical education at fifteen. . . .

Did the examination system serve a useful purpose? . . . The purpose of instituting the examinations . . . was to strike a blow against government by the hereditary aristocracy. . . .

The important point in China, as in Japan, was that the power of the aristocracy seriously constrained the emperor's power to appoint officials. . . . This was the situation when the Sui emperor, exploiting the fact that he had reestablished order and that his authority was at its height, ended the power of the aristocracy to become officials merely by virtue of family status. . . . He achieved this revolution when he enacted the examination system . . . and provided that only its graduates were to be considered qualified to hold governmental office. . . .

. . . The examination system was immeasurably progressive, containing as it did a superb idea the equal of which could not be found anywhere else in the world at that time.

Women in Early Japan
Jeffrey P. Mass

One of the most intriguing aspects of early Japanese history is the belief that originally women played important roles in that nation's politics and society. It is further believed that it was only with the introduction of Confucianism, and later Buddhism, both of which taught that women must be always inferior and subservient, that the status of Japanese women declined.

This reading explores the status of women in eary medieval Japan, prior to the diminution of their status, in relation to inheritance. In that way, the author Jeffrey P. Mass, tries to determine the situation women found themselves in during the Heian Period (794–1185).

> **Consider:** *The importance of inheritance and the rules governing them as they relate to the status of individuals: ways in which women's roles were limited; ways in which women and men were equal legally.*

We do not know how families were organized or how they transmitted property in the era before writing was introduced into Japan. Nevertheless, historians have offered a variety of hypotheses on these subjects, most emphasizing a communal system of possession and/or matrilineal descent patterns. The possibility of a matriarchy in pre-seventh-century Japan is perhaps the hub of this debate. Whatever the case, women were not inferior to men in matters involving property—a condition that might have continued if not for revolutionary changes within the polity. . . .

. . . In his study of Heian marriage practices McCullough has correctly observed that marriages were easily formed and easily broken, that polygamy was common, and that husbands and wives regularly lived apart or lived with the wife's family. Yet despite these clear obstacles to intimate, lasting relationships, it is obvious that gratitude and affection did at times induce husbands to bestow property on their wives. . . .

The reverse, however, was rare. We find almost no instances of wives leaving property to their husbands, even though women (through their parents) were inheritors of land. A major reason for this is that widows were more common than widowers, though the bias obviously ran deeper than that. In the only clear-cut case of a conveyance to a husband, the wife's rationale began with the absence of children. . . . By contrast, a husband who was also a father might favor a wife in addition to children.

It follows from the foregoing that there was little concept of community property issuing from a marriage. No land fell to the survivor unless explicitly devised, and no releases bore both a mother's and a father's signature. . . . Thus, property

SOURCE: Jeffrey P. Mass, *Lordship and Inheritance in Early Medieval Japan* (Stanford University Press, 1989), pp. 9, 15–18.

was received independently by each of the partners and also disposed of that way. Whether it might be managed by the husband during the course of the marriage is a different issue. . . . But even if property was so managed, one would need to prove deceit—as opposed to mere convenience—to make the case for some basic inequality. Joint management, like a merging of incomes, might just as easily have implied cooperation as something more sinister.

It follows, then, that it was only in the event of children that assets—by way of separate releases—might actually be combined. At the same time, with the emphasis so clearly on independent possession, no well-developed concept of dowry appeared, if by dowry we mean a marriage portion consisting of property. A bridegroom might expect to receive his wardrobe, residence, and a father-in-law to promote his career. But no land would change hands—at the point of the marriage or later. Brides did of course bring property into their marriages, but these were their own lands—daughters' shares, not wives'.

In fact, women were daughters and sisters before they were wives, mothers, and widows. There is no doubt that the Heian Japanese adhered to the sound principle that preference in inheritance be given to close women before distant males. This meant that a father or mother would normally bequeath to a daughter before a brother, nephew, or grandson. Moreover, daughters who inherited from fathers or mothers regularly received these legacies free of encumbrances. Much as in the case of wives who inherited, they were free to do with the legacies as they pleased. . . .

Despite the advantageous position of women in their familial roles, it remains true that they could not hold government office. Moreover, whereas courtier women could at least possess proprietorships or custodianships over estates, their provincial counterparts normally held no landed *shiki* whatever. These were both serious handicaps, since it meant that women could neither be appointed to nor inherit office; they were able to buy land or to have it released to them, but they could not enjoy the most prestigious and lucrative sources of wealth. At the same time, women were commonly referred to in documents as someone's wife or (especially) daughter, though their surnames were never those of their husbands. It was their brothers who received the best inheritances—generally even from their mothers. Thus, whereas women could become great landowners, their political power was limited.

The Maritime Expeditions
Philip Snow

Traditionally, Chinese rulers have had little interest in activities outside their borders unless it affected them directly. Since they considered their civilization superior, they felt no need to search out others and assumed others would come to them.

SOURCE: Philip Snow, *The Star Raft: China's Encounter with Africa* (New York: Grove Press, 1988). Copyright © 1988.

There were exceptions, however. The founding emperor of the Ming Dynasty made a concerted effort to reestablish tributary ties to China's immediate neighbors. The second Ming Emperor, Yong Le (Yung-lo, 1403–1424) went further, commissioning a Muslim eunuch named Zheng He (Cheng Ho) to mount seven expeditions over twenty-eight years that traveled to southeast Asia, India, the Arabian Gulf, and as far as the east coast of Africa. A handful of Chinese even reached Mecca.

These extraordinary expeditions, almost a century before the Europeans began to traverse the world, was possible because of the advanced state of Chinese navigational and nautical technology. Unfortunately, Chinese rulers were not very interested in exploring the world and after the Emperor's death, China turned inward once again, never again to attempt a similar feat.

Philip Snow, in this excerpt from his book TheStar Raft: China's Encounter with Africa, *compares Zheng He's expeditions with his more famous counterpart's, Christopher Columbus, many decades later.*

> **Consider:** *The capacity of the Chinese state to mount such an expedition; how this capacity was at variance with the willingness of the Chinese officials to use their technology; the difference between the European urge to search out other lands and the Chinese urge to have other people come to them.*

In 1414 a Chinese fleet pushed into the western Indian Ocean. It was commanded by Zheng He, Grand Eunuch of the Three Treasures. Three times already since 1405 Zheng He and his ships had descended on the ports of Indochina, Indonesia, south-west India and Ceylon. Now they were advancing into more distant regions, covering in the process a larger total quantity of water than any seafaring people had before.

Zheng He was the Chinese Columbus. He has become for China, as Columbus has for the West, the personification of maritime endeavour. Yet he differed from his Western counterpart in a number of major ways. Three-quarters of a century before Columbus crossed the Atlantic, this Ming dynasty admiral had at his disposal resources which make the Genoese explorer look like an amateur. Columbus had three ships. They had one deck apiece, and together weighed a total of 415 tons. Zheng He had sixty-two galleons, and more than a hundred auxiliary vessels. The largest galleons had three decks on the poop alone, and each of them weighed about 1,500 tons. They had nine masts and twelve sails, and are said to have measured 440 feet long by 180 feet wide. With a force of perhaps a hundred men, Columbus might have been grateful for the company of

> 868 civil officers, 26,800 soldiers, 93 commanders, two senior commanders, 140 'millerions' [captains of a thousand men], 403 centurions, a Senior Secretary of the Board of Revenue, a geomancer, a military instructor, two military judges, 180 medical officers and assistants, two orderlies, seven senior eunuch ambassadors, ten junior eunuchs and 53 eunuch chamberlains

who travelled in Zheng He's retinue, along with an unspecified number of signallers, interpreters, scribes, professional negotiators, purveyors, Chinese and foreign navigators, helmsmen, military and civil mechanics, naval captains, common sailors and cooks. Columbus's crew, whose diet included dirty drinking water and flour baked with sea water, might also have appreciated the abundance of grain, fresh water, salt, soya sauce, tea, liquor, oil, candles, firewood and charcoal which Zheng He brought with him in his attendant supply ships and water tankers.

Zheng He's voyages differed from Columbus's not only in scale but in kind. Each voyage was a huge collective operation, a state undertaking in the fullest sense. Zheng He was not just financially sponsored, as Columbus was, by a sympathetic government: he and his captains, eunuchs of the palace, were the agents and chosen personal servants of their emperor. He was not in the smallest degree an entrepreneur.

Nor, in fairness to Columbus, was he strictly an explorer. The real Chinese explorers were the anonymous merchants who slipped across the Indian Ocean centuries before Zheng He's time. The Grand Eunuch's crews advanced, as they later described it, through sky-high waves to the westernmost lands of the west and the northernmost lands of the north, far-off regions screened by a blue transparency of light vapours. But they cannot have shared with Columbus's men a dread of the unknown. They knew, in principle, what lay ahead. Calmly, bureaucratically, the Chinese had prepared themselves for the Moslem world beyond India. Zheng He himself was a Moslem. His father and grandfather had been to Mecca, and he was probably chosen admiral largely on the strength of his familiarity with the customs of Islamic countries. He in turn recruited Moslem translator-interpreters, a mullah called Hassan and another Chinese Moslem called Ma Huan who later wrote a memoir of the expeditions.

Far from being an exploration, this great outreaching of Chinese seapower was inspired by the most inward-looking of motives. . . . Prestige was probably the main consideration by now. The Ming as a newish dynasty may have needed prestige. . . . Prestige . . . was conferred through the arrival in China of foreign visitors with goods which the Chinese received as symbolic 'tribute'. . . . Supreme under heaven in their own opinion, the Chinese were none the less in quest of a sort of diplomatic recognition.

They also wanted trade. The great days of the merchant venturer were over, but the Chinese business instinct was still very much alive. Zheng He and his fellow eunuchs were scouring the Indian Ocean for luxury goods which the imperial court could consume and retail at a profit, and their galleons were called Treasure Ships for the wealth they carried home. Treasure Ships also carried Chinese export produce, and the eunuchs probably had the task of developing new outlets for handicrafts like silk and porcelain which China was now manufacturing to saturation point. They may just have thought of Africa. The rich East African coastal towns had dramatically expanded their imports of chinaware since their supplies of Islamic pottery were disrupted in the thirteenth century by the Mongol devastation of the Middle East. By the mid-fourteenth century porcelain from China was used in every important coastal settlement and was sometimes edging Islamic goods out of the market.

Chapter Questions

1. Both primary and secondary sources in this chapter focus on women in China and Japan. How might these sources be used to compare the position and roles of women in China and Japan during this period? What, in turn, might this reveal about family life and social conditions in China and Japan?

2. Draw on sources in this chapter to describe life for those in China who were not members of the elite class. What options were open to them? How did they cope with the position they were in?

3. There are many ways various groups in a society might express their discontent. In what ways might discontent or rebellion have been expressed, directly or indirectly, in China or Japan? How do the sources provide evidence for the occurrence of rebellions or the existence of discontent in these societies?

NINE

The Mongols, the Turks, and the Middle East, 1000–1500

In this chapter we focus on central Asia, long the birthplace of various no-madic tribes and peoples, for it is during this period between the eleventh and sixteenth centuries that these peoples move to center stage and have a great impact on other civilizations. Throughout the region that stretches from the eastern edge of the European continent to Mongolia, the period between the eleventh and sixteenth centuries saw the creation, expansion, and defeat of numerous empires as different peoples strove for greater power. The most important of these people were the Mongols and the Turks.

The Mongols experienced the most dramatic fluctuations of fortune. They were a nomadic people living in clans led by chieftains selected for their prowess. In 1206, Chinggis Khan (Genghis Khan), whose name means "uni-versal ruler," united Mongol clans. In the following decades, the Mongol armies marched east to Korea, south to China, and west through Russia and Persia, getting as far as Hungary. They spread their rule over much of this territorial expanse, unifying much of Asia during the thirteenth century. But by the beginning of the fourteenth century, Mongol power was already on the wane, though it was not until the fifteenth century that the remnants of Mongol power were broken in Russia.

Turkish people, led by various rulers, originated from the broad area be-tween Russia and Mongolia. After serving in the armies of Arabic overlords,

Seljuk-led Turks created a Middle Eastern empire in the eleventh century that stretched from the Bosphorus to Chinese Turkestan. Their empire eventually declined and was displaced, first by the Mongols in the thirteenth century, then for a period by other Turks led by Timur (Tamerlane), and finally by the Ottoman Turks in the fourteenth century. The Ottomans centered in Anatolia, eventually conquering the declining Byzantinian Empire and going on to establish a powerful, long-lasting empire that stretched from the Middle East well into southeastern Europe.

In this chapter we will examine the Mongols and Turks. How did these people rise from their nomadic roots to establish and rule vast empires? What sorts of images did they project? What qualities unified them and what did they have in common?

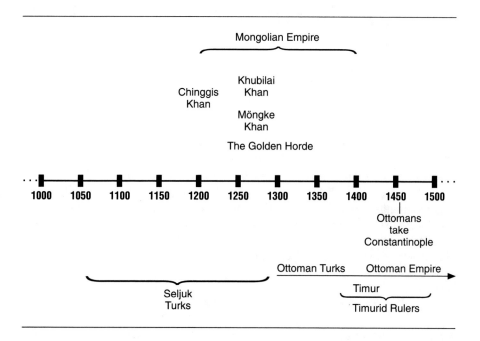

PRIMARY SOURCES

Turks and Arabs
al-Jāhiz

Early Turkish people lived in a broad area between Russia and Mongolia. Chinese records refer to them in the sixth century A.D., although the earliest Turkish writing dates from A.D. 730. Attempts to convert Turks to Buddhism and Christianity failed. But in the seventh century, Sunni Islam arrived through Persia and the Turks converted, even adopting Arabic script. From that point on, Arab rulers used Turks in their army until Turks had spread across central Asia into what were later Persian lands and finally Anatolia (Turkey). Well before the eleventh century, when they supplanted Arab caliphs as power holders in Baghdad, the Turks had gained a reputation as fierce nomadic warriors. This is reflected in the following comments on national character by the Persian scholar, al-Jāhiz of Basra (776–869).

> **Consider:** *How al-Jāhiz compares the Greeks, Chinese, and Turks; how the Turks resembled the Arabs; how useful these sorts of descriptions are.*

The Arabs . . . were not merchants, artisans, physicians, farmers—for that would have degraded them—, mathematicians or fruit-farmers—for they wished to escape the humiliation of the tax; nor were they out to earn or amass money, hoard possessions or lay hands on other people's; they were not of those who make their living with a pair of scales . . . they were not poor enough to be indifferent to learning, pursued neither wealth, that breeds foolishness, nor good fortune, that begets apathy, and never tolerated humiliation, which was dishonor and death to their souls. They dwelt in the plains, and grew up in contemplation of the desert. They knew neither damp nor rising mist, neither fog nor foul air, nor a horizon bounded by walls. When these keen minds and clear brains turned to poetry, fine language, eloquence and oratory, to physiognomy and astrology, genealogy, navigation by the stars and by marks on the ground . . . to horse-breeding, weaponry and engines of war, to memorizing all that they heard, pondering on everything that caught their attention and discriminating between the glories and the shames of their tribes, they achieved perfection beyond the wildest dreams. Certain of these activities broadened their minds and exalted their aspirations, so that of all nations they are now the most glorious and the most given to recalling their past splendors.

It is the same with the Turks who dwell in tents in the desert and keep herds: they are the Bedouins of the non-Arabs. . . . Uninterested in craftsmanship or

SOURCE: Charles Pellat, trans. *The Life and Works of Jahiz* (Berkeley, CA: University of California Press, 1969) pp. 96–97. Reprinted by permission.

commerce, medicine, geometry, fruit-farming, building, digging canals or collecting taxes, they care only about raiding, hunting, horsemanship, skirmishing with rival chieftains, taking booty and invading other countries. Their efforts are all directed towards these activities, and they devote all their energies to these occupations. In this way they have acquired a mastery of these skills, which for them take the place of craftsmanship and commerce and constitute their only pleasure, their glory and the subject of all their conversation. Thus have they become in the realm of warfare what the Greeks are in philosophy, the Chinese in craftsmanship, and the Arabs in the fields we have enumerated.

Mongol Wedding Ceremonies

For Mongols, as for many peoples, marriage ceremonies celebrated passage from youth to adulthood. These ceremonies also reflected the traditions of their nomadic life. For example, the term for marriage, gerleku, *refers to men and means "establishing a household." For women,* mordokhu, *means "to go off on a horse." Mongol weddings were auspicious occasions, as witnessed by the excerpt below. This dialogue dates from the time of Chinggis Khan and was meant to be spoken like poetry. The bride's and groom's representatives would change meter and rhyme, making the ceremony a friendly competition as well as an important ritual.*

> **Consider:** *The values and hopes expressed; the universal characteristics of ceremony; how the dialogue reflects Mongol life.*

WORDS THE GROOM'S REPRESENTATIVE IS TO SAY WHEN HE ENTERS THE BRIDE'S FAMILY YURT°:

On behalf of the groom's father, mother, and relatives,
in accordance with the tradition of our people
we cause your young son-in-law to grasp the good, sharp weapons,
to wear the sturdy, strong armor
to come forward to bow to the parents and relatives of the bride.

We now first present to the Buddha that you worship:
a beautiful lotus lamp and fragrantly ascending incense;
the long *khadagh,* eight jewels without and seven jewels within;
a fine white sheep selected from our beloved herds;
dry fruit selected from the choicest food.
In order to complete the ceremony of the marriage
to establish the immortal blessings of their future
we now present to all relatives and friends gathered here

SOURCE: Sechin Jagchid and Paul Hyer, *Mongolia's Culture and Society* (Boulder, CO: Westview Press, 1979) pp. 85–87. Reprinted by permission.

° The circular felt tent in which Mongol nomads live.

the holy, white *khadagh*, which has descended from heaven,
kumis and wine, which are the most delicious foods. . . .

WORDS OF THE BRIDE'S FATHER OR REPRESENTATIVE:

On this blessed occasion and on this auspicious day,
We desire to pronounce a benediction on our honored guests and our son-in-law.
May our son-in-law's family and property prosper,
May their storehouse overflow.
We now robe you from head to foot with exquisite clothing,
    fine armor, and a helmet.
Mounted on a swift, strong horse,
We have you carry the golden bow and silver arrows.
We wish you a bounteous future,
May your blessings increase day by day.
You, our friends, have come with deep significance
To complete the marriage ceremony where the bride and groom
    are joined.
We desire all your best blessings and wishes
To be bestowed upon the new couple
That they may receive the greatest benediction from heaven
And enjoy inexhaustible happiness.
We now present to you, our honorable guests, the *khadagh* of heaven
and *kumis*—the best tasting of food and drink.

WORDS OF THE BRIDE'S PARENTS WHEN SHE LEAVES THEIR HOME:

Our daughter, your father is as heaven
And your mother is as earth to you.
We, your parents and relatives, bestow upon you bounteous presents.
In so doing, we proclaim that this auspicious day is set to bring
    you great future happiness.
In accordance with the ordinances of the nation, and the
    tradition of the people,
We have decided that you, our beloved child, shall go afar
To be the offspring of both families by mutual consent. . . .

Men's daughters, raised in love
By the custom of the people
Must also marry into a distant clan and be their offspring.
As the rocks of the steep and solid peaks
Are crumbled by the hoofs of campaigning horses,
Thus our daughter, as a round jewel,
Raised in the palm of us, her parents,
Must be given in marriage to a distant clan. . . .

Take care always and be openhearted.
Thus, you may be friends with outsiders and honored by those within.

Persist in virtue, do not quarrel or struggle with others,
Then you will be loved by your husband
And praised by all, forever.

Timur the Great Amir
Ahmed ibn Arabshah

One of the most complex figures in the history of this region was Timur, or Tamerlane (1336–1405) as he became known in the West. A Turkish tribal leader who claimed descent from Chinggis Khan, his successes in battle and his renowned personal spirituality drew many followers. By 1360 Timur had managed to overcome his many foes and was named the Great Amir over his own empire. At first his rule was not unusually harsh. Making Samarkand his capital, he encouraged cultural activities, was an avid and skilled chess player, and demonstrated his political astuteness by giving greater authority to, and thereby winning the support of, the local Muslim religious leaders. Not satisfied with what he had, Timur began to wage war against his neighbors, all smaller and weaker than he. For the most part this was not a difficult task, but when there was considerable resistance, Timur displayed his capacity for both conquest and unspeakable cruelty. This is revealed in the following description by Ahmed ibn Arabshah, a fifteenth-century secretary to the Sultan of Baghdad, and in the subsequent visual source.

Consider: *The consequences of such conquests and cruelties; how Timur was able to succeed in battle.*

Then Timur [Tamerlane] turned the reins of outrage towards the city of Siwas, which was held, as I have said, by Amir Suliman, son of Bayazid, . . . who sent an envoy and informed his father of this danger, and urged him to render him assistance, while he was engaged in besieging Stambul, but he could not help him, because he himself wanted more troops and the places were far apart. Then he collected from his army his bravest men and fortified the city and citadel and prepared for battle and collected guards to sustain a siege and entrusted a part of the walls to each of his generals and Timur sent out spies from his army to confirm his suspicions, but when Amir Suliman saw the fineness of his army, he fled at the sight of it and decided to take himself to his father, stipulating with his generals and troops that they should guard the city for him, while he looked for forces and supplies and they could not but consent and remain behind and they could not follow him; but he sought safety for himself and escaped in hasty flight.

But Timur came to the city with his swelling floods of men on the seventeenth day of the month Zulhaja in the year 802 [1399] and when he had halted with ill-omened foot at Siwas he said: "I will storm this city on the eighteenth day."

Then he set up while besieging it signs of the last judgment and stormed it on

---

SOURCE: Ahmed Ibn Arabshah, *Tamerlane or Timur the Great Amir* (London: Luzac & Co., 1936), pp. 116–117.

the eighteenth day, after doing damage and havoc, on the fifth day of the week and the fifth of the month Muharram in the year 803 [1401] after swearing to the troops of the garrison, that he would not shed their blood and would protect them and preserve their families and goods; nevertheless when the storming was ended, when he had the soldiers in his power, he cast them all in chains and ordered a crypt under the earth to be dug for them, and ordered them to be hurled alive into those pits, as the leaders were hurled into the well of Badar. And the number of men hurled into those pits was three thousand. Then he loosened the reins of plunder and caused plunder, captivity, and havoc.

And this city was among the finest of great cities, set in a beautiful region, remarkable for public buildings, fortifications, famous qualities and tombs of martyrs renowned among all. Its water is pure, its air healthy for the bodily tempers; its people modest, lovers of magnificence and pomp and devoted to means of ceremony and reverence. And this city borders on the frontiers of three countries, Syria, Azerbaijan and Rum, but is now quite removed and overturned and its people scattered hither and thither, and is utterly destroyed and laid waste. . . .

VISUAL SOURCES

Cruelties of Conquest

This painting from the period depicts Timur's revenge on the people who opposed his conquest. To punish the people for their resistance, Timur resorted to mass murder, sometimes by sword, sometimes by walling up thousands in windowless towers and leaving them to slow deaths. If that wasn't enough, he also built pyramids of skulls as a warning against further resistance.

Consider: *The possible purposes of such acts; how this supplements the written account by Ahmed ibn Arabshah.*

Photo 9–1

Victoria and Albert Museum

Life in the Camp:
The Nomadic Tent
Mīr Sayyid ʿAlī

There is a very long history of tribal life in Persia and the most evocative aspect of that life was the tent. Tents were used by nomadic peoples as an easy means of relocating their housing and obtaining shelter from the elements. Tents were also used by rulers as they traveled around their domains. Tents were popular themes in Persian art, especially from the Timurid period to the middle of the sixteenth century. The tents most favored were the yurts of the Mongols. The importance of the tent is clearly seen in this painting by artist Mīr Sayyid ʿAlī from about 1540. Ths picture shows a nomad encampment with four yurts and all the various activities of camp life.

> **Consider:** *The different roles played by men and women as evidenced by their positions within the picture; what major aspects of civilization these roles reflect.*

Photo 9–2

The Arthur M. Sackler Museum, Harvard University, Gift of John Goelet, Formerly collection
of Louis J. Cartier.

Power in Central Asia and the Middle East

Between the eleventh and sixteenth centuries, Turkish and Mongol peoples moved throughout Asia and the Middle East, creating large, powerful empires. This is made clear in the following four maps. The first shows the empire of the Seljuk (Seljung) Turks in the mid-twelfth century. The second shows the huge Mongol Empire toward the end of the thirteenth and beginning of the fourteenth centuries. The third shows the relatively short-lived empire of Tamerlane toward the end of the fourteenth century. The fourth shows the empire of the Ottoman Turks during the sixteenth century. Together these maps reveal the fluidity of power in this area of the world during these centuries, as one empire succeeded the next.

> **Consider:** *The difficulties in conquering such large areas and then maintaining power; how the nomadic heritage of the Turks and Mongols may have facilitated such conquests but also made them relatively short-lived.*

Map 9–1   Power in Central Asia and the Middle East, circa 1150

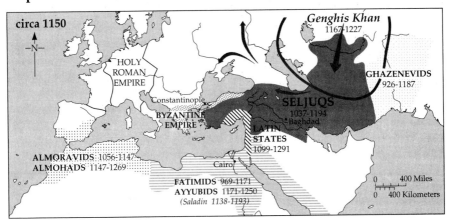

Map 9–2   The Mongol Empire in the Thirteenth Century

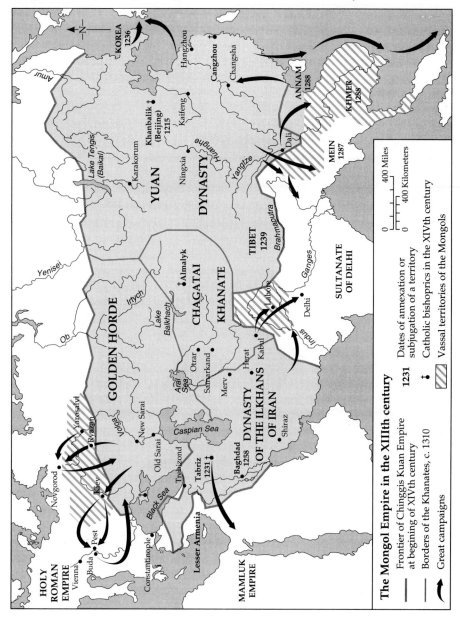

The Mongol Empire in the XIIIth century

——	Frontier of Chinggis Kuan Empire at begining of XIVth century
——	Borders of the Khanates, c. 1310

1231   Dates of annexation or subjugation of a territory

✝   Catholic bishoprics in the XIVth century

▨   Vassal territories of the Mongols

⟶   Great campaigns

Map 9–3   circa 1400

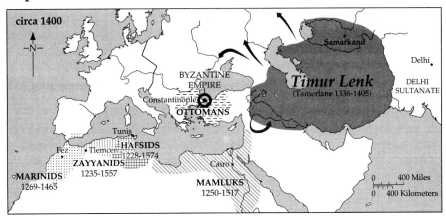

Map 9–4   circa 1550

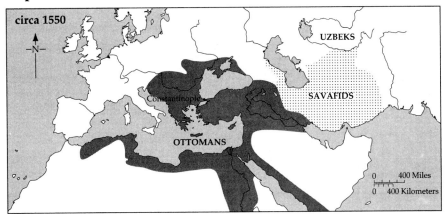

SECONDARY SOURCES

The Mongols and the Ottoman Turks

C. E. Bosworth

The popular image of the Mongols is often one of hordes of warriors inflicting mass de-
struction as they passed in conquest. The Ottoman Turks are also commonly perceived as
being terrorizing warriors. However, both of these conquering peoples established empires
that flourished for long periods of time. In the following selection, C. E. Bosworth com-
pares these popular misconceptions and realities as he examines the Mongols and the
Ottoman Turks.

> **Consider:** *The consequences of Mongolian rule; why the Ottoman Turks were so*
> *successful; why Western perceptions of these peoples might be distorted.*

The Mongol invasions of the thirteenth and fourteenth centuries constituted a
"time of troubles" for all the Islamic lands east of Egypt, out of which various
powerful and comparatively long-lived empires emerged. . . .

Despite the fact that the name of the Mongols ranks in the popular mind with
those of the Goths, Huns, and Vandals as perpetrators of mass destruction, this
initial violence subsided and the age of the Mongols had its favourable aspect.
Domination over such a great expanse of the Old World, from the Ukraine to
Korea, opened up the possibility of East-West cultural exchanges on an unprec-
edented scale. Chinese artistic techniques and motifs began perceptibly to affect
Islamic Persian art. People could move freely across Inner Asia as never before
or since, unhampered by political boundaries. Impelled by the search for Prester
John, the legendary Christian monarch who was tentatively identified with the
Mongol Great Khan, many Europeans travelled to Mongolia and have left us
fascinating accounts of life there. . . .

More than any other Muslim power of the late classical period, the Ottoman
Turks struck terror into the hearts of Christian Europe, so that the Elizabethan
historian of the Turks, Richard Knollys, described them as "the present Terror of
the World." Backed by the Turkish military qualities of self-discipline and endur-
ance, the Turkish invasions of Europe were indeed a potent threat, reaching on

SOURCE: R. M. Savory, ed. *Introduction to Islamic Civilisation* (Cambridge University Press, 1976), pp. 23–25.

two occasions to Vienna itself. The Ottomans began as a group of *ghāzīs* (i.e., corps of mystically inspired warriors) in northwestern Anatolia, confronting the truncated Byzantine empire there, and eventually eclipsing other Turkish principalities by their superior *élan* and experience in war. . . .

Much of this Ottoman vigour sprang from the use of a system of military slavery. . . . The Janissaries or "New Troops," a crack corps of highly trained soldiers and officials, were recruited from the Chinese populations of the Balkans and later, from those of Anatolia, from the late fourteenth down to the early eighteenth centuries. Like the Arabs in the first stages of their expansion, the Turks themselves were a military class comparatively thinly spread over what had grown to be a vast empire. Utilisation of the subject population was a brilliant device for tapping the manpower of the Balkans. Moreover, the lengthy and arduous training of a Janissary in a thoroughly Islamic atmosphere conduced to his adopting a soldierly type of Islam. It was the discipline and fire-power of these troops (the Ottoman army made use of artillery and hand-guns from the mid-fifteenth century onwards) which did much to create in Europe the image of Ottoman ferocity and invincibility.

Yet in its heyday, the Ottoman empire was the most powerful and lasting state known to the Islamic world since the early Arab Caliphate. It gave autocratic, but often good government to lands which had previously suffered internal chaos and dislocation, and only towards the end, when the political and economic pressure of the West contributed to administrative breakdown and internal economic decline, did the quality of Ottoman rule deteriorate.

Mongol Imperialism
Thomas T. Allsen

By the middle of the thirteenth century, Mongol armies were spreading across Eurasia. In 1251 Mongol leaders decided to advance southward into Persian lands at the meeting of Mongol princes that enthroned Mongke Khan. The main body of troops left Mongolia in 1253 and took two years to reach their destination across Central Asia; an extraordinary accomplishment logistically. By 1257, most Persian lands had been taken and the city of Baghdad placed under siege.

In a study of Mongke Khan's rule (1251–1259), Thomas T. Allsen, a scholar of Mongol history, examines the expansion of Mongol rule during this period, arguing that conquest and resource mobilization were perfected and brilliantly deployed. Allsen discusses both the logistical problems of getting across wide expanses of land and the problems the Mongols had in ruling the people they conquered.

SOURCE: Thomas Allsen, *Mongol Imperialism* (Berkeley, University of California and University of California Press, 1987) pp. 221–225.

Consider: *The difficulties in long-distance conquest and administration in the thir-teenth century; how the Mongols managed to succeed to the extent they did.*

Considering the size and cultural diversity of the empire, it is not surprising that the administrative system fashioned by the emperor and his associates was com-posed of widely diverse elements. The revenue system combined Mongol and central Asian Turkic practices, population registration followed Chinese tech-niques, and the military machine was patterned after long-established steppe traditions. Although the administrative system had a certain symmetry, it was by no means uniform throughout the empire, particularly at the lower levels. Some accommodation to local practice and tradition was unavoidable. Because the Mon-gols lacked both the skills and the numbers to supply the requisite bureaucratic personnel from within their own ranks, they were forced to rely upon subject peoples familiar with local conditions and languages to fill essential administrative posts. . . .

The administrative system also had to accommodate certain Mongol practices, some of which were clearly antithetical to bureaucratic efficiency and the quest for political centralization. For example, Möngke continued the policy of allotting territories and their inhabitants to Mongol princes and officials, despite the prob-lems the central government always had encountered in trying to control these appanages. The emperor even extended the practice by granting land to some trusted Chinese supporters. . . .

The Mongol tradition of hereditary succession to office was another practice that, to some degree, limited the central government's freedom of action. Thir-teenth-century sources abound in examples of sons succeeding fathers, or brothers succeeding brothers, in both military and civil offices. Möngke made no attempt to stop this practice. . . . It should be remembered, however, that even though one could gain access to office through inheritance, this was no guarantee that one would retain it for long if he were incompetent or disobedient. . . .

Although the administrative system was not perfectly uniform and had to ac-commodate practices that ran counter to efforts toward administrative centrali-zation and regularization, it was nonetheless effective and responsive to the com-mands of the central authorities. The basic components of Möngke's program of resource mobilization—introduction of the census, imposition of [taxes], conscrip-tion of large new armies, and issuance of new currency—were realized everywhere in the empire. Moreover, the resources generated by these measures were largely under the control of the central authorities. We know that Möngke's agents organized the census and assessed taxes in China, Iran, the Transcaucasus, and the Rus principalities. The disposition of the new armies raised at this time also was determined by the emperor. . . .

Viewed from a broad comparative perspective, Mongol methods of warfare have a character that is undeniably akin to the modern concept of total war. Mongol warfare had a political, economic, and psychological, as well as purely military, dimension. The Mongol people and their nomadic allies were fully mobilized. Under Möngke, the sedentary sector of the empire was placed on an equivalent footing. The magnitude and intensity of the effort to identify and exploit the empire's vast human and material resources likewise invites comparison with modern total wars. So, too, does the scale of Mongol operations in the 1250s, which in terms of the number of troops engaged and the distances involved was not again equaled until the wars of the Napoleonic era and not surpassed until the World Wars of the twentieth century.

Cultural Ties between Turkey, Iran, and Pakistan
Abdülkadir Karahan

At first glance, the differences between the cultures and languages of Turkey, Iran, and Pakistan seem greater than their similarities. Various armies, both military and religious, advanced across this portion of western Asia, bringing their own ideas. But how much influence did they have beyond the spreading of Islam, which all three peoples adopted?

One of the most difficult tasks for a historian is trying to trace cultural origins and identifying discernible patterns. In this excerpt, Istanbul University Professor Abdülkadir Karahan takes on the task for Turkey, Iran, and Pakistan. He argues that the similarities in culture, beyond the common religion, are greater than the differences, thereby creating an important link between the cultures.

> **Consider:** *How culture is spread; how these cultures interacted.*

The historical and cultural ties existing among the Moslem Indo-Pakistani peninsula, Iran, and Turkey are very old and exist on a broad scale. Initially, they had a religious character, and they developed in that direction. . . . [T]he people living in these various countries were in possession of the same religious culture, and . . . these various peoples . . . acted according to the teachings of the *Quran*. . . . Although various sects and religious orders sprang up (for instance, Turkish and Pakistani people are generally Sunnite, and Iranians are Shiite), these differences could neither undermine nor destroy the essential unity and complete system existing at the very basis of Islam, even if they seemed to weaken it from time to time. . . . These relations go back as far as the Gazneli, and particularly to the time of Gazneli Mahmud (970–1030). They became very strong during the Timur era (1405–1506). . . .

Literary and cultural contacts were quite lively in regions under Ottoman administration. . . . [S]ome rulers wrote books using the language of neighboring

SOURCE: Larry V. Clark and Paul Alexander Draghi, eds. *Aspects of Altaic Civilization II.* Proceedings of the XVIII PIAC, Bloomington, June 29–July 5, 1975 (Peeters, 1978), pp. 115–117. Reprinted by permission.

countries. . . . For instance, the poems of Shah Ismail (Hatâî) were very popular among Anatolian people. Furthermore, works written in Arabic, Persian and Turkish by the great poet Fuzulî . . . were among the books that the educated class enjoyed in Iran and Turkey. . . . Almost all intellectuals who lived in the Indo-Pakistani peninsula and Ottoman country and studied poetry mastered Arabic and Persian.

At the beginning, Persian was popular not only as a literary language but also as the language used in official correspondence and political life. . . . Persian had the privilege of becoming the literary and official language, and was even the language used for educational purposes until the nineteenth century. . . .

At the beginning, the Turkish literature of Anatolia was simple and addressed itself to people at large. As time went by, Ottoman Turkish developed. Ottoman Turkish had taken away many words and expressions from Arabic and Persian; therefore, a literary language that was in fact made up of three languages came into existence. . . . As a result, one witnessed the appearance of common literary arts, a common technique, common expressions, and even a mutual feeling and a mutual literary taste to some extent. . . .

A similar motif might be observed in architecture, as well as in fine workmanship pertaining to handicraft. . . .

The three kindred nations are close to one another from the point of view of clothes, kitchenware, gardening, etc. . . .

Common features pertaining to kindred cultures can be seen in birth rejoicings, circumcisions, weddings, and in ladies' adornments. Such similarities include gardening, and keeping in check excessive heat through the use of devices such as fountains and pools.

Muslim Arabs and Others
Albert Habib Hourani

It was in western Arabia during the late sixth and early seventh centuries that the Prophet Muhammed began teaching a set of beliefs that became known as Islam and were later recorded in the holy book called the Qur'an. Soon thereafter, armies began conquering Arabia and its adjacent territories in the name of this new religion. Before long, Islam spanned an area that stretched from Madrid to Baghdad. While political unity would not last long (by the tenth century there were several rival caliphates [leaders]), Islam and the Arabic language had become predominate from the Indian subcontinent through western Asia and north Africa, linking these disparate lands through religion, institutions, and trade. In most places, Islam learned to exist with other traditions and cultures.

In this excerpt, one of the world's most prominent historians of Arab history, Albert

SOURCE: Albert Hourani, *A History of the Arab People* (Cambridge, Mass.), Harvard University Press, Copyright © 1991. Reprinted by permission.

Habib Hourani, describes the multiplicity of peoples, cultures, and traditions that existed during the period following the eleventh century in the area we now know as the Middle East.

> **Consider:** *The profusion of religious traditions that emerged from this single area of the world; how they coexisted and prospered at times and conflict bitterly at other times.*

By the eleventh century Islam was the religion of the rulers, the dominant groups, and a growing proportion of the population, but it is not certain that it was the religion of a majority anywhere outside the Arabian peninsula. In the same way, while Arabic was the language of high culture and much of the urban population, other languages still survived from the period before the coming of the Muslim conquerors. By the fifteenth century the flood of Arabic Islam had covered the whole region, and for the most part it was Islam in its Sunni form, although adherents of doctrines evolved in the early centuries still existed. In south-eastern Arabia and on the fringes of the Sahara there were communities of Ibadis, claiming spiritual descent from the Kharijis who had rejected the leadership of 'Ali after the battle of Siffin, and had revolted against the rule of the caliphs in Iraq and the Maghrib. In Yemen, much of the population adhered to Shi'ism in its Zaydi form. Shi'ism in its 'Twelver' and Isma'ili forms, which had dominated much of the eastern Arab world in the tenth century, had receded; the 'Twelvers' were still numerous in parts of Lebanon, southern Iraq where they had their main shrines, and the west coast of the Gulf; and Isma'ilis still clung to their faith in parts of Yemen, Iran, and Syria, where they had been able to put up a local resistance to Sunni rulers, the Ayyubids in Syria and the Saljuqs farther east. (News of their activities, brought back to Europe during the time of the Crusades, gave rise to the name of 'Assassins' and the story, not found in the Arabic sources, that they lived under the absolute rule of the 'Old Man of the Mountains'.) Adherents of other offshoots of Shi'ism, the Druzes and Nusayris, were also to be found in Syria. In northern Iraq there were Yazidis, followers of a religion which had elements derived from both Christianity and Islam, and in the south the Mandaeans had a faith drawn from older religious beliefs and practices.

By the twelfth century the Christian Churches of the Maghrib had virtually disappeared, but a large part of the population of the Muslim kingdoms of Andalus were Christians of the Roman Catholic Church. Coptic Christians were still an important element of the Egyptian population by the fifteenth century, although their numbers were shrinking by conversion. Farther south, in the northern Sudan, Christianity had disappeared by the fifteenth or sixteenth century, as Islam spread across the Red Sea and down the Nile valley. All over Syria and in northern Iraq Christian communities remained, although in a diminished form. Some, mainly in the cities, belonged to the Eastern Orthodox Church, but others were members of those other Churches which had their origins in the controversies about the nature of Christ: the Syrian Orthodox or Monophysites, and the Nestorians. In Lebanon and other parts of Syria there was a fourth Church, that of the Maronites;

they had held the Monothelete doctrine, but in the twelfth century, when the Crusaders ruled the coasts of Syria, they had accepted Roman Catholic doctrine and the supremacy of the Pope.

Jews were spread more widely throughout the world of Arabic Islam. In the Maghrib a considerable part of the peasantry had been converted to Judaism before the coming of Islam, and there were still Jewish rural communities, as there were in Yemen and parts of the Fertile Crescent. Jews were found also in most of the cities of the region, for they played an important part in trade, manufacture, finance and medicine. The greater number of them belonged to the main body of Jews who accepted the oral laws and interpretation of them contained in the Talmud and maintained by those trained in Talmudic scholarship. In Egypt, Palestine and elsewhere, however, there were also Karaites, who did not accept the Talmud and had their own laws derived by their teachers from the Scriptures.

A large part of the Jewish communities were Arabic-speaking by this time, although they used forms of Arabic which were special to them and still used Hebrew for liturgical purposes. Among the Christians, too, Arabic had spread in the Fertile Crescent, Egypt and Spain; Aramaic and Syriac were shrinking as spoken and written languages, although used in liturgies, and the Coptic language of Egypt had virtually ceased to be used for any except religious purposes by the fifteenth century; many of the Christians of Andalus had adopted Arabic as their language, although the Romance languages they had inherited survived and were beginning to revive. At the margins of the Arabic flood, in mountain and desert districts, other languages were spoken: Kurdish in the mountains of northern Iraq, Nubian in the northern Sudan and various languages in the south, Berber dialects in the mountains of the Maghrib and the Sahara. Kurds and Berbers were Muslims, however, and to the extent to which they were educated they came within the sphere of the Arabic language.

Chapter Questions

1. Drawing on the sources in this chapter, how might the striking expansion of the Mongols and Turks against opposition from more established civilizations be explained?

2. As the sources indicate, this period of Asian history saw the advance of great armies sweeping across the Asian landmass, conquering peoples of every persuasion. These invasions, however cruel, also served as agents for the diffusion of ideas and goods. How might civilizations have been affected by these forced contacts? How might such contacts have affected the invaders themselves?

3. More often than not, information about the Mongols and Turks during this period comes to us from outside observers rather than the Mongols and Turks

themselves. Why might this be so? What problems does this pose for understanding these peoples and their civilizations? In light of this, are there any sources in this chapter that should be questioned even more than usual?

4. How might the invasions of the nomadic Mongols and Turks be compared to other invasions of nomadic peoples such as the Germanic tribes toward the end of the Classical era or the Aryans in early Indian history?

TEN

Europe's Middle Ages, 500–1300

By the sixth century, the decline of the Roman Empire in the West had long ended the political and cultural unity Greco-Roman civilization had brought to the Mediterranean basin and much of the West. In parts of the Mediterranean and eastern Europe, the Eastern Roman Empire maintained relative stability. Now centered at Constantinople, it would evolve into the Byzantine Empire and woud flourish until the eleventh century, when it would begin a long period of decline.

The civilization of the Middle Ages that formed in the rest of Europe between the sixth and thirteenth centuries was founded on the threefold legacy of the fifth and sixth centuries: Germanic customs and institutions, Roman culture and institutions, and Christian belief and institutions.

Early medieval institutions drew from this legacy and slowly took form. The Christian Church, supported by a growing bureaucracy, numerous monasteries, and vast land holdings, became increasingly powerful. Medieval monarchies formed, but for most of the Early Middle Ages were weak; local officials usually exercised political authority more effectively. Europeans gradually established feudal relations among themselves based on personal contractual obligations for military service or exchange of land. A relatively self-sufficient manorial economic and social system spread throughout many areas. Compared to the preceding Roman era, there was a broad cultural decline. Indeed, the Early Middle Ages (sixth to tenth centuries) were marked by disruptions and disorganization.

While there were temporary revivals, most importantly in the eighth and ninth centuries under the Carolingian King Charlemagne, it was not until the eleventh and twelfth centuries (the High Middle Ages) that Europe gained new dynamism. These two centuries were marked by population growth, external expansion, commercial revival, urban growth, religious reform, and cultural revival. During the thirteenth century these dynamic trends came to fruition. Politically, socially, and culturally, medieval civilization gained a striking maturity during this period of relative prosperity.

The sources in this chapter focus on four broad topics. The first has to do with power. What were the lines of religious and secular authority? In what ways did they compete; in what ways were they unified? The second concerns the society and economy of these centuries. Into what orders was medieval society organized? What was life like for the peasants? What roles were available to women? In what ways can the rise of early capitalism be traced? The third focuses on the Crusades, which began late in the eleventh century. How were the Crusades justified and what was their significance? The fourth concerns stability and change. Here the political and social con-

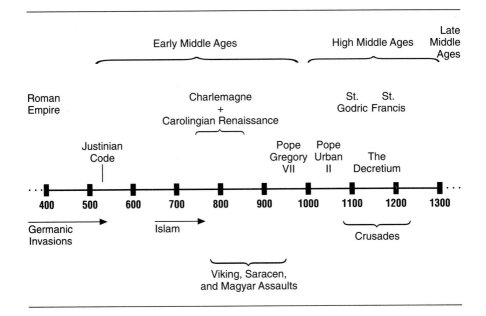

traction at the beginning of the Middle Ages, the expansion beginning with the eleventh century, and the contraction at the end of the period will be examined. The role of Byzantine civilization, for centuries a source of relative stability, will also be examined here.

This last topic will bring us to the eve of the fourteenth and fifteenth centuries, when medieval Europe experienced a painful and exciting transition. This will be our focus in the following chapter.

PRIMARY SOURCES

The Institutes of Justinian: Byzantium and the Legacy of Roman Law

Compared to western Europe, the Byzantine Empire to the east and south was a pillar of stability and continuity. A principal means of maintaining continuity between the Byzantine Empire and its predecessor, the Roman Empire, was through the use of the Justinian Code. Initiated in 528 during the reign of Emperor Justinian (527–565), this code contained a compilation of Roman laws, a growing collection of new laws, and a manual for students (the Institutes*). The following are selections from the Preamble and Book One of the* Institutes.

> **Consider:** *How the Germanic invasions of the fifth and sixth centuries were met in Byzantium; the purposes of the* Institutes; *the role of law in the Byzantine Empire.*

PREAMBLE

In the Name Of Our Lord Jesus Christ.

THE EMPEROR CÆSAR FLAVIUS JUSTINIANUS, VANQUISHER OF THE ALAMANI, GOTHS, FRANCS, GERMANS, ANTES, ALANI, VANDALS, AFRICANS, PIOUS, HAPPY, GLORIOUS, TRIUMPHANT CONQUEROR, EVER AUGUST, TO THE YOUTH DESIROUS OF STUDYING THE LAW, GREETING.

The imperial majesty should be not only made glorious by arms, but also strengthened by laws, that, alike in time of peace and in time of war, the state

SOURCE: *The Institutes of Justinian,* trans. Thomas C. Sandars (London: Longmans, Green, 1874), pp. 1–7.

may be well governed, and that the emperor may not only be victorious in the field of battle, but also may by every legal means repel the iniquities of men who abuse the laws, and may at once religiously uphold justice and triumph over his conquered enemies.

1. By our incessant labours and great care, with the blessing of God, we have attained this double end. The barbarian nations reduced under our yoke know our efforts in war; to which also Africa and very many other provinces bear witness, which, after so long an interval, have been restored to the dominion of Rome and our empire, by our victories gained through the favour of heaven. All nations moreover are governed by laws which we have either promulgated or arranged.

2. When we had arranged and brought into perfect harmony the hitherto confused mass of imperial constitutions, we then extended our care to the endless volumes of ancient law; and sailing as it were across the mid ocean, have now completed, through the favour of heaven, a work we once despaired of.

3. When by the blessing of God this task was accomplished, we summoned the most eminent Tribonian, master and ex-quæstor of our palace, together with the illustrious Theophilus and Dorotheus, professors of law, all of whom have on many occasions proved to us their ability, legal knowledge, and obedience to our orders; and we specially charged them to compose, under our authority and advice, Institutes, so that you may no more learn the first elements of law from old and erroneous sources, but apprehend them by the clear light of imperial wisdom; and that your minds and ears may receive nothing that is useless or misplaced, but only what obtains in actual practice. So that, whereas, formerly, the foremost among you could scarcely, after four years' study, read the imperial constitutions, you may now commence your studies by reading them, you who have been thought worthy of an honour and a happiness so great as that the first and last lessons in the knowledge of the law should issue for you from the mouth of the emperor.

4. When therefore, by the assistance of the same eminent person Tribonian and that of other illustrious and learned men, we had compiled the fifty books, called Digests or Pandects, in which is collected the whole ancient law, we directed that these Institutes should be divided into four books, which might serve as the first elements of the whole science of law.

5. In these books a brief exposition is given of the ancient laws, and of those also, which, overshadowed by disuse, have been again brought to light by our imperial authority.

6. These four books of Institutes thus compiled, from all the Institutes left us by the ancients, and chiefly from the commentaries of our Gaius, both from his Institutes and his Journal, and also from many other commentaries, were presented to us by the three learned men we have above named. We read and examined them, and have accorded to them all the force of our constitutions.

7. Receive, therefore, with eagerness, and study with cheerful diligence, these our laws, and show yourselves persons of such learning that you may conceive the flattering hope of yourselves being able, when your course of legal study is completed, to govern our empire in the different portions that may be entrusted to your care.

Given at Constantinople on the eleventh day of the calends of December, in the third consulate of the Emperor Justinian, ever August.

BOOK ONE

Justice is the constant and perpetual wish to render every one his due.

1. Jurisprudence is the knowledge of things divine and human; the science of the just and the unjust.

2. Having explained these general terms, we think we shall commence our exposition of the law of the Roman people most advantageously, if we pursue at first a plain and easy path, and then proceed to explain particular details with the utmost care and exactness. For, if at the outset we overload the mind of the student, while yet new to the subject and unable to bear much, with a multitude and variety of topics, one of two things will happen—we shall either cause him wholly to abandon his studies, or, after great toil, and often after great distrust of himself (the most frequent stumbling-block in the way of youth), we shall at last conduct him to the point, to which, if he had been led by an easier road, he might, without great labour, and without any distrust of his own powers, have been sooner conducted.

3. The maxims of law are these: to live honestly, to hurt no one, to give every one his due.

4. The study of law is divided into two branches; that of public and that of private law. Public law regards the government of the Roman Empire; private law, the interests of individuals. We are now to treat of the latter, which is composed of three elements, and consists of precepts belonging to natural law, to the law of nations, and to the civil law.

Feudal Contracts and Obligations

During the Middle Ages a system of feudalism developed, in part to fill the void created by the collapse of Roman authority and the weakness of centralized monarchies, and in part as a pragmatic outgrowth of various Roman institutions and German concepts of personal service and loyalty. Feudalism was essentially a series of contractual relationships between individuals, backed up by various ethical and legal doctrines. This is illustrated in the following documents dating from the seventh to the eleventh centuries.

Consider: *The benefits that each party to a feudal contract expected to gain; the ideals behind the feudal relationship; the conditions for termination of the contract*

SOURCE: Edward P. Cheyney, ed., "Documents Illustrative of Feudalism," in *Translations and Reprints from the Original Sources of European History.* Department of History of the University of Pennsylvania, ed., vol. IV, no. 3 (Philadelphia: University of Pennsylvania Press, 1898), pp. 3, 5, and 23–24.

or relationship; the social and political conditions during these centuries suggested by these documents; the ways individuals might have attempted to secure or improve their social position in this system.

A FRANKISH FORMULA OF COMMENDATION, SEVENTH CENTURY

Who commends himself in the power of another:

To that magnificent lord *so and so,* I, *so and so.* Since it is known familiarly to all how little I have whence to feed and clothe myself, I have therefore petitioned your piety, and your good-will has decreed to me that I should hand myself over or commend myself to your guardianship, which I have thereupon done; that is to say in this way, that you should aid and succor me as well with food as with clothing, according as I shall be able to serve you and deserve it.

And so long as I shall live I ought to provide service and honor to you, suitably to my free condition; and I shall not during the time of my life have the ability to withdraw from your power or guardianship; but must remain during the days of my life under your power or defence. Wherefore it is proper that if either of us shall wish to withdraw himself from these agreements, he shall pay *so many* shillings to the other party (*pari suo*), and this agreement shall remain unbroken.
. . .

CAPITULARY CONCERNING FREEMEN AND VASSALS, 816

If any one shall wish to leave his lord (*seniorem*), and is able to prove against him one of these crimes, that is, in the first place, if the lord has wished to reduce him unjustly into servitude; in the second place, if he has taken counsel against his life; in the third place, if the lord has committed adultery with the wife of his vassal; in the fourth place, if he has wilfully attacked him with a drawn sword; in the fifth place, if the lord has been able to bring defence to his vassal after he has commended his hands to him, and has not done so; it is allowed to the vassal to leave him. If the lord has perpetrated anything against the vassal in these five points it is allowed the vassal to leave him. . . .

LETTER FROM BISHOP FULBERT OF CHARTRES, 1020

Asked to write something concerning the form of fealty,[1] I have noted briefly for you on the authority of the books the things which follow. He who swears fealty to his lord ought always to have these six things in memory; what is harmless, safe, honorable, useful, easy, practicable. Harmless, that is to say that he should not be injurious to his lord in his body; safe, that he should not be injurious to him in his secrets or in the defences through which he is able to be secure; honorable, that

---

[1] The obligation of loyalty owed by a vassal to his feudal lord.

he should not be injurious to him in his justice or in other matters that pertain to his honor; useful, that he should not be injurious to him in his possessions; easy or practicable, that that good which his lord is able to do easily, he make not difficult, nor that which is practicable he make impossible to him.

However, that the faithful vassal should avoid these injuries is proper, but not for this does he deserve his holding; for it is not sufficient to abstain from evil, unless what is good is done also. It remains, therefore, that in the same six things mentioned above he should faithfully counsel and aid his lord, if he wishes to be looked upon as worthy of his benefice and to be safe concerning the fealty which he has sworn.

The lord also ought to act toward his faithful vassal reciprocally in all these things. And if he does not do this he will be justly considered guilty of bad faith, just as the former, if he should be detected in the avoidance of or the doing of or the consenting to them, would be perfidious and perjured.

Letters: Secular and Ecclesiastical Authority
Pope Gregory VII

Throughout the Middle Ages the line between secular and ecclesiastical authority was often unclear. During the eleventh century, the papacy grew in stature and power, particularly under Gregory VII's pontificate (1073–1085). Gregory VII, who brought the reforming spirit to his office, soon came into conflict with Emperor Henry IV of the Holy Roman Empire over who had the right to appoint people to high offices in the Church and who had control over properties and revenues connected with ecclesiastical offices. This controversy was not solved until well into the twelfth century, and similar struggles between Church and state continued to arise in succeeding centuries. The following set of papal propositions, found among the letters of Gregory VII (ca. 1075), indicates some of the powers the papacy was claiming for itself during this period.

Consider: *In what matters the papacy asserted its powers and over whom; the ways in which these powers might have threatened the powers of secular rulers.*

The Roman church was founded by God alone.

The Roman bishop alone is properly called universal.

He alone may depose bishops and reinstate them.

His legate, though of inferior grade, takes precedence, in a council, of all bishops and may render a decision of deposition against them.

He alone may use the insignia of empire.

The pope is the only person whose feet are kissed by all princes.

SOURCE: From James Harvey Robinson, ed., *Readings in European History*, vol. I (Boston: Ginn, 1904), p. 274.

His title is unique in the world.

He may depose emperors.

No council may be regarded as a general one without his consent.

No book or chapter may be regarded as canonical without his authority.

A decree of his may be annulled by no one; he alone may annul the decrees of all.

He may be judged by no one.

No one shall dare to condemn one who appeals to the papal see.

The Roman church has never erred, nor ever, by the witness of Scripture, shall err to all eternity.

He may not be considered Catholic who does not agree with the Roman church.

The pope may absolve the subjects of the unjust from their allegiance.

The Life of Saint Godric: A Merchant Adventurer
Reginald of Durham

By the eleventh century, Europeans were becoming involved in long-distance trade with the East, which had been monopolized by Byzantine and Muslim merchant fleets. The number of people involved in commerce grew during the eleventh and twelfth centuries, not only in the Mediterranean area but in northern Europe as well. In some cases, individuals were able to start with little and, over the years, amass considerable wealth. This is illustrated in the following selections from The Life of Saint Godric. *Godric lived during the twelfth century, closing out his career as a merchant by going on a pilgrimage to Jerusalem and giving his wealth to the Church. His biography was written by a friend and disciple, the monk Reginald of Durham.*

> **Consider:** *How this document might be used to show that the main elements of capitalism were present as far back as the twelfth century; what this document shows about the potential for social mobility during the Middle Ages.*

He chose not to follow the life of a husbandman, but rather to study, learn and exercise the rudiments of more subtle conceptions. For this reason, aspiring to the merchant's trade, he began to follow the chapman's way of life, first learning how to gain in small bargains and things of insignificant price; and thence, while yet a youth, his mind advanced little by little to buy and sell and gain from things of greater expense. For, in his beginnings, he was wont to wander with small wares around the villages and farmsteads of his own neighbourhood; but, in process of time, he gradually associated himself by compact with city merchants.

SOURCE: G. G. Coulton, *Social Life in Britain from the Conquest to the Reformation* (Cambridge, England: Cambridge University Press, 1918), pp. 415–419.

Hence, within a brief space of time, the youth who had trudged for many weary hours from village to village, from farm to farm, did so profit by his increase of age and wisdom as to travel with associates of his own age through towns and boroughs, fortresses and cities, to fairs and to all the various booths of the market-place, in pursuit of his public chaffer. . . . At first, he lived as a chapman for four years in Lincolnshire, going on foot and carrying the smallest wares; then he travelled abroad, first to St. Andrews in Scotland and then for the first time to Rome. On his return, having formed a familiar friendship with certain other young men who were eager for merchandise, he began to launch upon bolder courses, and to coast frequently by sea to the foreign lands that lay around him. Thus, sailing often to and fro between Scotland and Britain, he traded in many divers wares and, amid these occupations, learned much worldly wisdom. . . . For he laboured not only as a merchant but also as a shipman . . . to Denmark and Flanders and Scotland; in all which lands he found certain rare, and therefore more precious, wares, which he carried to other parts wherein he knew them to be least familiar, and coveted by the inhabitants beyond the price of gold itself; wherefore he exchanged these wares for others coveted by men of other lands; and thus he chaffered most freely and assiduously. Hence he made great profit in all his bargains, and gathered much wealth in the sweat of his brow; for he sold dear in one place the wares which he had bought elsewhere at a small price.

Then he purchased the half of a merchant-ship with certain of his partners in the trade, and again by his prudence he bought the fourth part of another ship. At length, by his skill in navigation, wherein he excelled all his fellows, he earned promotion to the post of steersman. . . .

And now he had lived sixteen years as a merchant, and began to think of spending on charity, to God's honour and service, the goods which he had so laboriously acquired. He therefore took the cross as a pilgrim to Jerusalem, and, having visited the Holy Sepulchre, came back to England by way of St. James [of Compostella].

The Decretum: Medieval Women—Not in God's Image
Gratian

In the eyes of the medieval Church, the position of women was a problem. On the one hand women were, in theory, spiritual equals to men: their souls were as worthy as men's. On the other hand, women were acknowledged as legally and socially subordinate to men:

SOURCE: Excerpts from *Not In God's Image* by Julia O'Faolain and Lauro Martines. Copyright © 1973 by Julia O'Faolain and Lauro Martines. Reprinted by permission of Harper & Row, Publishers, Inc.

for example, the priesthood was limited to men. In attitudes and in practice, the latter view of women as subject to men predominated. A particularly strong statement of this view can be found in the following selection from the Decretum, *a systematization of Church law written around 1140 by Gratian, a jurist from northern Italy.*

> **Consider:** *The image of women revealed in this document; how Gratian justifies this view of the position of women; some of the possible consequences of this attitude.*

Women should be subject to their men. The natural order for mankind is that women should serve men and children their parents, for it is just that the lesser serve the greater.

The image of God is in man and it is one. Women were drawn from man, who has God's jurisdiction as if he were God's vicar, because he has the image of the one God. Therefore woman is not made in God's image.

Woman's authority is nil; let her in all things be subject to the rule of man. . . . And neither can she teach, nor be a witness, nor give a guarantee, nor sit in judgment.

Adam was beguiled by Eve, not she by him. It is right then that he whom woman led into wrongdoing should have her under his direction, so that he may not fail a second time through female levity. [*Corpus Iuris Canonici*]

The Opening of the Crusades
Pope Urban II

The series of crusades in the eleventh century brought the West into greater contact with Byzantium and Islam. These crusades demonstrated the expansiveness of the West during the High Middle Ages as well as the increasing power and activism of the papacy. The first of these crusades was called for in 1095 by Pope Urban II in response to a request for help from the Byzantine Emperor Alexius Comnenus. At the Council of Clermont, Urban made the following plea, recorded by Robert the Monk.

> **Consider:** *How Urban justified his call for a crusade; what Urban might have hoped to gain from this crusade; to whom this plea was addressed.*

"Oh, race of Franks, race from across the mountains, race beloved and chosen by God,—as is clear from many of your works,—set apart from all other nations by the situation of your country as well as by your Catholic faith and the honor which you render to the holy Church: to you our discourse is addressed, and for you our exhortations are intended. . . .

SOURCE: From James Harvey Robinson, ed., *Readings in European History*, vol. I (Boston: Ginn, 1904), pp. 314–317.

"From the confines of Jerusalem and from the city of Constantinople a grievous report has gone forth and has repeatedly been brought to our ears; namely, that a race from the kingdom of the Persians, an accursed race, a race wholly alienated from God, 'a generation that set not their heart aright, and whose spirit was not steadfast with God,' has violently invaded the lands of those Christians and has depopulated them by pillage and fire. They have led away a part of the captives into their own country, and a part they have killed by cruel tortures. They have either destroyed the churches of God or appropriated them for the rites of their own religion. They destroy the altars, after having defiled them with their uncleanness. . . . The kingdom of the Greeks is now dismembered by them and has been deprived of territory so vast in extent that it could not be traversed in two months' time.

"On whom, therefore, is the labor of avenging these wrongs and of recovering this territory incumbent, if not upon you,—you, upon whom, above all other nations, God has conferred remarkable glory in arms, great courage, bodily activity, and strength to humble the heads of those who resist you? Let the deeds of your ancestors encourage you and incite your minds to manly achievements:—the glory and greatness of King Charlemagne, and of his son Louis, and of your other monarchs, who have destroyed the kingdoms of the Turks and have extended the sway of the holy Church over lands previously pagan. Let the holy sepulcher of our Lord and Saviour, which is possessed by the unclean nations, especially arouse you, and the holy places which are now treated with ignominy and irreverently polluted with the filth of the unclean. Oh, most valiant soldiers and descendants of invincible ancestors, do not degenerate, but recall the valor of your progenitors.

"But if you are hindered by love of children, parents, or wife, remember what the Lord says in the Gospel, 'He that loveth father or mother more than me is not worthy of me.' 'Every one that hath forsaken houses, or brethren, or sisters, or father, or mother, or wife, or children, or lands, for my name's sake, shall receive an hundredfold, and shall inherit everlasting life.' Let none of your possessions retain you, nor solicitude for your family affairs. For this land which you inhabit, shut in on all sides by the seas and surrounded by the mountain peaks, is too narrow for your large population; nor does it abound in wealth; and it furnishes scarcely food enough for its cultivators. Hence it is that you murder and devour one another, that you wage war, and that very many among you perish in intestine [internal] strife.

"Let hatred therefore depart from among you, let your quarrels end, let wars cease, and let all dissensions and controversies slumber. Enter upon the road to the Holy Sepulcher; wrest that land from the wicked race, and subject it to yourselves. That land which, as the Scripture says, 'floweth with milk and honey' was given by God into the power of the children of Israel. Jerusalem is the center of the earth; the land is fruitful above all others, like another paradise of delights. This spot the Redeemer of mankind has made illustrious by his advent, has beautified by his sojourn, has consecrated by his passion, has redeemed by his death, has glorified by his burial.

"This royal city, however, situated at the center of the earth, is now held captive by the enemies of Christ and is subjected, by those who do not know God, to the worship of the heathen. She seeks, therefore, and desires to be liberated and ceases not to implore you to come to her aid. From you especially she asks succor, because, as we have already said, God has conferred upon you above all other nations great glory in arms. Accordingly, undertake this journey eagerly for the remission of your sins, with the assurance of the reward of imperishable glory in the kingdom of heaven."

The Rule of St. Francis
St. Francis of Assisi

There were periodic Christian reform movements during the Middle Ages. The most important movement during the thirteenth century was initiated by the Franciscans, a group of pious laymen who gathered around Francis of Assisi (1181?–1226). Francis, who had been born into a merchant family and was headed for a secular career, had experienced a deeply emotional conversion, given up his worldly goods, and pursued a life of asceticism, preaching, and poverty. He and his followers did not withdraw to a cloistered life, but traveled extensively and were particularly active in urban areas. While still not formally approved by the Church, this organization constituted a potential threat. But by 1223, when the following version of St. Francis' rule was adopted, the papacy had officially recognized the Franciscans as an orthodox order.

> **Consider:** *Reasons why such an order might be so successful; the functions such an order might perform for society or for the Church; problems that could arise in religious orders as revealed by this document.*

This is the rule and life of the Minor Brothers, namely, to observe the holy gospel of our Lord Jesus Christ by living in obedience, in poverty, and in chastity. Brother Francis promises obedience and reverence to Pope Honorius and to his successors who shall be canonically elected, and to the Roman Church. The other brothers are bound to obey brother Francis, and his successors. . . .

I counsel, warn, and exhort my brothers in the Lord Jesus Christ that when they go out into the world they shall not be quarrelsome or contentious, nor judge others. But they shall be gentle, peaceable, and kind, mild and humble, and virtuous in speech, as is becoming to all. They shall not ride on horseback unless compelled by manifest necessity or infirmity to do so. When they enter a house they shall say, "Peace be to this house." According to the holy gospel, they may eat of whatever food is set before them.

I strictly forbid all the brothers to accept money or property either in person

---

Source: Oliver J. Thatcher and Edgar H. McNeal, eds., and trans., *A Source Book for Medieval History* (New York: Scribner's, 1905), pp. 499–507.

or through another. Nevertheless, for the needs of the sick, and for clothing the other brothers, the ministers and guardians may, as they see that necessity requires, provide through spiritual friends, according to the locality, season, and the degree of cold which may be expected in the region where they live. But, as has been said, they shall never receive money or property.

Those brothers to whom the Lord has given the ability to work shall work faithfully and devotedly, so that idleness, which is the enemy of the soul, may be excluded and not extinguish the spirit of prayer and devotion to which all temporal things should be subservient. As the price of their labors they may receive things that are necessary for themselves and the brothers, but not money or property. And they shall humbly receive what is given them, as is becoming to the servants of God and to those who practise the most holy poverty.

The brothers shall have nothing of their own, neither house, nor land, nor anything, but as pilgrims and strangers in this world, serving the Lord in poverty and humility, let them confidently go asking alms. Nor let them be ashamed of this, for the Lord made himself poor for us in this world. This is that highest pitch of poverty which has made you, my dearest brothers, heirs and kings of the kingdom of heaven, which has made you poor in goods, and exalted you in virtues. . . .

I strictly forbid all the brothers to have any association or conversation with women that may cause suspicion. And let them not enter nunneries, except those which the pope has given them special permission to enter. Let them not be intimate friends of men or women lest on this account scandal arise among the brothers or about brothers.

VISUAL SOURCES

Illustration from a Gospel Book: Christianity and Early Medieval Culture

During the Early Middle Ages art became quite religious. Indeed, many of the paintings that survive from that period are miniatures from religious manuscripts, as in the case of this picture of the four evangelists from an early ninth-century Carolingian Gospel book. Each evangelist is shown writing his Gospel, and each is accompanied by his symbol: Matthew by a man, John by an eagle, Luke by a bull, and Mark by a lion.

This picture reveals a number of things about the Early Middle Ages. First, it suggests something about the position of Christianity. To this recently Christianized civilization,

Photo 10–1

Ann Münchow

this scene could constitute a visual confirmation of biblical truth; the four evangelists are shown to have written, independently, similar accounts, thus testifying to the essential truth of the New Testament. Second, it exemplifies some of the uses of art in a strongly religious but relatively illiterate civilization: Here, the picture tells a story and important individuals are associated with identifying symbols. Third, the style and composition indicate that the artist was probably Byzantine or heavily influenced by Byzantine art. A Byzantine influence is also evident in a number of similar works that were part of the

Carolingian revival initiated by Charlemagne. This could indicate a recognition of the superiority of Classical and Byzantine cultural productions and perhaps a sense of cultural inferiority in western Europe.

Consider: *What this reveals about the purposes of art during this period.*

Medieval Life
Pol de Limbourg

While there was considerable change between the eleventh and fifteenth centuries, many fundamental aspects of life remained much the same. This late-medieval illustration by Pol de Limbourg from the Très Riches Heures du Duc de Berry, *a book of prayers for each day of the year, shows a typical October day. A peasant sows seeds in a small, recently plowed field. Just behind, a scarecrow in the form of an archer guards another field. In the background flows the Seine with some aristocrats on its bank under the walls of the Louvre, the Gothic castle of the French kings in Paris. The basic reliance on agriculture, the importance of the seasons, the sharp contrast between the social classes, and the increasingly large castles symbolizing military prowess and status remained typical of medieval life.*

Consider: *The nature of the peasant's life as portrayed by this artist; how an aristocratic viewer of this illustration might react.*

Photo 10–2

Chantilly, Musée Condé. Photographie Giraudon

Contraction and Expansion in the Middle Ages

Map 10–1 offers evidence for the urban decline that occurred throughout Europe during the Middle Ages. It shows Trier, Germany, founded by the Romans, as it was during the Early Middle Ages. It became smaller, and the ordered street plan of the Romans was abandoned. Some of the Roman buildings were retained and used; some new churches were constructed both inside and outside the city.

Map 10–2 illustrates the relative weakness and contraction of Europe on a broader scale. Pressure was being exerted by three non-Christian groups during the ninth and tenth centuries: the Saracens (Moslems) from the south, the Magyars from the east, and the Vikings (a general term for groups of Scandinavians known by various names) from the north. The Saracens, adding to the already conquered Spanish lands, took con-

Map 10–1   Urban Decline, the Early Middle Ages

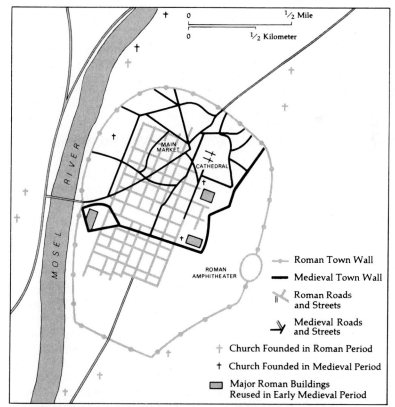

- Roman Town Wall
- Medieval Town Wall
- Roman Roads and Streets
- Medieval Roads and Streets
- † Church Founded in Roman Period
- † Church Founded in Medieval Period
- Major Roman Buildings Reused in Early Medieval Period

Map 10–2   Non-Christian Pressures, Ninth and Tenth Centuries

ICELAND

IRELAND   BRITAIN

VIKINGS

KIEVAN RUSSIA

FRANCE

MAGYARS

CORDOBA

BYZANTINE
EMPIRE

SARACENS

▤ Saracen Attacks and Invasions
▨ Devastation by Magyars
▦ Viking Activity and Occupation
•••••• Boundary of Christendom

0   500 Miles
0   500 Kilometers

trol of the western Mediterranean from Christian hands and disrupted life with numerous raids into large areas of southern Europe, particularly France and Italy. The Magyars made a number of destructive raids into parts of central, western, and southern Europe from their eastern homelands. The Vikings were the most mobile of all, moving into Slavic lands to the east, England to the west, and coastal areas in northern and western Europe, as well as competing with the Saracens in the Mediterranean region.

These two maps indicate some of the geopolitical problems affecting western Christendom in the Early Middle Ages. The difficulty Christian monarchs had in resisting these invasions contributed to the political decentralization and corresponding feudalization of the period. The invaders did not respect Christian holy places or officials, which added to the disruption of organized life. Similarly, commerce suffered, as it could no longer be safely carried out. All this contributed to the increased turning inward and contraction in Europe that were indeed geographic and political realities on both a local and an international scale. But with many of these invaders, particularly the Vikings, there was a merging of cultures and an influx of new strength as they eventually became Christianized and adapted to their new environments.

> **Consider:** The ways in which the geopolitical realities of Europe in the Early Middle Ages were conducive to the growth of feudalism; the ways in which maps can support the argument that the Early Middle Ages was a period of decline in the West.

MEDIEVAL EXPANSION

The first of the following two maps shows the growth of settlements in the Black Forest in Germany between the ninth and twelfth centuries; in fact, most of the growth took place during the eleventh and twelfth centuries. In this case, however, much of the settlement was planned and carried out by the dukes of Zähringen and some of the monasteries under their control, particularly St. Peter and St. George. By the end of the first half of the twelfth century, the Zähringens had founded the strategically located towns of Freiburg, Villingen, and Offenburg, which enabled them to gain control over the whole area.

Map 10–3   Planned Settlement (Germany)

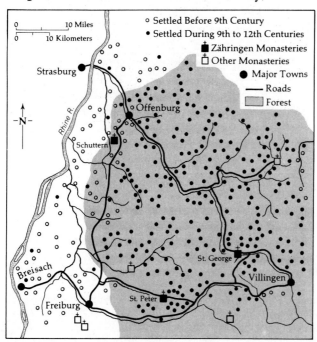

Map 10–4   External Expansion

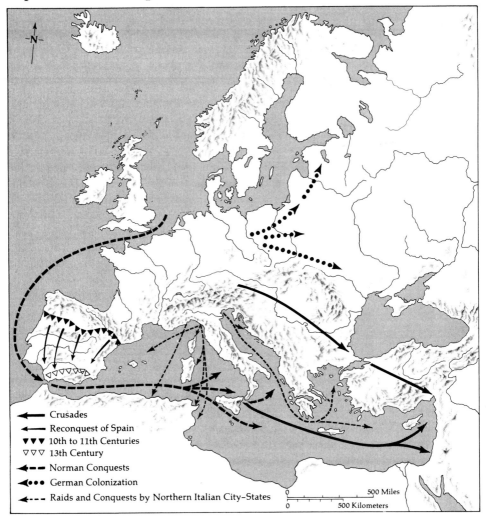

Legend:
- Crusades
- Reconquest of Spain
- ▼ ▼ ▼ 10th to 11th Centuries
- ▽ ▽ ▽ 13th Century
- ◄ – – Norman Conquests
- ◄ ● ● ● German Colonization
- ◄ – – – Raids and Conquests by Northern Italian City-States

0   500 Miles

0   500 Kilometers

Map 10–4 shows the external expansion of Europe and Christendom during this same period. This was carried out by the newly expanding Byzantine Empire; by the now Christianized Vikings (Normans); by military efforts with directly religious overtones, both national (the reconquest in Spain) and international (the crusades to the Holy Land); and by a combination of political and commercial expansion by Italian and north German cities and states.

The external and internal expansions complement each other and provide evidence of the general dynamism of the High Middle Ages.

Consider: *The ways in which maps can reveal both the expansion of a civilization and how the expansion took place; how differences between the Early and High Middle Ages are revealed when these maps are compared with Maps 10-1 and 10-2.*

SECONDARY SOURCES

Mohammed and Charlemagne: The Beginnings of Medieval Civilization
Henri Pirenne

Traditionally, the break between Roman civilization and the Middle Ages in the West has been dated to the Germanic invasions during the fifth century. According to this view, by the sixth century the West had experienced such change and decline in its political institutions, commerce, social life, and cities that Rome was at best a distant memory; the Early Middle Ages had begun. During the 1920s and 1930s this assumption was challenged by the Belgian historian Henri Pirenne (1862–1935). He argued that there was relative continuity during the fifth, sixth, and first half of the seventh centuries. The transition to the Middle Ages occurred between 650 and 750 as a result of the rise of Islam. Pirenne's thesis had wide acceptance for many years. Although historians have since cast doubt on important parts of this thesis, all medievalists must still deal with this interpretation.

Consider: *Pirenne's explanation of why the Germanic invasions did not create the break with antiquity; Pirenne's rationale for arguing that the transition was completed by 800; Pirenne's view of the most important ways in which the civilization of the Middle Ages differed from that of the fifth and sixth centuries.*

From the foregoing data, it seems, we may draw two essential conclusions:

SOURCE: From Henri Pirenne, *Mohammed and Charlemagne*, trans. Bernard Miall (London: George Allen & Unwin Ltd., 1958), pp. 284–285. Copyright © 1958. Reprinted by permission of Routledge.

1. The Germanic invasions destroyed neither the Mediterranean unity of the ancient world, nor what may be regarded as the truly essential features of the Roman culture as it still existed in the 5th century, at a time when there was no longer an Emperor in the West.

Despite the resulting turmoil and destruction, no new principles made their appearance; neither in the economic or social order, nor in the linguistic situation, nor in the existing institutions. What civilization survived was Mediterranean. It was in the regions by the sea that culture was preserved, and it was from them that the innovations of the age proceeded: monasticism, the conversion of the Anglo-Saxons, the *ars Barbarica*, etc.

The Orient was the fertilizing factor: Constantinople, the centre of the world. In 600 the physiognomy of the world was not different in quality from that which it had revealed in 400.

2. The cause of the break with the tradition of antiquity was the rapid and unexpected advance of Islam. The result of this advance was the final separation of East from West, and the end of the Mediterranean unity. Countries like Africa and Spain, which had always been parts of the Western community, gravitated henceforth in the orbit of Baghdad. In these countries another religion made its appearance, and an entirely different culture. The Western Mediterranean, having become a Musulman lake, was no longer the thoroughfare of commerce and of thought which it had always been.

The West was blockaded and forced to live upon its own resources. For the first time in history the axis of life was shifted northwards from the Mediterranean. The decadence into which the Merovingian monarchy lapsed as a result of this change gave birth to a new dynasty, the Carolingian, whose original home was in the Germanic North.

With this new dynasty the Pope allied himself, breaking with the Emperor, who, engrossed in his struggle against the Musulmans, could no longer protect him. And so the Church allied itself with the new order of things. In Rome, and in the Empire which it founded, it had no rival. And its power was all the greater inasmuch as the State, being incapable of maintaining its administration, allowed itself to be absorbed by the feudality, the inevitable sequel of the economic regression. All the consequences of this change became glaringly apparent after Charlemagne. Europe, dominated by the Church and the feudality, assumed a new physiognomy, differing slightly in different regions. The Middle Ages—to retain the traditional term—were beginning. The transitional phase was protracted. One may say that it lasted a whole century—from 650 to 750. It was during this period of anarchy that the tradition of antiquity disappeared, while the new elements came to the surface.

This development was completed in 800 by the constitution of the new Empire, which consecrated the break between the West and the East, inasmuch as it gave to the West a new Roman Empire—the manifest proof that it had broken with the old Empire, which continued to exist in Constantinople.

Sanctity and Power: The Dual Pursuit of Medieval Women

Jo Ann McNamara and Suzanne F. Wemple

Too often it has been assumed that the position of women changed little throughout the Middle Ages. In the following selection, two medieval historians, Jo Ann McNamara and Suzanne Wemple, argue that by the ninth century the situation for many women had vastly improved.

> **Consider:** *How marriage customs changed to the benefit of women; the social effects of changes in women's inheritance rights.*

By the ninth century a complex series of social advances had produced a vastly improved situation for the individual woman vis-à-vis the family interest to which she had previously been subordinated. Women were able to ensure their independence within the limits of whatever social sphere they occupied by their control of some property of their own. The Germanic custom of bride purchase practically disappeared. Instead of giving a purchase price to the bride's family, the groom endowed her directly with the bride gift, usually a piece of landed property over which she had full rights. To this, he frequently added the morning gift following the consummation of the marriage. In addition to the economic independence derived through marriage, the women of the ninth century enjoyed an increased capacity to share in the inheritance of property. Women had always been eligible to receive certain movable goods from either their own relatives or from their husbands but now law and practice allowed women to inherit immovables. A reason for this trend may be discerned from a deed from the eighth century in which a doting father left equal shares of his property to his sons and daughters. He justified his act by explaining that discrimination between the sexes was an "impious custom" that ran contrary to God's law and to the love he felt for all of his children.

Women's ability to inherit property had far-reaching social effects, which modern demographers are still investigating. Although a young women still could not marry a man against her family's will, her independence after marriage was greatly enhanced if she possessed her own property. After their father's death, Charlemagne's daughters were able to withdraw from the court of their brother and lead independent lives because Charlemagne had endowed them with substantial prop-

---

SOURCE: From "Sanctity and Power: The Dual Pursuit of Medieval Women," by Jo Ann McNamara and Suzanne F. Wemple, in *Becoming Visible: Women in European History* (eds. Renate Bridenthal and Claudia Koonz), pp. 103–104. Copyright © 1977 by Houghton Mifflin Company. Reprinted by permission.

erty. As widows, too, woman acquired increased status if they were allowed to control their sons' and their deceased husbands' property. The most dramatic example of this permanenty affected the political future of England. The daughter of Alfred the Great, Ethelflaeda, widow of the king of Mercia, devoted her long reign to cooperation with her brother in the pursuit of their father's policy of containing the Norse invaders. Together they established a strong, centralized kingdom centered on Wessex. After a life of campaigning against Danish, Irish, and Norwegian enemies, she succeeded in willing the kingdom away from her own daughter, the rightful heiress, and leaving it to her brother. This act destroyed the independence of Mercia with its rival claims to Anglo-Saxon supremacy and assured that the English kingdom would be dominated by Wessex and the line of Alfred. Ironically, Ethelflaeda's indisputable contribution to the future of England deprived another woman of her right to rule.

The Making of the Middle Ages: Serfdom
R. W. Southern

For large masses of people serfdom was the overriding condition of life during the Middle Ages. At times observers have tended to romanticize the Middle Ages and the bucolic life of the peasantry. But in the following selection R. W. Southern of Oxford University, author of the highly acclaimed The Making of the Middle Ages, *reflects most historians' views in arguing that serfdom was a condition characterized by servitude; the serf's lack of liberty was recognized by contemporaries as harmful and degrading. This selection illustrates the advantages of looking at the Middle Ages from the inside, from the point of view of the people of that time.*

> **Consider:** *The evidence Southern provides to support his argument; conditions that might have mitigated the negative aspects of serfdom.*

To nearly all men serfdom was, without qualification, a degrading thing, and they found trenchant phrases to describe the indignity of the condition. The serf's family was always referred to by lawyers as his brood, his *sequela*, and the poets delighted to exercise their ingenuity in describing the physical deformity of the ideal serf. Hard words break no bones, but they are hard to bear for all that, and they became harder as time went on. Men well knew, however theologians might seem to turn common notions inside out, the difference between the yoke of servitude and the honour of liberty—or, to use the expressive phrase of Giraldus Cambrensis, the *hilaritas libertatis:* "There is nothing," he wrote, "which so stirs

SOURCE: R. W. Southern, *The Making of the Middle Ages* (New Haven, Conn.: Yale University Press, 1953), pp. 106–107.

the hearts of men and incites them to honourable action like the lightheartedness of liberty; and nothing which so deters and depresses them like the oppression of servitude." If we consider only the practical effects of serfdom and notice how little the lines of economic prosperity follow those of personal status; if we reflect on the many impediments to free action, to which even the mightiest were subjected in such delicate matters as marriage and the bequeathing of property, it may seem surprising that the pride of liberty was so strong, and the contempt for serfdom so general: yet such was the case. However much the hierarchical principle of society forced men into relationships at all levels of society in which rights and restraints were inextricably mixed up, the primitive line which divided liberty from servitude was never forgotten.

The Meaning of the Middle Ages: The Crusades Minimized
Norman F. Cantor

Many historians have argued that the Crusades—particularly the First Crusade—had great significance. Above all, they were part of a European expansion that reflected new strength in comparison to competing civilizations. But not all historians agree. In recent years several historians have deemphasized the importance of the Crusades. This is exemplified in the following selection by Norman Cantor.

> **Consider:** *What, according to Cantor, was most important about the crusades; how this interpretation might be attacked.*

Historians used to believe that the Crusades reopened the Mediterranean to east-west trade after centuries of isolation and thus made a critical contribution to the economic and intellectual development of Europe. It is true that the Crusades were inspired in part by commercial motives: from the middle of the tenth century, Venetian and Genoese merchants had aspired to take over certain commercial ventures from the Arabs and Byzantines and to acquire new ports in the eastern Mediterranean. The Crusades helped the Italian merchants in both ambitions, but that does not imply that they opened up the Mediterranean—east-west trade had never completely disappeared, and in the ninth and tenth centuries, long before the Crusades, it was growing fast spurred on by the growth of the Italian cities.

It is true that the Christian world absorbed a great deal of Muslim philosophy, medicine, science, and literature in the late eleventh and twelfth centuries, but

---

SOURCE: From Norman F. Cantor, *The Meaning of the Middle Ages: A Sociological and Cultural History.* Copyright © 1973 by Allyn and Bacon, Inc., Boston. Reprinted with permission.

the Crusades did not contribute to this phenomenon—indeed, they probably inhibited it by stirring up religious fanaticism and hatred of Muslims. The intellectual exchange between Christians and Muslims did not take place among soldiers on a battlefield but in the cosmopolitan centers of southern Europe (especially those in Spain and Sicily) where Christians and Muslims lived side by side.

The tangible, institutional impact of the Crusades on the development of Europe was very slight: the institution of monarchy was affected almost not at all, and even the Church (apart from a slight rise in papal prestige) was not much affected by the Crusades in the twelfth century. Eventually two different kinds of crusading movements developed: external Crusades, directed mainly against Arabs, and internal Crusades against enemies within Christendom. The latter—the crusading ideal turned inward—had enormous impact upon the development of European civilization, but this was not fully realized until the thirteenth century.

The most important legacy of the crusading movement was the sanctification of violence in pursuit of ideological ends. This was not a new concept, but it took on new force when the pope and the flower of Christian chivalry acted it out in holy wars. The underlying concept outlived its religious origin, and eventually it was absorbed in the institution of monarchy. When the European kings grew more powerful, in the twelfth and thirteenth centuries, they secularized the concept of justifiable violence and extended it into the political sphere. The defense of the realm and its head became a moral duty, and the state gradually replaced the Church as a holy cause.

Byzantine East and Latin West
Deno J. Geanakoplos

In dealing with Byzantium, it is important to avoid seeing it only as a barrier to the further intrusion of Islam into the West or as a passive repository of Classical learning to be returned to the West with the fall of Constantinople in the Late Middle Ages. This civilization, though conservative in many ways, was of great importance in and of itself. In the following selection Deno Geanakoplos, a specialist in Byzantine history at Yale, interprets this civilization from this broad appreciative perspective.

> **Consider:** *The developments that justify considering Constantinople as the cultural capital of all Christendom during much of the Middle Ages; the ways in which Byzantium influenced Western cultural development.*

It is frequently asserted that from a cultural point of view the chief function of Byzantium was to serve for over one thousand years as the bulwark of Christendom against invading infidel hordes and in this capacity to preserve for the world the

SOURCE: Deno J. Geanakoplos, *Byzantine East and Latin West* (Oxford, England: Basil Blackwell, 1966), pp. 11, 53. Reprinted by permission.

literary and philosophic heritage of ancient Greece. There is not doubt of course of the signal service rendered by Byzantium as a preserver of Greek learning. After all, the Greek language and literature had virtually disappeared from the German-dominated West of the so-called Dark Ages. But Byzantium was certainly more than a mere passive repository of ancient civilization. On the contrary, as her culture developed, it reflected a remarkable amalgamation not only of the philosophy and literature of Greece, but of the religious ideals of Christianity—which in the East underwent a development significantly different from that of the Latin West—and thirdly, of a certain transcendent, mystical quality that may at least partly be attributed to the diverse influences of Syria, Egypt, the Jews, even Persia. These three elements, then, Greco-Roman classicism (including the governmental tradition of Rome), the Byzantine brand of Christianity, and what we may call the oriental component, were blended by the Byzantines into a unique and viable synthesis that made Constantinople, at least until 1204, the cultural capital of all Christendom. It was this many-faceted cultural amalgam . . . that enabled Byzantium to play a far from insignificant part in the formation of western civilization. . . .

Byzantium, through its amalgamation of classicism and the more original 'Byzantine' elements of its culture, above all its unique brand of Christianity which permeated every facet of medieval Greek life, was able, directly or indirectly, to influence a great many aspects of western cultural development: in certain types of art and architecture, in the sphere of industrial techniques, in law and statecraft, in navigational terms and regulations, the recovery of classical Greek literature and possibly the composition of the romance, in the development of a more refined mode of living and in some forms of religious piety and music as well as in religious thought. In these aspects of *most* of the cultural areas meaningful to medieval man there seems to have been some tangible specific evidence of Byzantine influence in one area or another of western European society. Once more, however, it should be emphasized that these influences ranged from the very minor in some spheres to the very substantial in others.

Ecological Conditions and Demographic Change
David Herlihy

Most historians feel that the medieval expansion ended between 1300 and 1350 and that changes occurred that marked the following century as one of contraction, disruption, and decline. Traditionally, these changes have been analyzed from political, military, and

SOURCE: David Herlihy, "Ecological Conditions and Demographic Change," in *One Thousand Years: Western Europe in the Middle Ages*, ed. Richard L. DeMolen (Boston: Houghton Mifflin, 1974), p. 32.

religious perspectives. In the following selection David Herlihy of Harvard focuses on the economic aspects of this change, particularly the economic limitations that prevented the medieval expansion from continuing much beyond the thirteenth century.

> **Consider:** *Obstacles hindering economic expansion by 1300; the social and political effects that might have stemmed from these economic changes; other factors that might account for the end of the medieval expansion.*

Medieval expansion, however, never achieved a true breakthrough, never reached what some economists today term the stage of "takeoff," in which a built-in capacity for continuing growth is developed. By around 1300, certain obstacles were beginning to hinder economic expansion. One was the relative stagnation of technology. In spite of important technological discoveries that introduced the Middle Ages, peasants in 1300 were working the land much as their ancestors had several centuries before. However, technological stagnation alone does not seem to have imposed a rigid ceiling on growth. Paradoxically, many peasants in the late thirteenth century were not working the soil according to the best known and available methods. Their chief handicap was not lack of knowledge but lack of capital, for the best methods were based upon the effective use of cattle to supply both labor and manure. Insofar as we can judge, many small cultivators of the thirteenth century could not afford cattle and had to work their plots with their own unaided and inefficient efforts.

A second limitation upon expansion was the failure to develop institutions and values that would maintain appropriate levels of investment, especially in agriculture. In spite of the growth of cities, a large part of Europe's lands was controlled by military and clerical aristocracies, which were not likely to reinvest their profits received in rent. The great landlords were rather prone to spend their rents on conspicuous but economically barren forms of consumption such as manor houses, castles, churches, wars, the maintenance of a lavish style of living. They were also likely to demand from the towns money in loans for such unproductive expenditures.

A third limiting factor seems to have been the growing scarcity of resources, especially good land. As the best soils were taken under cultivation, the still growing population had to rely increasingly upon poorer, marginal lands, which required more effort and capital to assure a good return. The European economy was burdened by a growing saturation in the use of its readily available resources, and it had neither the technology nor the capital to improve its returns from what it possessed. In the opinion of many historians today, this saturation in the use of resources not only ended the economic advance of the central Middle Ages but precipitated a profound demographic and economic crisis in the fourteenth century.

Chapter Questions

1. Drawing on sources in this chapter, what sorts of conflicts were there between secular and religious authorities during this period? How do you explain the relative strength of religious authorities in these conflicts?

2. For a long time it was believed that Europe's Middle Ages constituted an era of little change, offering little in comparison to the Greco-Roman civilization that preceded it and the Renaissance that succeeded it. In what ways might the sources in this chapter be used to reject this interpretation?

3. Using sources from this chapter and Chapter 6, how does this European civilization compare with the rapidly developing civilization of Islam, particularly between the seventh and tenth centuries?

ELEVEN

Medieval Europe in Transition, 1300–1500

The fourteenth century and the first half of the fifteenth saw decline, disruption, and disintegration in most of Europe. This period, usually referred to as the Late Middle Ages, has been described in terms such as "the decline of the Middle Ages" and "the waning of the Middle Ages." Certain developments support these descriptions. Population decreased significantly, due in great part to poor harvests, disease, and war. European expansion temporarily ended. The Roman Catholic Church faced a series of conflicts including heresy and internal divisions. Economic conditions varied greatly, contributing to the considerable social unrest of the period. Extended political conflicts led to an unusually intense period of wars. In short, these developments paint a picture in marked contrast to our image of the High Middle Ages.

While the decline during the Late Middle Ages was real, the same period witnessed an extraordinary outburst of cultural and intellectual creativity known as the Renaissance. The Renaissance started in the fourteenth century in the cities of northern Italy, where scholars and a social elite became more interested in the literature and ideas of ancient Greece and Rome. As interest in Classical civilization grew, so did a tendency to reject many of the ideas and practices of medieval civilization. While remaining deeply religious, people of the Renaissance concerned themselves more with the secular, physical world than medieval people did. This was reflected in the literature, art, and societies of northern Italian cities from the fourteenth century through the beginning of the sixteenth century. Similar cultural and intellectual developments occurred in northern Europe during the fifteenth century and through most of the sixteenth century, though with some different roots and characteristics.

To illustrate the disruptive developments of the Late Middle Ages, a number of documents in this chapter will be concerned with social problems of the period. One main focus will be the mid-fourteenth-century plague. How was it understood at the time? What were its psychological consequences? Other sources will touch on religious unrest, urban and rural revolts, and the incidence of crime.

For the Renaissance, emphasis will be on the traits historians define as typical of the Renaissance, such as literary humanism and humanistic education. Artistic and literary trends that reflect humanism are also explored. One of the central questions examined is to what extent the Renaissance should be distinguished from the Middle Ages. How should the Renaissance be interpreted as a whole?

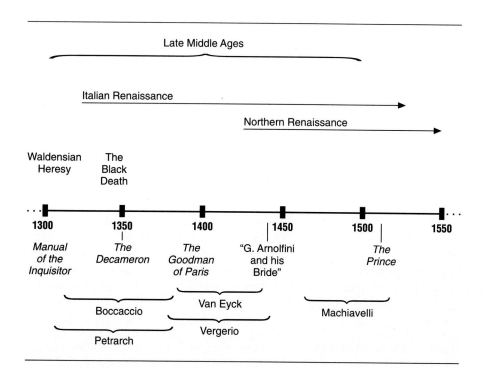

This examination of the Late Middle Ages and the Renaissance will take us into the sixteenth century. By then, Europe was already beginning an expansion that would extend its reach far outside of the western world. This will be our concern in following chapters.

PRIMARY SOURCES

Manual of the Inquisitor
Bernard Gui

One of the several problems facing the Roman Catholic Church in the fourteenth and fifteenth centuries was heresy. Always a concern for the Church, heresy became such a serious problem that the Church turned to formal institutions such as the Inquisition to deal with it. One of the best-known and longest-lasting heretical movements was that of the Waldensians in southern France and northern Italy. Originally, they were followers of Peter Waldo, who pursued a life of piety and religious belief. The Waldensians were officially condemned in the thirteenth century but survived to be persecuted in the fourteenth century. The following is a selection from the Manual of the Inquisitor, *compiled by Bernard Gui, a Dominican monk and bishop who became a zealous inquisitor in southern France from 1307 to 1324.*

> **Consider:** *The main crimes of the Waldensians according to Gui; the nature of the threat posed by these crimes; the similarities and differences between the threats posed by this heresy and those of the Conciliar Movement.*

Disdain for ecclesiastical authority was and still is the prime heresy of the Waldenses. Excommunicated for this reason and delivered over to Satan, they have fallen into innumerable errors, and have blended the errors of earlier heretics with their own concoctions.

The misled believers and sacrilegious masters of this sect hold and teach that they are in no way subject to the lord Pope or Roman Pontiff, or to the other prelates of the Roman Church, and that the latter persecute and condemn them unjustly and improperly. Moreover, they declare that they cannot be excommunicated by this Roman Pontiff and these prelates, and that obedience is owed to

SOURCE: Bernard Gui, *Manual of the Inquisitor*, in *Introduction to Contemporary Civilization in the West*, vol. I, 3rd ed., Contemporary Civilization Staff of Columbia College, Columbia University, ed. (New York: Columbia University Press, 1960), pp. 198–202, 204. Reprinted by permission.

none of them when they order and summon the followers and masters of the said sect to abandon or abjure this sect, although this sect be condemned as heretical by the Roman Church. . . .

Moreover, the sect does not accept canonical authority, or the decretals or constitutions of the Sovereign Pontiff, any more than the regulations concerning fasts and the observance of the feasts or the decrees of the Fathers. Straying from the straight road, they recognize no authority therein, scorn them, reject and condemn them.

Morever, the followers of the sect are even more perniciously mistaken concerning the sacrament of penance and the power of the keys. They declare they have received—this is their doctrine and their teaching—from God and none other, like the apostles who held it of Christ, the power of hearing the confessions of men and women who desire to confess to them, of granting them absolution and of prescribing penance. Thus they hear confessions, grant absolution and prescribe penance, although they have not been ordained as priests or clerics by a bishop of the Roman Church and although they are just laymen. They in no way claim to hold this power from the Roman Church, on the contrary, they deny it; and in fact, they hold it neither from God nor from His Church, since they have been cast out from the Church by this very Church, outside which there is neither true penance nor salvation.

Moreover, this same sect hold up to ridicule the indulgences established and granted by the prelates of the Church, saying they are worthless.

Moreover, they are in error with respect to the sacrament of the Eucharist. They claim, not publicly but secretly, that in the sacrament of the altar the bread and wine do not become body and blood of Christ when the priest who celebrates or consecrates is a sinner; and by sinner they mean any man who does not belong to their sect. Moreover, they claim, on the contrary, that any upright man, even a layman, without having received priestly ordination from the hands of a Catholic bishop, may consecrate the body and blood of Christ, provided he be of their sect. They believe that women too can do this, subject to the same condition, Thus they hold that any holy man is a priest.

The Decameron: The Plague in Florence
Giovanni Boccaccio

In the middle of the fourteeenth century, a devastating plague swept across Europe. In some cities almost half of the population was lost, and for those who were left alive the effects were long-lasting. One survivor was Giovanni Boccaccio (1313–1375), a well-

SOURCE: Giovanni Boccaccio, *The Decameron,* in *Stories of Boccaccio,* trans. John Payne (London: Bibliophilist Library, 1903), pp. 1–6.

known humanist of the Italian Renaissance. His best-known work is The Decameron, *written between 1348 and 1353 when the plague struck Florence. Boccaccio initiated the work with a description of the plague, an excerpt of which follows.*

> **Consider:** *How people reacted to the plague; the general understanding of the cause of the plague and how it spread.*

In the year then of our Lord 1348, there happened at Florence, the finest city in all Italy, a most terrible plague; which, whether owing to the influence of the planets, or that it was sent from God as a just punishment for our sins, had broken out some years before in the Levant, and after passing from place to place, and making incredible havoc all the way, had now reached the west. There, spite of all the means that art and human foresight could suggest, such as keeping the city clear from filth, the exclusion of all suspected persons, and the publication of copious instructions for the preservation of health; and notwithstanding manifold humble supplications offered to God in processions and otherwise; it began to show itself in the spring of the aforesaid year, in a sad and wonderful manner. Unlike what had been seen in the east, where bleeding from the nose is the fatal prognostic, here there appeared certain tumours in the groin or under the armpits, some as big as a small apple, others as an egg, and afterwards purple spots in most parts of the body; in some cases large and but few in number, in others smaller and more numerous—both sorts the usual messengers of death. To the cure of this malady, neither medical knowledge nor the power of drugs was of any effect; whether because the disease was in its own nature mortal, or that the physicians (the number of whom, taking quacks and women pretenders into the account, was grown very great) could form no just idea of the cause, nor consequently devise a true method of cure; whichever was the reason, few escaped; but nearly all died the third day from the first appearance of the symptoms, some sooner, some later, without any fever or accessory symptoms. What gave the more virulence to this plague, was that, by being communicated from the sick to the hale, it spread daily, like fire when it comes in contact with large masses of combustibles. Nor was it caught only by conversing with, or coming near the sick, but even by touching their clothes, or anything that they had before touched. . . .

These facts, and others of the like sort, occasioned various fears and devices amongst those who survived, all tending to the same uncharitable and cruel end; which was, to avoid the sick, and every thing that had been near them, expecting by that means to save themselves. And some holding it best to live temperately, and to avoid excesses of all kinds, made parties, and shut themseves up from the rest of the world; eating and drinking moderately of the best, and diverting themselves with music, and such other entertainments as they might have within doors; never listening to anything from without, to make them uneasy. Others maintained free living to be a better preservative, and would baulk no passion or appetite they wished to gratify, drinking and revelling incessantly from tavern to tavern, or in private houses (which were frequently found deserted by the owners, and therefore common to every one), yet strenuously avoiding, with all this brutal indulgence, to come near the infected. And such, at that time, was the public distress, that the laws, human and divine, were no more regarded; for the officers, to put them in force, being either dead, sick, or in want of persons to assist them, every one did just as he pleased. A third sort of people chose a method between these two: not confining themselves to rules of diet like the former, and yet avoiding the intemperance of the latter; but eating and drinking what their appetites required, they walked everywhere with odours and nosegays to smell to; as holding it best to corroborate the brain: for the whole atmosphere seemed to them tainted with the stench of dead bodies, arising partly from the distemper itself, and partly from the fermenting of the medicines within them. Others with less humanity, but perchance, as they supposed, with more security from danger, decided that the only remedy for the pestilence was to avoid it: persuaded, therefore, of this, and taking care for themselves only, men and women in great numbers left the city, their houses, relations, and effects, and fled into the country; as if the wrath of God had been restrained to visit those only within the walls of the city; or else concluding, that more ought to stay in a place thus doomed to destruction.

Thus divided as they were in their views, neither did all die, nor all escape; but falling sick indifferently, as well those of one as of another opinion; they who first set the example by forsaking others, now languished themselves without pity. I pass over the little regard that citizens and relations showed to each other; for their terror was such, that a brother even fled from his brother, a wife from her husband, and, what is more uncommon, a parent from his own child. Hence numbers that fell sick could have no help but what the charity of friends, who were very few, or the avarice of servants supplied; and even these were scarce and at extravagant wages, and so little used to the business that they were fit only to reach what was called for, and observe when their employer died; and this desire of getting money often cost them their lives. . . .

Not to dwell upon every particular of our misery, I shall observe, that it fared no better with the adjacent country; for, to omit the different boroughs about us, which presented the same view in miniature with the city, you might see the poor distressed labourers, with their families, without either the aid of physicians, or help of servants, languishing on the highways, in the fields, and in their own houses, and dying rather like cattle than human creatures. The consequence was that, growing dissolute in their manners like the citizens, and careless of everything, as supposing every day to be their last, their thoughts were not so much employed how to improve, as how to use their substance for their present support. The oxen, asses, sheep, goats, swine, and the dogs themselves, ever faithful to their masters, being driven from their own homes, were left to roam at will about the fields, and among the standing corn, which no one cared to gather, or even to reap; and many times, after they had filled themselves in the day, the animals would return of their own accord like rational creatures at night.

What can I say more, if I return to the city? unless that such was the cruelty of Heaven, and perhaps of men, that between March and July following, according to authentic reckonings, upwards of a hundred thousand souls perished in the city only; whereas, before that calamity, it was not supposed to have contained so many inhabitants. What magnificent dwellings, what noble palaces were then depopulated to the last inhabitant! what families became extinct! what riches and vast possessions were left, and no known heir to inherit them! what numbers of both sexes, in the prime and vigour of youth, whom in the morning neither Galen, Hippocrates, nor Aesculapius himself, would have denied to be in perfect health, breakfasted in the morning with their living friends, and supped at night with their departed friends in the other world!

The Goodman of Paris: Instructions on Being a Good Wife

Sources on the history of women during the Late Middle Ages are not abundant, and only recently have historians engaged in a fuller search for them. An exception is the relatively well known Goodman of Paris. *Written in the form of a letter by a Parisian merchant to his wife, it was an idealized manual of the duties of a wealthy wife from the point of view of an anonymous merchant. In the following excerpt from this late-fourteenth-century work, the author introduces and outlines what he will be discussing.*

> **Consider:** *The position and role of women at this time according to this document; the purposes of marriage according to this author.*

THE FIRST SECTION

The first section of the three is necessary to gain the love of God and the salvation of your soul, and also to win the love of your husband and to give you in this world that peace which should be in marriage. And because these two things, namely the salvation of your soul and the comfort of your husband, be the two things most chiefly necessary, therefore are they here placed first. And this first section contains nine articles.

The first article speaketh of worshipping and thanking our Saviour and his Blessed Mother at your waking and your rising, and of apparelling yourself seemingly.

The second article is of fit companions, and of going to Church, and of choosing your place, of wise behaviour, of hearing mass and of making confession.

The third article is that you should love God and his Blessed Mother and serve them continually and set and keep yourself in their grace.

The fourth article is that you should dwell in continence and chastity, after the ensample of Susanna, of Lucrece, and others.

SOURCE: Eileen Power, trans., *The Goodman of Paris* (London: Routledge & Kegan Paul, 1928), pp. 43–46. Reprinted by permission.

The fifth article is that you should love your husband (whether myself or another) after the ensample of Sarah, Rebecca and Rachel.

The sixth article is that you should be humble and obedient to him after the ensample of Griselda, of the woman who would not rescue her husband from drowning, and of the Mother of God who answered "fiat" etc., of Lucifer, of the *puys,* of the bailly of Tournay, of the monks and the husbands, of madame d'Andresel, of Chaumont and of the Roman woman.

The seventh that you be careful and heedful of his person.

The eighth that you be silent in hiding his secrets, after the ensample of Papirius, of the woman who laid eight eggs, of the Venetian woman, of the woman who returned from St James (of Compestollo), and of the advocate.

The ninth and last article showeth that if your husband try to act foolishly or so acteth, you must wisely and humbly withdraw him therefrom, like unto Melibeus and dame Jehanne la Quentine.

THE SECOND SECTION

The second section is necessary to increase the profit of the household, gain friends and save one's possessions; to succour and aid oneself against the ill fortunes of age to come, and it contains six [*sic*] articles.

The first article is that you have care of your household, with diligence and perseverance and regard for work; take pains to find pleasure therein and I will do likewise on my part, and so shall we reach the castle whereof it is spoken.

The second article is that at the least you take pleasure and have some little skill in the care and cultivation of a garden, grafting in due season and keeping roses in winter.

The third article is that you know how to choose varlets, doorkeepers, handymen or other strong folk to perform the heavy work that from hour to hour must be done, and likewise labourers etc. And also tailers, shoemakers, bakers, pastry-makers, etc. And in particular how to set the household varlets and chambermaids to work, to sift and winnow grain, clean dresses, air and dry, and how to order your folk to take thought for the sheep and horses and to keep and amend wines.

The fourth article is that you, as sovereign mistress of your house, know how to order dinners, suppers, dishes and courses, and be wise in that which concerns the butcher and the poulterer, and have knowledge of spices.

The fifth article is that you know how to order, ordain, devise and have made all manner of pottages, civeys, sauces and all other meats, and the same for sick folk.

THE THIRD SECTION

The third section tells of games and amusements that be pleasant enough to keep you in countenance and give you something to talk about in company, and contains three articles.

The first article is all concerned with amusing questions, which be shown forth and answered in strange fashion by the hazard of dice and by rooks and kings.

The second article is to know how to feed and fly the falcon.

The third article tells of certain other riddles concerning counting and numbering, which be subtle to find out and guess.

A Letter to Boccaccio: Literary Humanism
Francesco Petrarch

Literary humanism, a movement to revive Classical literature and the values expressed in Classical writings, was central to the early Renaissance. This trend, which originated in northern Italy during the fourteenth century, represented a broadening in focus from otherworldly concerns and people as religious beings, which was typical of the Middle Ages, to include the problems of people and nature in this world. The individual most commonly associated with it and perhaps most responsible for its spread was the Florentine Francesco Petrarch (1304–1374). Best known for his love sonnets to Laura, he also collected and translated many Classical works and wrote numerous letters—often extolling the Classical authors and even writing in their style. In the following selection from a 1362 letter to his friend Boccaccio, Petrarch offered reassurance and responded to charges typically made against humanistic learning.

Consider: *The nature of the charges Petrarch is refuting; how Petrarch related humanism to religion; Petrarch's perception of the benefits of literary humanism.*

Neither exhortations to virtue nor the argument of approaching death should divert us from literature; for in a good mind it excites the love of virtue, and dissipates, or at least diminishes, the fear of death. To desert our studies shows want of self-confidence rather than wisdom, for letters do not hinder but aid the properly constituted mind which possesses them; they facilitate our life, they do not retard it. Just as many kinds of food which lie heavy on an enfeebled and nauseated stomach furnish excellent nourishment for one who is well but famishing, so in our studies many things which are deadly to the weak mind may prove most salutary to an acute and healthy intellect, especially if in our use of both food and learning we exercise proper discretion. If it were otherwise, surely the zeal of certain persons who persevered to the end could not have roused such admiration. Cato, I never forget, acquainted himself with Latin literature as he was growing old, and Greek when he had really become an old man. Varro, who reached his hundredth year still reading and writing, parted from life sooner than

SOURCE: James Harvey Robinson and Henry Winchester Rolfe, *Petrarch: The First Modern Scholar and Man of Letters* (New York: Haskell House, 1898), pp. 391–395.

from his love of study. Livius Drusus, although weakened by age and afflicted with blindness, did not give up his interpretation of the civil law, which he carried on to the great advantage of the state. . . .

Besides these and innumerable others like them, have not all those of our own religion whom we should wish most to imitate devoted their whole lives to literature, and grown old and died in the same pursuit? Some, indeed, were overtaken by death while still at work reading or writing. To none of them, so far as I know, did it prove a disadvantage to be noted for secular learning. . . .

While I know that many have become famous for piety without learning, at the same time I know of no one who has been prevented by literature from following the path of holiness. The apostle Paul was, to be sure, accused of having his head turned by study, but the world has long ago passed its verdict upon this accusation. If I may be allowed to speak for myself, it seems to me that, although the path to virtue by the way of ignorance may be plain, it fosters sloth. The goal of all good people is the same, but the ways of reaching it are many and various. Some advance slowly, others with more spirit; some obscurely, others again conspicuously. One takes a lower, another a higher path. Although all alike are on the road to happiness, certainly the more elevated path is the more glorious. Hence ignorance, however devout, is by no means to be put on a plane with the enlightened devoutness of one familiar with literature. Nor can you pick me out from the whole array of unlettered saints, an example so holy that I cannot match it with a still holier one from the other group.

On the Liberal Arts
Peter Paul Vergerio

Closely associated with the rise of literary humanism was a new emphasis on the more broadly defined "liberal arts." This emphasis was manifested in a new concern with education; a change in educational curriculum constituted an institutional development that was enduring and that had wide-ranging effects. The first to express this emphasis systematically in an educational program was Peter Paul Vergerio (1370–1444). He taught in several Italian universities, and in his main treatise, On the Liberal Arts, *he rejected much of the content and methods of medieval education. Vergerio presents his views on the growing importance of the liberal arts in the following selection from a letter written to Ubertinus of Carrara.*

Consider: *What is particularly humanistic rather than scholastic or medieval about this view; how Vergerio justifies his choice of the three subjects in this proposed curriculum; what Petrarch might think of this letter.*

SOURCE: From William Harrison Woodward, *Vittorino de Feltre and Other Humanist Educators* (Cambridge; England: Cambridge University Press; New York: Bureau of Publications, Teachers College, Columbia University, 1963), pp. 96–97, 106–107. Reprinted by permission.

Your grandfather, Francesco I, a man distinguished for his capacity in affairs and for his sound judgment, was in the habit of saying that a parent owes three duties to his children. The first of these is to bestow upon them names of which they need not feel ashamed. For not seldom, out of caprice, or even indifference, or perhaps from a wish to perpetuate a family name, a father in naming his child inflicts upon him a misfortune which clings to him for life. The second obligation is this: to provide that his child be brought up in a city of distinction, for this not only concerns his future self-respect, but is closely connected with the third and most important care which is due from father to son. This is the duty of seeing that he be trained in sound learning. For no wealth, no possible security against the future, can be compared with the gift of an education in grave and liberal studies. By them a man may win distinction for the most modest name, and bring honour to the city of his birth however obscure it may be. But we must remember that whilst a man may escape from the burden of an unlucky name, or from the contempt attaching to a city of no repute, by changing the one or quitting the other, he can never remedy the neglect of early education. The foundation, therefore of this last must be laid in the first years of life, the disposition moulded whilst it is susceptible and the mind trained whilst it is retentive.

This duty, common indeed to all parents, is specially incumbent upon such as hold high station. For the lives of men of position are passed, as it were, in public view; and are fairly expected to serve as witness to personal merit and capacity on part of those who occupy such exceptional place amongst their fellow men. . . .

We come now to the consideration of the various subjects which may rightly be included under the name of 'Liberal Studies.' Amongst these I accord the first place to History, on grounds both of its attractiveness and of its utility, qualities which appeal equally to the scholar and to the statesman. Next in importance ranks Moral Philosophy, which indeed is, in a peculiar sense, a 'Liberal Art,' in that its purpose is to teach men the secret of true freedom. History, then, gives us the concrete examples of the precepts inculcated by philosophy. The one shews what men should do, the other what men have said and done in the past, and what practical lessons we may draw therefrom for the present day. I would indicate as the third main branch of study, Eloquence, which indeed holds a place of distinction amongst the refined Arts. By philosophy we learn the essential truth of things, which by eloquence we so exhibit in orderly adornment as to bring conviction to differing minds. And history provides the light of experience— cumulative wisdom fit to supplement the force of reason and the persuasion of eloquence. For we allow that soundness of judgment, wisdom of speech, integrity of conduct are the marks of a truly liberal temper.

The Prince
Machiavelli

The Italian Renaissance developed in an environment in which politics took on an increasingly competitive, secular tone. Within each Italian state, parties fought for power while at the same time the states fought each other for dominance or advantage. After 1492, Italy was invaded numerous times by Spain, France, and the Holy Roman Empire. These developments are reflected in the life and work of the great Renaissance political theorist Niccolò Machiavelli (1469–1527).

Born in Florence when it was under the rule of the Medicis, Machiavelli initiated his career in the Florentine civil service in 1498 during the period when the Medicis were out of power, replaced by a republican government. He rose to important diplomatic posts within the government, but was forced into retirement when the Medici family came back to power in 1512. He never gave up hope of returning to favor, and he wrote his most famous work, The Prince *(1513), in part as an application to the Medici rulers for a job in the Florentine government. The book has since become a classic treatise in political theory, above all for the way that it divorces politics from theology and metaphysics. The following selections from* The Prince *illustrate its style and some of its main themes.*

> **Consider:** *The ways in which this work reflects values or practices typical of the Renaissance; how these same principles might be applied to twentieth-century politics.*

It now remains to be seen what are the methods and rules for a prince as regards his subjects and friends. And as I know that many have written of this, I fear that my writing about it may be deemed presumptuous, differing as I do, especially in this matter, from the opinions of others. But my intention being to write something of use to those who understand, it appears to me more proper to go to the real truth of the matter than to its imagination; and many have imagined republics and principalities which have never been seen or known to exist in reality; for how we live is so far removed from how we ought to live, that he who abandons what is done for what ought to be done, will rather learn to bring about his own ruin than his preservation. A man who wishes to make a profession of goodness in everything must necessarily come to grief among so many who are not good. Therefore it is necessary for a prince, who wishes to maintain himself, to learn how not to be good, and to use this knowledge and not use it, according to the necessity of the case. . . .

It is not, therefore, necessary for a prince to have all the above-named qualities, but it is very necessary to seem to have them. I would even be bold to say that to possess them and always to observe them is dangerous, but to appear to possess them is useful. Thus it is well to seem merciful, faithful, humane, sincere, religious,

Source: From *The Prince and the Discourses* by Niccolò Machiavelli, translated by Luigi Ricci and revised by E. R. P. Vincent (Copyright © 1935), pp. 56, 65–66. Used by permission of Oxford University Press.

and also to be so; but you must have the mind so disposed that when it is needed to be otherwise you may be able to change to the opposite qualities. And it must be understood that a prince, and especially a new prince, cannot observe all those things which are considered good in men, being often obliged, in order to maintain the state, to act against faith, against charity, against humanity, and against religion. And, therefore, he must have a mind disposed to adapt itself according to the wind, and as the variations of fortune dictate, and, as I said before, not deviate from what is good, if possible, but be able to do evil if constrained.

A prince must take great care that nothing goes out of his mouth which is not full of the above-named five qualities, and, to see and hear him, he should seem to be all mercy, faith, integrity, humanity, and religion. And nothing is more necessary than to seem to have this last quality, for men in general judge more by the eyes than by the hands, for every one can see, but very few have to feel. Everybody sees what you appear to be, few feel what you are, and those few will not dare to oppose themselves to the many, who have the majesty of the state to defend them; and in the actions of men, and especially of princes, from which there is no appeal, the end justifies the means. Let a prince therefore aim at conquering and maintaining the state, and the means will always be judged honourable and praised by every one, for the vulgar is always taken by appearances and the issue of the event; and the world consists only of the vulgar, and the few who are not vulgar are isolated when the many have a rallying point in the prince.

VISUAL SOURCES

The Triumph of Death

With war, famine, and especially plague striking fourteenth- and fifteenth-century Europe, death became a common theme of art. Typically, the plague was viewed as God's punishment for human sins, and thus only the Church might do something about the plague. Yet religion and everything else seemed impotent against death. This is shown in the numerous illustrations focusing on the theme of death. This engraving of The Triumph of Death, from Petrarch's Trionfi, *was made by a Venetian artist between 1470 and 1480. Here king, clergy, and commoners all fall helplessly under Death's cart. The souls of the dead are taken either by angels, on the upper left, or devils, on the upper right.*

Consider: *Attitudes toward death reflected by such popular scenes; any ways these scenes reflect attitudes similar to those revealed by Boccaccio.*

Photo 11–1

British Museum, London

Giovanni Arnolfini and His Bride: Symbolism and the Northern Renaissance
Jan van Eyck

It should not be concluded even in art that the Renaissance constituted a sudden and complete break with the past. Even when in style and subject matter paintings reflect the realism, humanism, and individualism of the Renaissance, they also reflect medieval assumptions and concerns that remained.

This can be seen in a Northern Renaissance masterpiece, Giovanni Arnolfini and His Bride, *painted in 1434 by the Flemish artist Jan van Eyck. The scene appears to be quite secular: Giovanni Arnolfini, an Italian businessman residing in Bruges, is standing with his bride in a private bridal chamber taking marriage vows (at this time two people could contract a legitimate marriage outside the Church). Around them various objects that might typically be found in such a room are quite realistically depicted. To the medieval eye these objects have well-known symbolic meaning that give this scene considerable religious and cultural significance. The single lighted candle was the traditional nuptial candle, symbolizing Christ and implying divine light. The convex mirror reflected the chamber, testifying to the presence of two witnesses (one of whom was the artist, van Eyck, who tells us just above the mirror that "Jan van Eyck was here"), and represented the all-seeing eye of God. The shoes (to the left), so appropriate for the muddy streets of Bruges, are off, indicating that this couple is standing on holy ground. The dog in the foreground symbolizes fidelity. The ripening peaches to the left on the chest and window-sill represent fertility and perhaps paradise lost. On the post of a chair near the bed is a carved Margaret, patron saint of childbirth. The pose of the couple suggests relationships between husband and wife: He is dominating by his frontal pose; she is deferentially turned toward him.*

Thus this painting is both a realistic depiction of two individuals with distinct personalities (as revealed particularly in their faces) in a natural setting and a symbolic representation of the meanings of marriage in the fifteenth century, with all the religious implications. And that this is a portrait of an Italian merchant and his bride in a room furnished with items coming from all areas of Europe, in Bruges, a northern center of banking and commerce, reflects the growing importance and wealth of the middle class and international trade during this period.

Consider: *How this reflects a society and attitudes similar to those of the Middle Ages.*

Unrest in the Late Middle Ages

This map gives some idea of the geographic extent of the social and religious unrest in fourteenth-century Europe. England was affected by a combination of urban and rural revolts as well as religious heresy. Their geographic locations suggest that the revolts and the heresy may have been connected. What is not shown on this map would also add to

Photo 11–2

The National Gallery, London

the picture of turmoil and unrest: the numerous political and military disturbances, the religious divisions of the Great Schism (1378–1417), the spread of the plague, and the actual disappearance of settlements founded in the three preceding centuries.

   Consider: *Connections among political disturbances, religious divisions, plagues, and population loss that could be revealed by maps.*

Map 11–1   Social and Religious Unrest in Fourteenth-Century Europe

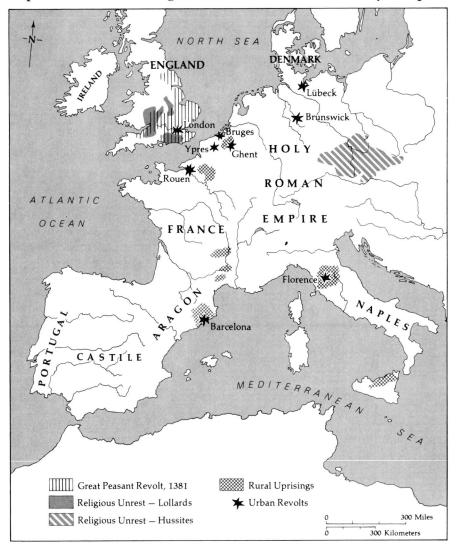

Food and Crime

This chart provides another indication of the disruptions affecting Europe in the fourteenth century. Here, rise and fall in the price of wheat and the number of crimes between 1300 and 1350 in Norfolk, England, are compared. Fluctuations in food supplies are thus revealed, as well as clear connections between the price of wheat and the number of crimes committed.

> **Consider:** *How the information in this chart might relate to social, political, or even religious unrest.*

Chart 11–1   Crime and the Price of Wheat in Fourteenth-Century Norfolk, England

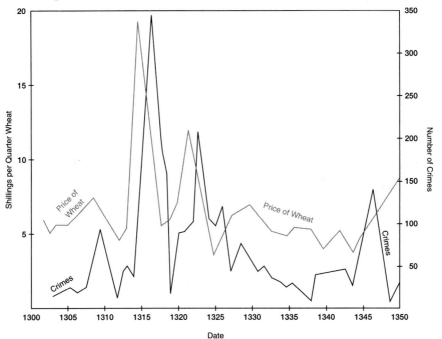

SECONDARY SOURCES

A Psychological Perspective of the Black Death
William L. Langer

Most historians have long been reluctant to view historical developments from a psychological perspective. In recent decades historians have been challenged to apply psychological insights to history. In 1957 William L. Langer, then president of the American Historical Association, issued such a challenge to historians in his presidential address to the annual convention. In the following selections from that address, Langer suggests how modern psychology might be used to interpret the Black Death and related developments.

Consider: *How a psychologist might explain various behaviors related to the Black Death; how* The Triumph of Death *fits with this interpretation.*

The Black Death was worse than anything experienced prior to that time and was, in all probability, the greatest single disaster that has ever befallen European mankind. In most localities a third or even a half of the population was lost within the space of a few months, and it is important to remember that the great visitation of 1348–1349 was only the beginning of a period of pandemic disease with a continuing frightful drain of population. . . .

At news of the approach of the disease a haunting terror seizes the population, in the Middle Ages leading on the one hand to great upsurges of repentance in the form of flagellant processions and on the other to a mad search for scapegoats, eventuating in large-scale pogroms of the Jews. The most striking feature of such visitations has always been the precipitate flight from the cities, in which not only the wealthier classes but also town officials, professors and teachers, clergy, and even physicians took part. The majority of the population, taking the disaster as an expression of God's wrath, devoted itself to penitential exercises, to merciful occupations, and to such good works as the repair of churches and the founding of religious houses. On the other hand, the horror and confusion in many places brought general demoralization and social breakdown. Criminal elements were

SOURCE: William L. Langer, "The Next Assignment," *The American Historical Review,* vol. LXIII, no. 2 (January 1958), pp. 292–293, 295–298. Reprinted by permission.

quick to take over, looting the deserted houses and even murdering the sick in order to rob them of their jewels. Many, despairing of the goodness and mercy of God, gave themselves over to riotous living, resolved, as Thucydides says, "to get out of life the pleasures which could be had speedily and which would satisfy their lusts, regarding their bodies and their wealth alike as transitory." Drunkenness and sexual immorality were the order of the day. "In one house," reported an observer of the London plague of 1665, "you might hear them roaring under the pangs of death, in the next tippling, whoring and belching out blasphemies against God." . . .

The age was marked, as all admit, by a mood of misery, depression, and anxiety, and by a general sense of impending doom. Numerous writers in widely varying fields have commented on the morbid preoccupation with death, the macabre interest in tombs, the gruesome predilection for the human corpse. Among painters the favorite themes were Christ's passion, the terrors of the Last Judgment, and the tortures of Hell, all depicted with ruthless realism and with an almost loving devotion to each repulsive detail. Altogether characteristic was the immense popularity of the Dance of Death woodcuts and murals, with appropriate verses, which appeared soon after the Black Death and which, it is agreed, expressed the sense of the immediacy of death and the dread of dying unshriven. Throughout the fifteenth and sixteenth centuries these pitilessly naturalistic pictures ensured man's constant realization of his imminent fate.

The origins of the Dance of Death theme have been generally traced to the Black Death and subsequent epidemics, culminating in the terror brought on by the outbreak of syphilis at the end of the fifteenth century. Is it unreasonable, then, to suppose that many of the other phenomena I have mentioned might be explained, at least in part, in the same way? We all recognize the late Middle Ages as a period of popular religious excitement or overexcitement, of pilgrimages and penitential processions, of mass preaching, of veneration of relics and adoration of saints, of lay piety and popular mysticism. It was apparently also a period of unusual immorality and shockingly loose living, which we must take as a continuation of the "devil-may-care" attitude of one part of the population. This the psychologists explain as the repression of unbearable feelings by accentuating the value of a diametrically opposed set of feelings and then behaving as though the latter were the real feelings. But the most striking feature of the age was an exceptionally strong sense of guilt and a truly dreadful fear of retribution, seeking expression in a passionate longing for effective intercession and in a craving for direct, personal experience of the Deity, as well as in a corresponding dissatisfaction with the Church and with the mechanization of the means of salvation as reflected, for example, in the traffic in indulgences.

These attitudes, along with the great interest in astrology, the increased resort to magic, and the startling spread of witchcraft and Satanism in the fifteenth century were, according to the precepts of modern psychology, normal reactions to the sufferings to which mankind in that period was subjected.

The Civilization of the Renaissance in Italy
Jacob Burckhardt

Modern interpretations of the Renaissance almost uniformly start with the Swiss historian Jacob Burckhardt's The Civilization of the Renaissance in Italy, *first published in 1860. Burckhardt rejected a chronological approach and pictured the Italian Renaissance of the fourteenth and fifteenth centuries as a whole, strikingly distinct from the preceding Middle Ages and clearly a superior civilization. Until the 1920s, historians almost unanimously accepted his interpretation. After that time various aspects of his thesis were attacked, particularly by medievalists. In recent decades, however, Burckhardt's work has gained new respectability, at least as an idealized cultural history of the Italian Renaissance. In any case, all historians who approach this topic must deal with Burckhardt's argument, some of the central points of which appear in the following excerpt.*

> **Consider:** *What most distinguishes the Italian Renaissance from the preceding Middle Ages according to Burckhardt; any support the primary dcuments might provide for this argument; how a proud medievalist might respond to this argument.*

In the Middle Ages both sides of human consciousness—that which was turned within as that which was turned without—lay dreaming or half awake beneath a common veil. The veil was woven of faith, illusion, and childish prepossession, through which the world and history were seen clad in strange hues. Man was conscious of himself only as member of a race, people, party, family, or corporation—only through some general category. In Italy this veil first melted into air; an *objective* treatment and consideration of the state and of all the things of this world became possible. The *subjective* side at the same time asserted itself with corresponding emphasis; man became a spiritual *individual,* and recognised himself as such. In the same way the Greek had once distinguished himself from the barbarian, and the Arabian had felt himself an individual at a time when other Asiatics knew themselves only as members of a race. . . .

In far earlier times we can here and there detect a development of free personality which in Northern Europe either did not occur at all, or could not display itself in the same manner. . . . But at the close of the thirteenth century Italy began to swarm with individuality; the charm laid upon human personality was dissolved; and a thousand figures meet us each in its own special shape and dress. Dante's great poem would have been impossible in any other country of Europe, if only for the reason that they still lay under the spell of race. For Italy the august

SOURCE: Jacob Burckhardt, *The Civilization of the Renaissance in Italy,* trans. S. G. C. Middlemore (London: George Allen and Unwin, Ltd.; New York: The Macmillan Co., 1890), p. 129.

poet, through the wealth of individuality, which he set forth, was the most national herald of his time. But this unfolding of the treasures of human nature in literature and art—this many-sided representation and criticism—will be discussed in separate chapters; here we have to deal only with the psychological fact itself. This fact appears in the most decisive and unmistakable form. The Italians of the fourteenth century knew little of false modesty or of hypocrisy in any shape; not one of them was afraid of singularity, of being and seeming unlike his neigbours.

The Renaissance in Perspective
Philip Lee Ralph

Many historians attacked Burckhardt's interpretation and the legacy built up around it, arguing that Burckhardt overemphasized how modern the Renaissance was. They stressed how much the Renaissance, even in Italy, was still part of the medieval world. While the harsh tone of these attacks has softened, most historians now agree that there was much more that was medieval in form and spirit in the Renaissance than Burckhardt believed. The following selection by Philip Lee Ralph exemplifies this more recent view.

Consider: *The ways in which the Renaissance was more medieval than modern; what was new or modern about the Renaissance; whether the documents better support Burckhardt's or Ralph's interpretation.*

The Renaissance, both in form and spirit, was far more medieval than modern; but this dictum—on which there is now wide but not universal agreement—is a relatively trivial point. To affirm it may give more due to the Middle Ages than is customary, but it by no means downgrades the Renaissance. While leaders of the Renaissance revived, admired, and employed the forms of classical antiquity, the classical tradition served them chiefly as an "energizing myth" (Chabod's term). They retained and embellished medieval conceptions and formulas. They remained within the framework of medieval civilization—not as prisoners but as legitimate heirs enthusiastically redecorating the old family mansion. While the medieval social and political order was beginning to crumble, and even while fascination with the golden age of Roman antiquity incited an anti-medieval bias, creative talents sought to give vivid expression to ideals and aspirations that had been active or latent all through the medieval centuries. These ideals, the product of a long philosophical and religious tradition, received new treatment. In a sense they were "secularized," drawn more directly into the orbit of individual consciousness and experience. What the boldest spirits of the Renaissance attempted was to bring to full realization the promise inherent in the wisdom of the ancients

SOURCE: Philip Lee Ralph, *The Renaissance in Perspective.* New York: St. Martin's Press, 1973, pp. 16–17.

and in the Christian tradition—to transform this promise from a distant hope to a present reality to be enjoyed by living men and women.

The leading exponents of Renaissance culture—known by the general term "humanists"—were indeed man-centered. But they were convinced that man is both the child of nature and the creature of God, and that through his twin heritage he càn reach a station of dignity and benevolence.

Chapter Questions

1. In what ways was the general character of the Late Middle Ages exemplified by the plague and reactions to it?
2. Drawing from sources in this chapter and the last chapter, in what ways was the Renaissance a new development strikingly different from the Middle Ages? How might the "newness" of these developments be minimized or reinterpreted as an evolutionary continuation of the Middle Ages?
3. Using the sources in this chapter, what was particularly "humanistic" about the cultural productions and attitudes of the Renaissance? How might some of the sources on Greco-Roman civilization in Chapters 4 and 5 be used to argue that the Renaissance was, in part, a return to the "humanistic" concerns of a previous era in the West?

TWELVE

Civilizations of Sub-Saharan Africa and the Americas, to 1500

During the first millennium A.D. a variety of civilizations arose in sub-Saharan Africa and the Americas. Before 1500 these civilizations were, for the most part, developing independently from civilizations on the Eurasian continent and northern Africa (though Islam had certainly penetrated into some northern and coastal areas of sub-Saharan Africa).

In sub-Saharan Africa, particularly in the western and central Sudan where the Saharan Desert gave way to grasslands and trade became of growing importance, several states formed, the most important of which was the empire of Ghana. In this area, the period between A.D. 1000 and 1500 was one of major political and economic changes. During this period, sometimes referred to as the "Middle Ages" in African history, various political leaders of centralized states emerged whose aim was to control the shape and character of states which had been founded in the centuries before. Even though centralized states were not necessarily the goal of all groups in African societies—as seen by the conflicts between rulers and various political, economic, and cultural elites—discussions of the functioning of state systems certainly dominate the available contemporary records as well as the later literature.

Most of the sources on sub-Saharan Africa focus on this process of state building and the role of rulers in this process, particularly in the states of Ghana and Mali in the western Sudan and Kiteve (Quiteve) farther south. The sources also explore cultural and religious aspects of these societies.

Historians and archaeologists generally agree that the people of the Americas were descendants of Asians who had crossed the land bridge where the Bering Straits are now located at least 20,000 years ago. The most advanced civilizations developed along the east coast of what is called Mesoamerica— central and southern Mexico, Guatemala, and Honduras—and along the western coast of South America in the Andes. The three major civilizations were the Maya (centered in what is now the Yucatan, Guatemala, and Belize), the Aztec (in what is now Mexico) and the Inca (extending from mid-Ecuador

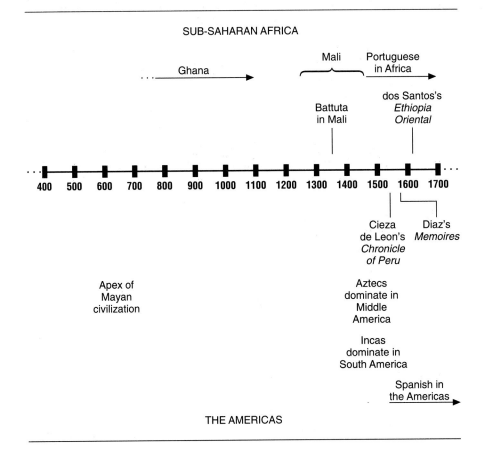

to mid-Chile). The Maya, who were the most artistic and scientifically oriented, were the most advanced early on with the apex of their growth and culture being about A.D. 600. They went into decline by about 850. The Aztec were more militaristic, creating a powerful state by about 1400. The Incas, based in the Andes highlands of Peru, rose to power in the early fifteenth century. They exerted remarkable control over the people in their region, forming an extraordinarily authoritarian, centralized state.

For the most part primary documents prior to 1500 are unavailable for these civilizations. It is necessary, therefore, to rely on archaeological evidence and reports by Europeans who first came into contact with these peoples in the decades after 1500. The sources on the Americas in this chapter focus on three topics. The first is the nature of the politics and culture of the major civilizations of the Americas before 1500. The second explores the differing economic and social systems of the native populations. The third looks at different theories on how the Western Hemisphere was populated over the millennia.

Together the sources in this chapter introduce the civilizations of sub-Saharan Africa and the Americas, which before 1500 were for the most part developing independently from civilizations on the Eurasian continent and Northern Africa. After 1500 these civilizations would be drawn into developments sweeping through the rest of the world.

PRIMARY SOURCES

A Muslim's View of the African Kingdom of Mali
Ibn Battuta

Between 1100 and 1400 several kingdoms developed in western Africa. Of these, Mali was the most widely known, in Africa as well as in the Muslim and Christian worlds. Ibn Battuta, who was born and raised in the north African town of Tunis, visited Mali in 1352–1353 as part of his travels to the major Muslim capitals of the time. His journeys took him as far afield as east Africa, India, and perhaps China. In his day, Mali was the most powerful and largest state of the western Sudan (a territory that encompasses modern Mauretania, Senegal, Mali, Guinea, Niger, and northern parts of Nigeria, Togo, Ghana, and Benin). Mali's rulers were known for their wealth in gold and for their control of the trans-Saharan trade, which linked the forest areas of west Africa with the wider world.

SOURCE: Muhammad ibn Abdullah ibn Battuta, "What I Approved of and what I Disapproved of Among the Acts of the Sudan," in J. F. P. Hopkins and Nehemia Levtzion, eds. and trans., *Corpus of Early Arabic Sources for West African History* (Cambridge, Cambridge University Press, 1982), pp. 285, 296–297 as excerpted.

In the following excerpt from his account of his travels, Ibn Battuta examines various features of Mali society.

Consider: *The role of the traveler as a diplomat, scholar, and newsreporter; what this reveals about Ibn Battuta's own concerns as a Muslim scholar; the position of women in an African-Muslim state at this time.*

WHAT I APPROVED OF AND WHAT I DISAPPROVED OF AMONG THE ACTS OF THE SŪDĀN

One of their good features is their lack of oppression. They are the farthest removed of people from it and their sultan does not permit anyone to practise it. Another is the security embracing the whole country, so that neither traveller there nor dweller has anything to fear from thief or usurper. Another is that they do not interfere with the wealth of any white man who dies among them. . . . They simply leave it in the hands of a trustworthy white man until the one to whom it is due takes it. Another is their assiduity in prayer and their persistence in performing it in congregation and beating their children to make them perform it. If it is a Friday and a man does not go early to the mosque he will not find anywhere to pray because of the press of the people. It is their habit that every man sends his servant with his prayer-mat to spread it for him in a place which he thereby has a right to until he goes to the mosque. Their prayer-carpets are made from the fronds . . . of the tree resembling the palm which has no fruit. Another of their good features is their dressing in fine white clothes on Friday. If any one of them possesses nothing but a ragged shirt he washes it and cleanses it and attends the Friday prayer in it. Another is their eagerness to memorize the great Koran. They place fetters on their children if there appears on their part a failure to memorize it and they are not undone until they memorize it.

I went into the house of the qadi on the day of the festival and his children were fettered so I said to him: "Aren't you going to let them go?" He replied: "I shan't do so until they've got the Koran by heart!" One day I passed by a youth of theirs, of good appearance and dressed in fine clothes, with a heavy fetter on his leg. I said to those who were with me: "What has this boy done? Has he killed somebody?" The lad understood what I had said and laughed, and they said to me: "He's only been fettered so that he'll learn the Koran!"

 . . . These people have remarkable and strange ways. As for their men, they feel no jealousy. None of them traces his descent through his father, but from his maternal uncle, and a man's heirs are the sons of his sister only, to the exclusion of his own sons. This is something that I have seen nowhere in the world except among the Indian infidels in the land of Mulaybār, whereas these are Muslims who observe the prayer and study fiqh and memorize the Koran. As for their women, they have no modesty in the presence of men and do not veil themselves in spite of their assiduity in prayer. If anybody wishes to marry one of them he may do so, but they do not travel with the husband, and if one of them wished to do so her family would prevent her.

The women there have friends and companions among the foreign men, just as the men have companions from among the foreign women. One of them may enter his house and find his wife with her man friend without making any objection. . . .

Ethiopia Oriental: Courtly Life in an African Kingdom
João dos Santos

When the Portuguese arrived in southeast Africa in the sixteenth century, the Zimbabwe civilization had already collapsed, leaving behind only the famous Zimbabwe ruins. The Portuguese thus encountered only the successor states which replaced it. João dos Santos, a Dominican priest of Portuguese nationality, provides some of the earliest detailed accounts of the states in the region. He spent a total of over ten years in east Africa between 1586 and 1609, when his Ethiopia Oriental *was published. The Kingdom of Kiteve (Quiteve) was one of a cluster of states on or around the highlands of modern Zimbabwe, most of which were subordinate to a loosely structured empire called Mwenemutapa. The ancient city and monumental buildings of Great Zimbabwe, in ruins already by the time dos Santos visited, is often used as a symbol of this complex and powerful culture. The following excerpt is dos Santos's eyewitness account of courtly life and manners of the Mwenemutapa states.*

> **Consider:** *The focus on justice and what this tells us about Africans' concepts of law and order; how ritual practices separated commoners from nobles; the role of women in courtly society.*

KINGDOM OF THE QUITEVE

The King of these parts [inland Mozambique and frontier with Zimbabwe] is of curled hair, . . . which worships nothing, nor hath any knowledge of God; yea, rather he carries himself as God of his Countries, and so is holden and reverenced of his Vassals. He is called Quiteve, a title royal and no proper name, which they exchange for this so soon as they become Kings. The Quiteve hath more than one hundred women all within doors, amongst which one or two are as his Queens, the rest as Concubines: many of them are his own Aunts, Cousins, Sisters and Daughters, which he no less useth, saying, that his sons by them are true heirs of the Kingdom without mixture of other blood. When the Quiteve dies, his Queens must die with him to do him service in the other world, who accordingly at the instant of his death take a poison (which they call Lucasse) and die therewith. The successor succeeds as well to the women as to the state. None else but the King may upon pain of death marry his Sister or Daughter. This Successor is commonly

SOURCE: In D. Robinson and D. Smith, eds., *Sources of the African Past* (Heineman, 1979), pp. 73–74. Originally in M. Theal, *Basutoland Records* (Capetown: Richards & Sons, 1883).

one of the eldest Sons of the deceased King, and of his great Women or Queens; and if the eldest be not sufficient, then the next, or if none of them be fit, his Brother of whole blood. The King commonly while he lives makes the choice, and trains up him to affairs of State, to whom he destines the succession. . . .

The same day the King dies, he is carried to a Hill where all the Kings are interred, and early the next morning, he whom the deceased had named his Successor, goes to the Kings house where the Kings Women abide in expectation, and by their consent he enters the house, and seats himself with the principal of them in a public Hall, where the King was wont to sit to hear Causes, in a place drawn with curtains or covered with a cloth, that none may see the King nor the Women with him. And thence he sends his Officers, which go through the City and proclaim Festivals to the New King, who is now quietly possessed of the Kings House, with the Women of the King deceased, and that all should go and acknowledge him for their King which is done by all the great Men then in Court, and the Nobles of the City, who go to the Palace now solemnly guarded, and enter into the Hall by licence of the Officers, where the new King abides with his Women; entering some, and some, creeping on the ground till they come to the middle of the Hall, and then speak to the New King, giving him due obeysance, without seeing him or his Women. The King makes answer from within, and accepts their service: and after that draw the Curtains, and shows himself to them; whereat all of them clap their hands, and then turn behind the Curtains, and go forth creeping on the ground as they came in; and when they are gone, others enter and do in like sort. In this ceremony the greatest part of the day is spent with feasting, music and dancing through the city. The next day, the King sends his Officers through the Kingdom to declare this his succession, and that all should come to the Court to see him break the Bow. Sometimes there are many Competitors, and then He succeeds whom the Women admit into the Kings House: for none may enter by Law without their leave, nor can be King without peaceable entrance; forceable entry forfeiting his Right and Title. By bribes therefore and other ways, they seek to make the Women on their side. . . .

Before the New King begins to govern, he sends for all the chiefs in the Kingdom, to come to the Court and see him break the Kings Bow, which is all one with taking possession of the Kingdom. In those Courts is a custom then also to kill some of those Lords or great Men, saying, that they are necessary for the service of the deceased King: whereupon they kill those of whom they stand in fear or doubt, or whom they hate, instead of whom they make and erect new Lords. This custom causeth such as fear themselves to flee the Land. Anciently the Kings were wont to drink poison in any grievous disasters, as in a contagious disease, or natural impotency, . . . or other deformity; saying, that Kings ought to have no defect; which if it happened, it was honour for him to die, and go to better himself in that better life, in which he should be wholly perfect. . . .

If the Cafars have a suit, and seek to speak with the King, they creep to the place where he is, having prostrated themselves at the entrance, and look not on him all the while they speak, but lying on one side clap their hands all the time

(a rite of obsequiousnesse in those parts) and then having finished, they creep out of the doors as they came in. For no Cafar may enter on foot to speak to the King, nor eye him in speaking, except the familiars and particular friends of the King.
. . .

They use three kinds of Oaths in Judgement most terrible, in accusations wanting just evidence. The first is called, Lucasse, which is a vessel full of poison, which they give the suspected, with words importing his destruction, and present death if he be guilty; his escape, if innocent: the terror whereof makes the conscious confess the crime: but the innocent drink it confidently without harm, and thereby are acquitted of the crime; and the plaintiff is condemned to him whom he falsely had accused; his wife, children, and goods being forfeited, one half to the King, and the other to the defendant. The second Oath they call, Xoqua, which is made by iron heated red hot in the fire, causing the accused to lick it being so hot with his tongue, saying, that the fire shall not hurt him if he be innocent; otherwise it shall burn his tongue and his mouth. This is more common, and is used by the Cafres. . . . The third Oath they call, Calano, which is a vessel of water made bitter with certain herbs, which they put into it, whereof they give the accused to drink, saying, that if he be innocent, he shall drink it all off at one gulp without any stay, and cast it all up again at once without any harm: if guilty, he shall not be able to get down one drop without gargling and choking. . . .

Political Practices in West Africa
Pieter de Marees

European sources provide us with detailed accounts of the various forms of government in west Africa which had emerged in the centuries before European contact. During the sixteenth century the area that became known as the Gold Coast, now modern Ghana, was divided into more than a dozen states with a common language and culture. Political organization was as varied as the size of the states, ranging from absolute monarchies to collective government by councils.

The following excerpt is from the writings of Pieter de Marees, a merchant who took service with the early Dutch traders. He visited this area of west Africa in the last years of the sixteenth century. This excerpt shows some of the political practices there and the balancing role kings had to play.

Consider: *The nature of west African political systems; the system's potential for transformation; the role of women in the king's household.*

SOURCE: *Pieter de Marees: Description and Historical Account of the Gold Kingdom of Guinea (1602),* edited by A. van Dantzig and A. Jones (1987), pp. 94–97. By permission of the British Academy.

The Kings are elected by the common people and by the highest vote; for the Kingdom does not devolve on friends [relatives] or descendants, and even some-one's children do not inherit. So, when the King is dead, they elect another to govern them and possess the Kingdom, and he takes possession of the Court, together with all that is in it. For his inauguration he must in the first place buy many Cows and much Palm wine and give these to his Subjects as a present; for they very much love a King who often fêtes them, but hate a King who is frugal and keen on accumulating Gold. They will not respect such a King and he is not loved by the common people: they bear him great hatred and jealousy, seeking every means of taking action against him, in order to drive him out and choose a better person who is to their liking. . . .

. . . Thus he who wishes to make himself loved by his people has to make it his custom to give a dinner every three months, when his Guards or Tollmen come to pay him what they have received on the beach as fines or from the Peasants as Tolls. His expenditure on it will depend on what he has received in that period. He invites . . . his Morinnis (a Morinni is a Nobleman or a member of his Council). Then he buys many Cows or Oxen and also all the Palm wine he can get in the Country, and this is shared among all members of the community. Then they are very merry and enjoy themselves, drumming and singing. The heads of the Cows are cleaned, nicely painted, bedecked with Fetisso and placed in the King's room in a row along the walls, instead of paintings, being of great honour to the King; so that strangers who come to the Court can see that he is a good King; thus he is much esteemed and honoured by his people. . . .

. . . His wives live with him in his Palace, and some also outside the Court; but these are the oldest wives, whom he does not love all that much and who can no longer please him. To each of the young and beautiful wives he normally gives separate living quarters, within his Palace, in order that they may serve him the better and [he] may have his comfort. These women do their husband the King great service and each fêtes him as best she can in order to be loved by him; so he does not lack any services or comfort. Each woman has her own goods and wealth, and each also maintains and brings up her own children. Those who are the favourites of the king [do not] stand in want of anything. Whenever these women go out they lean on the shoulders of other women who serve them and are their Slaves; likewise the children are carried on the shoulders of other blacks or Slaves of the King.

[The king] himself seldom goes out into the streets, but always stays in his house; sometimes he does sit in front of the door, but rarely. He is very well guarded, and day and night a watch is kept over his house by his Slaves, who always stand armed in the Court as well as in his Chamber. . . .

There is also one among them whom they call Viador . . . who keeps the King's gold and treasure, pays, receives and does the King's things [i.e. manages his affairs]. This man is the next after the King, and usually they go about even more covered with gold Rings around their arms, legs, feet and neck than the King himself.

His [the King's] children have to see to it that they find a means of earning something when they grow up and want to have something for themselves; for the King cannot just give them something to keep them idle, because the common people would not like to see that and would start to grumble for various reasons. The King would also wrong his Nobility by giving such presents to his children; yet he gives them their patrimony when they marry, as is customary. In addition the King gives each a Slave to serve them, but they do not enjoy any further advantage from the King their Father than this one Slave, and otherwise they receive the same as everybody gives to his children. As a result of this they are not esteemed or respected more than any other Man if they do not set to work once they come of age. The King keeps them to serve him, and if it happens that the King makes Peace with somebody, or with another Town or King, he employs his children, particularly his Sons, as Hostages, in order that they may begin to be honoured and attain a high status. The King can easily maintain his Court, Wives and Children from the revenue he receives [in the form] of all sorts of foodstuffs, such as Fruits, Fish, Palm Wine and Palm Oil. The *Millie* from which his bread is baked is previously sown and harvested for him. Things are done for him, free of charge, so that he does not stand in need of anything. Thus he has a good life (though a miserable one by our standards). When it happens that the King dies, he receives a fitting burial in accordance with their custom; at once another is chosen, but not someone from that same generation or a relation: they take any stranger they happen to like and they will not again take anybody who in any way belonged to the family of the deceased King. They then make him King and bring him into the Palace. This new King starts his Government with all that the deceased King enjoyed within his dominions. He takes everything, so that the children or heirs of the late King do not enjoy anything of his former prosperity or take any part of it except what he brought into it himself: this they take and share among themselves, in accordance with their custom. Thus these Kingdoms are not a heritage or fief and are not even inherited by friends [relatives] or children, but by a stranger.

The Chronicle of Peru: The Incas
Pedro Cieza de Leon

The Incas of South America established one of the most extensive and sophisticated empires in world history. By the time of Columbus's arrival, they had developed a political and economic system that extended along the edge of South America's western coast for about 2,500 miles. Much of our written information about the Incas comes from accounts of Western conquerors, explorers, and missionaries who streamed into South America dur-

SOURCE: Pedro Cieza de Leon, *The Second Part of the Chronicle of Peru*, Clements R. Markham, trans. and ed. (London: The Hakluyt Society, 1883), pp. 36–38, 42.

ing the sixteenth century. The following selection is a description of Incan culture by an early member of Spain's conquering armies who sought to document the complexity of the Incas even as they were about to be destroyed. Pedro Cieza de Leon (1518–1560) was involved in the several campaigns in Ecuador and Colombia between 1535 and 1547. He wrote what is now considered the authoritative account between 1547 and 1550 and based much of his writing on first-hand accounts he transcribed from the Incas themselves.

> **Consider:** *The nature of the Incan political system and its potential problems; what the existence of an extensive road system tells us about the nature of Incan civilization.*

It should be well understood that great prudence was needed to enable these kings to govern such large provinces, extending over so vast a region, parts of it rugged and covered with forests, parts mountainous, with snowy peaks and ridges, parts consisting of deserts of sand, dry and without trees or water. These regions were inhabited by many different nations, with varying languages, laws, and religions, and the kings had to maintain tranquillity and to rule so that all should live in peace and in friendship towards their lord. Although the city of Cuzco was the head of the empire, as we have remarked in many places, yet at certain points, as we shall also explain, the king stationed his delegates and governors, who were the most learned, the ablest, and the bravest men that could be found, and none was so youthful that he was not already in the last third part of his age. As they were faithful and none betrayed their trusts, and as they had the *mitimaes* on their side, none of the natives, though they might be more powerful, attempted to rise in rebellion; or if such a thing ever did take place, the town where the revolt broke out was punished, and the ringleaders were sent prisoners to Cuzco.

. . .

. . . All men so feared the king, that they did not dare to speak evil even of his shadow. And this was not all. If any of the king's captains or servants went forth to visit a distant part of the empire on some business, the people came out on the road with presents to receive them, not daring, even if one came alone, to omit to comply with all his commands.

So great was the veneration that the people felt for their princes, throughout this vast region, that every district was as well regulated and governed as if the lord was actually present to chastise those who acted contrary to his rules. This fear arose from the known valour of the lords and their strict justice. It was felt to be certain that those who did evil would receive punishment without fail, and that neither prayers nor bribes would avert it. At the same time, the Incas always did good to those who were under their sway, and would not allow them to be ill-treated, nor that too much tribute should be exacted from them. Many who dwelt in a sterile country where they and their ancestors had lived with difficulty, found that through the orders of the Inca their lands were made fertile and abundant, the things being supplied which before were wanting. In other districts, where there was scarcity of clothing, owing to the people having no flocks, orders were given that cloth should be abundantly provided. In short, it will be understood that as these lords knew how to enforce service and the payment of tribute, so they provided for the maintenance of the people, and took care that they should want for nothing. Through these good works, and because the lord always gave women and rich gifts to his principal vassals, he gained so much on their affections that he was most fondly loved.

One of the things which I admired most, in contemplating and noting down the affairs of this kingdom, was to think how and in what manner they can have made such grand and admirable roads as we now see, and what a number of men would suffice for their construction, and with what tools and instruments they can have levelled the mountains and broken through the rocks to make them so broad and good as they are. For it seems to me that if the Emperor should desire to give orders for another royal road to be made, like that which goes from Quito to Cuzco, or the other from Cuzco to go to Chile, with all his power I believe that he could not get it done; nor could any force of men achieve such results unless there was also the perfect order by means of which the commands of the Incas were carried into execution. For if the road to be made was fifty leagues long, or one hundred or two hundred, and though the ground was of the most rugged character, it would be done with diligent care. But their roads were much longer, some of them extending for over one thousand one hundred leagues along such dizzy and frightful abysses that, looking down, the sight failed one. In some places, to secure the regular width, it was necessary to hew a path out of the living rock; all which was done with fire and their picks. In other places the ascents were so steep and high that steps had to be cut from below to enable the ascent to be made, with wider spaces at intervals for resting-places. In other parts there were great heaps of snow, which were more to be feared, and not at one spot only, but often recurring. Where these snows obstructed the way, and where there were forests of trees and loose clods of earth, the road was levelled and paved with stones when necessary.

Memoirs: The Aztecs
Bernal Diaz del Castillo

The Aztecs arrived relatively late into the "middle American" world, around 1218. They slowly developed until the mid-1400s when they came to dominate the region. Although their empire was based on the plunder of war and human sacrifice, the Aztecs were also great lovers of beauty. By the time of Cortez's conquest of Mexico in 1519, there are indications that Aztec culture was about to decline. This selection, written a half-century later by Bernal Diaz (1492?–1581), a member of Cortez's conquering army, gives a sense of the highly developed civilization and splendor of the Aztec capital.

SOURCE: I. I. Lockhart, trans., *The Memoirs of the Conquistador Bernal de Castillo* (London: J. Hatchard and Son, 1844), pp. 220–221, 235–238.

Consider: *The similarities and differences between Spanish and Aztec culture; why Diaz was astonished at the splendor and wealth of this civilization.*

When we gazed upon all this splendour . . . we scarcely knew what to think, and we doubted whether all that we beheld was real. A series of large towns stretched themselves along the banks of the lake, out of which still larger ones rose magnificently above the waters. Innumerable crowds of canoes were plying everywhere around us; at regular distances we continually passed over new bridges, and before us lay the great city of Mexico in all its splendour. . . .

Motecusuma himself, according to his custom, was sumptuously attired, had on a species of half boot, richly set with jewels, and whose soles were made of solid gold. The four grandees who supported him were also richly attired, which they must have put on somewhere on the road, in order to wait upon Motecusuma; they were not so sumptuously dressed when they first came out to meet us. Besides these distinguished caziques, there were many other grandees around the monarch, some of whom held the canopy over his head, while others again occupied the road before him, and spread cotton cloths on the ground that his feet might not touch the bare earth. No one of his suite ever looked at him full in the face; every one in his presence stood with eyes downcast, and it was only his four nephews and cousins who supported him that durst look up. . . .

Our commander, attended by the greater part of our cavalry and foot, all well armed, as, indeed, we were at all times, had proceeded to the Tlatelulco. . . . The moment we arrived in this immense market, we were perfectly astonished at the vast numbers of people, the profusion of merchandise which was there exposed for sale, and at the good police and order that reigned throughout. The grandees who accompanied us drew our attention to the smallest circumstance, and gave us full explanation of all we saw. Every species of merchandise had a separate spot for its sale. We first of all visited those divisions of the market appropriated for the sale of gold and silver wares, of jewels, of cloths interwoven with feathers, and of other manufactured goods; besides slaves of both sexes. . . . Next to these came the dealers in coarser wares—cotton, twisted thread, and cacao. . . . In one place were sold the stuffs manufactured of nequen; ropes, and sandals; in another place, the sweet maguey root, ready cooked, and various other things made from this plant. In another division of the market were exposed the skins of tigers, lions, jackals, otters, red deer, wild cats, and of other beasts of prey, some of which were tanned. In another place were sold beans and sage, with other herbs and vegetables. A particular market was assigned for the merchants in fowls, turkeys, ducks, rabbits, hares, deer, and dogs; also for fruit-sellers, pastry-cooks, and tripe-sellers. Not far from these were exposed all manner of earthenware, from the large earthen cauldron to the smaller pitchers. Then came the dealers in honey and honey-cakes, and other sweetmeats. Next to these, the timber-merchants, furniture-dealers, with their stores of tables, benches, cradles, and all sorts of wooden implements, all separately arranged. . . .

In this market-place there were also courts of justice, to which three judges and several constables were appointed, who inspected the goods exposed for sale. . . . I wish I had completed the enumeration of all this profusion of merchandise. The variety was so great that it would occupy more space than I can well spare to note them down in; besides which, the market was so crowded with people, and the thronging so excessive in the porticoes, that it was quite impossible to see all in one day. . . .

Indeed, this infernal temple, from its great height, commanded a view of the whole surrounding neighbourhood. From this place we could likewise see the three causeways which led into Mexico. . . . We also observed the aqueduct which ran from Chapultepec, and provided the whole town with sweet water. We could also distinctly see the bridges across the openings, by which these causeways were intersected, and through which the waters of the lake ebbed and flowed. The lake itsef was crowded with canoes, which were bringing provisions, manufactures, and other merchandize to the city. From here we also discovered that the only communication of the houses in this city, and of all the other towns built in the lake, was by means of drawbridges or canoes. In all these towns the beautiful white plastered temples rose above the smaller ones, . . . and this, it may be imagined, was a splendid sight.

After we had sufficiently gazed upon this magnificent picture, we again turned our eyes toward the great market, and beheld the vast numbers of buyers and sellers who thronged them. The bustle and noise occasioned by this multitude of human beings was so great that it could be heard at a distance of more than four miles.

VISUAL SOURCES

West African Goldweights

These two brass sculptings are Ashanti goldweights. They both reveal typical activities of west African peoples. The first shows women pounding grain, an indication of the importance of agriculture for this society and one of the roles played by women. The second shows a man tapping a palm tree for wine, which was of social, cultural, and ceremonial importance. The fine sculpting and casting in brass of these weights indicates how sophisticated the Ashanti people were. The weights themselves testify to the importance of the gold trade in western Africa.

> **Consider:** *How these sculptings compare to the Mayan sculpting; the sorts of skills and concerns that were involved in producing these goldweights.*

Photo 12–1

Photo 12–2

Margaret Plass Collection, from "Through African Eyes," Leon E. Clark, ed.
(New York: Praeger, 1970).

The British Museum

The Western Sudan in the Fourteenth Century: Trade Routes and Politics

*Map 12-1 shows some of the major states of the western Sudan during the period between
A.D. 1000 and 1500. The locations of gold mines, salt mines, and major trade routes are
noted. The map reveals that there were a number of medium and large states during this
period, some in competition with each other. It also reveals the importance of controlling
trade between the south and north. This helps explain the power and importance of states
such as Ghana and Mali and how these states might be influenced by contact with other
African societies.*

Consider: *The combination of geography, economics, and politics that help explain
the rise of powerful states in this part of Africa.*

Map 12–1 West African Trade Routes

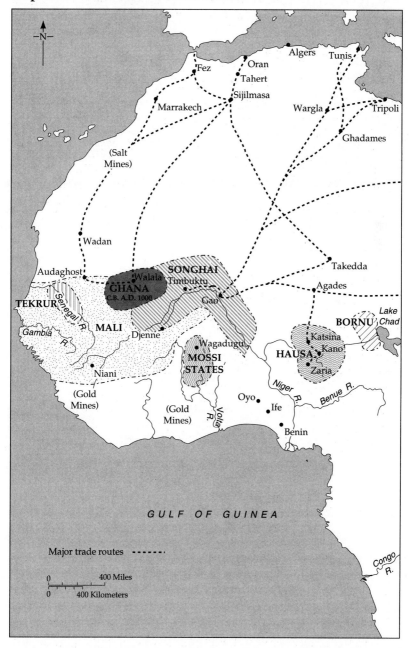

Major trade routes - - - - - -

0   400 Miles

0   400 Kilometers

Mayan Woman and Children

Much of our nondocumentary evidence about Mayan culture comes from sculptings, which provide important clues about Mayan society. This Mayan sculpture (Photo 12-3) from about 800–1000 A.D. shows a woman preparing tortillas. On her back is a child and in front of her is another. It indicates the many roles that women in Mayan culture had assumed by the end of the first millennium. Women were the caretakers of the children and were responsible for training the children in tasks essential for the success of the community. The sculpture also indicates the existence of a sophisticated agricultural system in the early Mayan culture. The woman is grinding maize, or corn, a domesticated crop that was basic to the Mayan diet. Maize had been cultivated by the Native Americans of the central Mexican plateau for approximately four thousand years before this sculpture was made.

> **Consider:** *Why the sculpture shows children intently observing the mother's work; what this sculpture might have meant to the Mayans.*

Photo 12–3

From "Woman in Pre-Columbian America" by Ferdinand Anton (New York: Abner Schram, 1973).

Map 12–2 Major Types of Subsistence on the Eve of Discovery

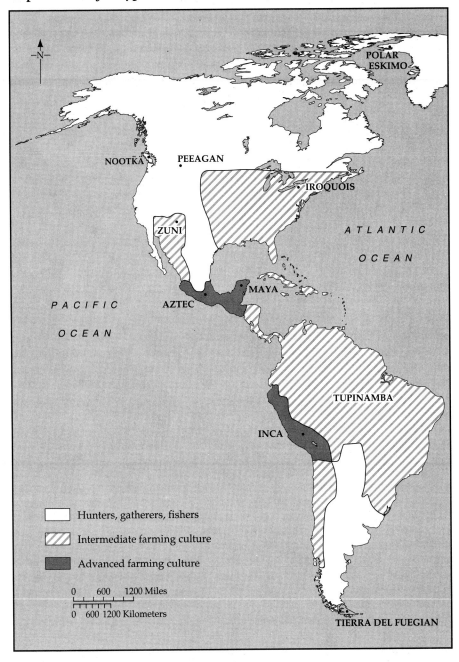

POLAR ESKIMO

NOOTKA

PEEAGAN

IROQUOIS

ZUNI

ATLANTIC

OCEAN

MAYA

AZTEC

PACIFIC

OCEAN

TUPINAMBA

INCA

Hunters, gatherers, fishers

Intermediate farming culture

Advanced farming culture

0   600   1200 Miles

0   600 1200 Kilometers

TIERRA DEL FUEGIAN

The Americas in 1490

The development of stable agricultural systems is essential for the success of any population. Map 12–2 illustrates the varied place of agriculture in the lives of the indigenous peoples of the Americas. Contrary to popular myths that depict the Native Americans primarily as "hunters and gatherers," the majority of the peoples of the New World had established stable agricultural communities. It is also significant that the most advanced agricultural communities were the civilizations with the most sophisticated road networks and urban centers. The Aztecs, Mayans, and Incas all built impressive cities that served as trading and political centers. The "intermediate" farming cultures frequently had developed political structure but lacked a sophisticated infrastructure.

> **Consider:** *What the existence of stable agricultural communities tell us about Native American political and social development.*

SECONDARY SOURCES

Origins of Cities and States in Western Africa
Roland Oliver

Ghana was the first of a series of empires that formed in the western Sudan—the band of grasslands bordering the Sahara Desert in western Africa. Clearly thriving by the eighth century A.D., its origins probably stretched back several centuries. Much of Ghana's strength derived from its urban origins and the trade it controlled. But how did these west African urban centers first develop? In the following selection, Roland Oliver addrsses this question.

> **Consider:** *How recent research has changed earlier interpretations; how both factors may be necessary to explain how Ghana became so powerful.*

It is in the belt of West Africa lying next to the Sahara that the problem of urban origins is most confusing, because it is here that the claims of outside influence shout loudest in the historical sources and have to be accorded at least some recognition. According to an earlier historiography which lacked the archaeological evidence available today, the Berbers, once equipped with the camel, opened the trans-Saharan routes, and caused the black peoples to the south of the desert to

SOURCE: Roland Oliver, *The African Experience: Major Themes in African History from Earliest Times to the Present* (New York, Icon Editions, HarperCollins, 1991), pp. 99–100.

reorganize themselves so as to take the best advantage of the long-distance trade. Hence the emergence of states in Ghana, Gao and Kanem, of which the first handled the trade with Morocco, the second that with Algeria and Tunisia, and the third that with Tripolitania and Egypt. The reorganization involved the enlargement of territory in order to protect trade routes, and the creation of entrepôt towns where camel-loads could be redistributed onto donkeys or into canoes, with a corresponding change in the ethnic character of the carriers. Today we see that the urban pattern of settlement long antedated the development of the trans-Saharan trade. On the one hand there were the oasis settlements, where the remnants of the old negro population of the southern Sahara had congregated. These . . . were essentially urban phenomena, and it is most likely that the capital of the Soninke kingdom of Ghana at Koumbe Saleh should be seen in this light. On the other hand, there were the urban settlements, equally those of black people, along the river lines which created special conditions suited for intensive agriculture in the otherwise arid Sahelian belt. . . . All these settlements would appear to have been founded by speakers of Niger-Congo languages, whose basic occupations were fishing and farming, who needed to defend themselves against the pastoralists of the surrounding savanna, but otherwise had little incentive to enlarge their little self-sufficient states. And beyond them to the east were the Chadic-speaking Sao, with their urban settlements along the water-lines of the Chad basin.

Power and Instability in Mali
Harry A. Gailey

The largest and most well known of the states in the western Sudan to succeed Ghana was the kingdom of Mali. Rising in the thirteenth century, this large, wealthy state flourished until its decline and disintegration in the fifteenth century. In the following selection, Harry A. Gailey analyzes the sources of Mali's strength and instability. He then goes on to describe and suggest reasons for Mali's decline.

Consider: *The ways in which Mali's strengths could also be sources of instability; how Mali's decline reflects the dynamics of power among competing and succeeding west African states.*

Throughout its history, Mali, not unlike European states of the same period, is a study of both strength and instability. The comparison can be extended further

SOURCE: Harry A. Gailey, *History of Africa from Earliest Times to 1800* (Mala Krieger Publishing, 1970), pp. 66, 69.

because the institutional problems in feudal Europe were of the same type as in Mali. Large states with a heterogeneous population are difficult to rule, particularly when communication between various parts of the polity are slow. In Mali there was early developed a bureaucracy of able administrators appointed by the king to deal with such problems as finance, defense, and foreign affairs. Conquered areas were administered in the name of the emperor by appointed governors and their aides. In time the higher positions came to be regarded by the officers as hereditary, and certain powerful factions operated openly at the courts of the Malian rulers. Strong emperors could keep these divisive forces in check either by playing one against the other or by overawing them by force. Weak rulers or men whose claim to the throne was questionable found it difficult to control the factions. . . .

Many interrelated factors were responsible for the decline and eventual eclipse of the great Mali kingdom. For one thing, the kingdom never really recovered from the civil strife in the period after 1360. In addition, the weakness of successive rulers was paralleled by dangers to the state from outside threats. The Berbers became more active in the fifteenth century, and the Mossi, who had never been conquered, grew bolder in their raids on Malian territory. By 1450 Walata, Timbuktu, and Macina were all independent of the emperor. In the 1470s Mossi armies plundered the central area of Mali and soon afterward the Wolof in Tekrur declared themselves independent. Aside from the ineptness of the late Malian rulers the major reason for the decline in the fortunes of Mali can be attributed to the growing power of the competitive Niger River state of Songhai.

The Earliest Americans
John Noble Wilford

The established archeological and scientific theory has been that Native Americans migrated across a frozen strait of land, now the Bering Strait, and then migrated south throughout the Americas. But recently, new discoveries are challenging this view and suggesting the possibility that the migration occurred earlier—some 15,000 to 32,000 years ago—and that migrants arrived in South America first.

Consider: *What kind of evidence scientists used to determine when the first migrants came and where they came from; the possible importance of these new discoveries and theories.*

SOURCE: John Noble Wilford, "New Finds Challenge Ideas on Earliest Americans," Copyright © 1985 by *The New York Times*, July 22, 1986, pp. C1, 13.

New discoveries in the Arctic and in South America are rekindling scholarly debate over some of the most intractable problems in American archeology: how and when did humans first enter the New World? What kind of people were they?

About the only thing archeologists agree on is that the earliest Americans originated in northeastern Asia and definitely arrived here before 11,500 years ago. The general assumption is that they migrated from Siberia to Alaska in the ice age of the late Pleistocene, when Asia was connected to North America by a broad plain stretching at what is now the Bering Strait.

Archeologists are sharply divided over when the migration occurred: whether it came early, at least 20,000 years ago and probably much earlier, or late, no more than 15,000 years ago. Geologists believe the Bering land bridge disappeared about 14,000 years ago when the massive glaciers melted and released so much water that sea levels rose several hundred feet worldwide.

Last month, French scientists reported evidence from a rock shelter in Brazil that, if confirmed by further analysis and excavation, would strongly support those who believe in an earlier human presence in the New World. Radio carbon dating put the age of charcoal associated with stone tools and other artifacts in the shelter at 32,000 years. Wall paintings at the site suggest that cave art in the Americas developed about the same time as it did in Europe, Asia and Africa.

At an excavation site in Chile, an anthropologist at the University of Kentucky, said he had found preliminary evidence of human occupation possibly as long ago as 33,000 years.

The discoveries in South America both challenged and confused archeological thinking. They have forced archeologists to reexamine old assumptions and wonder where they must dig next to establish more clearly when and where humans first came to America.

If humans were in South America as early as 32,000 years ago, where was the evidence that they had been in North America as early or earlier? They had to have been if there is any truth to the hypothesis of the Bering land bridge migration. Otherwise, archeologists might have no choice but to revive the generally discredited idea that the first humans came from across the Pacific, landing in South America and then moving north.

No firmly documented evidence shows the human presence in North America before 11,500 years ago. . . .

As the French scientists concluded in their report to Pedra Furada the new findings "strongly" suggest that the migration from Asia to North America occurred earlier than 32,000 years ago. But E. James Dixon, curator of archeology at the University of Alaska Museum in Fairbanks, said the discoveries cast some doubt on the Bering land bridge hypothesis and the north to south radiation of people throughout the Americas. . . .

An alternative hypothesis espoused most recently by Thor Heyerdahl, the Norwegian explorer, has the first Americans coming from Asia by boats across the Pacific.

Dennis Stanford, an archeologist with the Smithsonian Institution, said, "I find it hard to conceive of a transoceanic migration."

Although prehistoric Polynesians were accomplished navigators, scientists said, there is no evidence that people inhabited any of the Pacific Islands east of the Solomons until about 3,500 years ago. It is equally difficult, skeptics of the hypothesis added, to conceive of people from Australia, where there were humans 50,000 years ago, reaching the New World by way of Antarctica.

Moreover, studies of blood type, language and teeth all suggest a more direct link between the early Americans and Asians, primarily people of northern China and northeastern Siberia. This and the geologic evidence for the land bridge are considered the firmest foundation for the Bering migration hypothesis.

Christy G. Turner, a professor of anthropology at Arizona State University, concluded the founding Siberian-American people must have come from northern China 20,000 years ago, probably in three waves of migrations of different but related people. He based the conclusion on an examination of teeth from the skeletons of 9,000 pre-Colombian American Indians, Aleuts and Eskimos.

Judging by the differences and similarities of teeth, Dr. Turner said, the Aleuts and Eskimos must have descended from people who migrated directly from China along the southern rim of the Bering land bridge. Indians of the American northwest coast, a racial group known as NaDene, probably sprang from people who traveled from the Siberian forest through the interior of the land bridge. The rest of the American Indians probably descended from game hunters who moved across the northern edge of the land bridge.

Red, White, and Black: The Peoples of Early America
Gary Nash

We take for granted that people have the right to buy and sell land. Such a view is so fundamental to western European economics that it is hard to envision an alternative world view. Yet, this was not the case for Native Americans and the diverging understanding of the meaning of land ownership and, more broadly, private property, would lead to continual conflict. Over time, European settlers would fence in ranges, pen up wild horses, and hunt for private profit. This would undermine the entire livelihood of nomadic tribes that depended on freedom to move, hunt, and establish temporary communities. In this selection, Gary Nash, a historian of early American history at UCLA,

SOURCE: Gary B. Nash, *Red, White and Black, the Peoples of Early America*, 3rd ed. (Englewood Cliffs, Prentice-Hall, 1982), pp. 25–27. Copyright © 1982, 1992. Reprinted by permission of Prentice-Hall.

describes the clash of cultures and economic systems between white settlers and the native inhabitants of North America.

> **Consider:** *The differences between the Native American and European world views, views concerning land, and views concerning personal identity; in light of what we now know regarding ecological destruction, how you might evaluate the Native American view of the symmetry of nature.*

While Native American and European cultures were not nearly so different as the concepts of "savagery" and "civilization" imply, societies on the eastern and western sides of the Atlantic had developed different systems of values in the centuries that preceded contact. Underlying the physical confrontations that would take place when European and Native American met were incompatible ways of looking at the world. These latent conflicts can be seen in contrasting European and Indian views of man's relationship to his environment, the concept of property, and personal identity.

In the European view the natural world was a resource for man to use. "Subdue the earth," it was said in Genesis, "and have dominion over every living thing that moves on the earth." The cosmos was still ruled by God, of course, and supernatural forces, manifesting themselves in earthquakes, hurricanes, drought, and flood, could not be controlled by man. But a scientific revolution was under way in the early modern period, which gave humans more confidence that they could comprehend the natural world—and thus eventually control it. For Europeans the secular and the sacred were distinct, and man's relationship to his natural environment fell into the secular sphere.

In the Indian ethos no such separation of secular and sacred existed. Every part of the natural world was sacred, for Native Americans believed the world was inhabited by a great variety of "beings," each possessing spiritual power and all linked together to form a sacred whole. "Plants, animals, rocks, and stars," explains Murray Wax, "are thus seen not as objects governed by laws of nature but as 'fellows' with whom the individual or band may have a more or less advantageous relationship." Consequently, if one offended the land by stripping it of its cover, the spiritual power in the land—called "manitou" by some woodlands tribes— would strike back. If one overfished or destroyed game beyond one's needs, the spiritual power inhering in fish and animals would take revenge because humans had broken the mutual trust and reciprocity that governed relations between all beings—human and nonhuman. To exploit the land or to treat with disrespect any part of the natural world was to cut oneself off from the spiritual power dwelling in all things and "was thus equivalent to repudiating the vital force in Nature."

Because Europeans regarded the land as a resource to be exploited for man's gain it was easier to regard it as a commodity to be privately held. Private ownership of property became one of the fundamental bases upon which European culture rested. Fences became the symbols of exclusively held property, inheritance became the mechanism for transmitting these "assets" from one generation to another within the same family, and courts provided the institutional apparatus for settling property disputes. In a largely agricultural society property became the basis of political power. In fact, political rights in England derived from the ownership of a specified quantity of land. In addition, the social structure was largely defined by the distribution of property, with those possessing great quantities of it standing at the apex of the social pyramid and the mass of propertyless individuals forming the broad base.

In the Indian world this view of land as a privately held asset was incomprehensible. Tribes recognized territorial boundaries, but within these limits the land was held in common. Land was not a commodity but a part of nature that was entrusted to the living by the Creator. . . . Thus, land was a gift of the Creator, to be used with care, and was not for the exclusive possession of particular human beings.

In the area of personal identity Indian and European values also differed sharply. Europeans were acquisitive, competitive, and over a long period of time had been enhancing the role of the individual. Wider choices and greater opportunities for the individual to improve his status—by industriousness, valor, or even personal sacrifice leading to martyrdom—were regarded as desirable. Personal ambition, in fact, played a large role in the migration of Europeans across the Atlantic in the sixteenth and seventeenth centuries. In contrast, the cultural traditions of Native Americans emphasized the collectivity rather than the individual. Because land and other natural resources were held in common and society was far less hierarchical than in Europe, the accumulative spirit and personal ambition were inappropriate. . . . Hence, individualism was more likely to lead to ostracism than admiration in Indian communities.

Indians of the Americas: A Geopolitical Analysis
Roxanne D. Ortiz

Before Europeans came to the New World, Native Americans had already established diverse and often complex societies. Contrary to the prevailing myths presented in movies and books, many of the indigenous peoples had well-developed agricultural and political systems in place. This essay, by Roxanne D. Ortiz, a scholar at the California State Uni-

---

SOURCE: Roxanne D. Ortiz, *Indians of the Americas, Human Rights and Self-Determination* (New York: Praeger, 1984), pp. 1–4.

versity at Hayward, briefly surveys the variety of cultures that were dispersed in what is now the United States of America. In this excerpt, she argues that the economic and political systems of the native inhabitants were effective in distributing the societies' wealth and maintaining social cohesion.

> **Consider:** *The nature of these Native American cultures; how this picture of Native American cultures contrasts with popular images propagated through old and new movies and literature about the American frontier.*

The problem of interpreting the reality of America for Europeans, in the 16th Century as well as today, has been their insistence on justifying conquest, having encountered only scattered "hunting and gathering tribes" who had only "recently" migrated from Asia over the Bering Strait, and had as little claim as Europeans to the "new world" and its vast resources. Yet the reality has long been known and there are few mysteries about pre-colonial America if the above false assumptions are abandoned.

As on the three other major continental land masses of the world, civilization in America emerged from certain centres, which, in turn, created peripheries that the centres tended to incorporate; with periods of vigorous growth and integration, as well as decline and disintegration. At least a dozen such centres were functioning when the Europeans intervened. In North America, a remarkable federal state structure had incorporated five widely dispersed nations of thousands of agricultural villages, from the Great Lakes to the Atlantic, and as far south as the Carolinas and inland to Pennsylvania. This was the Iroquois Confederacy originally comprising five nations. Its capacity for dynamic transformation was demonstrated after the intervention by the Dutch, British and French. The Confederacy incorporated still another nation, the Tuscarora of the south, refugees from British colonization, and became the Six Nations of the Iroquois Confederacy. The Confederacy was a highly structured state system which allowed the multi-ethnic state to incorporate peoples and nations. Undoubtedly, it would have continued to incorporate and annex other peoples in North America. The remarkable aspect of the Iroquois state was its ability to avoid centralization by means of a clan-village system of democracy, based on collective ownership of the land; its products, stored in granaries, were distributed equitably to the people by elected authorities. "Clan mothers" played the key role of supervising all activities, having the final veto on any decision. . . . The population, at the period of European contact, was around two million. . . .

Bordering the Iroquois state to the west were the people of the Plains and prairies of central North America, from West Texas to the sub-Arctic. Several centres of state development in that vast region of bison-hunting peoples may be identified. In the prairies of Canada, the Cree; in the Dakotas, the Lakota and Dakota (Sioux); and to the west and south the Cheyenne and Arapaho peoples. What integrated each nation was its clan society and its annual Sun Dance. Many other bison-hunting peoples occupied various part of the territories, and territorial disputes occurred. Some peoples, such as the Potowatomie, turned almost entirely to commerce. These groups tended to be peacemakers and negotiators in disputes, speaking many languages, perhaps originating the sign language which became universal in the Western hemisphere in pre-colonial times; they are said also to have initiated the inter-tribal powwow, which persists today. In the whole region, the human population probably reached approximately one million, while the bison population was around 80 million.

To the south-east, bordering the Iroquois state, from the Atlantic Ocean to the Gulf of Mexico and west to the Mississippi river and Sioux country, is one of the most fertile agricultural belts in the world. Naturally watered, filled with plant and animal life, temperate in climate, this region provided the base for the vast accumulation of capital of the US, which used it for labour-intensive plantation cash crop production. Prior to the arrival of British planters with African slaves, however, the territory was a thriving civilization inhabited by five major nations that had incorporated most of their peripheral areas by 1600. These were the Muskogee-speaking Choctaw, Creek, and Chickasaw nations, in the south-central part of the region; the Cherokee, Algonkin-speaking like their Iroquois relatives, in the eastern half of the region; and the Natchez nation in the west, the Mississippi valley area. By currently accepted demographic figures, the total population of the region is estimated to have been two to three million, but may prove to have been much more. The Natchez nation alone—which was totally destroyed by colonization and the population sold into slavery—may have numbered several million. Since these were city- and town-dwelling peoples, their populations may have been larger than current estimates indicate. These states functioned much like those of the Iroquois Confederacy, based in the towns. Their system of decision-making was, however, based on popular consensus, the form of government that later baffled colonial agents who coud not find Indian officials to bribe or manipulate; probably partly accounting for the eventual deportation and relocation of these nations by the US.

In the Pacific north-west region of the North American continent, from Alaska to San Francisco, and along the vast waterways inland to the mountain barrier, a unitary culture of fishing peoples flourished. A state system as such is not apparent, although their ceremonial and trade linkages could have supported some sort of state structure. These were wealthy people living in a paradise of natural resources. Their population is estimated to have reached more than four million, with the majority in northern California and southern Oregon.

Chapter Questions

1. What kinds of sources do historians use to piece together the history of early civilizations in sub-Saharan Africa and the Americas? How do these compare with the sources used for the history of other early civilizations in Chapters 1, 2, and 3?

2. How might the kinds of sources used in this chapter help us to reevaluate the variety and sophistication of civilizations that existed in sub-Saharan Africa and the Americas prior to 1550? Speculate on what kind of new sources might be discovered and used for new interpretations of these civilizations.

3. How might the sources in this chapter be used to help explain the rise, the power, and the decline of sub-Saharan states prior to 1500? How might any patterns here compare to the rise, the power, and the decline of states in other areas of the world?

THIRTEEN

European Expansion and Global Encounters, 1500–1700

Between the mid-fifteenth and mid-sixteenth centuries much of Europe gained new political, economic, and technological strength. This enabled European states to support a new wave of expansion into the rest of the world. Led by Portugal and then Spain, these states sent explorers, missionaries, merchants, colonists, and armed forces throughout the world. In some cases, as for the civilizations of the Americas, the consequences would be immediate and profound. In other cases, as in China and Japan, the effects would be more indirect. But in the long run, this European expansion would mark a turning point in world history.

In Asia, contacts between Westerners and peoples of south and east Asia extended back for centuries, long before Marco Polo, the most widely known European traveler, reached China in the thirteenth century. Organized by merchants, missionaries, adventurers, or explorers, caravans crossed the vast plateaus of central Asia with the help of the local Turkic inhabitants. By the fifteenth century Arab speaking merchants and bankers had developed a monopoly on the east and south Asia trade. This changed in the fifteenth, sixteenth, and seventeenth centuries as the Portuguese, Spanish, Dutch,

British, and French moved in. During this same period the Russians were advancing eastward through Siberia, conquering as they went. A new Asian-European relationship had the potential of becoming a dialogue rewarding to all, but the relationship was marred from the beginning by ethnocentrism and the Europeans' propensity to force their will on the Asians. The long-established Asian societies were usually able to resist European efforts to establish control over them during this period.

In sub-Saharan Africa, the ability of Europeans to penetrate the continent beyond setting up coastal posts was limited by geographical factors, disease, and resistance from African kingdoms. However, this new contact with Europeans, and particularly the development of the slave trade, would become of importance to both Africans and Europeans.

In the Americas, Christopher Columbus's arrival in 1492 has often been used as the starting point for discussion of American history. Recently, historians have acknowledged that the indigenous peoples of North, Central, and South America had a rich culture that predated Europeans' arrival but

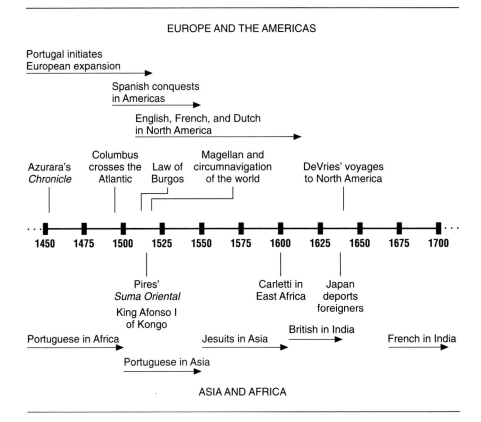

EUROPE AND THE AMERICAS

Portugal initiates
European expansion

Spanish conquests
in Americas

English, French, and Dutch
in North America

Azurara's   Columbus   Magellan and
Chronicle   crosses the   Law of   circumnavigation   DeVries' voyages
                  Atlantic   Burgos   of the world   to North America

1450   1475   1500   1525   1550   1575   1600   1625   1650   1675   1700

Pires'   Carletti in   Japan
Suma Oriental   East Africa   deports
                                                     foreigners
King Afonso I
of Kongo
                                    British in India
Portuguese in Africa   Jesuits in Asia   French in India

Portuguese in Asia

ASIA AND AFRICA

which has been neglected. As they established empires, Europeans from Spain, Portugal, France, Holland, and England had to adapt their own cultures to the existing environment of peoples and places in the western hemisphere. Europeans had to interact with the Native Americans they conquered and the Africans they brought to the Americas as slaves.

The sources in the chapter will examine three main topics. First, what were the motives for the European expansion? What did they have to gain? How did they justify their actions? Second, what observations did the people involved in these cross-cultural contacts make? What do these observations tell us about the societies being observed? What do they reveal about the observer's own assumptions? Third, what were the consequences of these global encounters? What were the effects in Europe? What were the effects outside of Europe?

This last topic will bring us toward a more detailed examination of developments in various parts of the world, which will be the focus of later chapters.

PRIMARY SOURCES

The Chronicle of the Discovery and Conquest of Guinea
Azurara

The great geographic expansion and conquests of the fifteenth and sixteenth centuries were initiated by Prince Henry (the Navigator) of Portugal (1394–1460). Although he did not personally participate in the explorations, he established a naval school and base of operations on the southwestern tip of Portugal from which he sent expeditions down the west coast of Africa. One of the clearest explanations of the motives for this effort has been provided by Gomes Eannes de Azurara, a friend of Prince Henry (referred to as "the Lord Infant"), who chronicled the voyages of 1452–1453 at the request of King Alfonso V.

> **Consider:** *The explanations that sound more like rationalizations than reasons for explorations; whether economic, military, and religious motives are complementary or contradictory; how this document reflects the history of a country engaged with Islam.*

Source: Gomes Eannes de Azurara, *The Chronicle of the Discovery and Conquest of Guinea*, vol. I, trans. Charles Raymond Beazley and Adgar Prestage (London: Hakluyt Society, 1896), pp. 27–29.

We imagine that we know a matter when we are acquainted with the doer of it and the end for which he did it. And since in former chapters we have set forth the Lord Infant as the chief actor in these things, giving as clear an understanding of him as we could, it is meet that in this present chapter we should know his purpose in doing them. And you should note well that the noble spirit of this Prince, by a sort of natural constraint, was ever urging him both to begin and to carry out very great deeds. For which reason, after the taking of Ceuta he always kept ships well armed against the Infidel, both for war, and because he had also a wish to know the land that lay beyond the isles of Canary and that Cape called Bojador, for that up to his time, neither by writings, nor by the memory of man, was known with any certainty the nature of the land beyond that Cape. Some said indeed that Saint Brandan had passed that way; and there was another tale of two galleys rounding the Cape, which never returned. But this doth not appear at all likely to be true, for it is not to be presumed that if the said galleys went there, some other ships would not have endeavoured to learn what voyage they had made. And because the said Lord Infant wished to know the truth of this,—since it seemed to him that if he or some other lord did not endeavour to gain that knowledge, no mariners or merchants would ever dare to attempt it—(for it is clear that none of them ever trouble themselves to sail to a place where there is not a sure and certain hope of profit)—and seeing also that no other prince took any pains in this matter, he sent out his own ships against those parts, to have manifest certainty of them all. And to this he was stirred up by his zeal for the service of God and of the King Edward his Lord and brother, who then reigned. And this was the first reason of his action.

The second reason was that if there chanced to be in those lands some population of Christians, or some havens, into which it would be possible to sail without peril, many kinds of merchandise might be brought to this realm, which would find a ready market, and reasonably so, because no other people of these parts traded with them, nor yet people of any other that were known; and also the products of this realm might be taken there, which traffic would bring great profit to our countrymen.

The third reason was that, as it was said that the power of the Moors in that land of Africa was very much greater than was commonly supposed, and that there were no Christians among them, nor any other race of men; and because every wise man is obliged by natural prudence to wish for a knowledge of the power of his enemy; therefore the said Lord Infant exerted himself to cause this to be fully discovered, and to make it known determinately how far the power of those infidels extended.

The fourth reason was because during the one and thirty years that he had warred against the Moors, he had never found a Christian king, nor a lord outside this land, who for the love of our Lord Jesus Christ would aid him in the said war. Therefore he sought to know if there were in those parts any Christian princes, in whom the charity and the love of Christ was so ingrained that they would aid him against those enemies of the faith.

The fifth reason was his great desire to make increase in the faith of our Lord Jesus Christ and to bring to him all the souls that should be saved,—understanding that all the mystery of the Incarnation, Death, and Passion of our Lord Jesus Christ was for this sole end—namely the salvation of lost souls—whom the said Lord Infant by his travail and spending would fain bring into the true path. For he perceived that no better offering could be made unto the Lord than this; for if God promised to return one hundred goods for one, we may justly believe that for such great benefits, that is to say for so many souls as were saved by the efforts of this Lord, he will have so many hundreds of guerdons in the kingdom of God, by which his spirit may be glorified after this life in the celestial realm. For I that wrote this history saw so many men and women of those parts turned to the holy faith, that even if the Infant had been a heathen, their prayers would have been enough to have obtained his salvation. And not only did I see the first captives, but their children and grandchildren as true Christians as if the Divine grace breathed in them and imparted to them a clear knowledge of itself.

Africa and Europe: The Problems of Alliances

Afonso I of Kongo

The Kingdom of Kongo was the largest and most powerful state in west-central Africa before 1500. The Kongolese met Europeans for the first time when Portuguese sailors led by Diogo Cão reached their country in 1483. By 1491, the ruler (the Mani Kongo*) had been baptized and accepted Christianity. King Afonso I, his son (ca. 1485–1543) was instrumental in making his state a Christian country, but often had to deal with a variety of problems, both with his own countrymen and with the Portuguese. Among the fruits of this contact were literacy, new building techniques, bureaucratic styles and titles and a host of lesser cultural infusions. In his attempts to maintain Christianity, Afonso often turned to either Portugal or Rome for assistance. The following selection touches on the conflicts that emerged between various Portuguese factions who had different allies among the Kongolese nobility, and the relationship between the African king and his European ally.*

> **Consider:** *What the document reveals about the strengths and weaknesses of this African-European alliance; the Kongolese experience with Christianity.*

Now we wish to tell your Highness about a certain Rui do Rego whom your Highness sent here to teach us and set an example for us, but as soon as he arrived here he wished to be treated like a nobleman and never wanted to teach a single

SOURCE: William H. McNeill and Mitsuko Iriye, *Modern Asia and Africa* (Oxford: 1971), pp. 56–59.

boy. During the Lenten season he came to us and asked for an ox, and we ordered one to be given to him. Then he said he was dying of hunger, and we ordered two sheep to be given to him, but that he was to eat them secretly, so that our people would not see him. Yet he, disregarding this, went and killed the ox in the middle of Lent, in front of all our nobles, and even tempted us with the meat; so that when our people saw it, those who were young and had only been Christians a short time all fled to their lands, and the older ones who remained with us said things that are not to be repeated, stating that we had forbidden them to eat meat, while the white men had plenty of meat, and that we had deceived them and they wanted to kill us. Then we, with much patience and many gifts, were able to pacify them, telling them that they should save their souls and not look at what that man was doing, and that if he wished to go to Hell then they should let him go.

We were so disgusted with all this that we could not see Rui do Rego again and ordered him to go to Chela,[1] so that he could board the first ship that arrived—for he had not taught as your Highness had ordered him to, but had caused to return to idols those whom we, with much fatigue, had converted. So he went and stayed at Chela—and at this time Simão da Silva[2] arrived with two ships and found the said Rui do Rego, who told him so many evil things and so many lies that there is no reckoning them, and that he had been cheated. And then Simão da Silva believed him, through the wrongheadedness of Rui do Rego and what he had said—but Rego did not tell him of the wickedness and heresy that he had practiced here. So that Simão da Silva did not wish to come to where we were (as your Highness had ordered him to) and sent the [ship's] physician with your letters, whom we sheltered as if he had been our brother. A vicar from the island [of São Tomé], who was present here, asked us to let him take the physician to his house to stay with him—but that ecclesiastic spoke so evilly of us to the physician that the physician's mind was changed, and he became persuaded that Simão da Silva should not come [to the capital]. And your Highness will know that it was Fernão de Melo who had ordered all this, since your Highness has no trading station here, and he has tainted goods [to sell?] and always steals from us.

Yet notwithstanding this, Sire, the physician fell ill with fever and could not return to Simão da Silva with an answer, and he wrote him a letter advising him not to come here; that we were a "João Pires" [a "Mr. Nobody," a nonentity], and that we did not deserve any of the things sent by your Highness.[3] The which letter he gave to one of our servants, and it came into our hands and we showed it to all of your Highness' servants who had come in the fleet. When we saw those things we well understood that they had been done at the command of Fernão de Melo—and we gave thanks to our Lord God for having been called a "João

---

[1] A coastal region south of the Zaire River.

[2] In 1512 the king of Portugal sent Simão da Silva, with several ships and many men and supplies, as ambassador to the king of the Congo.

[3] The king of Portugal had sent an impressive diversity of supplies, animals, luxuries, plants, and seeds with his ambassador to the Congo.

Pires" for His love. And all these things, lord and brother, we have suffered with good judgement and prudence, crying many tears—and we have reported nothing to our nobles and people, so that they may not conspire against us.

Then we sent one of our cousins with a young nobleman and wrote to Simão da Silva that, for the love of God, he should come and comfort us, and punish the people who were here, for we would not send him to ask anything of your Highness, except to ask that everyone be treated justly. Because of our entreaties, and those of Dom João our cousin, he left to come, but halfway here the fevers afflicted him with such force that he died. When we heard the news it broke our feet and hands,[4] and we suffered so much vexation that never again, not until this day, have we ever had any pleasure, because of the great disorders and evils later done by the men who came with him.

---

[4] A peculiar expression indicating great anguish.

The Suma Oriental
Tomé Pires

Vasco da Gama's voyage around the southern tip of Africa to India in 1498, ending the Arab monopoly on Indian trade, initiated a massive European expansion into Asia. Soon the Portuguese established a string of outposts and colonies that stretched around much of the world. In Asia alone these posts included Goa, on the west coast of India in 1510, Malacca on the west cast of Malaya in 1511, Macao off the coast of China in 1514, Timor in the eastern tip of Indonesia in 1520, and Japan in 1543.

Portuguese travelers to trading posts and urban centers often wrote about the lands and peoples they encountered, providing us with much of our evidence about these early contacts. Tomé Pires was a Portuguese apothecary to his country's royal family. He was also an explorer and wandered to Asia, living in Goa and Malacca, but also traveling extensively from 1511 to 1517. In 1517 he was dispatched as the Portuguese Ambassador to China where he was arrested after the Chinese authorities heard rumors that the Europeans were enslaving Chinese. He died in a Canton jail. In 1517 he submitted The Suma Oriental *(Account of the East) to the King of Portugal as an account of the trade and political situations in Asia to aid future Portuguese exploitation of Asia. Excerpts from this work follow.*

> **Consider:** *The concerns and attitude of Tomé Pires; the flavor of the trading posts he describes; the mixture of people already present in Asian ports before the Europeans arrived.*

SOURCE: Armando Cortesão, trans., *The Suma Oriental of Tomé Pires. An Account of the East, From the Red Sea to Japan, Written in Malacca and India in 1512–1515*, vol. II (London: Printed for the Hakluyt Society, 1944).

CAMBAY

I now come to the trade of Cambay. . . . All the trade in Cambay is in the hands of the heathen. Their general designation is Gujaratees, and then they are divided into various races—Banians, Brahmans and Pattars. . . . They are men who understand merchandise; they are so properly steeped in the sound and harmony of it, that the Gujaratees say that any offence connected with merchandise is pardonable. . . . They are diligent, quick men in trade. They do their accounts with figures like ours and with our very writing. They are men who do not give away anything that belongs to them, nor do they want anything that belongs to anyone else; wherefore they have been esteemed in Cambay up to the present, practising their idolatry, because they enrich the kingdom greatly with the said trade. There are also some Cairo merchants settled in Cambay, and many Khorasans and Guilans from Aden and Ormuz, all of whom do a great trade in the seaport towns of Cambay. . . .

They trade with the kingdom of the Deccan and Goa and with Malabar, and they have factors everywhere, who live and set up business—as the Genoese do in our part [of the world]— . . . taking back to their own country the kind of merchandise which is valued there. . . .

SIAM

Through the cunning [of the Siamese] the foreign merchants who go to their land and kingdom leave their merchandise in the land and are ill paid; and this happens to them all—but less to the Chinese, on account of their friendship with the king of China. . . .

There are very few Moors in Siam. The Siamese do not like them. There are, however, Arabs, Persians, Bengalees, many Kling, Chinese and other nationalities. And all the Siamese trade is on the China side, and in Pase, Pedir and Bengal. The Moors are in the seaports.

CHINA

They affirm that all those who take merchandise from Canton to the islands make a profit of three, four or five in every ten, and the Chinese have this custom so that the land shall not be taken from them, as well as in order to receive the dues on the merchandise exported as well as imported; and the chief [reason] is for fear lest the city be taken from them, because they say that the city of Canton is a rich one, and corsairs often come up to it. . . .

They say that the Chinese made this law about not being able to go to Canton for fear of the Javanese and Malays, for it is certain that one of these people's junks would rout twenty Chinese junks. They say that China has more than a thousand junks, and each of them trades where it sees fit; but the people are weak, and such is their fear of Malays and Javanese that it is quite certain that one [of our] ship[s] of four hundred tons could depopulate Canton, and this depopulation would bring great loss to China.

Not to rob any country of its glory, it certainly seems that China is an important, good and very wealthy country, and the Governor of Malacca would not need as much force as they say in order to bring it under our rule, because the people are very weak and easy to overcome. . . .

They say that there are people from Tartary (*Tartaria*) in the land of China . . . and these people are very white with red beards. They ride on horseback; they are warlike. And they say that they go from China to the land of the Tartars (*tartaros*) in two months, and that in Tartary they have horses shod with copper shoes, and this must be because China extends a long way on the northern side, and our bombardiers say that in Germany they heard tell of these people and of a city named by the Chinese *Quesechama,* and it seems to them that by this route they could go to their lands in a short time; but they say that by reason of the cold the land is uninhabited.

JAVA

The king of Java is a heathen. . . . These kings of Java have a fantastic idea: they say that their nobility has no equal. The Javanese heathen lords are tall and handsome; they are lavishly adorned about their person, and have richly caparisoned horses. They use krises, swords, and lances of many kinds, all inlaid with gold. They are great hunters and horsemen—stirrups all inlaid with gold, inlaid saddles, such as are not to be found anywhere else in the world. The Javanese lords are so noble and exalted that there is certainly no nation to compare with them over a wide area in these parts. . . .

The lords of Java are revered like gods, with great respect and deep reverence. The land of Java is thickly peopled in the interior, with many cities, and very large ones, including the great city of *Dayo* where the king is in residence and where his court is. They say that the people who frequent the court are without number. The kings do not show themselves to the people except once or twice in the year. They stay in their palace . . . and there they are with all the pleasures and with feasts, with great quantities of wives and concubines. They say that the king of Java has a thousand eunuchs to wait on these women, and these eunuchs are dressed like women and wear their hair dressed in the form of diadems. . . .

MALACCA

Those from Cairo bring the merchandise brought by the galleasses of Venice, to wit, many arms, scarlet-in-grain, coloured woollen cloths, coral, copper, quicksilver, vermilion, nails, silver, glass and other beads, and golden glassware.

Those from Mecca bring a great quantity of opium, rosewater and such like merchandise, and much liquid storax.

Those from Aden bring to Gujarat a great quantity of opium, raisins, madder, indigo, rosewater, silver, seed-pearls, and other dyes, which are of value in Cambay.

In these companies go Parsees, Turks, Turkomans and Armenians, and they come and take up their companies for their cargo in Gujarat, and from there they embark in March and sail direct for Malacca; and on the return journey they call at the Maldive Islands.

Women and Poverty in Japan
Francesco Carletti

The Asian–European relationship had the potential of becoming a dialogue rewarding to all sides, but in fact the relationship was marred from the beginning by each side lacking an understanding of the other's culture. The following selection is from the writings of Francesco Carletti who was born in Florence in 1572. He spent several years traveling with his father around the world, including East Asia in 1597–1598. Carletti is writing for an audience that has virtually no information about the Japanese and is relying on his accounts to formulate their own views. Here Carletti discusses poverty, women, and prostitution in Japan. Notice Carletti's hypocrisy since selling children and prostitution occurred in Europe as well.

> **Consider:** *The image of Japanese civilization this account might produce in European readers' minds; whether this reveals more about European visions of Japanese women than Japanese society; why the author might have chosen to write this account.*

[The Japanese] do not, however, hold in equal esteem the virtue of their daughters and sisters; or rather they take no account of this at all. Indeed it often happens that a girl's own father, mother, or brothers—without any feeling of shame on the part of any of those concerned—will without hesitation sell her as a prostitute before she is married, for a few pence, under the pressure of poverty, which is very severely felt throughout the whole country. And this poverty is the cause of the most shameless immorality—an immorality which is so gross and which takes such different and unusual forms, to pass belief.

But the Portuguese are my witnesses and cannot be gainsaid—especially those who come year by year from China, that is, from the island of Macao. . . . As soon as ever these Portuguese arrive and disembark, the pimps who control this traffic in women call on them in the houses in which they are quartered for the time of their stay, and enquire whether they would like to purchase, or acquire in any other method they please, a girl, for the period of their sojourn, or to keep her for so many months, or for a night, or for a day, or for an hour, a contract being

SOURCE: Bishop Trollope, trans. "The Carletti Discourse" published in *The Transactons of the Asiatic Society of Japan,* second series, vol. IX, 1932.

first made with these brokers, or an agreement entered into with the girl's relations, and the money paid down. And if they prefer it they will take them to the
girl's house, in order that they may see her first, or else they will take them to see
her on their own premises, which are usually situated in certain hamlets or villages
outside the city. And many of these Portuguese, upon whose testimony I am
relying, fall in with this custom as the fancy takes them, driving the best bargain
they can for a few pence. And so it often happens that they will get hold
of a pretty little girl of fourteen or fifteen years of age, for three or four *scudi*, or
a little more or less, according to the time during which they wish to have her at
their disposal, with no other responsibility beyond that of sending her back home
when done with. Nor does this practice in any way interfere with a girl's chances
of marriage. Indeed many of them would never get married, if they had not by
this means acquired a dowry, by accumulating 30 or 40 *scudi*, given to them from
time to time by these Portuguese, who have kept them in their houses for seven
or eight months on end, and who have in some cases married them themselves.
And when these women are hired by the day, it is enough to give them the merest
trifle, nor do they ever refuse to be hired on account of a variation in the price,
which is hardly ever refused by their relations, or by those who keep them as a
sort of stock in trade for these purposes in their houses, and to whom the money
is paid—the women being in effect all slaves sold for these purposes. And there
are, moreover, some of them who, by agreement with the brokers, ask for no
more than their food and clothing—neither of which costs much—while the whole
of their earnings go to the men who keep them.

To sum up, the country is more plentifully supplied than any other with these
sort of means of gratifying the passion for sexual indulgence, just as it abounds in
every other sort of vice, in which it surpasses every other place in the world.

Laws of the Burgos:
The Spanish Colonize Central
and South America

*As the first colonists in the New World, Spaniards sought to exploit the wealth of Central
and South America through the use of forced labor. This "encomienda" system, a system
of forced labor on extensive plantations, permitted Spanish settlers to compel native peoples to labor in gold and silver mines, agriculture, and in the home. This excerpt is from a
set of laws developed at Burgos, Spain in 1512. They became the basis for the legal system for Spanish America in the early colonial period.*

SOURCE: Lesley Byrd Simpson, trans. *The Laws of Burgos of 1512–1513*, (Westport, Conn.:
Greenwood Press).

Consider: *Spanish assumptions and concerns about these native peoples; what these laws tell us about how the native population actually lived under Spanish domination.*

Whereas, the King, my Lord and Father, and the Queen, my Mistress and Mother (may she rest in glory!), always desired that the chiefs and Indians of the Island of Española be brought to a knowledge of our Holy Catholic Faith, and, . . .

Whereas, it has become evident through long experience that nothing has sufficed to bring the said chiefs and Indians to a knowledge of our Faith (necessary for their salvation), since by nature they are inclined to idleness and vice, and have no manner of virtue or doctrine (by which Our Lord is disserved), and that the principal obstacle in the way of correcting their vices and having them profit by and impressing them with the doctrine is that their dwellings are remote from the settlements of the Spaniards who go hence to reside in the said Island, because, although at the time the Indians go to serve them they are indoctrinated in and taught the things of our Faith, after serving they return to their dwellings where, because of the distance and their own own evil inclinations, they immediately forget what they have been taught and go back to their customary idleness and vice, . . .

Whereas, this is contrary to our Faith, and,

Whereas, it is our duty to seek a remedy for it in every way possible, . . . the most beneficial thing that could be done at present would be to remove the said chiefs and Indians to the vicinity of the villages and communities of the Spaniards. . . .

First, since it is our determination to remove the said Indians and have them dwell near the Spaniards, we order and command that the persons to whom the said Indians are given, or shall be given, in encomienda, shall at once and forthwith build, for every fifty Indians, four lodges [*bohíos*] of thirty by fifteen feet, and have the Indians plant 5,000 hillocks (3,000 in cassava and 2,000 in yams), 250 pepper plants, and 50 cotton plants . . . and these shall be settled next the estates of the Spaniards who have them in encomienda, well situated and housed, and under the eyes of you, our said Admiral and judges and officers . . . and the persons who have the said Indians in their charge [in encomienda] shall have them sow, in season, half a *fanega* of maize, and shall also give them a dozen hens and a cock to raise and enjoy the fruit thereof, the chickens as well as the eggs; and as soon as the Indians are brought to the estates they shall be given all the aforesaid as their own property. . . .

Also, we order and command that the citizen to whom the said Indians are given in encomienda shall, upon the land that is assigned to him, be obliged to erect a structure to be used for a church. . . . Every Sunday and obligatory feast day they may come there to pray and hear Mass, and also to hear the good advice that the priests who say Mass shall give them; and the priests who say Mass shall teach them the Commandments and the Articles of the Faith, and the other things of the Christian doctrine. Therefore, in order that they be instructed in the things of the Faith and become accustomed to pray and hear Mass, we command that the Spaniards who are on the estates with the said Indians and have charge of them shall be obliged to bring them all together to the said church in the morning and remain with them until after Mass is said; and after Mass they shall bring them back to the estates and give them their pots of cooked meat, in such wise that they eat on that day better than on any other day of the week. . . .

Also, we order and command that, after the Indians have been brought to the estates, all the founding [of gold] that henceforth is done on the said Island shall be done in the manner prescribed below: that is, the said persons who have Indians in encomienda shall extract gold with them for five months in the year and, at the end of these five months, the said Indians shall rest forty days, and the day they cease their labor of extracting gold shall be noted on a certificate, which shall be given to the miners who go to the mines. . . .

Also, we order and command that all those on the said Island who have Indians in encomienda, now or in the future, shall be obliged to give to each of them a hammock in which to sleep continually; and they shall not allow them to sleep on the ground, as hitherto they have been doing. . . .

Voyages from Holland to America: The Dutch Colonize North America
David Pietersz de Vries

The Dutch were the first to colonize the area of the lower Hudson Valley in what are now the states of New York, New Jersey, and Connecticut in the United States. They established large estates and imported tenant farmers to work small parcels of land. Initially, Native Americans and the Dutch farmers traded together and lived in close proximity. Yet, new interests and new administrators led the Dutch to try to displace the Algonquins from their land. This document, about a massacre that took place in February of 1643 reveals the harsh practices of colonists who had little respect for the rights or humanity of those they considered to be "uncivilized."

> **Consider:** *The reasons for the author's opposition to the Governor's actions; whether the Governor's stand was based on self-interest or humanistic concerns.*

. . . So was this business begun between the 25th and 26th of February in the year 1643. I remained that night at the governor's, sitting up. I went and sat in the kitchen, when, about midnight, I heard a great shrieking, and I ran to the ramparts

---

SOURCE: David Pietersz de Vries, *Voyages From Holland to America*, Henry C. Murphy, trans. (New York, 1853), pp. 167–171.

of the fort, and looked over to Pavonia. Saw nothing but firing, and heard the shrieks of the Indians murdered in their sleep. I returned again to the house by the fire. Having sat there awhile, there came an Indian with his squaw, whom I knew well, and who lived about an hour's walk from my house, and told me that they two had fled in a small skiff; that they had betaken themselves to Pavonia; that the Indians from Fort Orange had surprised them; and that they had come to conceal themselves in the fort. I told them that they must go away immediately; that there was no occasion for them to come to the fort to conceal themselves; that they who had killed their people at Pavonia were not Indians, but the Swannekens, as they call the Dutch, had done it. . . . When it was day, the soldiers returned to the fort, having massacred or murdered eighty Indians, and considering they had done a deed of Roman valour, in murdering so many in their sleep; where infants were torn from their mother's breasts, and hacked to pieces in the presence of the parents, and the pieces thrown into the fire and in the water, and other sucklings were bound to small boards, and then cut, stuck, and pierced, and miserably massacred in a manner to move a heart of stone. . . . After this exploit, the soldiers were rewarded for their services, and Director Kieft thanked them by taking them by the hand and congratulating them. . . .

. . . As soon as the Indians understood that the Swannekens had so treated them, all the men whom they could surprise on the farm-lands, they killed; but we have never heard that they have ever permitted women or children to be killed. They burned all the houses, farms, barns, grain, haystacks, and destroyed everything they could get hold of. So there was an open destructive war begun. . . . When now the Indians had destroyed so many farms and men in revenge for their people, I went to Governor William Kieft, and asked him if it was not as I had said it would be, that he would only effect the spilling of Christian blood. Who would now compensate us for our losses? But he gave me no answer.

A Voyage to South America: Caste and Race in Latin America

Jorge Juan and Antonio de Ulloa

Unlike English North America, which excluded Native Americans from any participation in colonial society and enslaved anyone who had any African ancestors, Spanish and Portuguese South America developed a much more complex social caste and racial system. While the English colonies enforced strict distinctions between blacks and whites, the Spanish developed a more varied set of racial categories, which some historians have argued led to less segregation and racial hostility. This excerpt was written by two

SOURCE: Jorge Juan and Antonio de Ulloa, *A Voyage to South America*, vol. I (London, 1772), pp. 29–32.

Spanish officials after their inspection of the caste system of the Caribbean port Cartha-gena.

Consider: *The ways that the South American system allowed for a greater degree of interaction among people of different racial backgrounds; how the caste system reinforced social and class distinctions.*

The inhabitants may be divided into different castes or tribes, who derive their origin from a coalition of Whites, Negroes, and Indians. Of each of these we shall treat particularly.

The Whites may be divided into two classes, the Europeans, and Creoles, or Whites born in the country. The former are commonly called Chapitones, but are not numerous; most of them either return into Spain after acquiring a competent fortune, or remove up into inland provinces in order to increase it. Those who are settled at Carthagena carry on the whole trade of that place, and live in opulence; whilst the other inhabitants are indigent, and reduced to have recourse to mean and hard labor for subsistence. The families of the White Creoles compose the landed interest; some of them have large estates, and are highly respected.
. . . Some of these families, in order to keep up their original dignity, have either married their children to their equals in the country, or sent them as officers on board the galleons, but others have greatly declined. Besides these, there are other Whites, in mean circumstances, who either owe their origin to Indian families, or at least to an intermarriage with them, so that there is some mixture in their blood; but when this is not discoverable by their color, the conceit of being Whites alleviates the pressure of every other calamity.

Among the other tribes which are derived from an intermarriage of the Whites with the Negroes, the first are the Mulattos. Next to these the Tercerones, produced from a White and a Mulatto, with some approximation to the former, but not so near as to obliterate their origin. After these follow the Quarterones, proceeding from a White and a Terceron. The last are the Quinterones, who owe their origin to a White and Quarteron. This is the last gradation, there being no visible difference between them and the Whites, either in color or features; nay, they are often fairer than the Spaniards. The children of a White and Quinteron are also called Spaniards, and consider themselves as free from all taint of the Negro race. Every person is so jealous of the order of their tribe or cast, that if, through inadvertence, you call them by a degree lower than what they actually are, they are highly offended, never suffering themselves to be deprived of so valuable a gift of fortune. . . .

These are the most known and common tribes or castes; there are indeed several others proceeding from their intermarriages; but, being so various, even they themselves cannot easily distinguish them. . . .

These castes, from the Mulattos, all affect the Spanish dress, but wear very slight stuffs on account of the heat of the climate. These are the mechanics of the city; the Whites, whether Creoles or Chapitones, disdaining such a mean occupation, follow nothing below merchandise. But it being impossible for all to succeed, great numbers not being able to procure sufficient credit, they become poor and miserable from their aversion to those trades they follow in Europe; and, instead of the riches which they flattered themselves with possessing in the Indies, they experience the most complicated wretchedness.

The class of Negroes is not the least numerous, and is divided into two parts; the free and the slaves. These are again subdivided into Creoles and Bozares, part of which are employed in the cultivation of the haciendas, or estancias. Those in the city are obliged to perform the most laborious services, and pay out of their wages a certain quota to their masters, subsisting themselves on the small remainder. The violence of the heat not permitting them to wear any clothes, their only covering is a small piece of cotton stuff about their waist; the female slaves go in the same manner. Some of these live at the estancias, being married to the slaves who work there; while those in the city sell in the markets all kind of eatables. . . .

VISUAL SOURCES

Exploration, Expansion, and Politics

Aside from the various motivations for the voyages of discovery during the fifteenth and sixteenth centuries, a number of factors combined to make those voyages physically possible when earlier they were not. Technological discoveries significantly improved shipbuilding and navigation. But also important was the understanding and mapping of prevailing ocean currents and winds in relation to land masses. It was much easier to sail with, rather than against, currents and winds, and sailors counted on finding land masses for supplies along the way.

The early voyages tended to take advantage of currents and winds as shown in this map. Thus, for example, early voyages to North America usually took a more southerly route westward across the Atlantic and returned on a more northerly route, while Portuguese ships headed east to the Indian Ocean by following winds and currents to Brazil and then crossed the Atlantic farther south. Prevailing currents and winds also explain the difficulty of westward voyages around the tip of South America. These patterns of voyages also shed light on some of the geopolitical results of expansion. For example, even though Portugal's efforts were directed toward an eastern route to the Far East, she acquired Brazil (her only territory in the New World) to the west since it was on a route favored by winds and currents.

Consider: *How this map helps explain the pattern of exploration and colonization by the various European powers.*

Map 13-1 Overseas Explorations

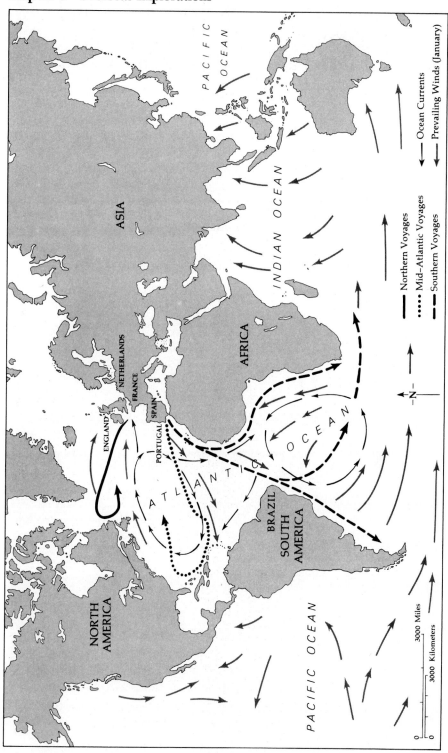

A Buddhist Temple:
European Views of Asia

When the first European travelers returned from Asia they brought with them tales of exotic lands and peoples that were so astonishing as to be barely believable. While Asian cultures were different enough from European cultures to elicit wonderment, travelers tended to exaggerate, and even distort, what they had seen. Europeans were interested in Asia as a source of precious goods (spice, tea, etc.), a market for excess European goods, and fertile ground for missionaries to proselytize. They rarely tried to understand what they were experiencing, and their contempt for non-European culture required distortion of their accounts lest anyone back home think these people were somehow equal to them.

Photo 13-1

From: *Pacific Voyages: The Encyclopedia of Discovery & Exploration* (London: Aldus Books Ltd., 1971).

This illustration is from the 1600s and depicts a Buddhist temple in China. The unknown European artist has seen fit to include two demons that look suspiciously European in origin on either side of the Buddha statue.

> **Consider:** *The impression the artist was trying to create in European viewers' minds.*

SECONDARY SOURCES

The Expansion of Europe
Richard B. Reed

In analyzing the overseas expansion of the fifteenth and sixteenth centuries, historians typically emphasize a combination of economic and religious factors to explain the motivation behind expansion while focusing on the establishment of adequate knowledge and technology as key conditions for its occurrence. In the following selection, Richard B. Reed argues that European expansion was a nationalistic phenomenon, and because of this, Portugal was able to become the early leader.

> **Consider:** *Why Italy and Germany did not participate in overseas expansion; how one might attack Reed's argument that Portugal was in a better position to initiate expansion than any other country; other factors that might help explain why Portugal led in overseas expansion.*

The expansion of Europe was an intensely nationalistic phenomenon. It was an aspect of the trend, most evident in the late fifteenth and early sixteenth centuries, toward the establishment of strong centralized authority in the "new monarchies," as they have been called, and the emergence of the nation-state. A policy of overseas expansion required a degree of internal stability and national consciousness that only a powerful central government could command. Portugal achieved this position long before her eventual competitors, and under the leadership of the dynamic house of Avis became a consolidated kingdom comparatively free from feudal divisions before the end of the fifteenth century. While Spain was still divided into a number of conflicting political jurisdictions, England and France

---

SOURCE: Richard B. Reed, "The Expansion of Europe," in *The Meaning of the Renaissance and Reformation*, ed. Richard L. DeMolen (Boston: Houghton Mifflin, 1974), p. 299. Reprinted by permission.

were preoccupied with their own and each other's affairs, and the Dutch were still an appendage of the Empire, the Portuguese combined the advantages of their natural geographic situation with their political and economic stability to initiate the age of discovery. Spain in the sixteenth century, and England, France, and the Netherlands in the seventeenth century, became active colonial powers only after each had matured into strong national entities, independent of feudal political and economic restrictions. . . .

The importance of the nation-state in Renaissance expansion is particularly apparent when the Italian city-states are considered. Venice and Genoa, cities that had contributed so many of the medieval travelers and early Renaissance geographers and mapmakers, did not participate directly in Europe's overseas expansion. Yet Italian names dominated the rolls of the early voyagers. Prince Henry employed Venetians and Florentines in his naval establishment, while Columbus, Vespucci, Verrazano, the Cabots, and many others sailed for Spain, France, and England. Italian cartography was the best in Europe until the second half of the sixteenth century, and a high proportion of the books and pamphlets that chronicled new discoveries emanated from the presses of Vicenza, Venice, Rome, and Florence. Italian bankers and merchants were also very active in the commercial life of the principal Iberian cities. A divided Italy was instrumental in making Renaissance expansion possible, but it could not take full advantage of its own endowments. Germans, too, figured prominently in the expansion of the sixteenth century, as the names of Federmann, Staden, Welser, and Fugger attest. But Germany, like Italy, was not united, and the emergence of these two nations as colonial powers had to wait until their respective consolidations in the nineteenth century.

While every nationality in Western Europe was represented in Renaissance expansion, it was by no means an international venture. On the contrary, it was very much an expression of that nationalistic fervor that characterized political developments in the fifteenth and sixteenth centuries. It was primarily a state enterprise, often financed privately but controlled and protected by the governments of the concerned powers. There was no cooperation between nations, and even after the upheaval of the Protestant Reformation, when political loyalties and alignments were conditioned by religious sympathies, there were no colonial alliances that provided for mutual Protestant or Catholic overseas policies.

The Changing Ecology of New England

William Cronon

Along with new habits, technologies and cultures, Europeans brought entirely new economic systems to New England. Together, these dramatically affected the environment of both the Native Americans and the colonists. We tend to think of ecological damage as being a product of twentieth century industrialism. In this excerpt, William Cronon summarizes the changes that New England underwent in the first two hundred years of contact between colonists and Native Americans. Both groups changed the "natural" environment. Significantly, he does not see all these changes as being beneficial or even benign.

Consider: *Cronon's view that Americans, in addition to being "the people of plenty, were a people of waste"; the significance of ecological changes.*

New England in 1800 was far different from the land the earliest European visitors had described. By 1800, the Indians who had been its first human inhabitants were reduced to a small fraction of their former numbers, and had been forced onto less and less desirable agricultural lands. Their ability to move about the landscape in search of ecological abundance had become severely constrained, so that their earlier ways of interacting with the environment were no longer feasible and their earlier sources of food were less easy to find. Disease and malnutrition had become facts of life for them.

Large areas particularly of southern New England were now devoid of animals which had once been common: beaver, deer, bear, turkey, wolf, and others had vanished. In their place were hordes of European grazing animals which constituted a heavier burden on New England plants and soils. Their presence had brought hundreds of miles of fences. With fences had come the weeds: dandelion and rat alike joined alien grasses as they made their way across the landscape. New England's forests still exceeded its cleared land in 1800, but, especially near settled areas, the remaining forest had been significantly altered by grazing, burning, and cutting. The greatest of the oaks and white pines were gone, and cedar had become scarce. Hickory had been reduced because of its attractiveness as a fuel. Clear-cutting had shifted forest composition in favor of those trees that were capable of sprouting from stumps, with the result that the forests of 1800 were physically smaller than they had been at the time of European settlement. The cutting of upland species such as beech and maple, which were accustomed to moist sites, produced drying that encouraged species such as the oaks, which preferred drier soils.

SOURCE: Excerpt from CHANGES IN THE LAND by William Cronon. Copyright © 1983 by William Cronon. Reprinted by permission of Hill and Wang, a division of Farrar, Straus & Giroux, Inc.

Deforestation had in general affected the region by making local temperatures more erratic, soils drier, and drainage patterns less constant. A number of smaller streams and springs no longer flowed year-round, and some larger rivers were dammed and no longer accessible to the fish which had once spawned in them. Water and wind erosion were taking place with varyng severity, and flooding had become more common. Soil exhaustion was occurring in many areas as a result of poor husbandry, and the first of many European pests and crop diseases had already begun to appear. These changes had taken place primarily in the settled areas, and it was still possible to find extensive regions in the north where they did not apply. Nevertheless, they heralded the future. . . .

The implications of this . . . ecological contradiction stretched well beyond the colonial period. Although we often tend to associate ecological changes primarily with the cities and factories of the nineteenth and twentieth centuries, it should by now be clear that changes with similar roots took place just as profoundly in the farms and countrysides of the colonial period. The transition to capitalism alienated the products of the land as much as the products of human labor, and so transformed natural communities as profoundly as it did human ones. By integrating New England ecosystems into an ultimately global capitalist economy, colonists and Indians together began a dynamic and unstable process of ecological change which had in no way ended by 1800. We live with their legacy today. When the geographer Carl Sauer wrote in the twentieth century that Americans had "not yet learned the difference between yield and loot," he was describing one of the most longstanding tendencies of their way of life. Ecological abundance and economic prodigality went hand in hand: the people of plenty were a people of waste.

China's Response to the West
John K. Fairbank and Ssu-yu Teng

At first China welcomed Europeans. The Chinese view was that their civilization was superior and non-Chinese had been coming for centuries looking to acquire aspects of this superior culture. The Europeans, the Chinese believed, were just the latest of these visitors. What the Chinese discovered, however, was that these travelers were different. They believed their own civilization was better and brought technologically advanced goods to prove it. Moreover they tried to convert the Chinese to Christianity, to Europeanize them, and to trade with them as equals. All this confused the Chinese court.

While the earliest Portuguese arrivals did not endear themselves to the Chinese, the Jesuits, particularly Matteo Ricci who became an advisor to the Emperor, respected and incorporated Confucian practices into Christian belief in a strategy designed to make

SOURCE: Ssu-yu Teng and John K. Fairbank, *Response to the West*, Cambridge, Mass.: Harvard University Press, Copyright © 1954, 1979 by the President and Fellows of Harvard College, © renewed 1982. Reprinted by permission.

conversion to Christianity appealing to the Chinese elite. Other orders, the Dominicans for example, opposed any dilution of Christian beliefs and the opposing factions contested their views in the Vatican. This struggle came to be known as the Rites Controversy which the Jesuits ultimately lost, leading to the expulsion of all missionaries from China.

This reading is by two of the more prominent American historians of China, John K. Fairbank and Ssu-yu Teng, and explores how the Chinese officials met these early European challenges and what influences these Europeans left in their wake.

Consider: *What it was about these new Europeans that made the Chinese uncomfortable and why; how Westerners influenced China; why that influence was not greater.*

The first extensive cultural contact between China and Europe began near the end of the sixteenth century, when the Jesuit missionaries, in the wake of the Portuguese, reached China by sea. Their dual function is well known: they not only diffused Western ideas in China, including elements of mathematics, astronomy, geography, hydraulics, the calendar, and the manufacture of cannon, but they also introduced Chinese (particularly Confucian) ideas into Europe. The Jesuits found it easier to influence China's science than her religion. Perceiving this, they used their scientific knowledge as a means of approach to Chinese scholars. Although a small number of their Chinese converts took part in the translation and compilation of religious and scientific books, the majority of the native scholars, entrenched in their ethnocentric cultural tradition, were not seriously affected by the new elements of Western thought. . . .

. . . [T]he immediate Jesuit influence in China was through items of practical significance, such as cannon, the calendar, or Ricci's map of the world. Why is so little trace of Christian doctrine to be found in the writings of Chinese scholars in the subsequent century? If this is to be explained by the fact that government suppression cut off contact and the relatively few professed converts had few successors, we still face the question why the minds of the non-Christian scholars were not more permanently influenced by Western knowledge or ideas. . . .

Opposition to the Jesuits and other Western missionaries was motivated partly by the xenophobic suspicion that foreigners were spies; partly by ethical scruples against Christian religious ceremonies which seemed contrary to Chinese customs such as the veneration of Heaven, ancestors and Confucius; and partly by professional jealousy, on the assumption that if Catholicism were to become prevalent in China, the decline of the doctrines of Confucius, Buddha, and Lao-tzu would damage the position of their protagonists. . . .

The Chinese Buddhist leadership appears to have been vehemently anti-Catholic. Meanwhile most Chinese scholars remained dogmatically opposed to the Westerners' religion. Lacking enthusiasm for their religion, they also disliked their science. . . . The conservatives objected to Western scientific instruments, arguing that clocks were expensive but useless, that cannon could not annihilate enemies but usually burned the gunners first, and that on Ricci's map of the globe China was not in the very center and was not large enough. They also objected to Western painting because it lacked forceful strokes. . . .

Behind all this condemnation of Western learning lay the basic political fact that the Manchu rulers of China could not tolerate the propagation of a foreign religion which asserted the spiritual supremacy of Rome over Peking. By 1640 Japan, under the Tokugawa, had proscribed Christianity and foreign contact (except for the Dutch in Nagasaki) as politically dangerous. In China by the end of the seventeenth century there were Catholic congregations in all but two of the provinces; the Roman Catholic faith was banned in the Yongzheng (Yung-cheng) period (1723–1735). . . .

All in all, the residual influence of the Western technology made available to China through the early missionaries seems to have been rather slight. Even when present, it was seldom acknowledged. Meanwhile an anti-Western political tradition had become well established.

The Closing of Japan
G. B. Sansom

In 1640, Japan deported all Europeans (except a handful of Dutch traders restricted to the island of Deshima in Nagasaki Bay) and forbid Japanese from leaving the country. There were also widespread persecutions of Japanese Christians. This has often been portrayed as a case of religious persecution. While it was certainly that, there were other factors as well. The reading which follows is from noted British Japanologist G. B. Sansom. Here he argues that the expulsion of Christianity from Japan was a political, rather than a religious, affair.

> **Consider:** *The motives, according to Sansom, for the anti-Christian acts; how missionary activity might be related to economic, military, and political activity.*

It will be seen that here was no consistent antagonism to a foreign creed, but a variable attitude based upon political grounds. . . . [T]he successes and failures of the Roman Catholic Church in India, China, and Japan have been closely related to the degree of political support that in the estimate of those countries was enjoyed by the missionaries. It is reasons such as these that best explain the apparent vacillations and inconsistencies of the Japanese ruling class in their treatment of Christian propaganda during the period we have been considering.

The action taken by Japan against Christianity cannot be considered separately from the exclusion policy to which it was a prelude. . . . [T]he anti-Christian edict of 1616 was inspired in part at least by fear of Spanish intervention in the domestic

SOURCE: George B. Sansom, *The Western World and Japan. A Study in the Interaction of European and Asiatic Culture* (1950), pp. 177–179.

affairs of Japan. The edict was re-enacted in 1624 because the Shogun had further grounds for suspecting Spain, or at any rate the Spanish in the Philippines, of aggressive designs; and this new edict was accompanied not only by the expulsion of all Spaniards but also by the stoppage of overseas travel by Japanese. The door was gradually being closed to both ingress and egress. The Shimabara rising that began in 1637 evidently caused further misgivings to the Shogunate, for it was followed in 1638 by the expulsion of all Portuguese, whether priests or traders. At the same time the prohibition of foreign travel was strengthened by imposing the death penalty on any Japanese who should attempt to leave the country or, having left it, should return. This embargo was extended to foreign trade by a law that forbade the building of any ship of more than 2,500 bushels' capacity and consequently prevented ocean voyages. Thus Japan deliberately cut herself off from intercourse with other nations rather than face the dangers it involved. In the history of relations between Europe and Asia this was the most decided rejection ever given by an Asiatic people to an approach by the Western world. . . .

. . . It is at first sight hard to understand why the Asiatic people who gave Europeans the most friendly welcome should have also given them the most violent dismissal. . . . It was clearly not due to a peculiar distaste for foreign intercourse, since that was resumed with remarkable alacrity once the country was reopened at a later date. It is true that, since the civilization of Japan was self-contained and her economy self-supporting, there was no compelling reason for cultural or commercial exchanges; and conservative sentiment, in Japan as in other countries, was naturally opposed to foreign influences, because to most people what is foreign is also disturbing. But the intense distrust which drove the Tokugawa shoguns to close their doors arose from no ordinary conservatism. They were moved by fear, and fear not of the contamination of national customs . . . but rather of domestic uprising against themselves.

By 1615 Ieyasu, the first Tokugawa Shogun, had after long struggle imposed the authority of his family upon all his feudal rivals. But neither he nor his successors felt entirely secure for several decades, and it was a cardinal feature of their policy to take every possible precaution against rebellion by one or more of the still powerful western feudatories. . . .

In 1637 the Tokugawa government had good reason to fear that one or [an]other of these great families might conspire with foreigners—Spanish, Portuguese, or Dutch—trade with them for firearms, get their help in procuring artillery and ships, and even call upon them for military or naval support. The leaders of the ruling house, firmly estabished as it was, did not feel strong enough to face this risk; and they took steps to remove it by closing the country to foreign influence, so far as that was possible.

The Effects of Expansion on the Non-European World

M. L. Bush

While the expansion of Europe was of great significance for European history, it was of even greater consequence for the non-European world touched by the explorers. However, its effects differed greatly in the New World, where the Spanish dominated, and the East, where the Portuguese were the leaders. In the following selection, M. L. Bush analyzes these differences.

> **Consider:** *Internal factors in non-Western societies that help explain these differences; contrasts between Portugal and Spain that help explain the different consequences for non-Western societies.*

The Castilian Empire in the West and the Portuguese Empire in the East had very different effects upon the world outside of Europe. In the first place, the Castilian expansion westwards precipitated a series of overseas migrations which were unparalleled in earlier times. For most of the sixteenth century, 1,000 or 2,000 Spaniards settled in the New World each year. Later this was followed by a large wave of emigrants from northwestern Europe, fleeing from persecution at home to the Atlantic sea-board of North America and the Caribbean, and a final wave of Africans forced into slavery in the West Indies and in Brazil. On the other hand, in the East, there was virtually no settlement in the sixteenth century. Europe impressed itself only by fort, factory and church, by colonial official, trader and missionary.

In the second place, the settlement of the New World had a severe effect upon native peoples, whereas in the East, European influence was very slight until much later times.

In the early 1520s, the conquistadors brought with them smallpox and typhoid. Between them these European diseases soon decimated the Indian population, particularly in the great epidemics of the 1520s, 1540s and 1570s. In central Mexico, for example, an Indian population which numbered 11,000,000 in 1519 numbered no more than 2,500,000 by the end of the century. In addition, the Indian was beset by enormous grazing herds of horned cattle which the white settler introduced. He escaped the herds by working for the white settler, but if this led him to the crowded labour settlements, as it quite often did, he stood less chance of escaping infection. Either through falling hopelessly in debt as a result of desiring the goods of the white man, or through entering the labour settlements on a permanent basis to avoid the herds and also the system of obligatory labour

SOURCE: M. L. Bush, *Renaissance, Reformation and the Outer World* (New York: Harper & Row, 1967), pp. 143–145. London: Blanford Press, Ltd., 1967.

introduced by the Spaniard,[1] there was a strong tendency for the Indian to become europeanised. He became a wage-earner, a debtor and a Christian. The Indian was exploited. But in the law he remained free. Enslavement was practised, but it was not officially tolerated. Moreover, the Franciscan order, a powerful missionary force in the New World, did its best to save the Indian from the evil ways of the white man. In Barthlomew de Las Casas and Francisco de Vitoria, the Indian found influential defenders; and through their schemes for separate Indian Christian communities, he found a partial escape from the white man. But the Indian mission towns, which were permitted by Charles V, were objected to by his successor, Philip II, and they only survived in remote areas.

With few exceptions, the way of life of the surviving Indians was basically changed by the coming of the white man. The outstanding exception was in Portuguese Brazil where the more primitive, nomadic Indians had a greater opportunity to retreat into the bush. There was also less settlement in Brazil, and generally less impression was made because of Portuguese preoccupations elsewhere, and also because of their lack of resources for empire-building on the Spanish scale. Furthermore, within the Spanish Empire, the European impressed himself less on the Incas in Peru than upon the Aztecs in Mexico. Because of the slow subjection of Peru, several Inca risings, the nature of the terrain, the smallness of the Spanish community, the process of europeanisation was much slower, and in the long run much less complete. The remnants of the Inca aristocracy became Spanish in their habits and Catholic in their religion, but the peasantry tended to remain pagan. In contrast to these developments, the westernisation of the East was a development of more modern times.

The West impinged upon the East in the sixteenth century mainly through the missionary. With the arrival of St. Francis Xavier in 1542 in India, an impressive process of conversion was begun. Concentrating upon the poor fishermen of the Cape Comorin coast, within ten years he had secured, it was said, 60,000 converts. The Jesuits fixed their attention on the East, choosing Goa as their main headquarters outside of Rome. Little was accomplished in Malaya, Sumatra and China in the sixteenth century, and Christianity soon suffered setbacks in the Moluccas after a promising start, but in Ceylon the conversion of the young king of Kotte in 1557 was a signal triumph, and so were the conversions in Japan. In the 1580s Jesuit missionaries in Japan claimed to have converted 150,000, most of whom, however, were inhabitants of the island of Kyushu.

Christianity was not a new religion in the East. There were extensive communities of Nestorian Christians, but they were regarded as alien as the Muslim by the Europeans. The new Christians by 1583 were supposed to number 600,000. But compared with the expansion of Islam in the East—a process which was taking place at the same time—the expansion of Christianity was a minute achievement.

---

[1] This system depended upon every Indian village offering a proportion of its menfolk or labour service for a limited amount of time throughout the year.

Finally, the Portuguese sea empire did little to transport Portuguese habits abroad. Their empire was essentially formed in response to local conditions. On the other hand, the Spanish land empire was to a much greater extent reflective of Castilian ways.

In the New World a carefully developed and regulated system of government was established in which it was seen that the care taken to limit the independent power of feudal aristocrats in the Old World should also be applied to the New. There was a firm insistence upon government officials being royal servants. However, the government of the New World became much more regulated from the centre than that of the old. There was less respect for aristocratic privilege. Less power was unreservedly placed in the hands of the nobility. In the New World, in fact, the weaknesses of government, at first, did not lie in the powers and privileges of the nobility but rather in the cumbersome nature of the government machinery. Nevertheless, in spite of these precautions, the New World, by the early seventeenth century, had become a land of great feudal magnates enjoying, in practice, untrammelled power.

Chapter Questions

1. Analyze the motives for the European expansion and the forces that stimulated and enabled the Europeans to carry out this expansion.

2. Compare the consequences of the new encounters in Asia, Africa, and the Americas. How do you explain the differences?

3. Drawing on the sources in this and the previous chapter, discuss what the observations made by Europeans tell us about the Europeans themselves and their own societies in addition to the societies they are observing.

FOURTEEN

Europe's Early Modern Era, 1500–1789

The Renaissance and the overseas expansion of Europe were two signs that Western civilization was emerging from the Middle Ages into a new era, stretching from the sixteenth to the eighteenth century, which Western historians have come to call Early Modern. There were several other signs. New monarchs created powerful national states that would endure for centuries. These states benefited from and took advantage of new economic developments such as the growth of commerce and the spread of capitalistic practices. The aristocracy, though still socially and culturally dominant, underwent internal changes and was challenged by a new middle class of merchants and entrepreneurs. The Roman Catholic Church, in decline during the last two centuries of the Middle Ages, was split apart by the Protestant Reformation. New ideas and ways of thinking about the world and the human condition led to the intellectual revolutions known as the Scientific Revolution and the Enlightenment.

In this chapter we will focus on three of these developments. The first is the Reformation. Initiated in 1517 by Martin Luther's challenges to official Church doctrine and papal authority, the Reformation spread in Germany, northern Europe, and other parts of Europe during the sixteenth century. The passion involved in the Reformation and the historical significance of this division in the western Christian Church have made the Reformation the object of intensive study. Here we will focus on the nature and appeal of the Protestant challenge and the Catholic response, the much debated question of causes, and the possible significance of the Reformation.

The second development is the rise of early modern political institutions. Emphasis will be on the competition over the source and exercise of political power—both in theory and in practice. Here the conflict was usually between monarchs and the nobility or, particularly in England, between royal and parliamentary authority. This will lead us to examine connections between political struggle, economic policy, and religious conflict. Additionally, some developments in intellectual history will be touched on, particularly as they relate to political theory.

The third development is the nature of Early Modern society. Although wars, economic development, and urbanization were forces of change, the structure of society changed little during these centuries. At the base of society were commoners—mostly the peasantry—and at the top was the still dominant aristocracy. Sources in this chapter will examine these groups as well as the Early Modern family and the position of women.

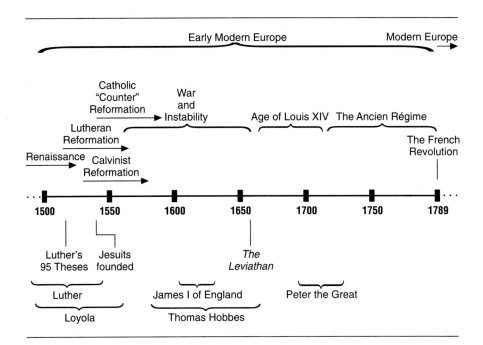

PRIMARY SOURCES

Justification by Faith
Martin Luther

The early leader of the Reformation was Martin Luther (1483–1546). Born in Germany to a wealthy peasant family, Luther became an Augustinian monk and a professor of theology at the University of Wittenberg. While at this post in 1517, he became involved in the indulgence problem with Tetzel and issued rather academic challenges in his ninety-five theses. News of this act quickly spread, and a major controversy developed. Although originally intending to stimulate only modest reforms within the Catholic Church, Luther soon found himself espousing doctrines markedly differing from those authorized by the Church and taking actions that eventually resulted in his expulsion from the Church.

Luther himself attributed his spiritual evolution to certain crucial experiences. The most important of these was his first formulation of the doctrines of "justification by faith," which constituted the core of his beliefs and much of the basis for Protestantism. In the following excerpts from his autobiographical writings, Luther describes this experience.

Consider: *What Luther meant by "justification by faith"; why this doctrine might have been so appealing to many Catholics; why this doctrine might have been threatening to the Catholic Church.*

I greatly longed to understand Paul's Epistle to the Romans and nothing stood in the way but that one expression, "the justice of God," because I took it to mean that justice whereby God is just and deals justly in punishing the unjust. My situation was that, although an impeccable monk, I stood before God as a sinner troubled in conscience, and I had no confidence that my merit would assuage him. Therefore I did not love a just and angry God, but rather hated and murmured against Him. Yet I clung to the dear Paul and had a great yearning to know what he meant.

Night and day I pondered until I saw the connection between the justice of God and the statement that "the just shall live by his faith." Then I grasped that the justice of God is that righteousness by which through grace and sheer mercy God justifies us through faith. Thereupon I felt myself to be reborn and to have gone through open doors into paradise. The whole of Scripture took on a new meaning, and whereas before the "justice of God" had filled me with hate, now it became to me inexpressibly sweet in greater love. This passage of Paul became to me a gate to heaven. . . .

SOURCE: From Roland H. Bainton, *The Age of Reformation* (New York: D. Van Nostrand Co., Inc., 1956), pp. 97–98. Reprinted by permission.

If you have a true faith that Christ is your Saviour, then at once you have a gracious God, for faith leads you in and opens up God's heart and will, that you should see pure grace and overflowing love. This it is to behold God in faith that you should look upon His fatherly, friendly heart, in which there is no anger nor ungraciousness. He who sees God as angry does not see Him rightly but looks only on a curtain, as if a dark cloud had been drawn across his face.

Constitution of the Society of Jesus

The Catholic Church was not passive in the face of the challenges from Protestant reformers. In a variety of ways the Church reformed itself from within and took the offensive against Protestants in doctrine and deed. Probably the most effective weapons of the Catholic Counter Reformation was the Society of Jesus (the Jesuits) founded by Ignatius Loyola (1491–1556). Loyola, a soldier who had turned to the religious life while recovering from wounds, attracted a group of highly disciplined followers who offered their services to the pope. In 1540, the pope formally accepted their offer. The Jesuits became an arm of the Church in combating Protestantism, spreading Catholicism to foreign lands and gaining influence within Catholic areas of Europe. The following is an excerpt from the Constitution of the Society of Jesus, approved by Pope Paul III in 1540.

> **Consider:** *The characteristics of this organization that help explain its success; how, in tone and content, this document differs from Luther's document.*

He who desires to fight for God under the banner of the cross in our society,— which we wish to distinguish by the name of Jesus,—and to serve God alone and the Roman pontiff, his vicar on earth, after a solemn vow of perpetual chastity, shall set this thought before his mind, that he is a part of a society founded for the especial purpose of providing for the advancement of souls in Christian life and doctrine and for the propagation of faith through public preaching and the ministry of the word of God, spiritual exercises and deeds of charity, and in particular through the training of the young and ignorant in Christianity and through the spiritual consolation of the faithful of Christ in hearing confessions; and he shall take care to keep first God and next the purpose of this organization always before his eyes. . . .

All the members shall realize, and shall recall daily, as long as they live, that this society as a whole and in every part is fighting for God under faithful obedience to one most holy lord, the pope, and to the other Roman pontiffs who succeed him. And although we are taught in the gospel and through the orthodox faith to recognize and steadfastly profess that all the faithful of Christ are subject to the Roman pontiff as their head and as the vicar of Jesus Christ, yet we have adjudged

SOURCE: James Harvey Robinson, ed., *Readings in European History*, vol. II (Boston: Ginn, 1904), pp. 162–163.

that, for the special promotion of greater humility in our society and the perfect mortification of every individual and the sacrifice of our own wills, we should each be bound by a peculiar vow, in addition to the general obligation, that whatever the present Roman pontiff, or any future one, may from time to time decree regarding the welfare of souls and the propagation of the faith, we are pledged to obey without evasion or excuse, instantly, so far as in us lies, whether he send us to the Turks or any other infidels, even to those who inhabit the regions men call the Indies; whether to heretics or schismatics, or, on the other hand, to certain of the faithful.

The Powers of the Monarch in England
James I

Turmoil, instability, and war (often civil war) characterized much of the period between the mid-sixteenth and mid-seventeenth centuries. In England, friction between the monarchy and Parliament increased under the Stuart kings, starting with James I. Already the Scottish monarch, James became King of England on the death of Elizabeth in 1603. James had a scholarly background and a reputation for his strong views about the monarchy. One of his clearest presentations of these views was in a speech to Parliament made in 1610. In it, he comments on the nature of the king's power, not simply in England but everywhere.

> **Consider:** *How James justifies the high position and vast powers he feels should rightly belong to kings; the limits to monarchical powers.*

The state of Monarchy is the supremest thing upon earth; for kings are not only God's lieutenants upon earth and sit upon God's throne, but even by God himself they are called gods. There be three principal similitudes that illustrate the state of Monarchy: one taken out of the Word of God and the other two out of the grounds of policy and philosophy. In the Scriptures kings are called gods, and so their power after a certain relation compared to the Divine power. Kings are also compared to the fathers of families, for a king is truly *parens patriae*, the politic father of his people. And lastly, kings are compared to the head of his microcosm of the body of man.

Kings are justly called gods for that they exercise a manner or resemblance of Divine power upon earth; for if you will consider the attributes to God you shall see how they agree in the person of a king. God hath power to create or destroy, make or umake, at his pleasure; to give life or send death; to judge all, and to be judged nor accomptable to none; to raise low things and to make high things low

---

SOURCE: From J. R. Tanner, *Constitutional Documents of the Reign of James I, A.D. 1603–1625* (Cambridge, England: Cambridge University Press, 1930), pp. 15–16. Reprinted by permission.

at his pleasure; and to God are both soul and body due. And the like power have kings; they make and unmake their subjects; they have power of raising and casting down; of life and death; judges over all their subjects and in all causes, and yet accomptable to none but God only. They have power to exalt low things and abase high things, and make of their subjects like men at the chess, a pawn to take a bishop or a knight, and to cry up or down any of their subjects as they do their money. And to the King is due both the affection of the soul and the service of the body of his subjects. . . .

As for the father of a family, they had of old under the Law of Nature *patriam potestatem,* which was *potestatem vitae et necis,* over their children or family, (I mean such fathers of families as were the lineal heirs of those families whereof kings did originally come), for kings had their first original from them who planted and spread themselves in colonies through the world. Now a father may dispose of his inheritance to his children at his pleasure, yea, even disinherit the eldest upon just occasions and prefer the youngest, according to his liking; make them beggars or rich at his pleasure; restrain or banish out of his presence, as he finds them give cause of offence, or restore them in favour again with the penitent sinner. So may the King deal with his subjects.

And lastly, as for the head of the natural body, the head hath the power of directing all the members of the body to that use which the judgment in the head think most convenient. . . .

The Powers of Parliament in England
The House of Commons

James's views on monarchical powers were not accepted by members of Parliament. Indeed, from the beginnng of his reign through the reign of his son Charles I, king and Parliament struggled over their relative powers. Along with other problems, this struggle culminated in the 1640s with the outbreak of civil war and the eventual beheading of Charles I. The nature of this struggle is partially revealed in the following statements issued by the House of Commons in 1604 to the new king, James I.

> **Consider:** *The powers over which the House of Commons and the king differed; the justifications used by James I and the House of Commons for their claims; any ways in which compromise was possible between these two positions.*

Now concerning the ancient rights of the subjects of this realm, chiefly consisting in the privileges of this House of Parliament, the misinformation openly delivered to your Majesty hath been in three things:

SOURCE: From J. R. Tanner, *Constitutional Documents of the Reign of James I, A.D. 1603–1625* (Cambridge, England: Cambridge University Press, 1930), pp. 220–222. Reprinted by permission.

First, That we held not privileges of right, but of grace only, renewed every Parliament by way of donature upon petition, and so to be limited.

Second, That we are no Court of Record, nor yet a Court that can command view of records, but that our proceedings here are only to acts and memorials, and that the attendance with the records is courtesy, not duty.

Thirdly and lastly, That the examination of the return of writs for knights and burgesses is without our compass, and due to the Chancery.

Against which assertions, most gracious Sovereign, tending directly and apparently to the utter overthrow of the very fundamental privileges of our House, and therein of the rights and liberties of the whole Commons of your realm of England which they and their ancestors from time immemorable have undoubtedly enjoyed under your Majesty's most noble progenitors, we, the knights, citizens, and burgesses of the House of Commons assembled in Parliament, and in the name of the whole commons of the realm of England, with uniform consent for ourselves and our posterity, do expressly protest, as being derogatory in the highest degree to the true dignity, liberty, and authority of your Majesty's High Court of Parliament, and consequently to the rights of all your Majesty's said subjects and the whole body of this your kingdom: And desire that this our protestation may be recorded to all posterity.

And contrariwise, with all humble and due respect to your Majesty our Sovereign Lord and Head, against those misinformations we most truly avouch,

First, That our privileges and liberties are our right and due inheritance, no less than our very lands and goods.

Secondly, That they cannot be withheld from us, denied, or impaired, but with apparent wrong to the whole state of the realm.

Thirdly, And that our making of request in the entrance of Parliament to enjoy our privilege is an act only of manners, and doth weaken our right no more than our suing to the King for our lands by petition. . . .

Fourthly, We avouch also, That our House is a Court of Record, and so ever esteemed.

Fifthly, That there is not the highest standing Court in this land that ought to enter into competency, either for dignity or authority, with this High Court of Parliament, which with your Majesty's royal assent gives laws to other Courts but from other Courts receives neither laws nor orders.

Sixthly and lastly, We avouch that the House of Commons is the sole proper judge of return of all such writs and of the election of all such members as belong to it, without which the freedom of election were not entire: And that the Chancery, though a standing Court under your Majesty, be to send out those writs and receive the returns and to preserve them, yet the same is done only for the use of the Parliament, over which neither the Chancery nor any other Court ever had or ought to have any manner of jurisdiction.

From these misinformed positions, most gracious Sovereign, the greatest part of our troubles, distrusts, and jealousies have risen. . . .

Austria Over All If She Only Will: Mercantilism
Philipp W. von Hornick

Mercantilism, a loose set of economic ideas and corresponding government policies, was a common component of political absolutism during the seventeenth century. Typical mercantilist goals were the acquisition of bullion, a positive balance of trade, and economic self-sufficiency. An unusually clear and influential statement of mercantilist policies was published in 1684 by Philipp Wilhelm von Hornick. A lawyer and later a government official, Hornick set down what he considered to be the nine principal rules for a proper economic policy. These are excerpted here.

> **Consider:** *The political and military purposes served by encouraging mercantilist policies; the foreign policy decisions such economic policies would support; the political and economic circumstances that would make it easiest for a country to adhere to and benefit from mercantilist policies.*

NINE PRINCIPAL RULES OF NATIONAL ECONOMY

If the might and eminence of a country consist in its surplus of gold, silver, and all other things necessary or convenient for its *subsistence,* derived, so far as possible, from its own resources, without *dependence* upon other countries, and in the proper fostering, use, and application of these, then it follows that a general national *economy* (*Landes-Oeconomie*) should consider how such a surplus, fostering, and enjoyment can be brought about, without *dependence* upon others, or where this is not feasible in every respect, with as little *dependence* as possible upon foreign countries, and sparing use of the country's own cash. For this purpose the following nine rules are especially serviceable.

First, to inspect the country's soil with the greatest care, and not to leave the agricultural possibilities or a single corner or clod of earth unconsidered. Every useful form of *plant* under the sun should be experimented with, to see whether it is adapted to the country, for the distance or nearness of the sun is not all that counts. Above all, no trouble or expense should be spared to discover gold and silver.

Second, all commodities found in a country, which cannot be used in their natural state, should be worked up within the country; since the payment for *manufacturing* generally exceeds the value of the raw material by two, three, ten, twenty, and even a hundred fold, and the neglect of this is an abomination to prudent managers.

SOURCE: Philipp W. von Hornick, "Austria Over All If She Only Will," in Arthur Eli Monroe, ed., *Early Economic Thought.* Reprinted by permission of Harvard University Press (Cambridge, Mass., 1927), pp. 223–225. Copyright © 1924 by The President and Fellows of Harvard College.

Third, for carrying out the above two rules, there will be need of people, both for producing and cultivating the raw materials and for working them up. Therefore, attention should be given to the population, that it may be as large as the country can support, this being a well-ordered state's most important concern, but, unfortunately, one that is often neglected. And the people should be turned by all possible means from idleness to remunerative *professions;* instructed and encouraged in all kinds of *inventions,* arts, and trades; and, if necessary, instructors should be brought in from foreign countries for this.

Fourth, gold and silver once in the country, whether from its own mines or obtained by *industry* from foreign countries, are under no circumstances to be taken out for any purpose, so far as possible, or allowed to be buried in chests or coffers, but must always remain in *cirulation;* nor should much be permitted in uses where they are at once *destroyed* and cannot be utilized again. For under these conditions, it will be impossible for a country that has once acquired a considerable supply of cash, especially one that possesses gold and silver mines, ever to sink into poverty; indeed, it is impossible that it should not continually increase in wealth and property. Therefore,

Fifth, the inhabitants of the country should make every effort to get along with their domestic products, to confine their luxury to these alone, and to do without foreign products as far as possible (except where great need leaves no alternative, or if not need, wide-spread, unavoidable abuse, of which Indian spices are an example). And so on.

Sixth, in case the said purchases were indispensable because of necessity or *irremediable* abuse, they should be obtained from these foreigners at first hand, so far as possible, and not for gold or silver, but in exchange for other domestic wares.

Seventh, such foreign commodities should in this case be imported in unfinished form, and worked up within the country, thus earning the wages of *manufacture* there.

Eighth, opportunities should be sought night and day for selling the country's superfluous goods to these foreigners in manufactured form, so far as this is necessary, and for gold and silver; and to this end, *consumption,* so to speak, must be sought in the farthest ends of the earth, and developed in every possible way.

Ninth, except for important considerations, no importation should be allowed under any circumstances of commodities of which there is sufficient supply of suitable quality at home; and in this matter neither sympathy nor compassion should be shown foreigners, be they friends, kinsfolk, *allies,* or enemies. For all friendship ceases, when it involves my own weakness and ruin. And this holds good, even if the domestic commodities are of poorer quality, or even higher priced. For it would be better to pay for an article two dollars which remain in the country than only one which goes out, however strange this may seem to the ill-informed.

Decree on the Invitation of Foreigners
Peter the Great

Russia stood on the eastern edge of Europe and spread well into Asia. By the sixteenth century, Russia had expelled the Mongols and begun a vast expansion. A century later the Russian Empire extended to the Pacific, but ambitious tsars continued to feel thwarted in their efforts to expand Russia westward. Many people perceived Russia to be behind technological and other developments occurring farther west in Europe. Tsar Peter the Great (1682–1725) was one of those who called for Russia to adopt certain western European institutions and practices. This is illustrated in the Decree on the Invitation of Foreigners, issued in 1702.

> **Consider:** *How Peter is trying to promote changes in Russia; Peter's motives for the changes he wants; problems Peter anticipates in getting people to accept foreigners.*

It is sufficiently known in all the lands which the Almighty has placed under our rule, that since our accession to the throne all our efforts and intentions have tended to govern this realm in such a way that all of our subjects should, through our care for the general good, become more and more prosperous. For this end we have always tried to maintain internal order, to defend the State against invasion, and in every possible way to improve and to extend trade. With this purpose we have been compelled to make some necessary and salutary changes in the administration, in order that our subjects might more easily gain a knowledge of matters of which they were before ignorant, and become more skillful in their commercial relations. We have therefore given orders, made dispositions, and founded institutions indispensable for increasing our trade with foreigners, and shall do the same in future. Nevertheless, we fear that matters are not in such a good condition as we desire, and that our subjects cannot in perfect quietness enjoy the fruits of our labors, and we have therefore considered still other means to protect our frontier from the invasion of the enemy, and to preserve the rights and privileges of our State, and the general peace of all Christians, as is incumbent on a Christian monarch to do. To attain these worthy aims, we have endeavored to improve our military forces, which are the protection of our State, so that our troops may consist of well-drilled men, maintained in perfect order and discipline. In order to obtain greater improvement in this respect, and to encourage foreigners, who are able to assist us in this way, as well as artists and artisans profitable to the State, to come in numbers to our country, we have issued this manifesto, and have ordered printed copies of it to be sent throughout Europe. And as in our residence of Moscow, the free exercise of religion of all other sects, although

SOURCE: George Vernadsky, ed., *A Source Book for Russian History From Early Times to 1917* (New Haven: Yale University Press, 1972), p. 347 as excerpted.

not agreeing with our church, is already allowed, so shall this be hereby confirmed anew in such wise that we, by the power granted to us by the Almighty, shall exercise no compulsion over the consciences of men, and shall gladly allow every Christian to care for his own salvation at his own risk.

Women of the Third Estate

The vast majority of eighteenth-century Europeans were not members of the aristocracy. Over 90 percent were peasants, artisans, domestics, and laborers—often referred to in France as members of the Third Estate. While both men and women of the Third Estate shared much, women's positions and grievances often differed from those of men. Articulate records of these women's grievances are difficult to find, but the flood of formal petitions preceding the French Revoluton of 1789 provides us with some rich sources. The following is a "Petition of the Women of the Third Estate to the King," dated several months prior to the outbreak of the French Revolution.

Consider: *What options seem available to women; the problems identified and solutions proposed; ways in which men's interests and women's interests might clash.*

1 January 1789. Almost all women of the Third Estate are born poor. Their education is either neglected or misconceived, for it consists in sending them to learn from teachers who do not themselves know the first word of the language they are supposed to be teaching. . . . At the age of fifteen or sixteen, girls can earn five or six sous a day. If nature has not granted them good looks, they get married, without a dowry, to unfortunate artisans and drag out a grueling existence in the depths of the provinces, producing children whom they are unable to bring up. If, on the other hand, they are born pretty, being without culture, principles, or any notion of morality, they fall prey to the first seducer, make one slip, come to Paris to conceal it, go totally to the bad here, and end up dying as victims of debauchery.

Today, when the difficulty of earning a living forces thousands of women to offer themselves to the highest bidder and men prefer buying them for a spell to winning them for good, any woman drawn to virtue, eager to educate herself, and with natural taste . . . is faced with the choice either of casting herself into a cloister which will accept a modest dowry or of going into domestic service. . . .

If old age overtakes unmarried women, they spend it in tears and as objects of contempt for their nearest relatives.

To counter such misfortunes, Sire, we ask that men be excluded from practicing those crafts that are women's prerogative, such as dressmaking, embroidery, mil-

SOURCE: Excerpts from *Not In God's Image* by Julia O'Faolain and Lauro Martines. Copyright © 1973 by Julia O'Faolain and Lauro Martines. Reprinted by permission of Harper & Row, Publishers, Inc.

inery, etc. Let them leave us the needle and the spindle and we pledge our word never to handle the compass or the set-square.

We ask, Sire . . . to be instructed and given jobs, not that we may usurp men's authority but so that we may have a means of livelihood, and so that the weaker among us who are dazzled by luxury and led astray by example should not be forced to join the ranks of the wretched who encumber the streets and whose lewd audacity disgraces both our sex and the men who frequent them.

VISUAL SOURCES

The Leviathan: Political Order and Political Theory
Thomas Hobbes

Although England avoided the Thirty Years' War, she had her own experiences with passionate war and disruption of authority. Between 1640 and 1660 England endured the civil war, the trial and execution of her king, Charles I, the rise to power of Oliver Cromwell, and the return to power of the Stuart king, Charles II. These events stimulated Thomas Hobbes (1588–1679) to formulate one of the most important statements of political theory in history.

Hobbes supported the royalist cause during the civil war and served as tutor to the future Charles II. Applying some of the new philosophical and scientific concepts being developed during the seventeenth century, he presented a theory for the origins and proper functioning of the state and political authority. His main ideas appear in Leviathan *(1651), the title page of which appears here. It shows a giant monarchical figure, with symbols of power and authority, presiding over a well-ordered city and surrounding lands. On close examination one can see that the monarch's body is composed of the citizens of this commonwealth who, according to Hobbes's theory, have mutually agreed to give up their independence to an all-powerful sovereign who will keep order. This is explained in the following selection from Hobbes's book, in which he relates the reasons for the formation of a commonwealth to the nature of authority in that commonwealth.*

> **Consider:** *Why men form such a commonwealth and why they give such power to the sovereign; how Hobbes's argument compares with that of James I; why both those favoring more power for the House of Commons and those favoring increased monarchical power might criticize this argument.*

Source: Thomas Hobbes, *The Leviathan*, vol. III of *The English Works of Thomas Hobbes*, ed. Sir William Molesworth (London: John Bohn, 1889), pp. 113, 151–153, 157, 159.

Photo 14–1

Whatsoever therefore is consequent to a time of war, where every man is enemy to every man; the same is consequent to the time, wherein men live without other security, than what their own strength, and their own invention shall furnish them withal. In such condition, there is no place for industry; because the fruit thereof is uncertain: and consequently no culture of the earth; no navigation, nor use of the commodities that may be imported by sea; no commodious building; no instruments of moving, and removing, such things as require much force; no knowledge of the face of the earth; no account of time; no arts; no letters; no society; and which is worst of all, continual fear, and danger of violent death; and the life of man, solitary, poor, nasty, brutish, and short. . . .

The final cause, end, or design of men who naturally love liberty, and dominion over others, in the introduction of that restraint upon themselves, in which we see them live in commonwealths, is the foresight of their own preservation, and of a more contented life thereby; that is to say, of getting themselves out from that miserable condition of war, which is necessarily consequent . . . to the natural passions of men, when there is no visible power to keep them in awe, and tie them by fear of punishment to the performance of their covenants, and observation of those laws of nature set down. . . .

For the laws of nature, as *justice, equity, modesty, mercy,* and, in sum, doing to others as we would be done to, of themselves, without the terror of some power to cause them to be observed, are contrary to our natural passions, that carry us to partiality, pride, revenge, and the like. And covenants, without the sword, are but words, and of no strength to secure a man at all. . . .

The only way to erect such a common power, as may be able to defend them from the invasion of foreigners, and the injuries of one another, and thereby to secure them in such sort, as that by their own industry, and by the fruits of the earth, they may nourish themselves and live contentedly; is, to confer all their power and strength upon one man, or upon one assembly of men, that may reduce all their wills, by plurality of voices, unto one will: which is as much as to say, to appoint one man, or assembly of men, to bear their person; and every one to own, and acknowledge himself to be author of whatsoever he that so beareth their person, shall act, or cause to be acted, in those things which concern the common peace and safety; and therein to submit their wills, every one to his will, and their judgments to his judgment. This is more than consent, or concord; it is a real unity of them all, in one and the same person, made by covenant of every man with every man, in such manner, as if every man should say to every man, *I authorise and give up my right of governing myself, to this man, or to this assembly of men, on this condition, that thou give up thy right to him, and authorise all his actions in like manner.* This done, the multitude so united in one person, is called a COMMONWEATH, . . . This is the generation of that great Leviathan, or rather, to speak more reverently, of that *mortal god,* to which we owe under the *immortal God,* our peace and defence. For by this authority, given him by every particular man in the commonwealth, he hath the use of so much power and strength conferred on him, that by terror thereof, he is enabled to perform the wills of them all, to peace at home, and mutual aid against their enemies abroad. And in him consisteth the essence of the commonwealth; which to define it, is *one person, of whose acts a great multitude, by mutual covenants one with another, have made themselves every one the author, to the end he may use the strength and means of them all, as he shall think expedient, for their peace and common defence.*

And he that carrieth this person, is called SOVEREIGN, and said to have *sovereign power;* and every one besides, his SUBJECT.

Happy Accidents of the Swing
Jean-Honoré Fragonard

The aristocracy remained dominant culturally during the Ancien Régime, commissioning most of the art of the period. It is not surprising, then, that the art reflected aristocratic values and tastes. Happy Accidents of the Swing *by Jean-Honoré Fragonard exemplifies a type of painting quite popular among France's eighteenth-century aristocracy.*

Fragonard was commissioned by Baron de Saint-Julien in 1767 to paint a picture of his mistress on a swing being pushed by a bishop who did not know that the woman was the baron's mistress, with the baron himself watching from a strategic place of hiding. In the picture the woman on the swing seems well aware of what is happening, flinging off her shoe toward a statue of the god of discretion in such a way as to cause her gown to billow out revealingly.

This painting reflects a certain religious irreverence on the part of the eighteenth-century aristocracy, for the joke is on the unknowing bishop. The significance of this irreverence is magnified by the fact that Saint-Julien had numerous dealings with the clergy, since he was at this time a government official responsible for overseeing clerical wealth.

The lush setting of the painting and the tenor of the scene suggest the love of romantic luxury and concern for sensual indulgence by this most privileged but soon to be declining part of society.

> **Consider:** *The evidence in this picture of the attitudes and lifestyle of the eighteenth-century French aristocracy.*

Photo 14–2

The Wallace Collection

SECONDARY SOURCES

The Continental Reformation: A Religious Interpretation
John M. Headley

Since the Reformation's occurrence in the sixteenth century, scholars have sought to ex-
plain it. Why did it occur? Why did some people convert to Protestantism while others
did not? Answers to these questions have been colored by religious preference as well as
by interpretive biases. The oldest, most traditional interpretation of the causes of the Ref-
ormation is a religious one, focusing on the doctrinal and spiritual factors involved. While
many of the older religious interpretations have been modified to take account of eco-
nomic, social, and political factors, many historians still stress religious causes as being
most fundamental in the Reformation. This is reflected in the following selection by John
M. Headley of the University of North Carolina.

> **Consider:** *The ways in which Lutheranism satisfied "men thirsting for God in a*
> *society saturated with religion"; connections that can be made between the Refor-*
> *mation and the Renaissance.*

The Reformation grew out of the depths of a church that sacramentally and legally embraced all of society. If the progress of this movement was shaped by the social-political currents of the age, its point of origin is to be found in a question of authority raised by a troubled conscience and not in particular abuses. The late medieval church, through a process of excessive institutionalization, had sacrificed spirit to structure and had come to confuse authority with its own practices and judgments. Confusion over the actual tradition of the church was aggravated in the schools by the rending of scripture into a collection of arguments and propositions for philosophical inquiry. In each process scripture, the ultimate source of knowledge of the faith, had lost its unity and integrity. A jumble of competing images cluttered people's minds, as well as the naves of churches. Luther's insight had the effect of restoring to the center of Christian experience not simply the unity and authority of scripture but also the overriding fact of Christ as personal Savior. At Augsburg, Leipzig, and Worms, he exalted scripture above all other authorities, patristic, canonistic, and papal, defying a church grown overly confident in the exercise of its massive power.

To a religiously-starved generation Christ now appeared neither as a pious

---

SOURCE: John M. Headley, "The Continental Reformation," in *The Meaning of the Renaissance and Reformation*, ed. Richard L. DeMolen (Boston: Houghton Mifflin, 1974), pp. 204–205. Reprinted by permission.

memory nor as a symbol in the mass but in the full and present reality of His person, communicated to the believer preeminently through the Bible—freshly and pungently translated and widely disseminated by the printing press. The direct encounter between Christ and the Christian who takes on the person of Christ was no longer a subject-object relationship, but one between persons in which Christ is always the same, a continuing reality. Here Luther and the Reformation struck a modern note and capitalized upon a strain in the experience of the Renaissance. What Catholic historians call "subjectivism," the profoundly spiritual event of personal appropriation, first emerged in the humanism of Petrarch, was shifted by Lorenzo Valla from classical texts to those of the early church, refocused by Erasmus on the example of Christ, and altered again by Luther to pertain to the gift of Christ. An essentially doctrinal reform, Christocentric and theocentric in character, it had an immense and immediate impact upon men thirsting for God in a society saturated with religion.

A Political Interpretation of the Reformation
G. R. Elton

In more recent times the religious interpretation of the Reformation has been challenged by political historians. This view is illustrated by the following selection from the highly authoritative New Cambridge Modern History. *Here, G. R. Elton of Canmbridge argues that while spiritual and other factors are relevant, primary importance for explaining why the Reformation did not did not take hold rests with political history.*

> **Consider:** *How Elton supports his argument; the ways in which Headley might refute this interpretation.*

The desire for spiritual nourishment was great in many parts of Europe, and movements of thought which gave intellectual content to what in so many ways was an inchoate search for God have their own dignity. Neither of these, however, comes first in explaining why the Reformation took root here and vanished there— why, in fact, this complex of antipapal 'heresies' led to a permanent division within the Church that had looked to Rome. This particular place is occupied by politics and the play of secular ambitions. In short, the Reformation maintained itself wherever the lay power (prince or magistrates) favoured it; it could not survive where the authorities decided to suppress it. Scandinavia, the German principalities, Geneva, in its own peculiar way also England, demonstrate the first; Spain, Italy, the Habsburg lands in the east, and also (though not as yet conclusively) France, the second. The famous phrase behind the settlement of 1555—*cuius*

SOURCE: From G. R. Elton, ed., *The New Cambridge Modern History*, vol. II, *The Reformation* Cambridge, England: Cambridge University Press, 1958), p. 5. Reprinted by permission.

regio eius religio—was a practical commonplace long before anyone put it into words. For this was the age of uniformity, an age which held at all times and everywhere that one political unit could not comprehend within itself two forms of belief or worship.

The tenet rested on simple fact: as long as membership of a secular polity involved membership of an ecclesiastical organisation, religious dissent stood equal to political disaffection and even treason. Hence governments enforced uniformity, and hence the religion of the ruler was that of his country. England provided the extreme example of this doctrine in action, with its rapid official switches from Henrician Catholicism without the pope, through Edwardian Protestantism on the Swiss model and Marian papalism, to Elizabethan Protestantism of a more specifically English brand. But other countries fared similarly. Nor need this cause distress or annoyed disbelief. Princes and governments, no more than the governed, do not act from unmixed motives, and to ignore the spiritual factor in the conversion of at least some princes is as false as to see nothing but purity in the desires of the populace. The Reformation was successful beyond the dreams of earlier, potentially similar, movements not so much because (as the phrase goes) the time was ripe for it, but rather because it found favour with the secular arm. Desire for Church lands, resistance to imperial and papal claims, the ambition to create self-contained and independent states, all played their part in this, but so quite often did a genuine attachment to the teachings of the reformers.

The World We Have Lost:
The Early Modern Family
Peter Laslett

The family is a tremendously important institution in any society. Changes in its structure and functions occur very slowly and gradually. With the passage of centuries since Early Modern times, we can see some sharp differences between the family of that period and the family of today. In the following selection Peter Laslett, a social historian from Cambridge who has written extensively on the Early Modern period, points out the differences.

> **Consider:** *The economic and social functions of the family revealed in this selection; how the structure of this family differs from that of a typical twentieth-century family.*

In the year 1619 the bakers of London applied to the authorities for an increase in the price of bread. They sent in support of their claim a complete description of a bakery and an account of its weekly costs. There were thirteen or fourteen people in such an establishment; the baker and his wife, four paid employees who were called journeymen, two apprentices, two maidservants and the three or four children of the master baker himself. . . .

The only word used at that time to describe such a group of people was "family." The man at the head of the group, the entrepreneur, the employer, or the manager, was then known as the master or head of the family. He was father to some of its members and in place of father to the rest. There was no sharp distinction between his domestic and his economic functions. His wife was both his partner and his subordinate, a partner because she ran the family, took charge of the food and managed the women-servants, a subordinate because she was woman and wife, mother and in place of mother to the rest.

The paid servants of both sexes had their specified and familiar position in the family, as much part of it as the children but not quite in the same position. At that time the family was not one society only but three societies fused together: the society of man and wife, of parents and children and of master and servant. But when they were young, and servants were, for the most part, young, unmarried people, they were very close to children in their status and their function. . . .

Apprentices, therefore, were workers who were also children, extra sons or extra daughters (for girls could be apprenticed too), clothed and educated as well as fed, obliged to obedience and forbidden to marry, unpaid and absolutely dependent until the age of twenty-one. If apprentices were workers in the position of sons and daughters, the sons and daughters of the house were workers too. John Locke laid it down in 1697 that the children of the poor must work for some part of the day when they reached the age of three. The sons and daughters of a London baker were not free to go to school for many years of their young lives, or even to play as they wished when they came back home. Soon they would find themselves doing what they could do in *bolting*, that is sieving flour, or in helping the maidservant with her panniers of loaves on the way to the market stall, or in playing their small parts in preparing the never-ending succession of meals for the whole household.

We may see at once, therefore, that the world we have lost, as I have chosen to call it, was no paradise or golden age of equality, tolerance or loving kindness. It is so important that I should not be misunderstood on this point that I will say at once that the coming of industry cannot be shown to have brought economic oppression and exploitation along with it. It was there already. The patriarchal arrangements which we have begun to explore were not new in the England of Shakespeare and Elizabeth. They were as old as the Greeks, as old as European history, and not confined to Europe. And it may well be that they abused and enslaved people quite as remorselessly as the economic arrangements which had replaced them in the England of Blake and Victoria. When people could expect to live for only thirty years in all, how must a man have felt when he realized that so much of his adult life, perhaps all, must go in working for his keep and very little more in someone's else's family?

Lords and Peasants
Jerome Blum

*The aristocracy made up a small percentage of Europe's population. Some 80 to 90 per-
cent of the people were still peasants. While peasants lived in a variety of different circumstances, most lived at not much more than a subsistence level. They were usually
thought of as at the bottom of society. In the following selection, Jerome Blum analyzes
attitudes held toward the peasants by seigniors (lords) and by peasants themselves.*

> **Consider:** *How lords viewed peasants in relation to themselves; how the lords'
> attitudes reflected actual social conditions; possible consequences of the negative
> attitudes held about peasants.*

With the ownership of land went power and authority over the peasants who
lived on the land. There were a multitude of variations in the nature of that
authority and in the nature of the peasants' subservience to their seigniors, in the
compass of the seigniors' supervision and control, and in the obligations that the
peasants had to pay their lords. The peasants themselves were known by many
different names, and so, too, were the obligations they owed the seigniors. But,
whatever the differences, the status of the peasant everywhere in the servile lands
was associated with unfreedom and constraint. In the hierarchical ladder of the
traditional order he stood on the bottom rung. He was "the stepchild of the age,
the broad, patient back who bore the weight of the entire social pyramid . . . the
clumsy lout who was deprived and mocked by court, noble and city." . . .

The subservience of the peasant and his dependence upon his lord were mir-
rored in the attitudes and opinions of the seigniors of east and west alike. They
believed that the natural order of things had divided humankind into masters and
servants, those who commanded and those who obeyed. They believed themselves
to be naturally superior beings and looked upon those who they believed were
destined to serve them as their natural inferiors. At best their attitude toward the
peasantry was the condescension of paternalism. More often it was disdain and
contempt. Contemporary expressions of opinion repeatedly stressed the ignorance, irresponsibility, laziness, and general worthlessness of the peasantry, and
in the eastern lands the free use of the whip was recommended as the only way
to get things done. The peasant was considered some lesser and sub-human form
of life; "a hybrid between animal and human" was the way a Bavarian official put
it in 1737. An eyewitness of a rural rising in Provence in 1752 described the
peasant as "an evil animal, cunning, a ferocious half-civilized beast; he has neither
heart nor honesty. . . ." The Moldavian Basil Balsch reported that the peasants of

SOURCE: Jerome Blum, *The End of the Old Order in Rural Europe.* Copyright © 1978 Princeton
University Press. Excerpt, pp. 29–31, 44–49, reprinted with permission of Princeton University
Press.

his land were "strangers to any discipline, order, economy or cleanliness. . . ; a thoroughly lazy, mendacious . . . people who are accustomed to do the little work that they do only under invectives or blows." A counselor of the duke of Mecklenburg in an official statement in 1750 described the peasant there as a "head of cattle" and declared that he must be treated accordingly. . . .

The conviction of their own superiority harbored by the seigniors was often compounded by ethnic and religious differences between lord and peasant. In many parts of central and eastern Europe the masters belonged to a conquering people who had established their domination over the native population. German seigniors ruled over Slavic peasants in Bohemia, Galicia, East Prussia and Silesia, and over Letts and Estonians in the Baltic lands; Polish lords were the masters of Ukrainian, Lithuanian, and White Russian peasants; Great Russians owned manors peopled by Ukrainians and Lithuanians and Poles; Magyars lorded it over Slovaks and Romanians and Slovenes—to list only some of the macroethnic differences. Few peoples of the rest of the world can match Europeans in their awareness of and, generally, contempt for or at least disdain for other ethnic and religious groups. . . . The dominant group, though greatly outnumbered, successfully maintained its cultural identity precisely because it considered the peasants over whom it ruled as lesser breeds of mankind, even pariahs. . . .

Schooling for most peasants was, at best, pitifully inadequate and usually entirely absent, even where laws declared elementary education compulsory. . . . [B]y far the greatest part of Europe's peasantry lived out their lives in darkest ignorance.

The peasants themselves, oppressed, contemned, and kept in ignorance by their social betters, accepted the stamp of inferiority pressed upon them. "I am only a serf" the peasant would reply when asked to identity himself. They seemed without pride or self-respect, dirty, lazy, crafty, and always suspicious of their masters and of the world that lay outside their village. Even friendly observers were put off by the way they looked and by their behavior. One commentator complained in the 1760's that "one would have more pity for them if their wild and brutish appearance did not seem to justify their hard lot."

Chapter Questions

1. Using the sources in this chapter, explain the Reformation and its spread in sixteenth-century Europe.

2. What arguments and tactics might someone supporting monarchical absolutism and someone opposing it use against each other?

3. How might sources in this chapter be used to compare the life of the aristocracy with that of commoners?

4. Speculate on how a history of Europe during this time might be written and understood by readers if historians drew primarily from sources dealing with the lives of commoners, such as some of the sources in this chapter.

FIFTEEN

Asia, 1500–1700

While these centuries marked major changes in the West and new encounters between East and West, it was not a period of major transformation in much of Asia. However, within the different Asian societies, important developments were taking place.

In China, the Ming Dynasty was characterized by relative stability and prosperity. Major building projects, such as the early fifteenth-century construction of the Forbidden City in Beijing (Peking), were undertaken. All cultural productions, and literature in particular, flourished—though more in quantity than in originality. The government fostered rigidity and remained relatively inward looking, apart from the vigilance needed against attack from Japanese pirates along the coast and from Mongols and Manchus from the north. By the mid-seventeenth century, the Manchus were victorious and established their own dynasty. They adopted the Confucian bureaucracy and ways of governing, were generally accepted by the Chinese, and eventually extended Chinese rule as far as Tibet.

In contrast, this period was one of greater change for Japan. The sixteenth century witnessed the emergence of strong military leaders. By 1600, Japan was unified by the Tokugawa house that created the Shogunate in 1603 and would rule for the next two hundred and fifty years. It outlawed Christianity, cut Japan off from the world, and established a centralized feudal state. Increasingly the samurai became, through education, government bureaucrats. And as the economy developed, a merchant class grew.

In India, the first Muslim rulers, the Delhi Sultanate (1211–1504), became ineffectual and were replaced by the Islamic Mogul (also Mughal—originally a Persian word for Mongols, but in the sixteenth century referred to the fierce Turkish tribe that conquered north India) Dynasty in 1526. Under Akbar, this rule was conciliatory toward the Hindus and encouraging of the arts. However, his seventeenth-century successors followed less tolerant policies and made costly attempts to expand their rule to the south, eventually leading to the collapse of Mogul power by the beginning of the eighteenth century and the spread of British power over India.

Finally, in the Middle East, Islamic powers not only remained strong but expanded their control. Most striking was the continued rise of the Ottoman

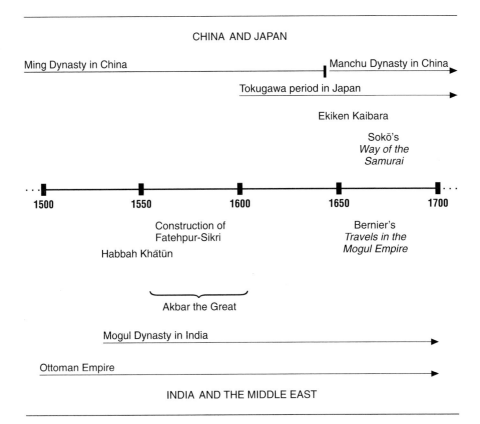

Empire, which by the last decades of the seventeenth century included all the southern and eastern Mediterranean basin and extended well into eastern Europe. However, the Ottomans themselves were under pressure from the expanding Russian Empire to the north and from the rise of the Islamic Safavid state in Iran. By the eighteenth century these Islamic powers had already begun a long-term process of decline.

The sources in this chapter focus on three topics. The first is social and political life in China and Japan. Here there is a particular focus on the role of women and the developing role of the samurai in Japan, as well as on family life in China. The second is Indian civilization, here also with some focus on women as well as the broader aspects of Indian culture. Finally, some sources will deal with Islamic civilizations, particularly the Ottoman Empire, which rose to heights during this period but also showed signs of long-term decline.

PRIMARY SOURCES

The Way of the Samurai
Yamaga Sokō

In the course of the seventeenth century, Confucianism became a greater influence as Japanese intellectuals began to develop an intellectual paradigm which was more reflective of their own culture. One of the first to do so was Yamaga Sokō (1622–1685). A man of enormous intellect and independence of thought, Yamaga became interested not only in the major philosophies of his day, but in military science as well.

Worried about the continual inaction of samurai under peaceful Tokugawa rule, Yamaga tried to forge a new identity for these warriors. This was markedly different from China where soldiers had very low status. Bringing together the ethics of Confucianism and the Japanese feudal tradition, Yamaga's writings are acknowledged as the beginnings of a creed known as bushido *(the way of the warriors). Yamaga's writings on the samurai also symbolize the transformation of the samurai in this period from a military aristocracy to government bureaucrats and political and intellectual leaders. The following excerpts are from* The Way of the Samurai, *which was the first attempt by Yamaga to develop his thoughts on this subject.*

SOURCE: *Sources of Japanese Tradition*, Ryusaku Tsuneda, et al., eds. (New York: Columbia University Press, 1961), pp. 398–401.

Consider: *The nature of a society that requires such strict codes of behavior from its people; how Yamaga justifies this description of the samurai's duties.*

The master once said: The generation of all men and of all things in the universe is accomplished by means of the marvelous interaction of the two forces [yin and yang]. Man is the most highly endowed of all creatures, and all things culminate in man. Generation after generation men have taken their livelihood from tilling the soil, or devised and manufactured tools, or produced profit from mutual trade, so that peoples' needs were satisfied. Thus the occupations of farmer, artisan, and merchant necessarily grew up as complementary to one another. However, the samurai eats food without growing it, uses utensils without manufacturing them, and profits without buying or selling. What is the justification for this? . . . The samurai is one who does not cultivate, does not manufacture, and does not engage in trade, but it cannot be that he has no function at all as a samurai. He who satisfied his needs without performing any function at all would more properly be called an idler. Therefore one must devote all one's mind to the detailed examination of one's calling.

Human beings aside, does any creature in the land—bird or animal, lowly fish or insect, or insentient plant or tree—fulfill its nature by being idle? Birds and beasts fly and run to find their own food; fish and insects seek their food as they go about with one another; plants and trees put their roots ever deeper into the earth. . . . All things are thus. Among men, the farmers, artisans, and merchants also do the same. One who lives his whole life without working should be called a rebel against heaven. Hence we ask ourselves how it can be that the samurai should have no occupation; and it is only then as we inquire into the function of the samurai, that [the nature of] his calling becomes apparent. . . .

If one deeply fixes his attention on what I have said and examines closely one's own function, it will become clear what the business of the samurai is. The business of the samurai consists in reflecting on his own station in life, in discharging loyal service to his master if he has one, in deepening his fidelity in associations with friends, and, with due consideration of his own position, in devoting himself to duty above all. However, in one's own life, one becomes unavoidably involved in obligations between father and child, older and younger brother, and husband and wife. Though these are also the fundamental moral obligations of everyone in the land, the farmers, artisans, and merchants have no leisure from their occupations, and so they cannot constantly act in accordance with them and fully exemplify the Way. The samurai dispenses with the business of the farmer, artisan, and merchant and confines himself to practicing this Way; should there be someone in the three classes of the common people who transgresses against these moral principles, the samurai summarily punishes him and thus upholds proper moral principles in the land. It would not do for the samurai to know the martial and civil virtues without manifesting them. Since this is the case, outwardly he stands in physical readiness for any call to service and inwardly he strives to fulfill the Way of the lord and subject, friend and friend, father and son, older and younger brother, and husband and wife. Within his heart he keeps to the ways of peace, but without he keeps his weapons ready for use. The three classes of the common people make him their teacher and respect him. By following his teachings, they are enabled to understand what is fundamental and what is secondary.

Herein lies the Way of the samurai, the means by which he earns his clothing, food, and shelter; and by which his heart is put at ease, and he is enabled to pay back at length his obligation to his lord and the kindness of his parents. . . . But if perchance one should wish public service and desire to remain a samurai, he should sustain his life by performing menial functions, he should accept a small income, he should limit his obligation to his master, and he should do easy tasks [such as] gate-keeping and nightwatch duty. This then is [the samurai's] calling. The man who takes or seeks the pay of a samurai and is covetous of salary without in the slightest degree comprehending his function must feel shame in his heart. Therefore I say that that which the samurai should take as his fundamental aim is to know his own function.

Greater Learning for Women
Ekiken Kaibara

There is some evidence which leads us to believe that in its earliest years, women enjoyed a fairly high status in Japanese society. With the introduction of feudalism and the emergence of a military society, along with the influence of Confucianism and Buddhism, that status deteriorated since militarization and both sets of beliefs denigrated women. Japan was soon emulating its neighbors and relegating women to a very low status.

The following excerpts are from a book entitled Greater Learning for Women *by Ekiken Kaibara, a seventeenth century intellectual, and purports to spell out the duties and functions of women in Japanese life. Until late in the nineteenth century, this book was widely used.*

> **Consider:** *Why these guidelines are so rigid; how men profit from these rules; what this reveals about Japanese society in general; the similarities with Ban Zhao's rules for women in China (Chapter 8).*

From her earliest youth a girl should observe the line of demarcation separating women from men, and never, even for an instant, should she be allowed to see or hear the least impropriety. The customs of antiquity did not allow men and women to sit in the same apartment, to keep their wearing apparel in the same place, to bathe in the same place, or to transmit to each other anything directly from hand to hand. . . . It is written likewise in the *Lesser Learning* that a woman must form no friendship and no intimacy except when ordered to do so by her

---

SOURCE: *Women and Wisdom of Japan (Greater Learning for Women)*, Ekiken Kaibara, trans. (London: John Murray, 1905), pp. 33–46.

parents or by middlemen. Even at the peril of her life must she harden her heart like rock or metal and observe the rules of propriety.

✿

In China marriage is called "returning," for the reason that a woman must consider her husband's home as her own, and that, when she marries, she is therefore returning to her own home. However low and needy her husband's position may be, she must find no fault with him, but consider the poverty of the household which it has pleased Heaven to give her as the ordering of an unpropitious fate. The sage of old taught that, once married, she must never leave her husband's house. Should she forsake the "way" and be divorced, shame shall cover her till her latest hour. With regard to this point, there are seven faults which are termed the "Seven Reasons for Divorce":

(i) A woman shall be divorced for disobedience to her father-in-law or mother-in-law. (ii) A woman shall be divorced if she fails to bear children, . . . (iii) Lewdness is a reason for divorce. (iv) Jealousy is a reason for divorce. (v) Leprosy or any like foul disease is a reason for divorce. (vi) A woman shall be divorced who, by talking overmuch and prattling disrespectfully, disturbs the harmony of kinsmen and brings trouble on her household. (vii) A woman shall be divorced who is addicted to stealing. . . .

✿

It is the chief duty of a girl living in the parental house to practise filial piety towards her father and mother. But after marriage her duty is to honour her father-in-law and mother-in-law, to honour them beyond her father and mother, to love and reverence them with all ardour, and to tend them with practice of every filial piety. . . .

✿

A woman has no particular lord. She must look to her husband as her lord, and must serve him with all worship and reverence, not despising or thinking lightly of him. The great lifelong duty of a woman is obedience. In her dealings with her husband, both the expression of her countenance and style of her address should be courteous, humble, and conciliatory, never peevish and intractable, never rude and arrogant—that should be a woman's first and chiefest care. When the husband issues his instructions, the wife must never disobey them.

✿

The five worst infirmities that afflict the female are indocility, discontent, slander, jealousy, and silliness. Without any doubt, these five infirmities are found in seven or eight out of every ten women, and it is from these that arises the inferiority of women to men. A woman should cure them by self-inspection and self-reproach.

A Woman's Voice in India
Habbah Khātūn

Habbah Khātūn lived in India during the reign of Akbar in the mid-sixteenth century. We know little of her life except that she was born into a well-to-do family and was married to a man in the same social class. She remained childless, which created difficulties in her marriage. The humiliation she felt in this situation was voiced in songs she sang while working with the other women in the field.

Her remarkable intelligence and talents led her to be ensconced in the palace of the ruling family of Kashmir. She developed her talents, giving a literary form to the Kashmiri language and developing a music system based on Persian and Indian styles. Her songs inspired much anti-Mogul feeling in northwest India. These are two of her songs, still sung today among the people of Kashmir.

> **Consider:** *How women in a male-dominated society can emerge as prominent figures; what these songs reveal about Khātūn's and the life of other women in sixteenth-century India.*

He has pierced every fibre of my body with the
    lightning of love:
I, hapless one, am filled with longing for him.
He glanced at me from the top of the wall—
I wish I could tie a turban round his head.
Why did he then turn his back on me?
I, hapless one, am filled with longing for him.
He glanced at me through my door—

Who told him where I lived?
Why has he left me in such anguish?
I, hapless one, am filled with longing for him.
He glanced at me through my window,
He who is lovely like my ear-rings;
He has made my heart restless:
I, hapless one, am filled with longing for him.
He glanced at me through the crevice in my roof,
Sang like a bird that I may look at him,
Then, soft-footed, vanished from my sight:
I, hapless one, am filled with longing for him.
He glanced at me while I was drawing water,
I withered like a red rose,
My body and soul were ablaze with love:

SOURCE: M. Mujeeb, *The Indian Muslims* (London: George Allen & Unwin, Ltd., 1967), pp. 328–329.

I, hapless one, am longing for him.
He glanced at me in the waning moonlight of early dawn,
Stalked after me like one obsessed.
Why did he stoop so low?
I, hapless one, am filled with longing for him!

&

I thought I was indulging in play, and lost myself.
  Oh for the day that is dying!
At home I was secluded, unknown,
When I left home, my fame spread far and wide,
The pious laid all their merit at my feet.
  Oh for the day that is dying!
Me beauty was like a warehouse filled with rare merchandise,
Which drew men from all the four quarters;
Now my richness is gone, I have no worth:
  Oh for the day that is dying!
My father's people were of high standing,
I became known as Habbah Khātūn:
  Oh for the day that is dying!

Travels in the Mogul Empire: Politics and Society in India
Francois Bernier

Francois Bernier (1620–1688) was a French physician who traveled widely through the Middle East and India from 1654 to 1669. He spent about twelve years in Mogul [Mughal] India, including time traveling with and observing the court of the Mogul ruler, Aurangzeb. Upon his return to France, he published his writings and letters on his travels.

In this undated (1670?) letter to French Finance Minister Jean Baptiste Colbert, Bernier describes some of his adventures and observations while traveling with Aurangzeb. This excerpt attempts to explain one of the major problems the Mogul rulers had with social stratification and the consequences of allowing a small elite too much power.

> **Consider:** *The connections between Indian politics, economics, and society revealed in this letter; how this letter might reflect Bernier's own concerns and assumptions.*

SOURCE: François Bernier, *Travels in the Mogul Empire* A.D. *1656–1668* (London: Oxford University Press, 1983), pp. 300–303.

. . . The *King,* as proprietor of the land, makes over a certain quantity to military men, as an equivalent for their pay; and this grant is called *jah-ghir,* or, as in Turkey, *timar;* the word *jah-ghir* signifying the spot from which to draw, or the place of salary. Similar grants are made to governors, in lieu of their salary, and also for the support of their troops, on condition that they pay a certain sum annually to the King out of any surplus revenue that the land may yield. The lands not so granted are retained by the King as the peculiar domains of his house, and are seldom, if ever, given in the way of *jah-ghir;* and upon these domains he keeps contractors, who are also bound to pay him an annual rent.

The persons thus put in possession of the land, whether as *timariots,* governors, or contractors, have an authority almost absolute over the peasantry, and nearly as much over the artisans and merchants of the towns and villages within their district; and nothing can be imagined more cruel and oppressive than the manner in which it is exercised. There is no one before whom the injured peasant, artisan, or tradesman can pour out his just complaints; no great lords, parliaments, or judges of local courts exist, as in *France,* to restrain the wickedness of those merciless oppressors, and the *Kadis,* or judges, are not invested with sufficient power to redress the wrongs of these unhappy people. This sad abuse of the royal authority may not be felt in the same degree near capital cities such as *Dehly* and *Agra,* or in the vicinity of large towns and seaports, because in those places acts of gross injustice cannot easily be concealed from the court.

This debasing state of slavery obstructs the progress of trade and influences the manners and mode of life of every individual. There can be little encouragement to engage in commercial pursuits, when the success with which they may be attended, instead of adding to the enjoyments of life, provokes the cupidity of a neighbouring tyrant possessing both power and inclination to deprive any man of the fruits of his industry. When wealth is acquired, as must sometimes be the case, the possessor, so far from living with increased comfort and assuming an air of independence, studies the means by which he may appear indigent: his dress, lodging, and furniture continue to be mean, and he is careful, above all things, never to indulge in the pleasures of the table. In the meantime, his gold and silver remain buried at a great depth in the ground; agreeable to the general practice among the peasantry, artisans and merchants, whether *Mahomeians* or *Gentiles,* but especially among the latter, who possess almost exclusively the trade and wealth of the country, and who believe that the money concealed during life will prove beneficial to them after death. A few individuals alone who derive their income from the King or from the *Omrahs,* or who are protected by a powerful patron, are at no pains to counterfeit poverty, but partake of the comforts and luxuries of life.

I have no doubt that this habit of secretly burying the precious metals, and thus withdrawing them from circulation, is the principal cause of their apparent scarcity in *Hindoustan.*

VISUAL SOURCES

Akbar Inspecting the Construction of Fatehpur-Sikri

Tulsi the Elder, Bandi, and Madhu the Younger

After witnessing the death of two previous male offspring, India's Mogul ruler, Akbar, had his most fervent wish fulfilled when on August 30, 1569 a son and heir-apparent was born. So inspired was he that a decision was made to build a grand edifice on the site of the birth just outside a town called Sikri. This magnificent structure, a classic example of Mogul architecture, became known as Fathabad, later Fatehpur, (City of Victory) and hence the name Fatehpur-Sikri. It became the Mogul capital. Construction took place from 1571–1576 and consisted of palaces, pavilions for various rituals, grand mosques, bazaar areas, gardens, and courtyards.

Akbar was himself interested in architecture and had commissioned many great building projects. This scene, painted in 1590, shows Akbar personally directing the building of the city and conferring with the stone masons while workers go about their business all around him.

Consider: *How people of different rank are distinguished; the role such building projects might play in a civilization.*

Architecture and the Imperial City

Since Confucian thinking created a society of rules of behavior and etiquette, it is not surprising that the architecture would follow this same pattern. Those who could afford it built houses surrounded by high walls, with the buildings around the inside of the walls and the middle left to a courtyard, or several courtyards if the family was wealthy enough. This was not a random architecture but a design of specific purpose and intent (see also the plan for the Chinese house, Chapter 3). There were traditions as to where each family member resided.

The imperial family followed these designs and traditions as well. When the Ming Dynasty decided to move the capital of China to Beijing (Peking—northern capital) in the fifteenth century, it had built an Imperial City with an inner Forbidden City, thus named since only members of the court and those on official business could enter. The Ming rulers built themselves residential palaces and ceremonial halls surrounded by a high wall, with a door leading to each point on the compass. This Forbidden City was home to the court and thousands of imperial eunuchs. Outside the gates to the larger Imperial

Photo 15-1

Victoria & Albert Museum, London/Art Resource

Map 15-1   The Imperial City

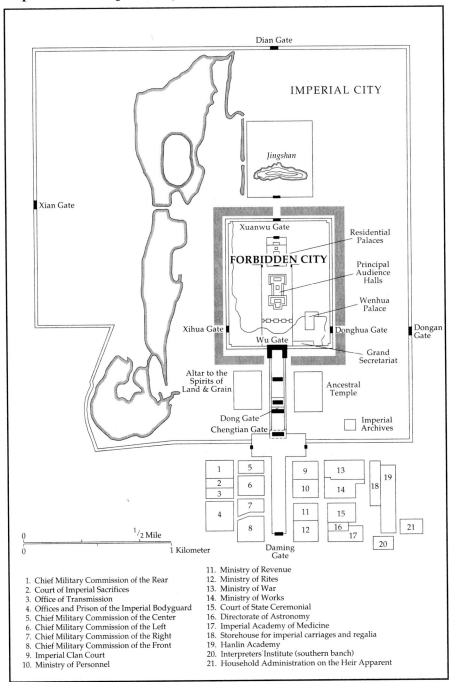

Dian Gate

IMPERIAL CITY

Jingshan

Xian Gate

Xuanwu Gate

Residential Palaces

FORBIDDEN CITY

Principal Audience Halls

Wenhua Palace

Xihua Gate

Donghua Gate

Dongan Gate

Wu Gate

Grand Secretariat

Altar to the Spirits of Land & Grain

Ancestral Temple

Dong Gate

Chengtian Gate

Imperial Archives

0   ¹/₂ Mile

0   1 Kilometer

Daming Gate

1. Chief Military Commission of the Rear
2. Court of Imperial Sacrifices
3. Office of Transmission
4. Offices and Prison of the Imperial Bodyguard
5. Chief Military Commission of the Center
6. Chief Military Commission of the Left
7. Chief Military Commission of the Right
8. Chief Military Commission of the Front
9. Imperial Clan Court
10. Ministry of Personnel
11. Ministry of Revenue
12. Ministry of Rites
13. Ministry of War
14. Ministry of Works
15. Court of State Ceremonial
16. Directorate of Astronomy
17. Imperial Academy of Medicine
18. Storehouse for imperial carriages and regalia
19. Hanlin Academy
20. Interpreters Institute (southern banch)
21. Household Administration on the Heir Apparent

City stood the offices of the Chinese bureaucracy; each designated a place according to its importance and status.

> **Consider:** *The traditional ideas that influence the design of these buildings; how they are built specifically to the rules of Chinese society.*

SECONDARY SOURCES

Islam in Indonesia
John R. Bowen

Indonesia is the world's largest archipelago stretching some 3,200 miles, encompassing about 13,700 islands of which about 6,000 are inhabited. Originally animist, Indonesians were converted to Hinduism in the third century by merchants and priests who arrived from southern India. From the fifth century, travelers bringing Buddhism, also from India, began arriving as well. From the end of the thirteenth century, Islam began appearing in the archipelago (in the form of Sufi mysticism), also by way of Indian merchants. Islam quickly began to eclipse its predecessors. The conversion to Islam in Indonesia did not, however, mean an end to Hindu-Buddhist beliefs and practices but, rather, a synthesis. Indonesians could embrace Islam without jettisoning their earlier customs, thereby incorporating their earlier beliefs with Islam.

In this selection, John R. Bowen, Professor of Anthropology at Washington University, St. Louis, examines the situation in Java where, more than any place in Indonesia, the Hindu-Javanese culture was kept alive. Bowen looks at two interpretations of what occurred in Java. Today some 85 percent of Indonesia's 190,000,000 people are Muslim, making it the largest Muslim state in the world.

> **Consider:** *The issue of religious synthesis and the ability of religions to adapt to local culture; the distinction between a culture and a religion.*

CASE STUDY: CULTURE AND RELIGION IN JAVA

One issue dividing students of Indonesian Islam is the degree to which some (the more traditional) religious forms are mixtures of Islamic and pre-Islamic ideas. This issue has arisen in particular with regard to Javanese religious life.

SOURCE: John R. Bowen, "Islam in Indonesia," Reprinted with permission from *Asia in the Core Curriculum. Case Studies in the Social Sciences.* Myron L. Cohen, ed. (Armonk, New York, M. E. Sharpe, 1992), pp. 100–102.

One position, developed by Clifford Geertz, is that Javanese society is . . . divided into three streams: the high culture of the Javanese nobles with its stress on mysticism and etiquette, the low culture of Javanese peasants with its many spirits and ritual meals, and the self-consciously Islamic culture of the merchants, students, and scholars, which saw itself as opposed to many features of the Javanese past. In this view, the basic elements of Javanese culture, including ritual meals, the art of shadow puppetry, and the ideas of power and rank suffusing the Javanese kingdoms evolved from indigenous and Hindu ideas, prior to the introduction of Islamic ideas. Islam was adopted as an additional religious layer rather late in Javanese history.

A second position holds that Javanese culture is suffused with Islamic ideas and in fact is the outcome of a process of religious adaptation. Advocates of this position argue that Islamic mystics, known as Sufis, propagated a form of Islam that was in keeping with Javanese interest in spirits and the power of unseen forces. They reinterpreted pre-Islamic ideas in Islamic terms. Thus, these scholars argue, the ritual meal in traditional Javanese culture was modified to conform to the custom as practiced throughout the Islamic world. Even the power of Javanese kings came to be viewed through an Islamic lens: the king was no longer an incarnation of a Hindu deity, but the "shadow of God on earth," an idea taken from Persian Muslim political thought.

What is clear is that Javanese religious life shows the adaptation of Islamic traditions to a particular set of Javanese emphases. Islam entered a Java where large kingdoms had already developed an elaborate court culture based on a mixture of animistic and Hindu ideas. Most Javanese Muslims acknowledge this cultural heritage, in which an emphasis on refinement and self-control is combined with Islamic ideas. For Javanese, authority involves the absorption of power within the self, the capacity to smoothly control others without being flustered or showing emotion. Refinement is epitomized by the lithe heros of shadow puppet theater, who effortlessly defeat giants; it is reflected in one's mastery of the elaborate system of speech levels in the Javanese language, and in the control of desires attained through meditation.

Sufism provided a Muslim framework that validated this idea of inward control. Meditation and abstinence refocus thought away from the outer world and toward one's inner self, and finally toward God. Some Sufi scholars taught that God was present in oneself. Whether or not one sees the present-day Javanese emphasis on self-control as pre-Islamic or as part of Sufism, it seems clear that a fit between indigenous and Sufi ideas was crucial to the propagatiom of Islam on Java.

Muslim rituals also have been shaped to fit indigenous concerns. On Java, the ritual meal, although present throughout the archipelago and indeed in other Muslim societies, takes on a Javanese character. The meal maintains social and emotional equilibrium, a persistent Javanese concern, by involving everyone in a neighborhood or village on an equal basis (despite their otherwise marked social inequalities). "When you give a ritual meal," said one Javanese quoted by Geertz, "nobody feels different from anyone else."

Funerals, though conducted according to Islamic rules, also reveal the Javanese concern for controlling emotion and reaching a state of detachment. The relatives of the deceased pass under his/her body several times when it is on the litter, give away money as a sign of their willingness to let the deceased go, and feature at the funeral meal a large, flattened-out rice cake that symbolizes the flat character of their emotions.

Marriage, Caste, and Society in India
V. P. S. Raghuvanshi

Indian society was in great part structured by the caste system. Determined by birth, one's caste was lifelong, inherited, and unbending. For Hindus, it was universal. No aspect of the caste system was more rigid than the issues of intercaste sexual relations and marriage. They went to the heart of maintaining caste lines. The following excerpt, written by V. P. S. Raghuvanshi, a prominent social historian of India, analyzes the connections between sexual relations, marriage, caste, and society. His focus is on India during the eighteenth century, but his analysis applies to the seventeenth and sixteenth centuries almost as well.

> **Consider:** *How and why marriage rules were so central to caste in Hindu society; the differences between functional castes and nonfunctional high castes.*

Caste governed the code of rules and conventions relating to marriage in Hindu society. In the 18th century, inter-caste matrimonial connections were beyond the comprehension of people and were liable to be visited by the sentence of excommunication. During the period we have evidence that the rules of caste, if violated in other respects, were leniently viewed but those in respect of marriage and sexual intercourse were rigorously enforced. . . . If a girl of high caste in Peshwas' dominions were detected in act of adultery, she could be sold and treated as a slave. In this sense caste implied hereditary continuation of families in the same group and prevented wide inter-mixture of blood. Marriage in the same caste was a social maxim of almost universal applicability among the Hindus. . . . Elsewhere caste suffered from various distinctions of rank even within its own sub-groups and these, in their turn, influenced marriage. As a general rule, among castes whose people were not privileged to be reckoned as "twice-born," the sub-castes had become entirely distinct endogamous groups. In this sense anything like a *Sudra* caste was non-existent. The various artisan and professional castes, loosely termed *Sudra*, by the end of the 18th century had organized themselves into

SOURCE: V. P. S. Raghuvanshi, *Indian Society in the Eighteenth Century* (New Delhi: Associated Publishing House, 1969), pp. 53–56.

separate endogamous[1] units of society. Their sub-divisions had become distinct castes. So strict was the rule that even sexual connection of the woman with a man outside her caste invariably entailed her excommunication from her own. This rule was rigidly observed even by those castes which were considered "altogether vile."

If matrimony within the group be construed as the fundamental test of caste, then the Kayasthas of Northern India, who might have been one caste before, had ceased to be so by the end of the 18th century. Their various sub-divisions like those of Srivastavas, Bhatnagars, Mathurs, Saxenas, Gaurs etc., had formed themselves into separate matrimonial groups and had thus become separate castes. Similarly in South India, the Panchalars, including people of the trades of goldsmiths, black smiths, carpenters, masons, although reckoned as one caste, did not admit of inter-group matrimonial relationship.

The relationship between sub-caste and marriage was, however, not necessarily uniform in the upper castes. In Bengal, the Brahmans, as also the Kayasthas, constituted single castes as distinctions of sub-castes were not material in regulating marriages within the same group. Hence those of higher birth (Kulins) were coveted by all inferior to them. Here Kulinism, although it encouraged a nefarious traffic in women, prevented the formation of rigid endogamous sub-groups. But this was not the case in Northern India or Central India. In Bihar, the Brahmans claiming descent from Kanauj had split into various local sub-divisions like Shukla, Anturvedi, etc., and even among them there were no inter-matrimonial relations. The other Brahman sub-castes, too, were endogamous subgroups. In Central India, also, we find that there was nothing like a uniform Brahman caste. The Brahmans had frittered into endless, strictly endogamous sub-castes. The same was true of the *Vaisya* community in Northern India. It was divided into several sub-divisions which were endogamous. The Rajputs were a solid exception. There sub-groups arranged on clan basis were exogamous, and marriage was regulated primarily on the basis of "purity of descent." This, too, could be overruled as a serious consideration if the girl of the lower class or family belonged to a rich influential family. Marriage outside the broad Rajput kin-group was, however, held in odium. Malcolm cites the degradation of the whole clan of Pamars in the social scale in Central India as their Chief, rulers of Dhar, married his daughter to a Maratha prince with whom "the poorest of the proud Rajput Chiefs" would refrain from eating together.

As such, we may say that caste was necessarily an endogamous group but among the functional castes, the sub-groups were also endogamous everywhere. In the non-functional high castes, the various sub-castes were not necessarily so everywhere, though in Northern India, among the Brahmans, *Vaisyas* and Kayasthas they had become so.

---

[1] "Endogamous" refers to marriage within a particular caste or group in accordance with set custom or law.

The Ottoman Empire and Its Successors

Peter Mansfield

The Ottoman Empire grew rapidly during the fifteenth and sixteenth centuries, reaching its height during the second half of the seventeenth century. Nevertheless, there were already signs of decline in the seventeenth century. In the following excerpt from The Ottoman Empire and Its Successors, *Peter Mansfield analyzes some of the causes for this long-term decline, here focusing on economic factors.*

> **Consider:** *The role of new trade routes and Ottoman taxation policies in the decline of the Empire; what the Ottoman Empire might have done to stem the decline.*

. . . The opening of a new trade route to Asia via the Cape by the Portuguese in the sixteenth century and the establishment of Dutch and British power in Asia in the seventeenth century "deprived Turkey of the greater part of her foreign commerce and left her, together with the countries over which she ruled, in a stagnant backwater through which the life-giving stream of world trade no longer flowed." At the same time the flood of cheap silver from the Spanish colonies in the New World caused a violent inflation, and disastrous devaluation of the currency of the Ottoman Empire. The consequent economic distress was compounded by the government's increasing demands for revenues from the already overtaxed peasantry for the swelling bureaucracy and armed forces. While the economies of the European powers made rapid progress in the seventeenth and eighteenth centuries, that of the Ottoman Empire actually declined. Agriculture deteriorated as the peasantry abandoned the countryside for the towns, but there was no compensating development of industry. Turkey's stagnant science and technology lagged increasingly behind the west, and it lacked any independent entrepreneurial class which might have led an industrial revolution. Western economic superiority was also manifested within the Ottoman Empire. In the sixteenth century, when the Empire was at the height of its powers, the Ottoman sultan granted special privileges to the French, English, Venetians and other non-Muslims, who had established themselves within the Empire to trade. These privileges—known as the Capitulations—exempted them from taxes imposed on Muslim Ottoman subjects and gave them the right to be tried in their own consular courts. As Ottoman power declined the privileges were reinforced. By the nineteenth century there were flourishing European business communities in many parts of the Empire which were virtually above the law.

SOURCE: Peter Mansfield, *The Ottoman Empire and Its Successors* (London: The Macmillan Press, Ltd., 1973), p. 7.

Chapter Questions

1. Several sources in this chapter deal with the position of and problems facing women in China, Japan, and India during this period. Is it fair to make comparisons here? How might it be argued that these sources reveal similar circumstances facing women in these civilizations?

2. How might the sources in this chapter be used to support the argument that even though Western civilization was expanding during these two centuries, most Asian civilizations continued to develop in line with their own internal, rather than external, forces?

3. Drawing on sources from this chapter and the previous chapters on the West, how might it be argued that European societies were becoming increasingly dynamic and flexible at the same time that societies such as those in India, China, and the Ottoman Empire were becoming more rigid and tradition bound? How might other sources be used to show that in many ways the lives of people in these civilizations and the problems they faced were similar?